Thinking Through Rituals

Many philosophical approaches today seek to overcome the division between mind and body. If such projects succeed, then thinking is not restricted to the disembodied mind but is in some sense done through the body. From a post-Cartesian perspective, then, ritual activities that discipline the body are not just thoughtless motions, but crucial parts of the way we think.

Thinking Through Rituals explores ritual acts and their connection to meaning and truth, belief, memory, inquiry, worldview, and ethics. Drawing on philosophers such as Foucault, Merleau-Ponty, and Wittgenstein, and sources from cognitive science, pragmatism, and feminist theory, it provides philosophical resources for understanding religious ritual practices like the Christian Eucharistic ceremony, Hatha Yoga, sacred meditation, and liturgical speech.

Its essays consider a wide variety of rituals in Christianity, Judaism, Hinduism, and Buddhism, including political protest rituals and gay commitment ceremonies, traditional Vedic and Yogic rites, Christian and Buddhist meditation, and the Jewish Shabbat. They challenge the traditional disjunction between thought and action, showing how philosophy can help to illuminate the relationship between doing and meaning which ritual practices imply.

Kevin Schilbrack is Associate Professor of Philosophy and Religious Studies at Wesleyan College, Georgia. The editor of *Thinking Through Myths: Philosophical Perspectives* (Routledge, 2002), he writes on the philosophical and methodological questions involved in the cross-cultural study of religions.

To my mother, a Kwan Yin

Thinking Through Rituals
Philosophical Perspectives

Edited by Kevin Schilbrack

Routledge
Taylor & Francis Group

NEW YORK AND LONDON

First published 2004
by Routledge
29 West 35th Street, New York, NY 10001

Simultaneously published in the UK
by Routledge
11 New Fetter Lane, London EC4P 4EE

Routledge is an imprint of the Taylor and Francis Group

© 2004 Edited by Kevin Schilbrack

Typeset in Sabon by
Florence Production Ltd, Stoodleigh, Devon
Printed and bound in Great Britain by
MPG Books Ltd, Bodmin, Cornwall

Library of Congress Cataloging in Publication Data
A catalogue record for this book is available from the British Library

British Library Cataloguing in Publication Data
A catalog record for this book has been requested

ISBN 0–415–29058–9 (hbk)
      0–415–29059–7 (pbk)

Contents

Contributors

Brian R. Clack is Tutor in Philosophy at St Clare's, Oxford. He is the author of *Wittgenstein, Frazer, and Religion* (Palgrave Macmillan, 1998), *The Philosophy of Religion: A Critical Introduction* (Blackwell, 1999), and *An Introduction to Wittgenstein's Philosophy of Religion* (Edinburgh University Press, 2000).

Nick Crossley is Senior Lecturer in Sociology at the University of Manchester. The author of several books, including *The Politics of Subjectivity: Between Foucault and Merleau-Ponty* (Avebury Studies in Philosophy, 1994), *Intersubjectivity: The Fabric of Social Becoming* (Sage, 1996), and *The Social Body: Habit, Identity and Desire* (Sage, 2001), Crossley works on social theory, embodiment, and the sociology of social movements.

Jonardon Ganeri is Reader in Philosophy at the University of Liverpool. The editor of B. K. Matilal's *The Character of Logic in India* (SUNY, 1998) and *Ethics and Epics: The Collected Essays of Bimal Krishna Matilal: Philosophy, Culture and Religion* (Oxford University Press, 2002), he is also the author of *Semantic Powers: Meaning and the Means of Knowing in Classical Indian Philosophy* (Oxford University Press, 1999), *Indian Logic* (Curzon, 2001), and *Philosophy in Classical India: The Proper Work of Reason* (Routledge, 2001).

Amy Hollywood is Professor of Theology and the History of Christianity at the University of Chicago Divinity School, specializing in mysticism, with strong interests in philosophy of religion and feminist theory. She is the author of *The Soul as Virgin Wife: Mechthild of Magdeburg, Marguerite Porete, and Meister Eckhart* (University of Notre Dame Press, 1995) and *Sensible Ecstasy: Mysticism, Sexual Difference, and the Demands of History* (University of Chicago Press, 2002).

Steven Kepnes is the Murray W. and Mildred K. Finard Professor in Jewish Studies in the Department of Philosophy and Religion at Colgate University. The author of *The Text as Thou* (Indiana University Press, 1992) and co-author of *Reasoning After Revelation: Dialogues in Postmodern Jewish Philosophy* (Westview Press, 1997), Kepnes is one of the founders of the movement of Textual Reasoning and co-editor of the *Journal of Textual Reasoning*.

T. C. Kline III is Assistant Professor of Philosophy at St Mary's College of Maryland. He is the co-editor with P. J. Ivanhoe of *Virtue, Nature, and Moral Agency in the* Xunzi (Hackett, 2000) and the editor of *Ritual and Religion in the* Xunzi (Seven Bridges, 2003). He is also series co-editor for the Society of Asian and Comparative Philosophy Monograph Series.

Robert N. McCauley is Professor of Philosophy at Emory University, specializing in philosophy of psychology and contemporary epistemology. He is co-author of *Rethinking Religion: Connecting Cognition and Culture* (Cambridge University Press, 1993) and of *Bringing Ritual to Mind: Psychological Foundations of Cultural Forms* (Cambridge University Press, 2002).

Ladelle McWhorter is Professor of Philosophy and Women's Studies at the University of Richmond. She is the author of *Bodies and Pleasures: Foucault and the Politics of Sexual Normalization* (Indiana University Press, 1999) and the editor of *Heidegger and the Earth: Essays in Environmental Philosophy* (Thomas Jefferson University Press, 1992).

Michael L. Raposa is Professor of Religion Studies at Lehigh University. He is the author of *Charles S. Peirce's Philosophy of Religion* (Indiana University Press, 1989), *Boredom and the Religious Imagination* (University of Virginia Press, 1999), and *Meditation and the Martial Arts* (University of Virginia Press, 2003).

Kevin Schilbrack is Associate Professor of Philosophy and Religious Studies at Wesleyan College. He writes on the philosophical and methodological questions involved in the cross-cultural study of religions, and he is the contributing editor of *Thinking through Myths: Philosophical Perspectives* (Routledge, 2002).

Frits Staal is Emeritus Professor of Philosophy at the University of California at Berkeley. He is the author of many books, including *Rules Without Meaning: Ritual, Mantras and the Human* (Peter Lang, 1989; 2nd edn, 1993), *The Science of Ritual* (Bhandarkar Oriental Research Institute, 1982), *Jouer avec le feu: pratique et théorie du rituel védique* (Institut de Civilisation Indienne, 1990), and *Agni: The Vedic Ritual of the Fire Altar* (Asian Humanities Press, 1983; Motilal Banarsidass, 2001).

Charles Taliaferro, Professor of Philosophy at St Olaf College, is the author of *Consciousness and the Mind of God* (Cambridge University Press, 1994), *Contemporary Philosophy of Religion* (Blackwell, 1997), and the co-editor of the *Blackwell Companion to Philosophy of Religion* (2003). He is also the current Book Review Editor of *Faith and Philosophy*.

Peter H. Van Ness taught philosophy of religion for over a decade at Union

Theological Seminary and Columbia University, during which time he published *Spirituality, Diversion, and Decadence* (SUNY, 1992) and edited and contributed to *Spirituality and the Secular Quest* (Crossroad, 1996). In 2000 he received a Master of Public Health degree in chronic disease epidemiology from the Yale University School of Medicine and he completed a postdoctoral fellowship in epidemiology there in 2002. Currently he has a faculty appointment as an Associate Research Scientist in the Yale School of Medicine and teaches courses on religion and health in both the School of Medicine and the Divinity School.

Acknowledgments

I would like to express my appreciation to Wesleyan College for the sabbatical that gave me the time and Harvard University's Center for the Study of World Religions for providing a space for work on this volume. Special thanks are due to Jennifer Mujica for help in preparing the manuscript. Thanks also to my sons Sasha and Elijah, for keeping me grounded in love, and to Teri Cole, who continues to inspire.

I would like to thank Pamela S. Anderson, Beverley Clack, and Routledge for granting permission to publish the paper by Amy Hollywood, which first appeared in Pamela S. Anderson and Beverley Clack (eds), *Feminist Philosophy of Religion: Critical Readings* (Routledge, 2004).

The paper by Kevin Schilbrack first appeared in 2004 in the *Journal of Ritual Studies*. Permission for the materials to be used here was granted by the Journal's editors, Dr Pamela J. Stewart and Prof. Andrew Strathern, and I would like to thank them for it.

The paper by Frits Staal is an expanded version of a paper that first appeared under the title "Simultaneities in Vedic Ritual" in the *Journal of Historical Pragmatics* 4:2 (2003) 195–210. I would like to thank the *Journal of Historical Pragmatics* for permission to reprint that paper.

Introduction

On the use of philosophy in the study of rituals

Kevin Schilbrack

I. Introduction

Rituals, like operas, are mixed and complicated events and, as a consequence, the study of rituals is an interdisciplinary job.[1] It includes sociology and psychology, history, and anthropology, performance studies and gender studies. And when those involved in the study of ritual list the disciplines relevant to the task, philosophy is not excluded – that is, the word "philosophy" can often be found on those interdisciplinary lists. But such lists can be misleading, for philosophy has so far contributed almost not at all to the study of rituals.

There is at present a lack of philosophical interest in ritual. Philosophers (including philosophers of religion) almost never analyze ritual behavior; those who study ritual almost never refer to philosophy.[2] The primary reason for this absence of a philosophical contribution to the study of rituals, in my judgment, is the assumption that ritual activities are thoughtless. That is, rituals are typically seen as mechanical or instinctual and not as activities that involve thinking or learning. This assumption reflects a dichotomy between beliefs and practices and, ultimately, a general dualism between mind and body, as Catherine Bell has noted (Bell 1992; cf. Grimes 1990: 1). But this inability to see rituals as thoughtful is unnecessary. My goal in this introduction, and ultimately, in this book, is to argue that there are rich and extensive philosophical resources available with which one might build bridges between ritual and thought, between practice and belief, and between body and mind. There are, I want to argue, several philosophical tools available for thinking through rituals.

One can begin to show the value of philosophy to ritual studies in a minimal way simply by noting that rituals are, whatever else they are, actions or practices in which people engage.[3] The last century of philosophy is sometimes described as having made the linguistic turn, that is, as reflecting the appreciation by both Continental and Anglophone philosophers that experience is always already mediated by language. But it is also true that many philosophers in the last century have made action or practice the central term of analysis. The century can also therefore be seen as making the practice turn, the appreciation that the world is revealed through activity (Schatzki *et al.* 2001). Richard J. Bernstein shows that action and praxis are central terms for analytic philosophers, Marxist philosophers, existentialists, and pragmatists (Bernstein 1971). Practice is seen as central to what it means to be human (May 2001). Contemporary philosophy is thus a congenial partner for those who want to understand ritual behavior.

One can begin to show the value of philosophy to ritual studies in a more perspicuous way. In my judgment, the central obstacle to a philosophical contribution to the study of rituals is the assumption that ritual activities are thoughtless, and this assumption turns on a set of modern views about what knowledge is. It is widely held that knowledge involves accurately representing the external world. Having representations, however, is something that only minds can do. Minds can represent or reflect the world – for example, by thinking "The cat is on the mat" – bodies cannot do this. Thus the assumption has been that bodily movements are not representations and therefore whatever is going on in the movements of rituals must be something other than thinking. And so the implication follows that philosophical tools are not needed. Rituals are consequently interpreted as non-cognitive behavior, for example, as expressions of people's emotions or neuroses, or as automatic activities, people mechanically "going through the motions." It is true that ritual is often interpreted as symbolic activity, and on this interpretation rituals may symbolize knowledge. But even in this latter case, the ritual actions are still treated as merely a vehicle for thought, but not a mode of thinking itself, like an illiterate person carrying a book. In a word, then, the primary obstacle to a philosophical contribution to the study of rituals is a theory of knowledge that has been called objectivism or the representational theory of knowledge. But if this is accurate, then it becomes clearer how philosophy has a contribution to make, because philosophy in the twentieth century made the pursuit of a non-objectivist or non-representationalist theory of knowledge a central concern. That is, hand in hand with the practice turn comes a set of philosophical movements with a convergent interest in overcoming the Cartesian dualistic account in which the mind is a disembodied spectator. Richard Rorty (1979), for example, argues that this is a goal that unites the projects of Wittgenstein, Heidegger, and Dewey, and this argument is developed further by Bernstein (1983) and Frisina (2002). On these postmodern accounts, knowledge is necessarily embodied, intersubjective, and active. As a consequence, I would argue, there are some overlooked philosophical tools for seeing ritual activity as thoughtful. To these I now turn.

II. Philosophical resources for the study of rituals

In this section I describe several philosophical movements that might help us, in different ways, to see rituals in their connections to thinking, learning, and knowing.[4] These are not, of course, the only philosophical resources – and may not even be the best ones.[5] Moreover, the philosophical approaches discussed below have tensions between them; I am not arguing that they can be unified into a single voice. Nevertheless, I suggest that they do provide valuable and sometimes overlooked resources and, for the purpose of studying ritual, they may help us avoid a representationalist theory of knowledge or other obstacles to seeing rituals as thoughtful. The sketches of these philosophies are so brief that they can do little more than serve to point to directions for future research. But I hope that they are not so cursory that they are misleading or frustrating but are long enough and suggestive enough to interest people in the prospects for attending to the philosophical aspects of ritual. The philosophical approaches that I consider here are the following nine: pragmatism, post-Wittgensteinian linguistic philosophy, existentialism, hermeneutic philosophy, Foucault's genealogical approach, phenomenology, cognitive science, feminist epistemologies, and comparative philosophy.

Pragmatist philosophers, as their name suggests, are primarily interested in understanding knowledge from the perspective of practical action. Seeking to overcome the idea of the knower as a spectator and to replace it with the idea of the knower as participant and problem solver is therefore a theme common to all the pragmatists (including here Peirce, James, Santayana, Whitehead, and Dewey). On a pragmatist approach, therefore, what the knower knows is not a static body of propositions but an ongoing process between the agent and its environment. Knowing and acting are not separate and the subject qua agent, engaged and purposive, is seen as a more *complete* subject. James Feibleman proposes that one read the pragmatists in this way:

> For if knowledge is to be derived from experience, as most philosophers as well as all experimental scientists pretty well agree that it is, then it must be the whole of experience, experience in all of its parts rather than only in some, that is meant. Action must be included as well as thought and sensation.
>
> (Feibleman 1976: 170)

In other words, just as the rationalists looked to reason as a source of knowledge, and the empiricists looked to the senses, the pragmatists add action as a third source of reliable knowledge.

Applying a pragmatist account of knowledge to rituals studies has not yet been explored in any depth (although see Jackson 1989). But such an approach has the potential to provide the conceptual tools to see rituals as activities in which ritualists are not simply repeating traditional gestures but are rather raising and seeking to settle a problem. From this Deweyan perspective, rituals seek to move the participants from disquiet to resolution, they involve the testing of hypotheses, and hence they are a form of inquiry (Dewey 1991). Thus a pragmatist philosophy of rituals might ask the questions: what problems are ritualists trying to solve, what afflictions or difficulties are they trying to overcome, and what do they learn in their rituals?

One of the greatest obstacles to a philosophy of ritual, in my judgment, has been the view that language must be about empirical facts if it is to be even possibly true. Given this view, ritual language (and religious language generally) is in a difficult situation. If it is not to be taken as meaningless babble, then ritual language must be either an attempt to describe empirical facts in the "external" world (in which case it is often contradicted by scientific descriptions) or a symbolic expression of feelings or values (in which case it is non-cognitive, that is, neither true nor false). Given this understanding of the limits of what meaningful language can be about, the twentieth century revolution in linguistic philosophy, signaled especially by the later writings of Ludwig Wittgenstein (Wittgenstein 1953), is of primary importance for the study of ritual. Wittgenstein rejects the idea that meaningful language must be descriptive, arguing that language has many legitimate uses:

> Giving orders, and obeying them – Describing the appearance of an object, or giving its measurements – Constructing an object from a description (a drawing) – Reporting an event – Speculating about an event – Forming and testing a hypothesis – Presenting the results of an experiment in tables and diagrams – Making up a story; and reading it – Play-acting – Singing catches – Guessing riddles – Making a joke; telling it – Solving a problem in arithmetic – Translating from one language to another – Asking, thanking, cursing, greeting, praying.
>
> (1953: 11–12 [27])

On Wittgenstein's view, these different uses of language follow their own rules, just as different games do, but that is no fault, especially when one sees that these ways of speaking and thinking arise from particular practices or forms of life in which they have their sense. Wittgenstein did not develop a philosophy of rituals, but he did comment on them suggestively, and criticized the assumption that rituals involve science-like hypotheses or attempts to control the natural world (Wittgenstein 1979; for insightful discussions, see Cioffi 1998; Clack 1999).

Peter Winch applied Wittgenstein's pluralistic understanding of language to the study of social action (including religion) and to the study of rituals (1958, 1970; the best assessment of Winch is Lerner 2002). Winch argues that rituals are often criticized for being irrational, impractical, or non-scientific behavior, but one should not use criteria taken from one practice to criticize another. Focusing on Zande witchcraft rituals, Winch argues that one should interpret them as rational in their context. Specifically, Winch argues that they express an attitude about contingencies in general, rather than seeking to control or predict a particular contingency (like an illness).

Another example of a post-Wittgensteinian linguistic philosophy that appreciates the variety of uses of language and that has therefore proven useful for ritual studies is John Austin's analysis of speech-acts (Austin 1965; cf. Searle 1969, 1979). Austin argues that words can have what he calls "illocutionary" force, in that one can do things with them. When one christens a ship or pronounces a couple married, for example, the words one uses bring about real changes in the world. Ruth Finnegan argues for the value of this approach for the study of ritual precisely in that it avoids the limited view of language mentioned above. Given Austin's approach, she says, prayer and sacrifice need not be explained (or explained away) as being merely "expressive" or "symbolic" and thus very different from most everyday speech acts; rather they can be brought under the same general heading as such acts as "announcing," "saying goodbye" or greeting. ... Austin's analysis helps us out of the dilemma of having to allocate all speech utterances into just one or the other of two categories: descriptive or expressive (or symbolic) utterances.

(Finnegan 1969: 550)

As Benjamin Ray says, "the performative power of ritual language [is] its ability to rearrange people's feelings and command psychological forces to make things happen in people's lives" (2000: 110; see also Ray 1973; Tambiah 1979; and for a critique, Grimes 1990 ch. 9).

The recognition of the performative and other non-descriptive functions of words in rituals is important. However, many of the post-Wittgensteinian approaches to ritual sidestep and do not challenge the positivist idea that ritual uses of language are disconnected from the world and therefore non-cognitive. If the idea of cognitive ritual language is to be an interpretive option, what is needed is a way of understanding how rituals can make or reveal a world, not only in the psychological sense that Ray mentions, but also in an ontological or metaphysical sense that ritual behavior creates and reveals ways of being in the world. Here existentialism may help.

Existentialist philosophy is a reaction to philosophical and scientific systems that forget the concrete individual in their pursuit of abstract systems of thought. The primary value of existentialism for our purposes follows from its conception of the human condition as an embodied, social, and active being-in-the-world (Heidegger 1962; cf. Todes 2001). This understanding calls into question dualisms that have blocked an appreciation of rituals as thoughtful. In the first place, being-in-the-world seeks to move beyond a Cartesian, representationalist, or objectivist model of knowledge (Bernstein 1983). Second, the existentialist approach denies the romantic split between one's "inner," secret self and one's "outer," public action. Subjectivity is really "intersubjectivity," as Sartre says. And third, it undermines the idea that what is given to experience is value neutral. What is immediately given is rather a ready-to-hand life-world revealed by our projects. This connection between facts and values is important for the study of practices that claim to reveal fundamental norms.

In the middle of the twentieth century, existentialism received a warm reception in both theology and religious studies, and so some may assume that as a tool for the study of ritual existentialism has already been put to good use. It is true that Mircea Eliade took as his task the rediscovery of the existential dimensions of ritual life in archaic societies and that he adopts Heideggerian language in his analysis of the sacred and the profane as two modes of being in the world (Eliade 1959: esp. 8–18). But the implications of being-in-the-world for understanding ritual actions as thoughtful – and in particular the existentialist idea that the body is the subject of consciousness (Sartre 1956: 303–59; Wider 1997) – have not yet been appreciated. For Sartre, the body is not identified as an unthinking *res extensa*, which would be the body defined as an object among other objects, the body defined "in-itself" from the outside. Rather, the body indicates (to use Sartre's nice phrase) "the possibilities which I am" of moving and otherwise engaging with the world. The body is the seat of one's conscious engagement with the world; it is that by which objects are revealed to me, that which "makes there be a world" (303–6). From this perspective, "knowledge and action are only two abstract aspects of an original, concrete relation" (308). This provides a way of speaking of ritual action and ritual knowledge as growing out of and shaping a level of intentionality that is more basic than the linguistic.[6]

Existentialist approaches to the study of ritual will tend to see rituals as part of a search for meaning. On an existentialist view, being human perpetually and necessarily involves giving oneself projects and purposes, living toward the future, and creating oneself through one's actions. Insofar as ritual is not merely a conservative bolster for the status quo but, as more and more are arguing, can be conducive to change and even to revolution (e.g. Lincoln 1989, 2000, 2003: ch. 6), one might therefore draw on existentialism to argue that ritual can be a way for people to navigate change and to choose who they will be so as to create a future not like their past. Here is relevant Sartre's belief that even one's "thrownness" is not a limit on one's freedom, for one always chooses what meaning one's situation will have.

Hermeneutic philosophy is another movement influenced by Heidegger's analysis of projective understanding that shows promise for ritual studies. Though Schleiermacher and Dilthey originally developed hermeneutics in the nineteenth century for the interpretation of texts, and Heidegger and Gadamer adapted it for the interpretation of human understanding more generally, it is primarily Paul Ricoeur who has applied hermeneutics to the study of human action. Ricoeur argues that meaningful actions may become the objects of study "through a kind of objectification similar to the fixation that occurs in writing" (1991: 151); this objectification is possible, he says, because actions themselves have a propositional content and structure. Ricoeur therefore proposes using the written text as the paradigm for understanding human action and reading as the paradigm for the human sciences, arguing that with this approach human action is opened "to anybody who *can read*" (1991: 155; emphasis in the original).

As with existentialism, some may feel that hermeneutics is not a new tool for the study of ritual. It is true, for example, that Clifford Geertz defines culture as an "acted document" and a "system of signs" and so conceives of the ethnographer's task as providing a vocabulary in which what ritual action "says" can be expressed (1973: 27). Geertz credits Ricoeur, "from whom this whole idea of the inscription of action is borrowed and somewhat twisted" (1973: 19), and he conceives of action as a form of social discourse. Hermeneutics of ritual in this sense has been criticized, however, insofar as it reduces sensual, embodied actions to textual, disembodied signs. Ruel Tyson, for example, raises the question whether the most important aspect of social action is "its 'said,' its conceptual, statable, propositional content, and the conceptual structures, sponsoring it and making it decipherable" (Tyson 1988: 105). For Tyson, a semiotic theory of ritual intellectualizes actions – not in the sense that it reads them as bearing a sense that they do not really have, but in that it ignores the gap between the performative domain of action and the relatively bloodless domain of writing. Similarly, Paul Stoller argues that treating the body as a text strips it of its smells, tastes, textures, and pains (1997: xiv). And he asks: "is it not problematic to use the body as text metaphor in societies in which the body is felt and not read?" (Stoller 1997: 5–6).

If a hermeneutic philosophy can shed light on rituals without distorting them, therefore, it needs to develop a hermeneutics of performance that does not lose the richness of ritual action. One suggestion about how to do so comes from William Schweiker, who argues not that ritual performance should be seen as a kind of text but that both rituals and texts should be seen as "mimetic" in that they both involve the creative practice of imaginative understanding. Hermeneutics, then, understood as a mimetic play (using Gadamer's term, *Spiel*) of understanding in its own right, can provide a vocabulary that can do justice to the textual, the performative, and the rule-following features of a culture (Schweiker 1987, 1988; on ritual mimesis see also Stoller 1997: 65–7). Another proposal for a non-textual hermeneutics of performance comes from Lawrence Sullivan, who points out that throughout most of human history "the problems of meaning, understanding, communication and interpretation have been thrashed out without references to texts and without resort to text as a primary metaphor" (1990b: 41). Students of culture should therefore recognize that human reflection is found not only (and not even primarily) in books, but also in other meaningful activities like canoe-making, pottery, basket-making, weaving, house construction, musical performance, and astronomy, all of which can be taken as reflective interpretations of their makers' worlds:

> The notion of text now stifles the attempt of religious studies to confront the full range of religious experiences and expressions – even those recorded in texts ... [and it] diverts us onto a wide detour that escapes a confrontation with other modes of intelligibility.
>
> (Sullivan 1990b: 46, 50)

Sullivan proposes that hermeneutics flower into an approach that recovers the sensual dimension of religion (Sullivan 1986) and that in the same way that new ways of understanding symbolic life were opened by Freud's hermeneutics of dreams, a non-textual reality, a hermeneutics of the sensual world might do the same:

> I am suggesting that religious studies could look not only at dreams but at shadows, at flowers, at sounds, at pottery and basketry, at smells and

light, at the crafts and domestic sciences, and regard them as symbolic vehicles for the full load of human experience.

(Sullivan 1990b: 51)

These revisions of hermeneutic philosophy of rituals have yet to be fully assayed.

It is in part because of his dissatisfaction with hermeneutics, however, that Michel Foucault develops his genealogical approach (see especially Foucault 1979, 1980, 1998). Foucault's objection to hermeneutics is that it treats disciplined practices, in which people are trained to have certain affects, desires, and competencies, as if they were really symbolic activities with hidden meanings that need to be decoded. His genealogical method therefore differs from hermeneutics because it seeks not the meaning or interpretation or understanding of the practice, what the practice "says," but rather the *effect* of the practice, what the practice does to those who participate in it.[7] As Hubert Dreyfus notes,

> Since the hidden meaning is not the final truth about what is going on, finding it is not necessarily liberating, and can, as Foucault points out, lead away from the kind of understanding that might help the participant resist pervasive practices whose only end is the efficient ordering of society.
>
> (Dreyfus 1984: 80)

In other words, on a genealogical approach, social practices like rituals do not repress what they are really about (as they are said to, for example, in the hermeneutics of suspicion of Freud and Marx). Rather, they reveal their strategies in the very production of trained bodies.

Thus a Foucauldian analysis of rituals is centrally about controlling bodies, and it focuses on power. But Foucault is distinctive in that on his account power is not coercive:

> What makes power hold good, what makes it accepted is simply the fact that it does not weigh on us as a force that says no, but that it traverses and produces things, it induces pleasure, forms of knowledge, produces discourse. It needs to be considered as a productive network which runs through the whole social body, much more than a negative instance whose function is repression.
>
> (1980: 19)

Through small, quotidian "micro-practices," power works by creating the possibilities for people to live as a certain kind of subject. (Susan Bordo (1993) provides some especially good examples of this point.) A strength of Foucault's approach is thus the explicit attention it gives to rituals' role as disciplinary practices. In this light, how people stand, move, hold their hands, and so on, is moved from the category of "the natural" to the category of the social, and as having an effect on people's "souls." As Foucault says, genealogy seeks the significance of events "in the most unpromising places, in what we tend to feel is without history – in sentiments, love, conscience, instincts" (Foucault 1998: 369). Thus it permits students of ritual to see the body as inscribed with cultural signs and ritual is a central tool of inscription (for Foucault's treatment of religion, see Foucault 1999).

Some critics argue, however, that a weakness of Foucault's approach is that it lacks the sense of a thinking body. Some complain that subjectivity is eliminated altogether. Foucault does use the phrase "the mindful body," but by it he does not mean a body that is full of mind, but a body that is "minded" in the sense of watched over, under surveillance, or self-monitored (as a contrast, see Scheper-Hughes and Lock 1987). Despite Foucault's attention to the body, ultimately he does not see the body as a source of human agency. As Chris Shilling puts it:

> Once the body is contained within modern disciplinary systems, it is the mind which takes over as the location for discursive power. Consequently, the body tends to be reduced to an inert mass which is controlled by discourses centred on the mind. However, this mind is itself disembodied; we get no sense of the mind's location within an active human body. To put it bluntly, the bodies that appear in Foucault's work do not enjoy a prolonged visibility as corporeal entities. Bodies are produced, but their own powers of production, where they have any, are limited to those invested in them by discourse. As such, any body is dissolved as a causal phenomenon into the determining power of discourse, and it becomes extremely difficult to conceive of the body as a material component of social action.
> (Shilling 1993: 80)

In this respect, its critics say, genealogy does not move beyond the problematic modernist dualisms of mind and body mentioned at the beginning of this chapter.

By contrast, phenomenology argues for the ineliminability of the body as subject. For phenomenologists like Maurice Merleau-Ponty, the mind is not the only or even the primary source of engagement with the world. As Merleau-Ponty says, "The body is our general medium for having a world" (Merleau-Ponty 1962: 146). And Merleau-Ponty explains that the body opens up a meaningful world for us in three senses:

> Sometimes it is restricted to the actions necessary for the conservation of life, and accordingly it posits around us a biological world; at other times, elaborating upon these primary actions and moving from their literal to a figurative meaning, it manifests through them a core of new significance: this is true of motor habits such as dancing. Sometimes, finally, the meaning aimed at cannot be achieved by the body's natural means; it must then build itself an instrument, and it projects thereby around itself a cultural world.
> (Merleau-Ponty 1962: 146)

Thus our bodies determine what presents itself in our world sometimes in terms of their innate structures, as when some part of the world is presented as providing a place to rest; sometimes the world is mediated in terms of acquired skills common to bodies in general, as when some part of the world is presented as providing a place for sitting or for dancing; and sometimes the world is mediated in terms of acquired skills that are culturally specific, as when some part of the world is presented as providing a place for sitting in zazen (see Dreyfus and Dreyfus 1999). All three dimensions of corporeal subjectivity would be present in a ritual.

Thomas Csordas (1999) explains why a phenomenological approach to ritual is so important. Since the 1970s, the metaphor of the text has come to dominate the study of culture. On this perspective, and as we saw above in the discussion of hermeneutics, a culture is treated as a system of signs or symbols that can be read. In the past 20 years, there has been a shift from discussion of "signs" and "symbols" to "discourse" and "representation," but such post-structuralist terms are still broadly semiotic. The metaphor of the text is, as Csordas says, a hungry metaphor, "swallowing all of culture to the point where it became possible and even convincing to hear the deconstructionist motto that there is nothing outside the text" (1999: 146). When one holds that discourse does not disclose the world but rather constitutes it, then the notion of experience drops out. Without phenomenology, therefore, it is difficult to pose the question about the limits of discourse. It seems to be fallacious to ask whether there is anything beyond or outside discourse or to ask what discourse refers to. In the study of rituals, then, phenomenology can provide a dialogical partner for those approaches that treat ritual as cultural inscription and do not take into account the materiality of the lived body (cf. Csordas 1994; for an excellent treatment of how a phenomenological approach to subjectivity like Merleau-Ponty's *can* be combined with Foucault's, see Crossley 1994).

Cognitive science was not originally receptive to the study of embodied thought, but in the last ten to twenty years there has been evidence of a paradigm shift. The traditional model of thinking in cognitive science is often labeled "cognitivism," in which thinking is understood as computation, that is, the manipulation of internal symbolic representations. On this approach, the model of the mind is the computer, and the "world is (just) a source of inputs and an arena for outputs, the body is (just) an organ for receiving the inputs and effecting the outputs" (Clark 1998: 36). But there has been a growing appreciation of this approach's shortcomings. Emerging as alternatives is a variety of approaches that challenge the identification of thinking and representing. In its place are proposed a range of alternatives that either minimize (Clark 1997) or, in the extreme case, eliminate internal representations (e.g. van Gelder 1995; for a critique, see Clark and Toribio 1994). On these new models, thinking is necessarily dynamically related to a body in a world. As Tim van Gelder writes, "In this vision, the cognitive system is not just the encapsulated brain; rather, since the nervous system, body, and environment are all constantly changing and simultaneously influencing each other, the true cognitive system is a single unified system embracing all three" (van Gelder 1995: 373; similarly, Haugeland 1998: ch. 9). For this reason, Francisco Varela and his colleagues call thinking "enaction," a term that emphasizes their view that thinking "is not the representation of pregiven world by a pregiven mind but is rather the enactment of a world and a mind on the basis of a history of the variety of actions that a being in the world performs" (Varela *et al.* 1991: 9).

Moreover, Mark Johnson argues that not only must a mind be in a body to think, but that body metaphors are the very substance of abstract thinking.[8] He argues that from our sensorimotor activity there emerge patterns in our knowing interactions with the world. That is, as we orient ourselves spatially and temporally, direct our perceptual focus, move our bodies, and manipulate objects for various purposes, we also develop structures to our experiences. For example, the bodily experience of tracking an object visually from point A along a path to point B produces the pattern, or what Johnson calls an "image schemata," of *source-path-goal*. This pattern or schemata gives rise to metaphors such as "purposes are directions" (as when one says "I am *on the way* to get a Ph.D.") or "arguments are journeys" (as when one says "I can *follow* what you are saying"). Such metaphors constitute our under-standing of intentional action and structure even our most abstract reasoning. Bodily experience is thus the basis for cognitive activity.

These developments in cognitive science are pregnant for the study of rituals. Tamar Frankiel (2001) hypothesizes that the ritualized body is deeply invested precisely in image schemata. Rituals teach people to embody the distinctions in basic schemata such as up/down, inside/outside, and center/periphery, and in this way the rituals reinforce and elaborate the basic patterns through which people perceive their world. Different societies emphasize different schemata. For example, one society may focus on scale and hierarchy, extending and developing that pattern in its metaphors, while another focuses on the schemata of center and periphery (Frankiel 2001: 82). In this way, Johnson's theory can provide a vocabulary for the comparative study of rituals that lets us see how bodily movements give shape to – or more: give rise to – thinking through rituals (see also Andresen 2001).

Susan Bordo points out that feminists began to develop a critique of the "politics of the body" long before it was in philosophical fashion (Bordo 1993: 15–23). There has consequently been an enormous amount of theo-retical work by feminists on the body (e.g. Davis 1997; Price and Shildrik 1999; Schiebinger 2000), and by feminist philosophers on the body (e.g. Daly 1978; Jaggar and Bordo 1989; Young 1990; Sawicki 1991; Grosz 1994, 1995; Butler 1993, 1999; Weiss 1999; McWhorter 1999; Sullivan 2001), though relatively little of it has been explicitly on rituals. Feminist philosophy has much to offer ritual studies. For example, feminist epistemologists have stressed the political, racial, and gendered specificity of the knowing subject. They have argued for the socially constructed nature of the knower and so, in this context, one can see two possible directions for feminist epistemological

contributions to the study of ritual knowledge. In the first place, some feminist philosophers call for and are beginning to provide the resources for
appreciating bodily forms of knowing. As Elizabeth Grosz writes,

> a feminist philosophy of the body ... must avoid the impasse posed by
> dichotomous accounts of the person which divide the subject into the
> mutually exclusive categories of mind and body. Although within our
> intellectual heritage there is no language in which to describe such
> concepts, no terminology which does not succumb to versions of this
> polarization, some kind of understanding of *embodied subjectivity*, of
> *psychical corporeality*, needs to be developed.
>
> (Grosz 1994: 21–2)

In the second place, some feminist philosophers have also argued for an
intrinsically gendered form of knowing. Grosz writes,

> Once the universal is shown to be a guise for the masculine and knowl-
> edges are shown to occupy only one pole of a (sexual) spectrum instead
> of its entirety, the possibility of other ways of knowing and proceeding
> – the possibility of feminine discourses and knowledges – reveals itself.
>
> (Grosz 1994: 38)

Meredith McGuire has suggested such an idea for the ethnographic study of
religions: "Women's uses of intuition may also be gender-linked, due to the
culturally patterned ways that women attend to their bodies and use their
bodies to attend to the world" and "bodily ways of knowing may produce
intuitions, a form of knowledge that could be sound bases for ethnographic
exploration and analysis" (McGuire 2002: 209; cf. McGuire 1990, 1996).

Perhaps the richest philosophical resources for the study of ritual can be
found in an often overlooked source for philosophy, namely, religious traditions themselves. As Lawrence Sullivan points out, religions (and especially
religions other than Christianity) "have all been taken, in the main, as data
to be explained rather than as theoretical resources for the sciences that
study them" (Sullivan 1990a: 87). But religious traditions have not merely
been practicing their rituals unreflectively; they themselves often have long
philosophical traditions of analyzing the nature and the function of rituals.
There is, then, a body of Buddhist philosophical reflections on ritual, as well
as Daoist philosophical traditions, Islamic ones, and so on. Thus Sullivan's
question presents itself: "What role will other cultures be allowed to play
in answering these questions about the nature of different modes of knowing
and the relations among them?" (Sullivan 1990a: 87).[9]

The study of non-western religious philosophies often takes place under the
rubric of comparative philosophy. Borrowing from Thomas Kasulis, one can
say that comparative philosophy has both a heuristic and a provocative function (Kasulis 1993: xi–xii). In its heuristic function, comparative philosophy
can help one understand rituals better simply by seeing them from more than

one cultural perspective. In its provocative function, however, comparative philosophy can have dramatic effects, shaking one out of preconceptions and leading one to shift one's perspective on an issue that might otherwise be stuck in stalemate. Kasulis gives the example of the work of the contemporary Buddhist philosopher, Yuasa Yasuo, on the mind–body relationship (Yuasa 1987, 1993; cf. Nagatomo 1992). Yuasa argues that western philosophers have tended to ask the question of the relation between mind and body in terms of the intrinsic or essential relation between the two, and they have looked for insight in ordinary situations. By contrast, eastern philosophers who reflect on mind–body relations – precisely because they pursued their philosophy in a context of religious practice – have tended to treat mind–body relation as something that varies with one's level of achievement, and they have looked for insight in the skills of exceptional individuals. In this way, Kasulis argues, non-western religious philosophies can provide new perspectives and reorientations in one's conceptual categories (Kasulis 1987). Moreover, religious philosophical approaches are more likely to tie ritual to what the religion understands as true, good, and beautiful, which is to say, to metaphysics, ethics, and aesthetics (see e.g, Kasulis *et al.* 1993; Law 1995; Coakley 2000). And I suspect that the idea of thinking through rituals is one that many religious philosophers would find natural (see e.g. Clooney 1990).

Having come to the end of this overview, it may be worthwhile to summarize my assessments of these nine general approaches. In my judgment, pragmatism lets us interpret ritual as a form of inquiry and is the most promising and underappreciated approach for those who are interested in ritual as a knowledge-generating practice. Post-Wittgensteinian linguistic philosophy lets us interpret ritual uses of language in terms of "language games" and "speech acts," and so as rational in their own right, and "illocutionary force" identifies an important aspect of ritual language. But in seeking to distinguish ritual uses of language from scientific uses, this approach surrenders too much to science and often leaves us with ritual as merely the expression of attitudes. Existentialism helps us interpret rituals as modes of being-in-the-world, which is to say, as a synthesis of mind and body. Moreover, the existentialist idea that the body is the subject of consciousness has not yet been fully appreciated and is ripe for use in the study of rituals. Hermeneutics lets us "read" rituals, on an analogy with texts, as meaningful, communicative activities, a valuable and almost unavoidable approach for contemporary academics, but if a hermeneutics of performance is not developed, the analogy of ritual to text threatens to drain ritual of its sensuous and performative elements. Foucault's genealogical approach lets us see the ways in which rituals work as power-laden "disciplinary regimes" and "technologies of the self" that create people as subjects (in both senses of the term). Some of its proponents hold that this approach invalidates existentialist, hermeneutic, and phenomenological approaches, but if it is taken as one tool that complements the others, it is the best account of how rituals shape people's desires, experiences, and sense of self. Phenomenology develops the existentialist notion of being-in-the-world so as to speak of embodiment as the ground of (inter)subjectivity. Because it attends to the ritual body as it is lived, it is a necessary ingredient in any complete philosophy of ritual. Feminist philosophy provides resources for understanding the gendered subject. Of all the approaches surveyed here, feminist philosophy provides perhaps the strongest case that there is more than a single way of knowing. Recent work in cognitive science not only ties the philosophy of mind to the empirical sciences but also puts brain, body, and world together again in a way that should be congenial to the study of rituals. Lastly, comparative philosophy lets the philosophical study of rituals get schooled by and draw on sophisticated traditions of reflection on the nature and function of rituals. Such approaches are more likely to move beyond the social and psychological functions of rituals to connect ritual activities to the metaphysical nature of things.

The essays in this volume draw from these philosophical resources as they develop their approaches to understanding rituals.

III. The papers collected here

In "Ritual, body technique, and (inter)subjectivity," Nick Crossley interprets rituals as a form of what Marcel Mauss calls "body techniques." On this view, rituals necessarily involve patterned movements and postures that are culturally specific *uses* of the body. Crossley quotes Mauss's statement that "[t]he body is man's first and most natural instrument. Or more accurately, not to speak of instruments, man's first and most natural technical object, and at the same time technical means, is his body." But Crossley points out that this conception of the body as a tool can be problematic if it suggests that the body is merely a tool, a thoughtless vehicle through which the mind pursues its projects. Crossley argues that the phenomenology of Maurice Merleau-Ponty can help to stave off this kind of dualism. In Merleau-Ponty's analysis, one experiences one's body not as an object but as the very texture of one's experience. It is the body itself that "intends a world." A phenomenological approach like this one holds that our primary way of knowing and understanding the world consists in prereflective practical know-how. Rituals understood as body techniques when seen in this light, therefore, would be the practical uses that the thinking body makes of itself. With this phenomenologically informed understanding of Mauss's idea, one can appreciate body techniques as forms of practical reason (an idea also taken up and developed in the paper by Amy Hollywood). That is, the idea of body techniques suggests that reason is not exhausted by conscious and reflective thought but includes the acquired cultural competencies that cannot be separated from the body. Body techniques, including rituals, are our simultaneously physical and social way of being in the world, rendering the world intelligible and constituting it as a meaningful context for action.

If rituals are seen as forms of practical reason, techniques for achieving practical results, then they involve practical knowledge. Crossley argues that this will be not just knowledge of how to do the ritual itself, but also knowledge of how to relate to the natural and – especially – the social world. Rituals involve knowledge of social rules and social roles; for example, rituals of deference embody an understanding of authority in a given society and this is why rituals have such a crucial role in the maintenance and reproduction of society. Crossley argues that rituals play this role by effecting transformations in people's subjective and intersubjective states. For this reason, rituals, precisely as repositories of knowledge, can be used to tap into the corporeal potential for different ways of being, to transform one's individual or collective mode of intending the world. Rituals can be used to invoke or to ward off particular intentional states, which Crossley develops in terms of emotional and imaginative intentionality. In this way, Crossley illustrates a value towards which this book as a whole aims, namely, the use of philosophy to clarify the terms with which rituals are studied. His work shows in particular how the social scientific and the philosophical approaches to rituals cannot be wholly separated insofar as the social sciences always already take positions on philosophical questions.

Amy Hollywood approaches ritual from the perspective of a feminist philosopher of religion. She notes that other feminist philosophers of religion have followed the mainstream of analytic and continental philosophy of religion in focusing on religious belief and giving little attention to ritual. Taking the work of Pamela Sue Anderson and Grace Jantzen as examples, Hollywood shows that feminist philosophers of religion have aimed at expanding the grounds of moral and religious reflection to include bodily affects, emotion, and desire. Nevertheless, they offer accounts of the object of religious belief that eschew talk of existing realities and end up with religious objects that are merely "ideal," "mythical," or "abstract." But such accounts amount to a redefinition of religious belief or a recommendation for what religious belief should be, and not a fair description of what religious believers understand themselves to be focused on.

In light of this disconnect between religion as it is lived and "religion" as it is seen in philosophy of religion, Hollywood argues that the descriptive responsibilities of philosophy of religion require attention to ritual practices. "For many religious people, practice takes precedence over belief; a philosophy of religion that does not account for the function and meaning of practice will never be adequate to its object." Moreover, her proposal is that the turn to practice actually elucidates the nature of the object of religious belief. Drawing on the work of Marcel Mauss and Talal Asad, Hollywood argues that insofar as bodily practices train people to be certain kinds of subjects, they also provide philosophers with a way to develop a broader conception of practical reason. On Hollywood's account, practical reason should be understood not merely as a matter of principles (for example, universalizability), but also as the means for achieving a broad range of objectives, and so as involving learned modes of being in the world. In this way, the work of Mauss and Asad complements that of Anderson and Jantzen: the feminist philosophers of religion critique mainstream philosophy of religion for ignoring the roles of the body, emotion, and desire (and so for not appreciating the gendered constitution of religious belief), and Mauss and Asad provide a positive account of how those elements might be included by showing how bodily techniques serve in the formation of subjectivity and practical reason. Hollywood illustrates how religious practice can both shape religious subjects and provide the experiences that validate the way of life that produces them with the example of the meditative practices of Margaret Ebner, the thirteenth-century German mystic.

Ladelle McWhorter begins her paper, "Rites of passing: Foucault, power, and same-sex commitment ceremonies," by pointing out that the widespread view that ritual practice is in decline in the modern, rationalized world presupposes an understanding of ritual as non-rational action. Taking the perspective of Michel Foucault, however, one sees not a decline in ritual activities but a change in their style. The question is not how ritualized the modern world is, but how the modern world ritualizes. For Foucault, ritual practices represent techniques, first through mechanical and then normalizing disciplines, for making human interaction manageable, which is to say, both obedient to authority and productive.

Despite the suspicion towards ritual practices that McWhorter inherits from Foucault, her project is not simply a critique of "power/knowledge" in ritual practices. Unlike others, she also finds in Foucault the possibility of using rituals for self-cultivation: rituals, that is, as a form of work on oneself, as the invention of new modes of being. In her terms, this would be not rituals as "rites of passage" to a pre-established end, but rituals as "rites of passing," as self-transformation without an ultimate telos. Such rituals can aid in resistance by strengthening participants in self-disruptive and self-reconstructive ways. In Foucault's later writings, he asserts that ritual, as a technology of self- and community-shaping, can be part of an ethical *askesis*, part of a transformative discipline. Ritual for Foucault can be a practice of freedom. Finding resistance in rituals understood in this way, McWhorter argues,

> The task for those who would oppose the power of normalization is to maximize ethics' tendencies to resist identification – in other words, to place the emphasis on ethical practice as self-transformation rather than on whatever outcome such practices might be hoped to have. The task is to find ways of living, exercises, *askeses* that unsettle us, move us, change us in ways that keep us perpetually open to some degree of unsettlement, movement, and change, rather than tie us firmly to one identity, one truth, and one life trajectory.

McWhorter develops this hope with attention to same-sex commitment ceremonies. Drawing autobiographically on her own experiment, she seeks to take seriously Foucault's analysis of power and find means of empowerment within it. She asks,

> Is such a ritualized profession of one's commitment, which is automatically also a declaration of one's homosexual status or identity, a way

of opposing normalization – or of playing into it? And to the extent that these rites *are* marriage ceremonies, do they simply affirm and reinforce the state's right to regulate so-called private life?

Her paper is thus like the title of the first chapter of her book, "How I served as an anchor point for power and emerged as a locus of resistance" (McWhorter 1999), in that it draws on Foucault to explore what the positive – that is, non-normalizing, freeing – effects of such rites might be. Can they serve as *askeses*, ethical practices, a mode of transformation that emphasizes pass*ing* rather than pass*age*, open possibility rather than finality, completion, or static goal?

In "Scapegoat rituals in Wittgensteinian perspective," Brian R. Clack uses the biblical example of a scapegoat ritual to take an independent approach to Ludwig Wittgenstein's philosophical approach to rituals, that is, an approach in which Wittgenstein is treated as original and insightful but as nevertheless needing to be appropriated critically. Wittgenstein's philosophy of religion is often seen as providing resources for the defense of religious beliefs and practices, for it seems to treat religious ways of speaking and thinking – the religious "language game" – as immune to criteria of what is real or true that are not already religious. Famously, Wittgenstein objects to James Frazer's assumption in *The Golden Bough* that ritual practices are based on mistakes. Nevertheless, Clack argues that Wittgenstein's understanding of religious practices is misunderstood. Clack argues that it is true that Wittgenstein opposes Frazer's intellectualist interpretation of rituals. But it is not true that Wittgenstein always considers the ordinary religious language of rituals as alright as it is, for Wittgenstein refers to the scapegoat ritual as an example of a practice that is confused. This ritual, Wittgenstein says, reflects "a false picture, similar to those that cause errors in philosophy." What is the confusion? Some Wittgensteinians interpret Wittgenstein as saying that this ritual is confused because it gets an animal, which cannot be a moral agent, to carry sin. But Clack shows that this interpretation is crypto-Christian (the problem for Wittgenstein is not that only a human can carry another human's sin) and, moreover, Wittgenstein is surely not suggesting that errors in philosophy are caused by a process analogous to thinking confusedly that an animal can feel the responsibility of sin. Instead, Wittgenstein criticizes the scapegoat ritual as an example of a common linguistic confusion, namely, the conceptual problem that arises when one is bewitched by the surface grammar in a use of language to reify abstract nouns as if they were entities. The confusion is that the scapegoat ritual treats sin as if it were a physical object that one can carry for another. But here, then, one sees that the scapegoat ritual is not an isolated example of this problem: as Frazer details, it is one of a huge number of rituals with a similar logic and therefore, for Wittgenstein, a similar confusion. Wittgenstein's criticism of the scapegoat ritual therefore opens the door to a Wittgensteinian critique of a great swath of rituals, not excluding Christian rituals. Moreover, Wittgenstein's understanding of the confusion of these rituals is not very far from Frazer's understanding of the mistake in them. Thus Clack concludes that

> [t]he apparently throwaway remark about the scapegoat, seized on by the Wittgensteinian to evade the charge of fideism, is, as we have seen, in fact deeply subversive of humanity's religious life; it reveals Wittgenstein to be no great friend and defender of the faith, and if pressed strongly, as we have here done, it shakes the very foundations of the Christian faith.

In this way, Clack's interpretation of Wittgenstein avoids the usual labels of expressivism and fideism and rather points the way to a Wittgensteinian natural history of ritual (cf. Wittgenstein 1953: 125 [§415]).

In "Ritual inquiry: the pragmatic logic of religious practice," Michael Raposa recommends Charles Peirce's pragmatism as a philosophy that lets one understand rituals precisely as thoughtful actions. On Peirce's account, a belief is not an inner representation of a state of affairs but rather a program for action. For example, the belief "that the house is there" means that one is disposed to look for the house in a certain way and expects to find it in the given place. A belief is in this sense a rule for action. One's beliefs are embodied in one's conduct, and one's *deeply held* beliefs are embodied in the *patterns and habits* of their conduct. Given this understanding of belief, however, rituals that seek to mold behavior or to form habits in the ritualists are internally and not accidentally tied to belief. That is, if beliefs are habits, to mold people's behavior and to form their habits is to shape their beliefs. From this perspective, then, Raposa is able to say that rituals are "a thinking through and with the body."

The behavior that rituals shape, Raposa points out, is not merely physical behavior. Many rituals also represent a discipline of one's attention, training one's powers of perception, getting people to look in one place rather than another for insight. Rituals develop one's cognitive skill of how to see. Ritual understood in this way is not merely the inculcation of teachings, strengthening membership and creating a secure space but also (to use Peirce's language) an invitation to musement. It is in this sense that Raposa says that rituals are a form of inquiry. Like the cognitive skills developed in a laboratory, ritual skills facilitate insight and discovery. Like Ganeri in his paper, then, Raposa is willing to speak of the logic of rituals. According to Ganeri, Vedic rituals possess a logic in the sense that they provide a paradigmatic (or one might say "closed") model for practical reason. For Raposa, by contrast, rituals possess a logic in the sense that they provide a guiding (or one might say "open") model for spiritual development. Like the rules for inquiry in scientific practice, rituals guide and develop one's cognitive capacities.

In "Ritual metaphysics," Kevin Schilbrack argues that ritual practices often serve as a means for religious communities to pursue metaphysics, which is to say, investigations into the character of things in general. There are two ways in which one might see rituals as pursuing metaphysics. In the first, ritual communities treat the bodies of the ritual participants as objects – specifically, as texts upon which are inscribed cultural meanings. This idea that bodies are trained to carry marks or elicit signs, this semiotic approach to the social body, is common in the study of culture, but the idea that the bodily inscriptions can be about metaphysical matters has fallen into desuetude as part of the general contemporary prejudice against metaphysics. Recovering the idea of a metaphysical aspect of ritual bodies is therefore important, if religions actually do use their rituals to impress upon their practitioners a metaphysical view of the nature of things. On the second sense of ritual metaphysics, religious communities can also pursue metaphysics by treating the bodies of the ritual participants not as ritually inscribed objects, but rather as subjects, which is to say, as the locus of the thinking consciousness itself. On this account, it is through the directed somatic activities of the ritual that one learns about the metaphysical nature of things. Rituals are metaphysical in this sense, then, to the extent that they provide an opportunity for embodied inquiry into the character of that which is. The two parts of this paper therefore concern two senses of ritual knowledge, namely, a knowledge taught through rituals and a knowledge pursued through rituals, and these senses correspond to the double sense of "metaphysics" as both the product of an inquiry into the nature of things and the process of such an inquiry.

In the final section of the paper, Schilbrack holds that the two forms of ritual metaphysics described above do not wait on the emergence of a leisured, intellectual class, but can tacitly operate in the everyday practice of rituals. Drawing on the analysis of ritualizing activities by Catherine Bell, Schilbrack argues that metaphysics can be pursued and taught through the ritual participants' engagement with the structure of their ritual environment. Whether these structures are completely created by the ritualizing itself and in no sense discovered is another question, but the point is that metaphysics as a form of inquiry can be practiced not only explicitly by intellectuals or scholars, but also implicitly by ritual practitioners in general.

Robert McCauley's paper, "Philosophical naturalism and the cognitive approach to ritual," differs from the approach taken in many of the other papers in this book. Whereas other contributors seek to uncover what they call the reason or the logic in rituals, McCauley is not here interested in ritual as a resource for or a kin to philosophy. Ritual, he says, "seems to be . . . transparently irrational conduct." Yet McCauley argues that the philosophical study of ritual is not exhausted by interpreting the meaning of such conduct in its home context, nor by an analysis of its conceptual infrastructure. People also have explanatory and predictive interests; we want to know why these unusual practices are done, and why they are done in the specific way they are. In service of those interests, McCauley gives an account of philosophical naturalism, the philosophical view that there is no better method for understanding what exists than the scientific method. From the perspective of philosophical naturalism, the study of ritual is not reduced to the sciences, but it is constrained by them, and in particular the sciences like psychology and cognitive science that seek to explain and predict how people think.

In this naturalistic context, then, McCauley outlines a cognitive approach to ritual. He proposes that human beings naturally process actions in terms of agency, and one common way in which actions are cognitively structured is this: agent A does an action with instrument B to patient C. Religious rituals do not tamper with this structure. What makes rituals distinctive is that they introduce special entities – entities with "counter-intuitive properties" – as either A, B, or C. For example, an action in which a woman regularly gives food to her son would not (typically) be counted as a religious ritual, but an action in which she regularly gives food to invisible spirits would be. McCauley then uses this framework to make predictions. For example, he predicts that rituals with special entities as either their agents or connected to their (proximal) agents – that is, with special entities in the A position – will typically be performed on an individual patient only once; comparatively speaking, these rituals will tend to involve a great deal of pageantry, sensory stimulation, and emotion; and the performance will tend to be remembered distinctly. Those rituals with special entities in the B or C positions will be the reverse: they will typically be repeated several times for an individual patient, with much less pageantry, stimulation, and emotion, and the individual performances will be remembered indistinctly. This one example then serves as an indication of the promise of what the emerging cognitive sciences can offer to those interested in studying rituals naturalistically as the products of human minds.

In "Theories and facts on ritual simultaneities," Frits Staal makes some observations about how Vedic rituals are actually practiced and then draws from these facts an unusual implication for theories of ritual. Staal begins by observing that the rules followed in Vedic rituals are followed by the priests, not by the Gods. The Gods are typically not even understood to be hearers of the ritual. But "if there are no hearers in Vedic ritual, then there are no speakers." In other words, if there are no hearers, then Vedic ritual should not be understood as a form of communication. Ritual is not like a dialogue or a conversation. And Staal puts this in even stronger terms: if language is communication or expression of knowledge, then the words and the gestures in rituals are not even a form of language.

This negative point can also be seen, Staal says, in the fact that the (communicative) use of language typically displays people speaking in succession, not simultaneously, but in the Soma ritual to which he attends (and perhaps by extension to rituals in general) the words are often spoken simultaneously. These simultaneities, moreover, are structural, not haphazard or accidental; the priests are not *trying* to communicate. Another example is the avoidance of gaps in the recitation of mantras, which is accomplished by making sounds continuous and protracted, despite the consequence that the meaning of what is said is obscured. Again, communication is not the goal. Other cases of structural simultaneity, such as placing of sticks while one chants, are like stage directions. They are devices for counting and do not carry semantic messages. In general, then, the important thing to the priests is that they do and chant what they do and chant properly, that is, according to the rules of the ritual, but not that they do so according to the rules of communication. In marshalling these facts, then, Staal's overall goal is to add fuel to his thesis that rituals are not symbolic or meaning-conveying activities; they are concerned instead with following rules of the ritual for their own sake. Thus rituals should be understood not as symbolic activities – not as a use of language at all – but, like birdsong, as an inherently pleasurable activity not performed for any instrumental or extrinsic end.

T. C. Kline III's "Moral cultivation through ritual participation: Xunzi's philosophy of ritual" focuses on the work of Xunzi as an entry to Chinese philosophy of ritual. Xunzi (310–219 BCE) is the philosopher in the Confucian tradition who developed the most sophisticated account of the value of ritual practices. Borrowing a term from Thomas Kasulis, Kline labels the *Xunzi* a work of "metapraxis." Metapraxis Kasulis distinguishes from metaphysics: the former serves to justify one's practices, the latter one's beliefs. Kline shows that in his philosophy of ritual Xunzi weaves both forms of discourse together in order to provide a defense or an apologetics of the Confucian path.

Xunzi's metaphysics consists of a cosmic triad of Heaven, Earth, and humans. The forces of Heaven and those of Earth operate according to their own fixed patterns; these forces are not anthropomorphic and so they are morally neutral. According to Xunzi, however, human nature is "bad" in that, if undisciplined, it leads to conflict. As Kline puts it, "we find ourselves born into a disordered cosmos with an innate set of inclinations and capacities that do not naturally or spontaneously lead to harmonious interactions with each other or with the rest of the natural world." The Confucian path or *dao*, then, is a ritual order designed by ancient sage kings to shape human behavior and to provide a foundation for good government precisely by bringing humans into harmony with Heaven and Earth. The Confucian ritual tradition is therefore not merely a set of manners, nor is it limited to its social or political value, but is also the means for rightly ordering the human relationship to the cosmos.

Xunzi defends Confucian ritual practices (that is, he offers a metapraxis) by arguing that participation in these rituals is the best tool for moral cultivation. Unlike Mengzi, his Confucian opponent, Xunzi holds that one lacks innate moral tendencies. One therefore needs the Confucian rituals (and Confucian teachers) as external devices first to constrain and eventually to transform one's natural inclinations. Like the steam and the press that can straighten crooked wood, the prescriptions of ritual train one to control one's desires, so that proper behavior becomes "second nature." And Xunzi is clear that such rituals are not merely physical: they aim to transform one's understanding and thereby to transform one's patterns of approval and disapproval. In this way, the Confucian rituals aim to create noble people (*junzi*), which is to say, to create selves that are complete, beautiful, and fully human.

In "The ritual roots of moral reason: lessons from Mīmāṃsā," Jonardon Ganeri argues that Vedic rituals are a source of moral reason. Like Kline, that is, Ganeri argues that ritual has an intimate connection to ethics. But whereas Kline connects participation in Confucian rituals to the cultivation of moral virtues, Ganeri connects interpretation of Vedic rituals to the development of intellectual virtues. Here is how he sees the connection. Ritual is often taken as mechanical repetition of an invariant tradition, but as Ganeri reminds us, "whenever a ritual is performed, there are decisions to be made – about what to leave in, and what to leave out, about how to adapt the model to the circumstances." Hence since hermeneutics is inevitable, the practice of ritual requires deliberation about how to apply the ritual rules and how to perform the ritual, and so it requires the use of reason. Ganeri's thesis is that a model of ritual reason, introduced and developed by the Mīmāṃsā school of interpreters in order to make decisions about Vedic practice, is then taken as a method of reasoning about "what is to be done" (*dharma*) in non-ritual contexts. In this way, rituals are the paradigm of right action, and the ability to think about how to do these right actions is then taken as paradigmatic for thinking about other proper actions. Ritual law is the training ground for reason.

To what extent can one extrapolate from Ganeri's example a general account of "reason in ritual"? Can one draw a lesson from Mīmāṃsā for the study of rituals in other contexts? I judge that Ganeri's thesis will be useful for the study of ritual reason in other contexts, if two conditions are met. First, in the case of Mīmāṃsā, rituals are taken as paradigms of right action. As in a divine command theory in ethics, the Mīmāṃsā interpreters begin from the assumption that the ritual law is perfect, though it must be applied to one's own particular situation. Second, they develop an explicit model or set of rules for right reasoning about the ritual law. This model or set of rules then can be extended to reasoning about non-ritual matters. My expectation is that these two conditions – the perfection of the ritual law and the development of hermeneutic rules for reasoning about it – can be found in other ritual traditions and that therefore there will be other cultural traditions in which moral reason actually grows from ritual roots.

Writing from within mainstream contemporary philosophy of religion as one who bemoans the field's neglect of ritual, Charles Taliaferro develops a distinctively Christian philosophical account of rituals. On his account, participation in Christian rituals like the Eucharist or Baptism is a means of pursuing certain goods or excellences – what Taliaferro calls virtues. These goods or virtues are:

1   the good of acting in concord with God's will
2   the good of praising one's benefactor (and taking pleasure in giving that praise)
3   the good of ritually seeking ends external to ritual
4   the good of integrating one's affective and corporeal life in one's religious identity, that is, the good of embodying one's relation to God, and

5   the good of constituting, as a church, the body of Christ in the world, that is, the good of being God's embodiment.

Taliaferro's Christian philosophy understands Christian rituals unapologetically in Christian terms. As he puts it, "entering the world of Christian practice cannot be wholly separated from Christian theology." The philosophy of ritual that he proposes therefore exemplifies the view that ritual activities cannot be fully understood apart from their cognitive contexts. To take Taliaferro's example, participating in the ritual of the Eucharist involves making claims either implicitly or explicitly about God's activity as Creator, Sustainer, and Redeemer of the cosmos. In contrast, therefore, to a position like Frits Staal's, in which participating in rituals only requires one to follow the rules or the "syntax" of rituals without subscribing to a view of the ritual's meaning, Taliaferro argues that rituals are intentional activities. Like the use of language, rituals refer beyond themselves. Consequently, on Taliaferro's account, to describe someone as participating in a particular ritual requires one to say that the participants not only understand the basic rules of ritual activity, but also that they intend to live the life the ritual professes. This is why participating in rituals involves the pursuit of virtues.

According to Steven Kepnes, in his "Ritual gives rise to thought: liturgical reasoning in modern Jewish philosophy," ritual does not merely *express* thought; it also serves as a "primal engine for thinking" in that Jewish liturgies create a lived space that allows for the projection and experience of religious ideals. This thought-full space has been of special interest to modern Jewish philosophers, Kepnes argues, for it connects Jewish thought, on the one hand, to the traditional attention to the Torah and, on the other hand, to modern understandings of reason and ethics. Kepnes develops his slogan that ritual gives rise to thought with attention to three modern German Jewish philosophers: Moses Mendelssohn (1729–86), Hermann Cohen (1842–1918), and Franz Rosenzweig (1886–1929).

For the Enlightenment avatar Mendelssohn, following Jewish ceremonial law induces people to engage in reflection and, crucially, it is able to do so without falling into the danger of idolatry. Images of the divine may lead to idolatry, and even words in their explicit and fixed declarations take from the believer the task of searching. But rituals "merely" point to the divine and thereby stimulate a communal and active quest for religious truth. For the neo-Kantian Cohen, Jewish ritual observance complements and completes the work of philosophy – ritual does what reason requires but cannot itself do. Reason may teach that one *ought* to love all of humanity, but how does one learn this universal compassion? According to Cohen, rituals like the festival of Shabbat mediate the abstractions of reason to our concrete situations by imaginatively projecting the ideals of justice and social equality and by thereby awakening love in the participants. For the post-Hegelian Rosenzweig, Jewish liturgy has a task that goes beyond service to philosophy's ethical or rational goals, though one can through philosophy appreciate it. Ritual opens one up to eternity, connecting one's present to a history and a future, and giving one's experience of time a sense of shape and drama. Observing Jewish rituals thereby provides a mode of being in the world that transforms one's relationships with other people, with the natural world, and with God into I–Thou relationships.

Peter Van Ness's "Religious rituals, spiritually disciplined practices, and health" is a philosophically informed appreciation of what social epidemiology might contribute to the study of rituals. Social epidemiologists study the social factors related to health in a population and, in particular, the distribution and determinants (such as the risk factors and protective factors) of disease. Van Ness points out that the social epidemiologist's quest for generalizable knowledge can complement that of the social scientist (e.g. the medical anthropologist) who focuses on the local and the particular. Van Ness draws on Catherine Bell's characterization of ritual-like activities as formal, traditional, invariant, rule-governed activities that express and evoke experiences of the sacred. But Van Ness adds another feature not included by Bell: he points out that such activities tend not to be isolated but are usually configured within larger wholes. In his phrase, rituals are often "nested periodic behaviors." Understanding rituals in this way, moreover, enables one to integrate the three theoretical perspectives on ritual that Bell identifies and, according to Van Ness, too rigidly segregates. As nested periodic behaviors, rituals structure people's temporal existence and can also serve unintended social functions, including health.

Van Ness argues that one can also understand spiritually disciplined practices – his example is Hatha Yoga – as ritual activities that have been interiorized or personalized. Consequently, his account of nested periodic behaviors would also apply in some respects to spiritually disciplined practices. Both rituals and spiritual disciplines, then, "are human efforts to cope with natural and social changes that threaten aspects of human equilibrium and well-being." Thus, while other contributors to this volume have spoken of rituals as having an impact on one's habits of belief, Van Ness focuses on rituals as instilling the habits of a healthy body. Van Ness's thesis is that participating in such rituals and spiritual disciplines helps people cope with stress. (Presumably Van Ness's thesis could also be adapted to explain the health *problems* caused by religion as well, insofar as some rituals increase stress, perhaps deliberately.) This connects participation in rituals and spiritual disciplines to a discipline that is political or ethical. Like McWhorter, then, Van Ness sees rituals as a potential form of resistance, and he looks to ritual observance as resisting the breakneck rhythms of consumerist culture by cultivating habits that resist unhealthy patterns of behavior.

Notes

1   Rituals are also notoriously difficult to define. In sympathy with those who hold that the concept of ritual is a social construction, and in order to give the contributors to this book free rein, I did not constrain them to a single definition of ritual.

2 Thus there is an almost complete absence of philosophical approaches in, for example, *The Journal of Ritual Studies* or in Ronald Grimes's *Readings in Ritual Studies* (1996). This neglect is reciprocated by philosophers, including philosophers of religion, in whose textbooks religion almost never includes ritual (or worship or liturgy or religious practice) as an object of philosophical reflection. The assumption that ritual and philosophy have nothing to do with each other perhaps explains the comment from a reviewer of the book proposal for this present book, wondering whether there *could be* a philosophy of ritual.

3 Characterizing ritual in this minimal way avoids the dispute as to whether rituals are symbolic (Beattie, Firth, Leach) or not (Staal, Bloch).

4 Perhaps the closest thing in Ritual Studies at present to a philosophy of ritual (as opposed to a science of ritual, which Staal (1982) points out began in ancient India) is Ronald Grimes' proposal for Ritual Criticism (Grimes 1990). Grimes develops the idea of normative reflection on ritual, saying "[u]nlike theory, the aim of which is to explain, the aim of criticism is to assess" (1990: 15–6). And Grimes emphasizes that the popular idea that ritual and critical thought (like religion and critical thought) are mutually exclusive is a mistake. Not only does ritual permit criticism, it implies and requires criticism. There is thus a critical dimension to ritual itself (1990: 1). Nevertheless, though Ritual Criticism may be philosophically informed, it is perhaps best understood on analogy with Literary Criticism.

5 Left out are Marxist philosophy and other philosophical treatments of ritual aspects of political and economic behavior (like Chwe 2001), aesthetics (like Williams and Boyd 1993), process philosophy (like Frankenberry 2000), or the large field of analytic philosophy of action.

6 Thomas Busch notes that, though existentialism may have begun as a defense of the individual, the later existentialists develop not only a philosophy of lived experience and embodiment but move beyond this to what he calls "incorporation," that is, "the transcendence of individual experience in the discursive circulation of Being," "a call to shared communicative life" (Busch 1999), a development of potential value for the study of rituals.

7 Talal Asad writes in this genealogical vein and argues that the hermeneutic approach reflects a Christian agenda: "the claim to have penetrated through some formal appearance to the essential reality within . . . has been central to [Christian] theological discourse . . . The idea that symbols need to be decoded is not, of course, new, but I think it plays a new role in the restructured concept of ritual that anthropology has appropriated and developed from the history of Christian exegesis" (Asad 1993: 59–60).

8 Thomas Csordas is critical of Johnson and Lakoff. He writes that their

> work has introduced the notion that the cognitive categories on which cultural knowledge is based are themselves grounded in the body (Johnson 1987; Lakoff 1987), and this has led to an understanding of culture as the body in the mind. This is surely an advance, but it allows the body to remain merely a source, the objective raw material of representations, rather than the seat of subjectivity and the ground of intersubjectivity. . . . In this respect, to embrace the paradigm of embodiment [i.e. Csordas's recommended phenomenological approach] as a move from representation toward being-in-the-world would be to endorse a further step in the progression from "culture from the neck up" to "the body in the mind," moving finally to recognition of "the mind in the body."
>
> (1999: 150–1)

For Johnson's appreciation of phenomenology, see 1999: 81–2.

9 The questions to which Sullivan alludes in this sentence are the following: "Studies about the body raise pressing questions. What precisely is it that the body knows? What kind of knowledge is bodily knowledge? Is bodily knowledge cognitively

valuable? Is it critical knowledge? In what way are bodily knowledge and scientific knowledge of the body (or of anything else, for that matter) related? How will we come to know, in a discursive, conceptual way, the knowledge of the body? Can we know without remainder, in this discursive way, what the body knows? Is the knowledge that remains untranslatable into our discursive, scientific languages, important knowledge? If it is important, how may it be gathered into our experience for edification and for evaluation? Then there is the question that has plagued modern and postmodern philosophy: How could we *know* that we know what the body knows? Could any certain and valid knowledge of bodily knowing – that is could any cognitively valuable knowledge of either the process or the contents of bodily knowing – be anything other than a form of bodily knowledge itself?" (Sullivan 1990a: 86).

Bibliography

Andresen, J. (ed.) (2001) *Religion in Mind: Cognitive Perspectives on Religious Belief, Ritual, and Experience*, Cambridge: Cambridge University Press.

Asad, T. (1993) "Toward a Genealogy of the Concept of Ritual," in T. Asad (ed.) *Genealogies of Religion: Discipline and Reasons of Power in Christianity and Islam*, Baltimore: Johns Hopkins University Press.

Austin, J. L. (1965) *How to Do Things with Words*, New York: Oxford University Press.

Bell, C. (1992) *Ritual Theory, Ritual Practice*, New York: Oxford University Press.

Bernstein, R. (1971) *Praxis and Action: Contemporary Philosophies of Human Action*, Philadelphia: University of Pennsylvania Press.

—— (1983) *Beyond Objectivism and Relativism: Science, Hermeneutics, and Praxis*, Philadelphia: University of Pennsylvania Press.

Bordo, S. (1993) *Unbearable Weight: Feminism, Western Culture and the Body*, Berkeley: University of California Press.

Busch, T. W. (1999) *Circulating Being: From Embodiment to Incorporation: Essays on Late Existentialism*, New York: Fordham University Press.

Butler, J. (1993) *Bodies that Matter: On the Discursive Limits of 'Sex'*, New York: Routledge.

—— (1999) *Gender Trouble*, New York: Routledge.

Carrette, J. (2000) *Foucault and Religion: Spiritual Corporeality and Political Spirituality*, London: Routledge.

Chwe, M. S.-Y. (2001) *Rational Ritual: Culture, Coordination and Common Knowledge*, Princeton: Princeton University Press.

Cioffi, F. (1998) *Wittgenstein on Freud and Frazer*, Cambridge: Cambridge University Press.

Clack, B. R. (1999) *Wittgenstein, Frazer and Religion*, New York: Macmillan.

Clark, A. (1997) *Being There: Putting Brain, Body, and World Together Again*, Cambridge, Mass.: MIT Press.

—— (1998) "Embodiment and the Philosophy of Mind," in A. O'Hear (ed.), *Current Issues in Philosophy of Mind*, 35–52. Cambridge: Cambridge University Press.

Clark, A. and Toribio, J. (1994) "Doing without Representations?" *Synthese* 101: 401–31.

Clooney, F. X. (1990) *Ritual Thinking: Rediscovering the Purva Mimamsa of Jaimini*, Vienna: Sammlung De Nobili Institut fur Indologie der Universitat Wien.

Coakley, S. (ed.) (2000) *Religion and the Body*, Cambridge: Cambridge University Press.

Crossley, N. (1994) *The Politics of Subjectivity: Between Foucault and Merleau-Ponty*, Aldershot: Avebury.

Csordas, T. J. (1990) "Embodiment as a Paradigm for Anthropology," *Ethos* 18: 5–47.

—— (1994) "Introduction: The Body as Representation and Being-in-the-world," in T. J. Csordas (ed.), *Embodiment and Experience: The Existential Ground of Culture and Self*, Cambridge: Cambridge University Press.

—— (1999) "Embodiment and Cultural Phenomenology," in G. Weiss and H. F. Haber (eds), *Perspectives on Embodiment: The Intersections of Nature and Culture*, New York: Routledge.

Daly, M. (1978) *Gyn/Ecology: The Metaethics of Radical Feminism*, Boston: Beacon Press.

Davis, K. (ed.) (1997) *Embodied Practices: Feminist Perspectives on the Body*, London: Sage.

Dewey, J. (1991) *Logic: The Theory of Inquiry*, Carbondale, IL: Southern Illinois University Press.

Dreyfus, H. (1984) "Beyond Hermeneutics: Interpretation in Late Heidegger and Recent Foucault," in G. Shapiro and A. Sica (eds), *Hermeneutics: Questions and Prospects*, 66–83, Amherst: University of Massachusetts Press.

Dreyfus, H. L. and Dreyfus, S. E (1999) "The Challenge of Merleau-Ponty's Phenomenology of Embodiment for Cognitive Science," in G. Weiss and H. F. Haber (eds), *Perspectives on Embodiment: The Intersections of Nature and Culture*, New York: Routledge.

Eliade, M. (1959) *The Sacred and the Profane: The Nature of Religion*, trans. W. R. Trask, New York: Harper and Row.

Feibleman, J. K. (1976) *Adaptive Knowing: Epistemology from a Realistic Standpoint*, The Hague: Nijhoff.

Finnegan, R. (1969) "How to Do Things with Words: Performative Utterances among the Limba of Sierra Leone," *Man* 4: 537–52.

Foucault, M. (1979) *Discipline and Punish: The Birth of the Prison*, New York: Vintage Books.

—— (1980) *The History of Sexuality, Vol. 1: An Introduction*, trans. R. Hurley, New York: Vintage Books.

—— (1998) "Nietzsche, Genealogy, History," in J. D. Faubion (ed.), *Essential Works of Foucault: 1954–84, Vol. 2: Aesthetics, Method, and Epistemology*, 369–91, New York: The New Press.

—— (1999) *Religion and Culture*, London: Routledge.

Frankenberry, N. K. (2000) "The Process Paradigm, Rites of Passage, and Spiritual Quests," *Process Studies* 29: 347–57.

Frankiel, T. (2001) "Prospects in Ritual Studies," *Religion* 31: 75–87.

Frisina, W. G. (2002) *The Unity of Knowledge and Action: Toward a Nonrepresentational Theory of Knowledge*, Albany, N.Y.: State University of New York Press.

Gatens, M. (1996) *Imaginary Bodies: Ethics, Power, and Corporeality*, London: Routledge.

Geertz, C. (1973) *The Interpretation of Culture*, New York: Basic Books.

Grimes, R. L. (1990) *Ritual Criticism: Case Studies in its Practice, Essays on its Theory*, Columbia, S.C.: University of South Carolina.

—— (ed.) (1996) *Readings in Rituals Studies*, Upper Saddle River, NJ: Prentice Hall.

Grosz, E. (1994) *Volatile Bodies: Toward a Corporeal Feminism*, Bloomington: Indiana University Press.

—— (1995) *Space, Time, and Perversion: Essays on the Politics of Bodies*, New York: Routledge.

Haugeland, J. (1998) *Having Thought: Essays in the Metaphysics of Mind*, Cambridge, MA: Harvard University Press.

Heidegger, M. (1962) *Being and Time*, trans. J. Macquarrie and E. Robinson, London: SCM Press.

Jackson, M. (1989) *Paths Toward a Clearing: Radical Empiricism and Ethnographic Inquiry*, Bloomington: Indiana University Press.

Jaggar, A. M. and Bordo, S. R. (eds) (1989) *Gender/Body/Knowledge: Feminist Reconstructions of Being and Knowing*, New Brunswick, NJ: Rutgers University Press.

Johnson, M. (1987) *The Body in the Mind: The Bodily Basis of Meaning, Imagination, and Reason*, Chicago: The University of Chicago Press.

—— (1991) "Knowing through the Body," *Philosophical Psychology* 4: 3–18.

—— (1999) "Embodied Reason," in G. Weiss and H. F. Haber (eds), *Perspectives on Embodiment: The Intersections of Nature and Culture*, New York: Routledge.

Kasulis, T. P. (1987) "Editor's Introduction," in Y. Yuasa, *The Body: Toward an Eastern Mind-Body Theory*, Albany, N.Y.: State University of New York Press.

——, Ames, R. T., and Dissanayake, W. (eds) (1993) *Self as Body in Asian Theory and Practice*, Albany, N.Y.: State University of New York Press.

Lakoff, G. (1987) *Metaphors We Live By*, Chicago: University of Chicago Press.

—— and Johnson, M. (1999) *Philosophy in the Flesh: The Embodied Mind and Its Challenge to Western Thought*, New York: Basic Books.

Law, J. M. (ed.) (1995) *Religious Reflections on the Human Body*, Bloomington: Indiana University Press.

Lerner, B. D. (2002) *Rules, Magic, and Instrumental Reason: Peter Winch's Philosophy of the Social Sciences*, London: Routledge.

Lincoln, B. (1989) *Discourse and the Construction of Society: Comparative Studies of Myth, Ritual, and Classification*, Oxford: Oxford University Press.

—— (2000) "On Ritual, Change, and Marked Categories," *Journal of the American Academy of Religion* 68: 487–510.

—— (2003) *Holy Terrors: Thinking about Religion after September 11*, Chicago: University of Chicago Press.

McGuire, M. B. (1990) "Religion and the Body: Rematerializing the Human Body in the Social Sciences of Religion," *Journal for the Scientific Study of Religion* 29: 283–96.

—— (1996) "Religion and Healing the Mind/Body/Self," *Social Compass* 43: 101–16.

—— (2002) "New-Old Directions in the Study of Religion: Ethnography, Phenomenology, and the Human Body," in J. V. Spickard, S. Landres, and M. B. McGuire (eds), *Personal Knowledge and Beyond: Reshaping the Ethnography of Religion*, New York: New York University Press.

McWhorter, L. (1999) *Bodies and Pleasures: Foucault and the Politics of Sexual Normalization*, Bloomington: Indiana University Press.

May, T. (2001) *Our Practices, Our Selves: Or, What It Means to Be Human*, University Park, PN: The Pennsylvania State University Press.

Merleau-Ponty, M. (1962) *Phenomenology of Perception*, London: Routledge & Kegan Paul.

Nagatomo, S. (1992) "An Eastern Concept of the Body: Yuasa's Body Scheme," in M. Sheets-Johnstone (ed.), *Giving the Body Its Due*, Albany, N.Y.: State University of New York Press.

Price, J. and Shildrik, M. (eds) (1999) *Feminist Theory and the Body: A Reader*, New York: Routledge.

Raposa, M. L. (1999) *Boredom and the Religious Imagination*, Charlottesville: University of Virginia Press.

Ray, B. (1973) "'Performative Utterances' in African Rituals," *History of Religions* 13: 16–35.

—— (2000) "Discourse about Difference: Understanding African Ritual Language," in K. C. Patton and B. C. Ray (eds), *A Magic Still Dwells: Comparative Religion in the Postmodern Age*, Berkeley: University of California Press.

Ricoeur, P. (1991) "The Model of a Text: Meaningful Action Considered as a Text," in *From Text to Action: Essay in Hermeneutics, II*, Evanston, Ill.: Northwestern University Press.

Rorty, R. (1979) *Philosophy and the Mirror of Nature*, Princeton: Princeton University Press.

Sartre, J.-P. (1956) *Being and Nothingness: An Essay on Phenomenological Ontology*, New York: Philosophical Library.

Sawicki, J. (1991) *Disciplining Foucault: Feminism, Power, and the Body*, London: Routledge.

Schatzki, T. R., Cetina, K. K., and van Savigny, E. (eds) (2001) *The Practice Turn in Contemporary Theory*, London: Routledge.

Scheper-Hughes, N. and Lock, M. M. (1987) "The Mindful Body: A Prolegomenon to Future Work in Medical Anthropology," *Medical Anthropology Quarterly* 1: 6–41.

Schiebinger, L. (ed.) (2000) *Feminism and the Body*, Oxford: Oxford University Press.

Schweiker, W. (1987) "Sacrifice, Interpretation, and the Sacred: The Import of Gadamer and Girard for Religious Studies," *Journal of the American Academy of Religion* 55: 791–810.

—— (1988) "Beyond Imitation: Mimetic Praxis in Gadamer, Ricoeur, and Derrida," *The Journal of Religion* 68: 21–38.

Searle, J. (1969) *Speech Acts: An Essay in the Philosophy of Language*, Cambridge: Cambridge University.

—— (1979) *Expression and Meaning: Studies in the Theory of Speech-acts*, Cambridge: Cambridge University Press.

Shilling, C. (1993) *The Body and Social Theory*, London: Sage.

Staal, F. (1982) *The Science of Ritual*, Poona, India: Bhandarkar Oriental Research Institute.

Stoller, P. (1997) *Sensuous Scholarship*, Philadelphia: University of Pennsylvania Press.

Sullivan, L. E. (1986) "Sound and Senses: Toward a Hermeneutics of Performance," *History of Religions* 26: 1–33.

—— (1990a) "Body Works: Knowledge of the Body in the Study of Religion," *History of Religions* 30: 86–99.

—— (1990b) "Seeking an End to the Primary Text: Or, Putting an End to the Text as Primary," in F. E. Reynolds and S. L. Burkhalter (eds), *Beyond the Classics? Essays in Religious Studies and Liberal Education*, Atlanta: Scholars Press.

Sullivan, S. (2001) *Living In and Through Skins*, Bloomington: Indiana University Press.

Tambiah, S. (1968) "The Magical Power of Words," *Man* 3: 175–208.

—— (1979) "A Performative Approach to Ritual," *Proceedings of the British Academy* 65: 113–69.

Todes, S. (2001) *Body and World*, Cambridge, Mass.: MIT Press.

Tyson, R. W., Jr. (1988) "Culture's 'Hum and Buzz' of Implication: The Practice of Ethnography and the Provocations of Clifford Geertz's 'Thick Descriptions,'" *Soundings* 71: 95–111.

van Gelder, T. (1995) "What Might Cognition Be, If Not Computation?" *Journal of Philosophy* 92: 345–81.

Varela, F. J., Thompson, E., and Rosch, E. (1991) *The Embodied Mind: Cognitive Science and Human Experience*, Cambridge, Mass.: MIT Press.

Weiss, G. (1999) *Body Images: Embodiment as Intercorporeality*, New York: Routledge.

Wider, K. (1997) *The Bodily Nature of Consciousness: Sartre and Contemporary Philosophy of Mind*, Ithaca: Cornell University Press.

Williams, R. G. and Boyd, J. W. (1993) *Ritual Art and Knowledge*, Columbia, S.C.: University of South Carolina Press.

Winch, P. (1958) *The Idea of a Social Science and its Relation to Philosophy*, London: Routledge & Kegan Paul.

—— (1970) "Understanding a Primitive Society," in B. Wilson (ed.), *Rationality*, Oxford: Blackwell.

Wittgenstein, L. (1953) *Philosophical Investigations*, Oxford: Blackwell.

—— (1979) *Remarks on Frazer's* Golden Bough, trans. A. C. Miles, Atlantic Highlands, NJ: Humanities Press.

Young, I. M. (1990) *Throwing Like a Girl and Other Essays in Feminist Philosophy and Social Theory*, Bloomington: Indiana University Press.

Yuasa Y. (1987) *The Body: Toward an Eastern Mind-Body Theory*, Albany, N.Y.: State University of New York Press.

—— (1993) *The Body, Self-Cultivation and Ki-Energy*, Albany, N.Y.: State University of New York Press.

1 Ritual, body technique, and (inter)subjectivity

Nick Crossley

I. Introduction

It is one of the most obvious features of rituals that they are "embodied," that is, that we do them and that this "doing" is a bodily act. Rituals involve gestures, postures, dances, patterns of movement. If we are to make sense of rituals, it follows, we need to engage with this corporeality; that is, we need to make sense of rituals specifically as embodied practices. Until recently, this would have been difficult for philosophers and social scientists. With a few notable and important exceptions, "the body" and "embodiment" were not thematized or explored to any great extent within philosophical and social scientific discourse in the past. Tides have, however, turned. A multitude of perspectives now compete over the truths of corporeal life.

In this chapter, building upon earlier work on embodiment (esp. Crossley 1995, 2001), I seek to elucidate the nature of ritual, qua embodied practice. The perspective I use for this analysis combines insights from the phenomenology of Maurice Merleau-Ponty (1962, 1965), the sociology of Émile Durkheim (1915) and Marcel Mauss (1979), and the pioneering work of Pierre Bourdieu – which itself pulls together the insights of the other two camps. Through the tools that these different theorists provide, I hope to be able to reveal that and how rituals embody the practical wisdom of the individuals who perform them and the societies from which they derive. Rituals, I will argue, are a form of embodied practical reason.

The interplay of sociology and philosophy, or more specifically phenomenology, within the paper will, I hope, demonstrate both the respective value of these approaches and one of the key ways in which they can be made to work together in a mutually informing manner. Specifically, as this paper belongs to a collection on philosophical conceptions of ritual, I hope that the paper demonstrates how phenomenological philosophy allows us simultaneously to clarify, deepen, and question concepts and analyses that have been generated within a more sociological framework. Phenomenology can dissect and unravel sociological concepts and observations to a greater degree than might ordinarily be the case, generating new insights in doing so. However, to give sociology its due, the very process of doing so entails that phenomenology is prepared to learn from sociology, to accept the empirical discipline of this science, and to philosophize around "phenomena" which are always already defined and constituted through social scientific work.

The chapter begins with a brief reflection upon Mauss' (1979) conception of 'body techniques." I outline Mauss' notion and attempt to use the work of Merleau-Ponty, in particular, to expand and deepen it. This allows me to frame ritual analytically and to raise a question which is central to the rest of the chapter, namely, what purpose do rituals serve? What are they "for"? In response to my own question, I begin by suggesting that rituals embody a practical understanding of the societies in which they are situated, and suggest that they may have a role therein of restoring and protecting order. From this point I then consider, in greater detail, the potentially transformative effect of some rituals upon human subjectivity. The power of rituals to establish order and contribute to the maintenance of social stability, I argue, stems in part from their power to tap into the deeper corporeal basis of human subjectivity. Finally, in an attempt both to illustrate my arguments and to counter the possibility that I might seem to be suggesting that rituals are, in some sense, necessarily "conservative," I consider the extended example of protest rituals.

Prior to doing any of this, however, I should add an important qualification. The meaning of the concept of ritual belongs to the "fuzzy logic" (Bourdieu 1992) of everyday language use. We use "ritual" to identify a wide range of quite different forms of social practice and individual behavior: everything from the "exotic" magical or religious practices of "other" cultures, through both the high ceremonies or festivals and the bureaucratic procedures of our own, to everyday "interaction rituals" (Goffman 1967), personal habits, compulsive behaviors, and even the psychotherapeutic procedures intended to cure such compulsions. Doubtless we could identify common threads running through each of these types of practice, not least, for example, their repetitive nature; but repetition is scarcely exclusive to ritual activity, unless we are prepared to call all forms of repetitive activity "rituals," and the question must necessarily be posed of whether anything is. Are there properties of those activities we call rituals which are both sufficiently exclusive to them and sufficiently inclusive of them to constitute their essence and thus afford us the possibility of a watertight definition? The answer, I suggest, is that this is highly unlikely in light of the above-mentioned diversity of uses of the term "ritual." It seems more likely that, like Wittgenstein's (1953) "games," rituals enjoy a family resemblance rather than a fixed and clear essence. We would be ill-advised, therefore, to attempt to define ritual in a neat or conclusive fashion. Rather, we must work with its "fuzziness." Furthermore, for this reason it is also inadvisable to attempt an analysis of ritual that would apply to all cases. We cannot say that "all rituals are like this" or "all rituals have this function." The meaning, function, and characteristics of rituals will be different in different cases. Indeed, even the same ritual may change in these respects over time, as rituals necessarily belong to the flow of historical time. It is my contention that my analysis applies, in varying degrees, to a great many diverse types of ritual, but it would be unwise, given this fuzziness, to suggest that it applies to them all. My analysis, both taken as a whole and in its various elements, will apply to some rituals more than others. I will offer examples and illustrations of this applicability along the way, and will conclude, as noted earlier, with an extended consideration of the applicability of my analysis as a whole to the example of protest rituals.

II. Body techniques

The starting point for my analysis is the contention that rituals are a form of what Marcel Mauss (1979) has termed "body techniques." At one level, I use this term simply to denote that rituals are embodied. They entail bodily activity, patterned movements, or postures. Prayer, for example, might involve kneeling, closing one's eyes, and clasping one's hands, whilst rituals of greeting entail a bow or a handshake. In some cases, the meaning of the movement or posture may be more important in a ritual than its precise mechanical manifestation. It may be important, for example, that deference is clearly demonstrated or that a duty of some form is performed, without much importance attaching to the precise manner in which deference is expressed or duty performed. In other cases, specific bodily forms may be prescribed but only generally: for example, one must bow, but the precise details of the bow are unimportant. Often, however, ritual entails not only that something is done, but also that it is done in a highly specific way, by means of quite specific gestures and movements. Participants in a ritual know, because they have learned precisely how to, for example, bow in *this* ritual or clasp their hands or hold the objects and instruments used in the ritual.

The concept of body techniques has further implications than this, however. Mauss defines them as (culturally) specific "uses" of the body and, as such, likens them to tools. Body techniques, Mauss writes, are the "ways in which from society to society men [sic] know how to use their bodies" (Mauss 1979: 97). Cultural variations in the ways that people walk, talk, swim, run, carry, make love, spit, sleep, etc., indicate that groups learn to use their bodies in specific ways, for specific purposes, he argues, in much the same way that they learn to use the other raw materials in their environment. Indeed, Mauss claims that "[t]he body is man's first and most natural instrument. Or more accurately, not to speak of instruments, man's first and most natural technical object, and at the same time technical means, is his body" (Mauss 1979: 104). This is interesting and prompts a key question which this chapter will attempt to address; namely, what are rituals used for? What purpose do they serve? Where this may be obvious with respect to some body techniques, such as hunting methods or swimming styles, it is less so for many rituals which do not manipulate the external world or modulate our relationship with it in any obvious way. The concept of the body as a "tool" is one which Mauss fails to elaborate, however, and is potentially problematic, as indeed is the notion that the body has uses, is an "object," or is a "means." Although, as I note below, other aspects of Mauss' account suggest an interesting challenge to Cartesian dualism, this particular notion could be read in a Cartesian way, implying that "the body" is a mere tool or vehicle through which something "other," a mind or mental being, pursues its projects.

An elucidation of this problem and the basis of a solution to it can be found if we open our analysis up to the insights of phenomenology, and particularly the work of Merleau-Ponty (1962, 1965) and the later Husserl (1970, 1973). The Cartesian, Merleau-Ponty (1962) observes, views the human body, including his/her own body, as an object. Indeed, they regard it as merely one more object in the world, akin to the rocks and stones of their natural environment, albeit perhaps an object with which they are in closer contact. Descartes (1968 [1648]) claims to have arrived at this view via a process of philosophical meditation upon his experience. He knows that his body is distinct from himself, he argues, because he has been led, through the course of his meditations, to doubt the existence of his body but not the existence of his self. Indeed, as the *cogito* famously establishes, as long as he thinks, whether to doubt or affirm, he cannot doubt his own existence as a thinking being. Thus, his mind or self and body can exist independently and must be distinct. As Husserl (1970) argues, however, Descartes' meditations were prejudiced by prior acceptance of certain of the claims of the emerging sciences of his day, including Galileo's claims regarding "matter" and the nature of the body (see also Ryle 1949). Descartes' meditations are not the radical philosophical meditations, prior to science and capable of grounding it, that Descartes suggests. They already presuppose certain of the fundamental definitions and assumptions of science, and this structures their trajectory. It is only because Descartes already assumes that "his body" is "mere matter" and because he thereby believes that it is distinct from his conscious being that he is able to doubt its existence without thereby risking the self-contradiction of denying his own existence. A more radical philosophical reflection upon subjective experience, which suspends belief in all scientific claims and definitions, Husserl continues, reveals this conception of "bodies" to be an abstraction which ignores important features of "bodies" as actually experienced. More importantly, as Merleau-Ponty's (1962) extension of Husserlian ideas shows, it is not true of our experience of our own bodies. We do not, in the first instance, experience "our body" for Merleau-Ponty. Our body is not an external object in our experience. Rather our experience is, in the first instance, an embodied experience of a world which transcends us, that is, a world beyond our own embodied being. Sensuous experience is directed outwards and the body is the very texture of this experience. It intends a world. Insofar as we do have experiences of "our bodies," furthermore, this is always itself an embodied experience. Indeed, we must say in such cases that "the body" experiences itself:

> I am not front of my body, I am in, or rather *I am it*. . . . We do not merely behold as spectators the relations between the parts of our bodies and the correlations between the visual and tactile body: we are ourselves

the unifier of these arms and legs, the person who both sees and touches them. .... *If we can still speak of interpretation in relation to the body, we shall have to say that it interprets itself.*

(Merleau-Ponty 1962: 150; my emphasis)

The same, I suggest, must be said of "uses" of the body. If "use" and "tool" are appropriate terms to use in relation to body techniques, we will have to say that the body makes use of itself. Another less cumbersome way of putting this would be to say that body techniques are acquired and embodied cultural competencies. Thus, to say that rituals are body techniques is to say that they are manifestations of embodied cultural competence and understanding, uses which we, qua bodies, make of ourselves for specific purposes.

A final important element that Mauss adds to his definition of body techniques is that they are both social and habitual in nature, and belong to the realm of practical reason. That is to say, they belong to the realm of the habitus:

I have had this notion of the social nature of "*the habitus*" for many years. Please note that I use the Latin word – it should be understood in France – *habitus*. The word translates infinitely better than "*habitude*" (habit or custom), the "*exis*," the "acquired ability" and "faculty" of Aristotle (who was a psychologist). It does not designate those metaphysical *habitudes*, that mysterious "memory", the subject of volumes or short and famous theses. These "habits" do not vary just with individuals and their imitations; they vary between societies, educations, proprieties and fashions, prestiges. In them we should see the techniques and work of collective and individual practical reason rather than, in the ordinary way, merely the soul and its repetitive faculties.

(Mauss 1979: 101)

This quotation, notwithstanding my earlier point about Mauss' possibly dualistic formulation, suggests an interesting challenge to Cartesianism. Mauss is suggesting that at least some of our patterns of bodily activity constitute forms of reason – reason which, qua habit, is irreducible to our conscious and reflective life and which, consisting as it does in uses which the body makes of itself, cannot be separated from the body. Again he fails to offer much clarification of this point, but again Merleau-Ponty's (1962) work can be used to provide this clarity. The human manner of being-in-the-world, Merleau-Ponty argues, is constituted by way of knowledge, understanding, and intention (in the phenomenological sense). Human beings are not "in" the world as an object might be "in" a box. Our world exists for us as a meaningful pole of our experience, as something we know and understand. For the Cartesian, such "knowledge" and "understanding" are properties of the mind and, as such, are distinct from our bodily life. Furthermore, they are generally conceived in propositional or thetic terms, as knowledge-that or conceptual understanding. Against this, Merleau-Ponty, echoing Wittgenstein (1953), Ryle (1949), and also Heidegger (1962), argues that our primary grasp upon the world, our primary way of knowing and understanding it, consists in practical know-how and mastery. And this, in turn, is irreducibly embodied. To know or understand, in this primary sense, is to be able to do something, and that doing is necessarily a bodily doing. Furthermore, it is often a doing which is done without reflective or conscious intention and whose "principles" we cannot articulate in conscious terms by way of concepts. Indeed, our reflective-discursive grasp upon the world is, for Merleau-Ponty, founded upon our prior mastery of language qua body technique. What we "do" with language, we "do" in an embodied way. It is as bodies that we enjoy a practical mastery of language. Speech is an acquired use of the body, a cultural-corporeal competence. And so too is the perceptual grasp upon the world that our reflection and discourse reflect and discourse upon. Perception entails acquired *uses* of the body, body techniques. Even the capacity to distinguish colors is an acquired use of the body for Merleau-Ponty:

> To learn to see colours is to acquire a new way of seeing, *a new use of one's own body*: it is to recast the body image. Whether a system of motor or perceptual powers, our body is not an object for an 'I think', it is a grouping of lived through meanings which moves towards its equilibrium.
>
> (Merleau-Ponty 1962: 153; my emphasis)

Where Mauss (1979) refers to "habitus" in his formulation of "body techniques," Merleau-Ponty refers to "habit." What Merleau-Ponty means by "habit" is much the same as what Mauss means by "habitus," however. Specifically, he seeks to challenge naive and mechanistic conceptions of habit, such as those posited in the work of the psychological behaviorists (for example, Pavlov 1911). Habit, he argues, is not a mechanical linking of stimulus and response but rather a sediment of active learning experiences and thus a practical form of embodied know-how and understanding:

> We say that the body has understood and habit has been cultivated when it has absorbed a new meaning and assimilated a fresh core of significance.
>
> (Merleau-Ponty 1962: 146)

If habit is neither a form of knowledge nor an involuntary action what then is it? It is knowledge in the hands, which is forthcoming only when bodily effort is made, and cannot be formulated in detachment from that effort. The subject knows where the letters are on the typewriter as we know where one of our limbs is, through knowledge bred of familiarity which does not give us a position in objective space.

> (Merleau-Ponty 1962: 144)

We said earlier that it is the body which understands in the acquisition of habit. This way of putting it will appear absurd, if understanding is subsuming a sense datum under an idea, and if the body is an object. But the phenomenon of habit is just what prompts us to revise our notion of 'understand' and our notion of the body. To understand is to experience the harmony between what we aim at and what is given, between the intention and the performance – and the body is our anchorage in a world.

(Merleau-Ponty 1962: 144)

Body techniques then, are forms of practical and pre-reflective knowledge and understanding. They are our way of being-in-the-world, that is, of acting in the world, rendering it intelligible and constituting it as a meaningful context for action. They render the world meaningful and stable for us, providing us with relatively stabilized ways of "making out" in the world and of coping with the situations that we find ourselves thrown in. They "anchor" us in situations which are simultaneously physical and social:

Although the body does not impose definite instincts upon us, as it does other animals, it does at least give to our life the form of generality, and develops our personal acts into stable dispositional tendencies. In this sense our nature is not long established custom, since custom presupposes the form of passivity derived from nature.

(Merleau-Ponty 1962: 146)

Moreover, as the word "habit" suggests, we generally use body techniques without recourse to thought or reflection and, at least in some cases, the know-how they embody remains unintelligible and inaccessible to our reflective, discursive consciousness. For example, I have acquired several techniques ("strokes") and a general knack of swimming, but I do not need to think about how to perform these techniques when doing so and I cannot translate my practical understanding of water, buoyancy, motility, etc., as manifest in my ability to swim, into discourse. Similarly, whilst my hands "know" the layout of my word-processor keyboard, I cannot *say* where the letters are and thinking about typing, if anything, is an impediment to doing so. We draw upon body techniques, knowing to use them in particular situations, without first thinking about or planning to do so, and we perform them in a similarly pre-reflective manner. We may even use body techniques without becoming aware, in any reflective sense, that this is what we are doing.

Body techniques may, in some cases, have an individual aspect to them. However, Mauss is keen to identify their social patterns of distribution, and this is a theme which has also been picked up in the work of the French sociologist Pierre Bourdieu – who has also developed the concept of the habitus, drawing upon both Mauss and Merleau-Ponty to do so. Looking at body techniques associated with a wide range of social activities, Bourdieu has shown how they vary across different social groups, particularly social classes.

It is my contention, as noted earlier, that we can fruitfully explore "ritual" in these terms, that is, as a form of body technique. This raises an important question, however, of just what uses or purposes ritual has for us. If, as I have argued, ritual is a form of knowledge, mastery, and understanding, then *what do we understand, know, and master by way of ritual?* Rituals generally lack the direct and obvious instrumental value of certain other "body techniques": for example, hunting or cooking techniques. Therefore, both their uses and the "understanding" they embody are less clear. Isn't ritual precisely something ornamental and thus something which has no purpose? It is my contention that the answer to this question is "no." Rituals have important practical uses. In what follows I will attempt to spell out my case for this.

III. Ritual understanding

As I noted in the introduction to this chapter, rituals are diverse and their definition fuzzy. Consequently, we should not attempt to offer a uniform answer or analysis for all rituals. What many rituals manifest, however, particularly public and social rituals, is an understanding of the social world to which the agent belongs, that is, of its values, beliefs, distinctions, social positions, and hierarchies. Furthermore, at the same time, they constitute the practical know-how necessary for the reproduction of that social world. Whilst most rituals may appear to have little instrumental value in relation to our dealings with the natural world, they have a demonstrable instru-mental value in relation to our dealings with each other in the social world. We can look at this at a number of different levels.

In the first instance, fairly evidently, the performance of ritual requires a basic embodied know-how. Agents know how to perform the ritual, how to initiate it, when it is appropriate (and inappropriate) to initiate it, how to allocate roles in relation to it, etc. In part, this is a matter of embodied competencies. Agents learn how to perform certain types of act, which hand to move where, how to co-ordinate part-moves into a whole. At the same time, however, it is equally a matter of understanding social norms regarding the appropriateness of certain forms of conduct and achieving a practical grasp of the semiotic codes which constitute the meaning of acts within a given ritual context. Agents learn how to read the activities of others involved in the ritual and how to respond appropriately. This may entail conceptual or reflective understanding but it may not and in either case it must neces-sarily also entail the pre-reflective and embodied practical reason of the ritual qua body technique. Agents must be able to do the ritual, not just theorize it. The "doing" of the ritual, in this respect, will be an active, and, to a degree, improvised accomplishment of the agents involved in it, but at the same time it will be an improvised "doing" which is very much structured by the history of the social group in question as it is embodied in their norms and collective habitus.

At a deeper level, some forms of ritual know-how and understanding can be regarded to be knowledge and understanding of the wider society in which the ritual is situated. The ritual deference afforded monarchs and political leaders, for example, embodies an understanding of the social position of those leaders, qua leaders, and indeed of the power structure of society. To bow before an authority is to understand, in a practical and corporeal way, both the nature of authority in general and the nature of this specific authority before whom one is prostrate. Furthermore, in effect it is to affirm that structure, to communicate one's acceptance of it and thereby "cast one's vote" in favor of its continuation. Authority consists, at least on many occasions and in some part, precisely in the deference that is embodied, understood, and communicated in the bow. In this respect, ritual is practical knowledge of particular types of social relationship, a practical knowledge which is necessary for the perpetuation of those types of social relationship. It is embodied knowledge of the social world which is, at the same time, a practical technique for reproducing aspects of that world.

A variation of this can be found in such rituals as the handshake. The meaning of the handshake varies across context. It can, for example, be a way of greeting people or a way of establishing an agreement or deal. Learning these meanings and how to recognize them in context is clearly integral to the acquisition of this particular body technique. To be able to "do" the ritual of handshaking, competently, requires that one understands what one is doing by doing this across a variety of contexts. At the same time, however, to use the handshake as a ritual for fixing an agreement entails a tacit understanding of the nature of agreements as practiced within a particular society or social group and the sanctions which can be brought against those who fail to stick to agreements. Again, the ritual entails embodied knowledge of the social world which, at the same time, is a necessary constitutive element of that world – since society would be impossible if its members did not understand such things as agreements. Furthermore, we might argue that the handshake is a ritual which, qua body technique, social agents have collectively developed for the specific purposes of cementing agreements. Where some body techniques, such as hunting techniques, mediate the relationship of the agent to the natural world, ritual techniques, at least in this case, mediate the relationship of the agent to other agents and to the social world. The wider social world is particularly implicated here insofar as it is the group which effectively constitutes the force of obligation embodied within the ritual. In addition to handshakes, this argument might apply equally to wedding ceremonies, perhaps funerals, various rites of passage or initiation and, indeed, any form of ritual which marks a change of transformation in social relationships (and by implication statuses). The ritual is the technique for achieving the transformation.

We should perhaps add here that part of the value of the ritual, qua body technique, is its capacity to "condense" meaning and circumvent verbal negotiation. The meanings of the handshake, the funeral rite, the wedding ceremony, etc., are multiple and complex. Indeed, in certain respects they are too extensive, complex, and subtle to be spelled out. Like many linguistic usages, including our use of the term "ritual," they obey a "fuzzy logic"

(Bourdieu 1992), irreducible to an exhaustive list of rules. We cannot spell them out. By way of ritual, however, we can seal them without having to spell them out. The ritual brings them to pass. Furthermore, because the ritual typically circumvents negotiation we can seal them in largely non-negotiable terms, drawing upon a power of society or the social group which is prior to and deeper than our capacity for rational negotiation and agreement.

As it stands, this account remains incomplete. How, we might ask, does the ritual achieve this? By what magic? I will attempt to answer this later in this chapter when I discuss the power of ritual to invoke both emotion and imagination. Rituals can effect social transformations, I will argue, because they effect transformations in our subjective and intersubjective states. They allow us to make imaginative leaps, investing arbitrary moments or figures with an element of (social) necessity. Before we discuss this, however, it is important to complete this first stage of our analysis.

I have just suggested that ritual is a technique, a form of practical reason, for achieving particular kinds of effect, both short and long term, within a social group. This entails, in the first instance, that ritual, or the initiation of a ritual is, to use the words of Pierre Bourdieu, a "call to order": "The social world is riddled with *calls to order* that function as such only to those who are predisposed to heeding them as they *awaken* deeply buried corporeal dispositions, outside the channels of consciousness and consent" (Bourdieu 1998: 54–5; his emphasis). Bourdieu does not directly identify these "calls to order" with ritual, but it is my contention that rituals and specifically the initiation of rituals fit very closely with what he has in mind here. To initiate a ritual is to make a powerful normative appeal to very deeply rooted cultural dispositions. Others within the ritual community "ought" to respond and will experience the social pressure of this "ought" acutely. To remain seated during a national anthem, to give one example of a call to order, requires considerable restraint. One's "natural" inclination is to rise. It is second nature to respond to calls to order "appropriately." The effect here, as described by Bourdieu, is not "mechanical submission to an external force" but neither is it a matter of "conscious consent" (ibid.). He seeks to locate human life – realistically, in my view – somewhere between absolute mechanism and absolute voluntarism. Ritual activities are meaningful, purposive, and "mindful" in contrast to the mere mechanical responses posited in, for example, behaviorist conceptions of "reflexes." And yet, contrary to the intellectualist tradition, they are not steered by or thematized within reflective thought. They are precisely pre-reflective. More specifically, Bourdieu identifies them with socially structured "dispositions" which operate below the level of conscious volition. To initiate a ritual is to tap into these dispositions and, thereby, to attempt to steer and channel the conduct of others. It is precisely to call them to order.

Émile Durkheim's (1915) work on the religious rituals of aboriginal totemic clans provides an interesting illustration and extension of this point. Durkheim writes of the "collective effervescence" associated with rituals and festivities. The initiation of at least ceremonial rituals, he argues, brings about a change, both emotional and practical, in the life of the group – one is reminded of Christmas in a Christian culture. Ordinary tasks are abandoned in favor of preparations for the ritual, and the degree of privatization and individualization within the group is lessened, in favor of interactions which are both more extensive and intensive. In some cases, Durkheim observes, these rituals follow a set temporal pattern. Those rituals which mark the changes in the seasons, for example, will have relatively fixed times. In both these cases and a fortiori in the case of more situationally occasioned rituals, however, it is noteworthy that ritual activity is particularly prominent at times when the life of the group is in some way threatened: for example, by a death, a food shortage, a major infraction of social rules, a change in the wider social or natural environment. Rituals, in other words, call members of a group to order at times when order is (potentially) threatened and, at least if the collective life of the group is to be maintained, needs to be reasserted. They have the purpose or function of binding members of a group (back) into the group.

Durkheim analyzes this process exclusively at the societal level. He is concerned with the functions of ritual for society. This arguably blinds him to the role of social agency in the initiation of rituals and, according to many critics, raises problems of functional or teleological explanation. He can appear to argue that the social need for binding rituals or "calls to order" is, at the same time, the cause of those rituals. However, we need not follow him along this path. To the contrary, we might argue that integral to the practical know-how embodied in particular ritual forms is a sense or feeling of when their use is appropriate. Rituals, in other words, are not triggered by "society's need" for them but rather by a practical sense of "the need" for a specific ritual that specific social agents have acquired through their own participation in both a society and its rituals. Agents know in a pre-reflective way when and how to mobilize specific rituals in the interests of maintaining social order and they know, in a pre-reflective way, when society or the order of a social group is under threat. They "feel" when a ritual is required. Furthermore, following the more critical and cynical implication of Bourdieu's (1998) analysis, we might argue that it is not merely society's need which is protected by ritual calls to order but equally the need of specific (often dominant or elite) social groups within society. Agents who experience their hegemony slipping may mobilize rituals as a way of calling those whom they dominate back to order, re-establishing the stability of their rule. National anthems and the rituals surrounding them, for example, are techniques which elites have either invented or appropriated as a means of affirming authority and order. By using the anthem at public events they effectively use those events as a means of bolstering their own position.

This, to reiterate, does not necessarily imply conscious computation. As with our other body techniques, we can call upon rituals to address the specific problems we face at any point of time without being perfectly clear, at a reflective and self-conscious level, that this is what we are doing. The ritual may "feel" appropriate without our being reflectively aware of the purpose to which we and/or many before us have put it. Indeed, it may be utilized automatically, without feeling and feeling may only emerge when, for whatever reasons, the ritual fails or is not executed, its utility becoming apparent in the breach. Even at their most habitual, however, many rituals remain body techniques for manipulating and generating order in the social world.

IV. Ritual emotion

It is not simply the "conduct" of the group which is steered in this way, however, at least not in a narrow sense. Through the medium of our conduct, rituals tap into and affect our intentional (in the phenomenological sense), emotional, and imaginative lives. Consider Merleau-Ponty's reflections upon his nightly bedtime ritual:

> I lie down in bed, on my left side, with my knees drawn up; I close my eyes and breathe slowly, putting my plans out of my mind. But the power of my will or consciousness stops there. As the faithful, in the Dionysian mysteries, invoke the God by miming scenes from his life, I call up the visitation of sleep by imitating the breathing and pos- ture of the sleeper. The god is actually there when the faithful can no longer distinguish themselves from the part they are playing, when their body and their consciousness cease to bring in, as an obstacle, their particular opacity, and when they are totally fused in the myth. There is a moment when sleep 'comes', settling on this imitation of itself which I have been offering to it, and I succeed in becoming what I was trying to be.
>
> (Merleau-Ponty 1962: 163–4)

Merleau-Ponty cannot go to sleep by deciding to do so. Sleep is not a matter of voluntary choice or decision, and neither, for that matter, is wakefulness. Both belong to the pre-volitional aspect of subjectivity which subtends choice and decision. They are transformations of one's state of being effected by bodily processes beyond one's conscious awareness or control. Our bodies situate us in the waking world and the world of sleep quite independently of any decisions we might make. And yet the transition to sleep is not completely beyond Merleau-Ponty's power. He can attempt by indirect means to act upon the pre-volitional level of his subjectivity and thereby to trans- form it. He can "call upon" sleep as the faithful call upon Dionysus. And he can do so by way of ritual. He attempts to put himself in situation by way of ritual imitation of the state of sleep.

Sleep is, admittedly, one of the more extreme transformations that our subjective life undergoes. Sleep is a form of withdrawal from the "paramount reality" of the waking world – even if, as Merleau-Ponty notes, the fact that we can be woken from sleep by events in the waking world suggests that this withdrawal is never complete. There is a more general point here, however, about the way in which rituals may be used to induce specific subjective states, particularly emotional states. In his account of sleep rituals, for example, Merleau-Ponty refers to Dionysian rituals, invoking the ecstatic element of certain religious rituals, which are remarked upon in such classic social scientific accounts of ritual as those of Durkheim (1915). Durkheim writes with a sense of wonder at the manner in which a collective mood of excitement overtakes the participants in the aboriginal totemic festivals, in an almost magical way. Merleau-Ponty, in my view, offers an account of that magic, rooting it in the bodily nature of the rituals involved. By performing "ecstatic rituals," that is, rituals which mimic ecstasy, agents are able to tap into their corporeal potential for ecstatic ways of being, putting themselves into an ecstatic state. And they perform the ritual as a way of inducing the state. The same might be said, in a different vein, of funeral rituals, which invoke attitudes of solemnity, or perhaps the calming rituals of yoga, prayer, and meditation. In each case, a ritual use is made of the body for the express purpose of tapping into bodily processes which, in turn, effect a transformation of subjective state.

What is transformed here is our mode of intending the world, that is, of experiencing it and constituting it as an object of experience. Emotions are not "inner states" for Merleau-Ponty, but rather intentional threads connecting us to and projecting us towards the world. They consist in ways of acting towards, perceiving, thinking about, and being affected by the world. To seek to modify our emotional states in this way, therefore, is to seek to modify, however temporarily, our intentional connection to our situation. Rituals are thus body techniques for modifying our relationship to the world. They manifest a practical grasp upon or embodied understanding of our incarnate subjective or psychological state and its potentialities. Indeed, they are precisely practical forms of psychology.

In the above cases, ritual is used positively to invoke a particular emotional state. It may equally be used, however, to fend off or circumvent a particular emotional state. It is commonplace, for example, to view at least some "compulsive" rituals, whether of an extreme or more mundane form, as ways of fending off anxiety. The compelled individual performs their ritual, for example of cleansing or dressing, as a means of keeping at bay the rising tide of panic they feel approaching. Furthermore, there is at least a hint of this same point, transposed to the collective level, in Durkheim's (1915) account of ritual. Rituals can serve the function of preserving social order by fending off the anxieties or other potentially harmful emotions and impulses which periodically threaten to erupt and disturb that order. Anger and ill feeling within the group, for example, may be buried by way of ritual, and harmonious or at least ordered relationships restored. In these instances, it might be appropriate to refer to the "repressive" action of rituals. Indeed, in an important challenge to Freudian orthodoxy, and particularly to its concept of "repression," Billig (1999) analyzes rituals in just this way. The problematic paradox of an "unconscious" created by the repression of potentially distressing thoughts and feelings – namely, that one must consciously be aware of repressed material in order to repress it, such that it cannot therefore be repressed – is answered according to Billig if we attend to the role of habits and rituals in our lives. Rituals can effectively serve to repress undesirable contents of consciousness, keeping them below the threshold of thematic awareness, by deflecting our attention and focusing and framing our experience in particular ways. At the same time, however, given that they are habitual and are initiated or mobilized "automatically," without thought, they can serve this function without it being necessary for us to be aware that this is what they are doing. We acquire a habitual repertoire of rituals for dealing with potentially distressing situations before it becomes necessary to consciously confront them. Furthermore, we do so at both the individual and the social-collective level. Social groups, or at least agents qua members of social groups, like individuals, know how to use rituals to maintain a particular intersubjective equilibrium and avoid potentially distressing or disintegrative affective states. Social effects are achieved by way of (inter)subjective transformations. Again, ritual is practical and embodied psychology. It is a form of understanding of human subjectivity, of self, other, and we.

V. Ritual imagination

The subjective and intersubjective transformations achieved by way of ritual are not limited to emotional manipulation, however, at least not as narrowly conceived. Ritual can invoke an imaginative intentionality, effecting a "magical" transformation of situation. An obvious example of this might be the Dionysian worshippers discussed by Merleau-Ponty in the above passage. Through the power of ritual as an imaginative act, make-believe misrecognized as worship, they bring their God into being for themselves, experiencing His existence intensely and acutely. Similarly, when secular monarchists participate in the rituals and festivities of their king or queen, they imaginatively generate a "majesty" which they misrecognize as emanating from the person whom they, by way of ritual, invest with it. And again, as Bourdieu (Bourdieu *et al.* 1991) has argued, it is the ritual of the museum or gallery, as practiced by its visitors, which generates and imputes to the works the aura which those same visitors experience as emanating from the works. Deities, monarchs, high art, and all of the sacreds of culture require, for their proper appreciation, an imaginative "attitude" or "intentional stance," and it is ritual, as a body technique for modulating emotional and imaginative intentions, which is able to call up this attitude. Ritual situates agents imaginatively. It is for this reason, I suggest, that Pascal (1987) argued that he did not kneel and pray because he believed in God but rather believed in God because he kneeled and prayed. The ritual frames the experience which, in turn, shapes the belief. Pascal is able to believe in God because, by way of the ritual of prayer, he "experiences" God. It is for this same reason, moreover, that individuals may experience discrepancy or dissonance between what they believe "rationally" and their "faith" or what they "feel." Ritual, as an imaginative-embodied act, entails a "suspension of disbelief" and an investment of imagination which opens up "alternative realities" and experiences which cannot necessarily be reconciled with the experiences and deliberations of "paramount reality" (Schutz 1962) or the mundane and everyday world. Ritual is a technique, a body technique, for achieving this.

What we also begin to see here is the manner in which rituals, qua imaginative practices, allow us to invest meaning and structure in the world (as we experience it), in an embodied and sensuous way, and thereby also perhaps allow us to gloss over and/or misrecognize what some have identified as the necessarily "culturally arbitrary" bases of the social formation to which we belong (see Bourdieu and Passeron 1996). Rituals, by way of their capacity to tap into and concentrate the imagination, invest the world with a recognizable sense and structure. They effect a peculiarly social form of "magic." Sartre (1993) gives a good example of this, drawing upon those rituals which serve to mark time or events for human societies: for example, birthday rituals, rites of passage, harvest rituals, Christmas. The temporal landmarks which punctuate and thereby give order and meaning to our lives, he argues, are in many respects quite arbitrary and necessarily so. It is not clear, for example, at what exact point we pass our exams, or commit ourselves to another person for life or even at what point we die – given that different cultures mark the moment of death differently (Hertz 1960). Lived time comprises flows rather than discrete events. As such, however, lived time thereby lacks meaning and structure in an important sense. Without punctuation, there is no meaning. Rituals allow us to overcome this. They allow us to mark time, to punctuate our lives, affording them a temporal shape and thus meaning. The moment or event is constituted by the ritual. A boy becomes a man at the moment he endures whatever ritual obligations of passage his culture demands. However, rituals are only able to do this to the extent that we can believe in them, that is to say, that we can abandon ourselves to them. The importance of the ritual is not simply that it stands as an arbitrary marker, that "here will do," but equally that it taps into and focuses the emotions and the power of imagination that allows members of a social group to believe, if only for the moment, that something has indeed happened in the world beyond them. Ritual effectively allows us to achieve what would otherwise be an impossible task. It marks arbitrary moments with an element of necessity. If this were an operation of reflective consciousness, it would surely be doomed to failure since questioning consciousness would constantly bring the arbitrariness of the situation back into focus. Why here? Why now? Why not yesterday or tomorrow? Because it operates at the pre-reflective level, however, because it is acted out habitually rather than thought about, ritual bypasses this questioning and the desired effect is achieved. In certain respects, this is bad faith or self-deception. It is arguably a necessary form of self-deception, if our lives are to assume any meaningful shape, however, and it is equally a form of self-deception necessary to the constitution of human societies and their evidently "arbitrary" cultural forms.

This point relates to my earlier argument regarding the handshake, marriage ceremony, etc. The techniques "work," in part, because they are sanctioned to work by society. Because we agree, in what Wittgenstein (1953) called our "forms of life," that they will work. But they equally have a subjective and intersubjective validity for us because, qua techniques, they situate us within the collective imagination of our society, calling forth from us an imaginative intending of the world, just as Merleau-Ponty's sleep rituals put him into sleep.

VI. Ritual as body technique

To sum up my argument, hitherto, I have suggested in this paper that rituals are best considered as a form of "body technique." That is to say, they are embodied forms of practical reason shared within a particular social group and perhaps varying across different social groups. The concept of body techniques, as developed in the work of Marcel Mauss (1979), tended to refer to techniques with a specific and relatively obvious "physical" purpose. Mauss's body techniques are, for the most part, techniques corresponding to the basic physical manipulation of our environment, albeit sometimes in ways which express observance of cultural codes and beliefs. With rituals, however, I have suggested that we have body techniques whose principle purposes concern the manipulation of our individual psychological and our social states, our subjective and intersubjective being. Rather than harboring the forces of the "natural world," so to speak, as techniques of fire building might be said to do, rituals are body techniques which harbor the powers and potentialities of both our own subjectivity, as an embodied way of being-in-the-world, and those of the social world. In saying this, I perhaps come close to the claims of some of the more old-fashioned sociological and anthropological perspectives on ritual, particularly those of functional analysis. I hope, however, that by conceptualizing rituals in terms of body techniques I have both opened up the issue of ritual and its effects in a way not amenable to functional analysis, and also that I have restored to the analysis of ritual a sense of practical individual agency. Rituals don't just happen. They are initiated by agents who know how to initiate them and know what, albeit perhaps in a pre-reflective and embodied way, they are for. Furthermore, rituals can only be initiated amongst populations who have this same embodied know-how, that is, who have acquired the particular ritual in question as a body technique and who are thus disposed to respond to the initiation of a ritual as a call to order.

The extent to which the use of ritual is consciously reflected upon will vary between cases, as indeed will the flexibility with which they can be used. Nevertheless, the effectiveness of ritual depends in large part upon our capacity to "suspend disbelief" and abandon ourselves pre-reflectively to it, and this assumedly puts limits upon the extent to which it can be reflectively and cynically manipulated. Indeed, reflective and deliberative rationality is, to some extent, the enemy of ritual, since it precisely refuses to suspend disbelief and identifies the culturally arbitrary nature of ritual.

VII. Radical rituals

My analysis hitherto has perhaps tended to suggest that rituals are primarily conservative in nature. At one level, this is true. As repetitions, rituals conserve specific action patterns through time. However, in pluralistic and internally conflictual societies, such as most of those we are aware of, the action patterns preserved may be oppositional patterns, oriented towards change. Rituals can conserve and bolster an impetus towards confrontation and challenge. Protest, for example, very often assumes a ritual form, and the sociological analysis of social movements reveals numerous aspects of ritual behavior therein. In what remains of this paper, I will offer a brief analysis of protest and movement rituals, both as a way of illustrating some of the arguments made in the chapter and as a way of reinforcing the view that rituals can, paradoxically, conserve an impetus for change (see also Crossley 2002).

Recent analyses of protest have suggested that its forms vary across different societies and historical epochs. Each society and epoch, it is argued, has its own specific "repertoire of contention" (Tilly 1978, 1995). In itself this is significant for the claims of this chapter as it effectively establishes that each society has its own habitual stock of "protest rituals." In addition, however, it is noteworthy that many public protests and demonstrations manifest a variety of repetitive expressive forms akin to those found in other public rituals. Demonstrators sing (sometimes quite specific songs), they chant, march, gesture, wave banners and flags, etc.

At one level, this might be analyzed simply in terms of the need of protestors to have their voices heard, and thus their need to generate a form of public spectacle. Protest rituals, from this point of view, are body techniques which embody an understanding or know-how of socially acceptable and legitimate ways of publicly expressing dissent. Like the handshake, they embody an understanding of "how we do these sorts of things in our society." Moreover, they embody an understanding of the political system as a democracy, and of the ways in which private citizens can form a public to challenge or confront elites therein. Protestors know how to challenge the system and rituals are an integral practical element of that knowledge.

Protests are more than simple expressions of dissent, however. There is a very clear sense in which they must generate, or at least regenerate, the anger or outrage which they express. Like Merleau-Ponty, with his sleep rituals, protestors use their songs, chants, and gestures to put themselves, affectively, into protest situations, to whip up the mood or atmosphere, individual and collective, necessary to an expression of dissent. I do not mean to suggest by this that there is anything inauthentic about the outrage expressed.

Protestors may be moved to protest by very immediately felt emotional responses to events. However, whatever emotions have stirred an individual to decide to protest in the first place will have had considerable time to "cool" by the time of the protest. A great many unrelated events, demanding different emotional intentions, will have been engaged in between the decision to protest and the protest itself. Even the organization of the protest event itself will often have required polite negotiation and cold-headed reflection upon times, places, arrangements, legalities, and logistics. Modern protests are not, generally speaking, spontaneous expressions of immediately felt reactions. Thus, feelings need to be rekindled or regenerated. To show that they are angry or outraged or saddened, protestors need to be able to tap into their emotions and publicly display them. This is just what protest rituals allow them to do. They activate or reactivate the appropriate emotions. Furthermore, they ensure a solidaristic expression of the emotions in question. Even individuals who agree upon the nature of certain events as, for example, unjust, and who agree that protest is necessary, might react with a different emotion or express their emotion differently; but the public expression of feeling, in the form of protest, demands relative homogeneity and, again, the protest ritual serves this end. It generates a (largely) intersubjectively shared state. Protest rituals are thus important body techniques by and through which protestors practically understand and manipulate their collective emotional state to achieve that state best suited to the specific purposes of the issue they have at hand.

In some circumstances, this public generation of emotion by way of ritual may also serve the additional function of staving off or repressing other thoughts and emotions. McAdam (1988), for example, in his work on the "Freedom Summer"[1] volunteers, notes that songs and other collective rituals often served as a way of fending off the fear and anxiety which protestors, three of whom were murdered in the first few days of the action, felt in the face of threats from police and the local white population, not to mention the general hardships they experienced when living amongst the poor black populations of the southern United States. The experience of the Freedom Summer project was shocking and terrifying for many, and they had good reason to be both terrified and shocked. Their lives were potentially in danger. But the rituals of the volunteer groups, particularly collective song singing, were an important technique available to them for repressing that fear and thus pushing on with their task at hand. They could effect a transformation of their state of being, both bodily and shared, by way of ritual. Again then, protest rituals are effectively body techniques for psychological self-management.

In addition to emotion, protest rituals serve important imaginative functions for protestors, constituting a collective sense of the "we" of protest, and the "them" of opponents. In a world where many of the targets of protest are either abstract or too extensive or dispersed to be directly addressed (for example "capitalism," "the system," "multinationals," "patriarchy," "militarism"), protest rituals effectively evoke the collective imagination required to focus upon the enemy or constitute a more concrete proxy target. The use of effigies and particularly their ritual destruction in public protests is one good example of this. The effigy itself and the effect of its destruction clearly presuppose an imaginative attitude. The effigy becomes the target by way of the magic of the make believe of the protest ritual. And ritual is precisely the technique through which this magic, this imaginative transformation, is achieved. Through ritual protestors submit themselves to an imaginative attitude. There are more mundane examples, however. Buildings which protestors, in other contexts, might walk past on a daily basis, for example, can become, by force of ritual imagination, the focus of the emotions generated on the protest, a symbol of the target of the protest. The "ritual" attacks upon McDonald's restaurants in recent anti-corporate protests is one example of this. The rituals of the protest (re)constitute the meaning of a situation and the manner in which it is intersubjectively intended by those party to it. And as such they are precisely body techniques available to protestors and organizers for these purposes.

Hitherto, I have focused only upon the situational significance of protest rituals. However, as Herbert Blumer (1969) recognized, these rituals can have a more durable function, insofar as they serve to create and/or sustain a sense of *esprit de corps* amongst protestors, constituting them as a social movement (see also McAdam 1989). Rituals can both serve as a "call to order" amongst a protest community, and also generate a dispositional receptivity to such calls to order. They do this, in part, simply by way of repetition and habit formation, but they do it equally by way of the above-mentioned transformations of emotional and imaginative intention and the effect this has upon those who undergo them. Like Pascal's (1987) religiosity, the motivations of the protestors are as much created and nourished by their protest activities, perhaps especially their protest rituals, as vice versa. And in this respect, protest (and related) rituals are quite indispensable to protest communities. As much of the literature in this area suggests, mobilizing and maintaining commitment is one of the hardest tasks facing both individual protestors and collective movement communities. Rituals are one of the key tools available to protestors for these purposes.

What I am effectively suggesting here, then, is that rituals are body techniques which political activists can use to act both upon themselves and others, in an effort to generate and sustain their impetus qua individual and collective movement. Rituals are subjective and intersubjective technologies which, qua physical actions, tap into the deeper corporeal basis of our (inter)subjective lives, effecting desired transformations. In some cases, these uses of ritual may be planned or reflected upon. However, integral to the learning of rituals, qua body techniques, is the habitual "feel" for their appropriateness and the capacity to use them without needing to reflect upon doing so. To know how to protest, how to mobilize the rituals of protest appropriately, is to be disposed to do so at the appropriate moments without need of reflective intervention.

VIII. Conclusion

In this chapter, I have explored the nature of rituals qua "body techniques," that is, embodied forms of practical reason which social agents draw upon in the context of their everyday lives. In contrast to some body techniques, such as techniques of cooking, hunting or fishing, I have argued, rituals have little obvious instrumental function in relation to our dealings with the natural world and the "understanding" they embody is often therefore far from clear. However, I have sought to show how rituals are important techniques for manipulating our subjective and intersubjective lives and, by way of these (at least sometimes), our social world also. To be able to use ritual is to have a practical grasp upon at least some aspects of subjectivity and intersubjectivity and some capacity to channel and use them for specific purposes. In this respect rituals do have an important instrumental value. In the final section of the chapter, I attempted to illustrate this by reference to protest rituals and the various ways in which they serve to shape the (inter)subjectivities of those involved in them.

Note

1   The 'Freedom Summer' project of 1964 involved predominantly white, well-off students from elite universities in the north of the USA traveling down to the South for the period of the summer to offer political assistance to the oppressed but resisting black population there. They experienced a considerable threat from local white populations, including the police.

Bibliography

Billig, M. (1999) *Freudian Repression*, Cambridge: Cambridge University Press.
Blumer, H. (1969) "Collective Behaviour" in A. M. Lee (ed.), *Principles of Sociology*, 65–120, New York: Barnes and Noble.
Bourdieu, P. (1977) *Outline of a Theory of Practice*, Cambridge: Cambridge University Press.
—— (1992) *The Logic of Practice*, Cambridge: Polity.
—— (1998) *Practical Reason*, Cambridge: Polity.
—— , Darbel, A., and Schnapper, D. (1991) *The Love of Art*, Cambridge: Polity.
—— and Passeron, J-C. (1996) *Reproduction*, London: Sage.
Crossley, N. (1995) "Body Techniques, Agency and Intercorporeality," *Sociology* 29: 133–50.
—— (1996) *Intersubjectivity*, London: Sage.
—— (2001) *The Social Body: Habit, Identity and Desire*, London: Sage.
—— (2002) *Making Sense of Social Movements*, Buckinghamshire: Open University Press.
Descartes, R. (1968 [1648]) *Discourse on Method* and *The Meditations*, Harmondsworth: Penguin.
Durkheim, E. (1915) *The Elementary Forms of Religious Life*, New York: Free Press.
Goffman, E. (1967) *Interaction Ritual*, New York: Anchor Books.
Heidegger, M. (1962) *Being and Time*, Oxford: Blackwell.
Hertz, R. (1960) *Death and the Right Hand*, Glencoe, IL: Free Press.

Husserl, E. (1970) *The Crisis of the European Sciences and Transcendental Phenomenology*, Evanston: Northwestern University Press.

—— (1973) *Experience and Judgement*, Evanston: Northwestern University Press.

Jasper, J. (1997) *The Art of Moral Protest*, Chicago: University of Chicago Press.

McAdam, D. (1988) *Freedom Summer*, New York: Oxford University Press.

—— (1989) "The Biographical Consequences of Activism," *American Sociological Review* 54: 744–60.

Mauss, M. (1979) "Body Techniques," in *Sociology and Psychology*, 95–123, London: Routledge.

Merleau-Ponty, M. (1962) *The Phenomenology of Perception*, London: Routledge.

—— (1965) *The Structure of Behaviour*, London: Methuen.

Pascal, B. (1987) *Pensées*, Harmondsworth: Penguin.

Pavlov, I. (1911) *Conditioned Reflexes*, Oxford: Oxford University Press.

Ryle, G. (1949) *The Concept of Mind*, Harmondsworth: Penguin.

Sartre, J-P. (1993) *The Emotions: Outline of A Theory*, New York: Citadel.

Schutz, A. (1962) "On Multiple Realities," *Collected Papers, Vol. I*, 207–59, The Hague: Martinus Nijhoff.

Tilly, C. (1978) *From Mobilisation to Revolution*, Reading: Addison Wesley.

—— (1995) "Contentious Repertoires in Great Britain, 1758–1834," in M. Traugott (ed.), *Repertoires and Cycles of Collective Action*, 15–42, Durham: Duke University Press.

Wittgenstein, L. (1953) *Philosophical Investigations*, Oxford: Blackwell.

2 Practice, belief, and feminist philosophy of religion

Amy Hollywood

I. Introduction

The two most important and comprehensive feminist interventions in the philosophy of religion – Pamela Sue Anderson's *A Feminist Philosophy of Religion* and Grace Jantzen's *Becoming Divine: Toward a Feminist Philosophy of Religion*[1] – follow the mainstream of analytic and continental philosophy of religion in focusing on belief.[2] Anderson arguably remains closer to that tradition than does Jantzen. Rather than changing the aims of philosophy of religion, Anderson insists that gender must become a crucial analytic category within accounts of the process of justification. More centrally (and more audaciously), she argues that philosophical arguments grounded in feminist concerns must not only justify, but also evaluate belief and its constitution. Jantzen, on the other hand, eschews justification, arguing that feminist philosophy of religion has different aims than does its Anglo-American counterpart. For Jantzen, philosophy of religion is theological and practical; properly pursued, it will lead to the "becoming divine" of women rather than the justification of religious belief. Yet Jantzen too focuses her attention on "religious discourse and the symbolic of which it is a part." The goal of feminist philosophy of religion is less to justify or to argue for the truth or falsity of belief than to "restructur[e] that myth in ways that foster human dignity – perhaps in ways that oblige and enable us to become divine" (Jantzen 1999: 22).[3] Questions of justification thereby give place to questions of moral or political adequacy. Jantzen suggests the primacy of moral or political over epistemological justification, whereas in Anderson the two exist side by side.

Jantzen, however, is finally unable to avoid the epistemological issues she wishes to displace. Ultimately, she and Anderson both address the issue of the "truth" or "objectivity" of belief. Yet neither provides a satisfactory account of the ontological status of the objects of religious belief. Both Anderson and Jantzen challenge the split between reason and desire that would render belief solely a matter of rationality and conscious cognition, yet they remain on the level of the discursive, the symbolic, or the mythic, giving little attention to the place of ritual and practice in religion.

My contention here is that these two problems are closely related. The unsatisfactory nature of current arguments about the ontological status of the objects of religious belief – in feminist philosophy of religion and in the philosophical study of religion more generally – is tied to the neglect of practice and ritual. Put in another way, attention to the role of practice and ritual in religion will force feminist philosophers to understand religious belief and its objects in new ways. Given the more immediately bodily nature of ritual and other forms of religious practice, moreover, any philosophy of religion attendant to them will be forced to acknowledge and to theorize those differences inscribed in and on bodies (often through rituals and bodily, mental, and spiritual practices themselves). We will then be better able to understand why religion is such an important site for the inculcation of bodily differences and to analyze the relationship between religious practice, belief, and sexual – as well as other – differences (themselves objects of belief inculcated on bodies through the bodily, mental, and discursive repetition of norms) (Hollywood 2002b).

II. The ontological status of the objects of religious belief

Anderson deals directly with the issue of the ontological status of the object of belief, asking in relationship to the work of Luce Irigaray, "To what extent, if any, can one say that the female or feminine divine exists?" Anderson begins by distinguishing between a variety of different ways in which something might be said to exist. Existence might be: real or empirical; ideal; fictional; mythical; illusory; or historical (which for Anderson entails something like a collectively held illusion) (Anderson 1998: 118). Anderson will be most interested in the ideal and the mythical conceptions of existence, bringing them together in a modified Kantianism by means of which she attempts to safeguard the legitimacy of religious belief and the reality of its objects without committing herself to empiricist claims about the existence or nature of the divine.[4]

Anderson begins with Kant's assertion that transcendental ideas (like that of God's existence) do not constitute knowledge, but are regulative principles that direct human understanding toward the summation and limits of what can be known. Various post-Kantian accounts of the transcendental ideas as regulative principles, she argues, provide sufficient "ground to treat myth as a regulative principle and not to equate it with constitutive knowledge of supersensible reality" (Anderson 1998: 137). When we talk about God or the divine, we talk not about entities available to our senses and hence to empirical knowledge, but rather about the conditions of knowledge – both pure and practical (moral) – themselves. In stark contrast to Kant, Anderson wishes to allow an epistemological and moral role for desire. She insists, moreover, that this desire is neither psychologistic nor narcissistic, but grounded in the shared embodiment of human beings and hence susceptible to universalization. For feminist philosophy, she argues, "authentically conceived and strongly objective theistic beliefs of women would not come from psychological need alone, nor from epistemological ignorance but, significantly, from a rational passion for justice" (Anderson 1998: 213).[5] Moreover, "reason, in its substantive form of yearning, represents the human potential for justice and freedom or liberty. These potentials are Enlightenment ideals; in Kantian terms, they are regulative ideals" (Anderson 1998: 137). When feminist philosophers talk about God, then, they are talking about the potential for human self-flourishing and human justice by means of which moral and political life should be regulated. In this sense, Anderson claims to maintain objectivity and ontological realism while at the same time avoiding any assertion of the empirical reality of supersensible beings at odds with the presumptions of her own Kantianism.

Anderson's inventive solution to the problem of theological realism and the ontological status of the divine depends on the close correlation of two central Kantian principles. Kant's argument about God's existence as a regulatory principle of pure reason occurs in the *Critique of Pure Reason*, yet Anderson's larger argument is grounded in his *Critique of Practical Reason* and its complex moral argument for the justification – even necessity – of accepting the postulate of God's existence (see Kant 1950: 532–70; 1956: 130–8). The *Critique of Practical Reason* rests on two presumptions: 1) that reason in its practical dimension demands that human beings follow the moral law given to them by reason and 2) that rationality demands the moral law be capable of fulfillment. (For Kant, it would be irrational for human beings to pursue an end they know is incapable of attainment.) Fulfillment of the moral law, however, depends on human freedom and the possibility of a perfect conjunction between virtue and happiness – the highest good, according to Kant. The latter in turns depends on the immortality of the soul and on the existence of God. Only if a being exists in which the phenomenal (the realm of happiness) and the noumenal (that of human freedom) come together can the highest end be possible. Although freedom, immortality, and God's existence cannot be known by pure reason, then, reason in its practical dimension requires that we postulate their existence. In this sense, moral ideals readily available to reason serve as the grounds for religious belief.

For Kant, we can never know empirically that God exists. The very constitutive categories of understanding preclude knowledge of God, for God, as eternal and omnipresent, stands outside of these categories and thus can never become an object of knowledge. In the *Critique of Pure Reason*, Kant argues for God's existence as a regulative ideal of pure reason, that which marks the limits of reason and the sum total of its audacious – if unfulfillable – desire. The *Critique of Practical Reason* argues that we must accept as a postulate, a necessary hypothesis, that God exists, albeit in a manner never knowable by human beings. In both the *Critique of Pure Reason* and the *Critique of Practical Reason*, moreover, these ideals – be they epistemological or moral – are ideals the *existence of which* renders pure reason or practical reason and the moral life themselves rational. In other words, despite his insistence on the limitations of reason, Kant's God must be hypothesized as existing. Kant's realism is, then, arguably much more radical and far-reaching than Anderson's.

Despite crucial differences between Anderson's and Jantzen's projects, Jantzen falls back on a similar modified Kantianism when it comes to the question of the nature of divine existence. Rereading Ludwig Feuerbach's account of the divine as the projection of human ideal becoming, Jantzen argues that in speaking of the divine we "speak . . . of ideals, indeed regulatory ideals in a Kantian sense. Projections need to be those which embody our best and deepest aspirations, so that we are drawn forward to realize them" (Jantzen 1999: 92). Like Anderson, Jantzen brings together the concept of God's existence as an epistemological regulatory ideal for pure reason with God's existence as a postulate necessary to the rationality of the moral law. Within the terms of practical reason, what is ideal is not the concept of God, but that of the moral law itself, its complete fulfillment, and its coincidence with absolute happiness (i.e. the highest good). God can only be said to be an ideal of practical reason in that God's existence renders the highest good possible.

Like Anderson, Jantzen also hopes to show that attention to the communities of faith for whom religious projections are meaningful enables feminist philosophy of religion to avoid the charge of relativism, arguing cogently that "partiality of insight is not the same as absence of criteria" for adjudicating competing truth claims, or, as she prefers to put it, symbolic systems (Jantzen 1999: 223).[6] She is not interested in defending philosophical realism, however, and so saves herself from some of the worries faced by Anderson. Yet with Jantzen as with Anderson we are left with the problem that their accounts of belief – and most crucially their accounts of the ontological nature of the objects of religious belief – do not correspond to what people most often mean when they say that they believe in God. (This, incidentally, includes Kant. Although he gives different grounds for belief than would those not directly influenced by his work, his understanding of *what* is believed comes closer, I think, to the kind of theological realism espoused by many – if not most – religious people.)

Arguably, as constructive philosophical theologians, neither Anderson nor Jantzen need be concerned by my critique. They might easily respond that their projects entail an ameliorative reconception of what is meant by religious belief. Yet the question remains open what kind of power these putatively regulative ideals have if we do not believe in their realist instantiations. For Kant, once again, without belief in God's existence, reason becomes self-contradictory. Reason in its practical dimension, in particular, would demand a course of action that it would be irrational to pursue, given that without God's existence the moral law's ends are unfulfillable. At the same time, however, Kant argues that to know God through pure reason would itself jeopardize morality, for we would then act out of a fear or love of God rather than from duty alone. (Hence Kant's insistence that we need to postulate the existence of God not in order to make moral action desirable, but rather to render it fully rational [Kant 1956: 136].)[7] Jantzen takes advantage of an ambiguity within the *Critical of Practical Reason* and argues that hope in the possibility of an ideal's realizability by human nature is all that is required for either religion or morality.

Jantzen's argument depends on the conflation of Feuerbach's theory of projection with a modified Kantianism. Yet she overlooks a crucial dimension of Feuerbach's theory of religion in her appeal to the divine as a realizable projection of human ideals. For Feuerbach, reason alone is inadequate to explain religious belief; *desire* motivates projection and with it the insistence on the ontological independence of that which is projected. As Van Harvey shows, for Feuerbach pain and ecstasy fuel humanity's projection of a divine other. When one human being encounters another,

> the individual I experiences a powerful inrush of two types of feeling: on the one hand, a painful feeling of limitation and inadequacy over against the unlimitedness of the species and, on the other, an ecstatic sense of the attractiveness of the species, an attractiveness grounded in the individual's joy in the exercise of his/her own distinctive powers. But because the idea of the species is an abstraction and as such has very little emotional power, it is seized upon by the imagination and transformed into the idea of a single being. The individual, driven by his/her desire to live and his/her sense of finitude, finds in the perfection of the divine being a substitute for the true bearer of these predicates, the species, as well as an assurance of his/her worthiness and immortality as an individual.
>
> (Harvey 1995: 110)

Unlike the forms of Christianity analyzed by Feuerbach, Jantzen is not interested in asserting the unlimitedness and immortality of the species. Yet ideals – however limited – remain abstract. Feuerbach suggests that to attain emotional force they require concretization in an object of belief held to be ontologically independent of the believer.[8]

Perhaps most importantly, what if we understand philosophy of religion less as an attempt to justify or redefine belief, than as an attempt to account philosophically for those aspects of human existence broadly characterized as religious? Philosophy of religion understood in this way cannot move so quickly from the descriptive to the prescriptive, for it is responsible to religious phenomena as lived by practitioners and believers. From this perspective, the question of the ontological status of the objects of religious belief cannot be resolved by redefining the nature of divine existence in terms of regulatory ideals (be they epistemological or moral). Nor can religion be equated solely with belief. For many religious people, practice takes precedence over belief; a philosophy of religion that does not account for the function and meaning of practice will never be adequate to its object.

As I suggested earlier, the issues of the ontological status of the objects of religious belief and of the centrality of practice to religion are intimately related. The early twentieth-century French sociologist, a son-in-law and intellectual heir of Émile Durkheim, Marcel Mauss makes the argument most starkly:

> I believe precisely that at the bottom of all our mystical states there are body techniques which we have not studied, but which were studied fully in China and India, even in very remote periods. This socio-biological

study should be made. I think that there are necessarily biological means of entering into "communion with God."

(Mauss 1979: 122; cited in Asad 1993: 76)

If mystical states are understood as God's existence made bodily and spiritually inescapable, then this leads to the possibility that skepticism about or disbelief in God's existence is itself, as Talal Asad puts it, "a function of untaught bodies" (Asad 1993: 77).[9]

III. Bodily practice, the *habitus*, and practical reason

Asad uses Mauss's argument about the constitutive power of bodily practice in order to intervene in two related debates within contemporary anthropology, the first having to do with the supposed primacy of belief over practice and the second with the putative distinction between ritual and instrumental human actions. Both debates stem from modern Western European Protestantism's rejection of ritualism and insistence on the primacy of faith. Understanding religion primarily through the models provided by their own religious tradition (regardless of how distanced individual philosophers and proto-anthropologists may have been from that tradition), early students of religion assumed the centrality of belief to religion (see, for example, Preus 1987). Ritual action, understood as a debased form of religiosity, needed to be distinguished from instrumental action; the former operates symbolically, the latter practically. In other words, rituals are understood to be actions that must be interpreted in terms of pre-existing systems of belief rather than described in terms of what they do (the presumption being that they do not do anything) (Asad 1993: 55–79). Mauss's rejection of the clear cut distinction between instrumental and ritual action makes it possible for Asad to contest claims to the primacy of belief within religion (a contestation increasingly demanded by students of religion on empirical grounds – even, as I will show, in the study of Protestant Christianity).

For Mauss, "the body is man's first and most natural instrument. Or more accurately, not to speak of instruments, man's first and most natural technical object, and at the same time technical means, is his body" (Mauss 1979: 104; cited in Asad 1993: 75). Mauss is interested in those forms of bodily practice marked by culture (as well as by biology and psychology) yet not easily read in terms of symbolic meaning: gait, athletic styles, manners of sleeping and eating, clothing, and birth and nursing patterns. These forms of bodily practice form subjectivity, inculcate virtue, and embody belief. They constitute what Mauss calls the habitus:

Please note that I use the Latin word ... *habitus*. The word translates infinitely better than "*habitude*" [habit or custom], the "*exis*" the "acquired ability" and "faculty" of Aristotle (who was a psychologist). ... These "habits" do not vary just with individuals and their imitations; they vary especially between societies, educations, proprieties, and fashions, prestiges. In them we should see the techniques and work of collective and individual practical reason rather than, in the ordinary way, merely the soul and its repetitive faculties.

(Mauss 1979: 101; cited by Asad 1993: 75)[10]

As Asad explains, Mauss's understanding of the *habitus* enables social scientists "to analyze the body as an assemblage of embodied attitudes, not as a medium of symbolic meanings" (Asad 1993: 75). The distinction between bodily practices in the Maussian sense and ritual thus breaks down; for Asad, both are disciplinary practices through which bodies, dispositions, and subjectivities are formed and transformed (Asad 1993: 131).[11] Rituals, like bodily practices, do not carry symbolic meanings but instead *do* things. They create certain kinds of subjects, dispositions, moods, emotions, and desires. Put in another way, they are like performative speech acts, for that to which they refer is constituted through the action itself.[12]

As Asad shows, Mauss provides the framework for an historicized Kantianism or "an anthropology of practical reason." Practical reason is not, as it is for Kant, a principle of universalizability by means of which ethical rules can be determined, but rather an

historically constituted practical knowledge, which articulates an individual's learning capacities. According to Mauss, the human body was not to be viewed simply as the passive recipient of "cultural imprints," still less as the active source of "natural expressions" that are "clothed in local history and culture," as though it were a matter of an inner character expressed in a readable sign, so that the latter could be used as a means of deciphering the former. It was to be viewed as the developable means for achieving a range of human objectives, from styles of physical movement (e.g. walking), through modes of emotional being (e.g. composure), to kinds of spiritual experience (e.g. mystical states). This way of talking seems to avoid the Cartesian dualism of the mind and objects of the mind's perception.

(Asad 1993: 76)[13]

Mauss's arguments also de-stabilize any rigid distinction between "body sense and body learning" (Asad 1993: 76). Bodily experience is physiological and cultural; the body can – and arguably must – be taught and the various cultural lessons learned by the body shape one's experience. Physical pain, for example, is a universal physiological phenomenon, yet according to Asad anthropological and psychological research demonstrates "that the perception of pain threshold varies considerably according to traditions of bodily training – and also according to the pain history of individual bodies" (Asad 1993: 76). Pain, understood simultaneously as one of the most universal and one of the most subjective aspects of human experiences, is always also inflected by culture.[14]

Following Mauss, then, Asad embodies and historicizes practical reason and he does so by insisting on the centrality of bodily practices and rituals as forms of discipline. The body is humanity's first technical means and object because through disciplined body practices bodies acquire aptitudes, emotions, dispositions, and beliefs (although it should be noted that the relationship between dispositions and beliefs requires further discussion and refinement). On first sight, then, the *habitus* represents a much broader conception of practical reason than that found in Kant. One might argue that while Kant articulates reason in its practical dimension as providing a universally available means of determining the moral law (through the process of universalizability), Mauss and Asad show that practical reason also, and perhaps more fundamentally, involves learned modes of being in the body and in the world.[15] Seen from this perspective, Asad's work nicely complements that of Anderson and Jantzen, both of whom wish to expand the grounds for religious and moral reflection to include bodily affects, emotion, and desire. Asad, by insisting on the necessity of body practices and rituals to the formation of practical reason, provides the concrete grounds for this extension in a way not provided by Anderson and Jantzen.

Yet to what extent and in what ways is Asad's conception of practical reason broader than Kant's? Asad's arguments are indebted to the work of philosopher and historian Michel Foucault as well as to that of Mauss. Foucault offers a rough typology of different modes of morality that might be helpful in elucidating the relationship between Mauss's and Asad's conception of practical reason and that of Kant. Foucault argues that the term "morality" covers three different realities. First, there are the values and rules of action that are set forth as normative for a particular group, a "prescriptive ensemble" that Foucault calls a "moral code." Morality also refers to "the real behavior of individuals in relation to the rules and values that are recommended to them," what Foucault terms "the morality of behaviors." Finally, there "is the manner in which one ought to 'conduct oneself' – that is, the manner in which one ought to form oneself as an ethical subject acting in reference to the prescriptive elements that make up the code" (Foucault 1986: 25–6). In other words, social groups not only prescribe *what* one should do, but also attempt to form subjects who will perform certain kinds of actions in preference to others. The practices or exercises through which ethical subjects are formed also shape *how* and *toward what end* these subjects will act.

Descriptions of morality can be either descriptions of "codes," of "moral behaviors," or of "'ethics' and 'ascetics', understood as a history of the forms of moral subjectivation and of the practices of the self that are meant to ensure it" (Foucault 1986: 29). A history or anthropology of ethics and ascetics, of

the way in which individuals are urged to constitute themselves as subjects of moral conduct would be concerned with the models proposed for setting up and developing relationships with the self, for self-reflection, self-knowledge, self-examination, for the decipherment of the self by oneself, for the transformation that one seeks to accomplish with oneself as object.

(Foucault 1986: 29)

One is called on not only to perform certain actions or to follow certain prohibitions, but *to be* a particular kind of moral subject, and within any given culture the models, techniques, and practices (remember that in ancient Greek, *askesis* means "practice" or "exercise") through which this form of subjectivity is inculcated can be uncovered by the historian or anthropologist. These practices not only form ethical subjects of a particular sort, but also promise them certain pleasures or goods. Thus, Foucault argues, technologies of the self "permit individuals to affect, by their own means, a certain number of operations on their own bodies, their own souls, their own thoughts, their own conduct, and this in a manner so as to transform themselves, modify themselves, and to attain a certain state of perfection, happiness, purity, supernatural power" (Foucault 1985: 367). Although certain cultures might give more weight to the "code" and others more weight to "askesis" and the formation of the self, generally both operate together within flourishing moral systems.

Seen in light of Foucault's threefold account of morality, one might be tempted to argue that Kant's moral theory is all about codes whereas Mauss and Asad create a space for thinking about askesis. Yet Kant does not simply provide a method for determining the maxims according to which one should act, but also argues that a particular mode of being in the world is decisive for determining the moral nature of one's actions. To behave on behalf of anything other than the moral law, Kant argues, is to act heteronomously. Morality depends on autonomy, on acting out of duty to the moral law itself. Human action must be determined solely by practical reason and the demands it makes on the subject. In providing the means for determining the moral law, then, Kant provides not only a code but also an askesis through which moral subjects are created. Kant not only tells us how to determine the proper moral code, but the very same operation also forms us as subjects who act in a particular way and toward particular ends. For Kant, then, code (or at least the means for determining the code) and askesis are inseparable. The form of askesis he recommends requires detachment from the body, emotion, and desire. It entails a bodily and mental discipline by means of which the subject becomes detached from his or her body. Thus Kant's form of askesis, like the notion outlined by Foucault, broadens Mauss's conception of practice to include mental and spiritual exercises that effect the body but are not generally acknowledged themselves to be bodily practices. (It is important to recognize, moreover, that the principle of universalizability is not reducible to the principle of detachment, although there are close relationships between the two. Moreover, there are aspects of body practice that go beyond the parameters of that with which Kant concerns himself in his writings on practical reason. The relationship between this more broadly construed conception of *habitus* and Kant's moral law requires further elucidation.) Kant generally does not acknowledge that the form of subjectivity he wishes to inculcate is a learned mode of being in the world. Instead, he argues it is the mode of subjectivity demanded by human reason itself, rightly understood. At the same time, Kant's deep interest in education as central to the work of enlightenment suggests his at least partial recognition that bodily and intellectual training is necessary to the successful attainment of moral subjectivity, despite his insistence that a revolution in human disposition is required rather than merely its reform.

Mauss and Asad, in deuniversalizing the claims of practical reason, enable us to see that the moral law and moral dispositions – even those called for by Kant – are learned. An Asadian reading of Kant, then, would demand attention to his account of the practices – bodily and intellectual – through which the mind removes itself from the body, emotion, and desire in order to determine the moral law and to attain the proper disposition for its enactment. Seen from this perspective, Anderson's and Jantzen's critique of Kant is directed toward the debilitating effects of his particular account of the moral life. They both insist that the body, emotion, and desire must play a role in practical moral reasoning and in the religious life. What Mauss and Asad offer is an account of the role of bodily, mental, and spiritual practices and rituals in the transformation of the moral, religious, and intellectual life. Not only are we unable fully to understand Kant's moral philosophy and philosophy of religion without an understanding of the role of askesis within them, we also cannot hope to bring the body, emotion, and desire back into morality and religion solely through an analysis and critique of symbols and beliefs.

IV. Embodying belief

Asad substantiates his claims about the constitutive role of practice in the formation of moods, emotions, dispositions, and beliefs through an analysis of medieval Christian monastic practice as codified within the *Rule of Benedict*.[16] As he argues, monastic practice formed and reformed Christian dispositions, among them humility, patience, and contrition. Following the *Rules* prescriptions involves undertaking a set of performative actions through which will, desire, intellect, and mind are transformed and (re)constituted. In other words, one becomes a certain kind of person, responds bodily, affectively and intellectually in certain ways, and comes to hold certain beliefs by engaging in certain prescribed behaviors. (Of course, a certain set of beliefs determines one's decision to engage in these practices in the first place, rendering the relationship between body and practice even more complex than I can here articulate.) The monk who weeps over his sinfulness will become contrite; humiliating oneself before the abbot and the community (through manual labor, acts of homage to the abbot, and public confession) generates humility. Although Asad's detailed arguments are too complex for full elaboration here, his central, well-attested point is that "emotions, which are often recognized by anthropologists as inner, contingent events, could be progressively organized by increasingly apt performances of conventional behavior" (Asad 1993: 64; for full discussions of the role of humility in Christian monasticism, see 125–67).

Asad's examples focus on how subjects are constituted and/or transformed through practice, yet he follows Mauss in suggesting the more radical claim that religious experiences constitutive of and validating belief are constituted through practice. Substantiating evidence for this claim can be found within the texts of the Christian Middle Ages, together with some evidence for the ways in which bodily differences – in this case sexual difference – may be both inculcated and presumed by prescriptive practices. Clear indications of the role of bodily practices and rituals in the inculcation of belief can be found in medieval meditative handbooks, saint's lives, and mystical texts. I'll focus here on just one example, chosen to highlight certain crucial features of meditative practice and the variable relationship between meditation and sexual difference within the later Middle Ages.

Margaret Ebner (1291–1351) was a German Dominican nun whose religious practice and experience followed closely the traditions of meditative practice and mystical experience found in the writings of thirteenth-century religious women. In her *Revelations*, however, Ebner provides more concrete descriptions of the relationship between meditative practice and mystical experience than we find in women's and men's mystical texts from the previous century. Ebner explicitly articulates the way in which her intense meditation on Christ's Passion leads to her inability *not* to see, hear, and feel Christ's Passion and ultimately to experience it in and on her own body.

The process begins with a conscious concentration of Ebner's energies on visual representations of Christ's suffering:

> Every cross I came upon I kissed ardently and as frequently as possible. I pressed it forcibly against my heart constantly, so that I often thought I could not separate myself from it and remain alive. Such great desire and such sweet power so penetrated my heart and all of my members that I could not withdraw myself from the cross. Wherever I went I had a cross with me. In addition, I possessed a little book in which there was a picture of the Lord on the cross. I shoved it secretly against my bosom, open to that place, and wherever I went I pressed it to my heart with great joy and with measureless grace. When I wanted to sleep, I took the picture of the Crucified Lord in the little book and laid it under my face. Also, around my neck I wore a cross that hung down to my heart. In addition, I took a large cross whenever possible and laid it over my heart. I clung to it while lying down until I fell asleep in great grace. We had a large crucifix in choir. I had the greatest desire to kiss it and to press it close to my heart like the others. But it was too high up for me and was too large in size.
>
> (Ebner 1993: 96; cf. Strauch 1882: 20–1)

The one sister in whom Margaret confides this desire refuses to help her, fearing that the act would be too much for one as physically frail as Margaret. Yet, Margaret claims, what can't be possible while awake was granted to her in a dream:

> It seemed as if I were standing before the cross filled with the desire that I usually had within me. As I stood before the image, my Lord

Jesus Christ bent down from the cross and let me kiss His open heart and gave me to drink of the blood flowing from His heart.

(Ebner 1993: 96; cf. Strauch 1882: 21)[17]

The movement from actively pursued practice to unconsciously enacted experience first occurs, then, in Ebner's dream life. We see here a feature of religious practice suggested by Asad and highlighted by Saba Mahmood in her study of the modern Islamic women's piety movement in Egypt: the goal of consciously pursued bodily practices and rituals is ultimately to render conscious training unnecessary.[18] In Ebner, this movement nears completion when Christ's passion becomes inescapably present to her. In the Lent of 1340, while at matins, Margaret explains,

the greatest pain came over my heart and also a sorrow, so bitter that it was as if I were really in the presence of my Beloved, my most heartily Beloved One, and as if I had seen his suffering with my own eyes and as if it were all happening before me at this very moment.

(Ebner 1993: 114; cf. Strauch 1882: 52)

Following in the meditative tradition on Christ's life and death promulgated by the Franciscan and Dominican orders during the later Middle Ages, Ebner seems here to have achieved a perfect *meditatio* in which external aides, be they visual or auditory, are no longer required in order for Christ's passion to be viscerally present to her.

Ebner goes even further, however, claiming not only to see Christ's passion, but to share in it. At first, she finds herself unable not to cry out when she hears of or sees (either through the physical eye or the mind's eye) Christ's passion before her. These outcries lead to physical suffering that renders her body itself Christ-like:

But when I was given to loud exclamations and outcries by the gentle goodness of God (these were given to me when I heard the holy suffering spoken about), then I was pierced to the heart and this extended to all my members, and then I was bound and ever more grasped by the silence. In these cases, I sit a long time – sometimes longer, sometimes shorter. After this my heart was as if shot by a mysterious force. Its effect rose up to my head and passed on to all my members and broke them violently. Compelled by the same force I cried out loudly and exclaimed. I had no power over myself and was not able to stop the outcry until God released me from it. Sometimes it grasped me so powerfully that red blood spurted from me.

(Ebner 1993: 114 and Strauch 1882: 54)

With blood gushing forth from her body, Margaret seems here to become a visible representation of Christ's suffering for those around her.[19] Her identification with the Passion shifts from identification with the onlookers to one with Christ himself.

Ebner claims, like Francis of Assisi a century before her, to achieve an identification with Christ's Passion in which her own body becomes a representation of Christ's suffering for those around her. This cross-gender identification occurs seemingly without question in Ebner's text, suggesting a gender fluidity that renders culturally plausible the valorization of women's suffering bodies.[20] In fact, the situation in the later Middle Ages is more complex than this sole example might suggest. Whereas women did find ways to associate their suffering bodies and souls with that of Christ, other contemporary practices and discourses suggest that at least some men mistrusted these identifications and argued that women should identify, not with Christ on the cross, but with Mary at the foot of the cross.[21] Often couched in terms of concern for the danger done to women's bodies by their excessive suffering and asceticism, texts like Henry Suso's *Life of the Servant* reserve the role of Christ-like bodily and spiritual suffering for men (in this case, for Suso himself), with Suso's Christ-like body becoming itself the center of women's devotional life.

Early in his life, Suso had engaged in intense ascetic bodily practices, like Ebner rendering his body bloody in imitation of contemporary representations of Christ on the cross. In addition, he inscribed Christ's name on his chest with a stylus. In the second part of the *Life,* he eschews such violent practices, particularly for his female followers, yet the sanctification of his body through these practices remains salient. So toward the end of his life we see his "holy daughter" (Elsbet Stagel, who may have in part authored the *Life of the Servant*) sewing "this same name of Jesus in red silk onto a small piece of cloth in this form, IHS, which she herself intended to wear secretly." Moreover, she makes further images of the name of Jesus for distribution:

> She repeated this countless times and brought it about that the servant put them all over his bare breast. She would send them all over, with a religious blessing to his spiritual children. She was informed by God: whoever thus wore this name and recited an Our Father daily for God's honor would be treated kindly by God, and God would give him his grace on his final journey.
>
> (Suso 1989: 173–4; for the German text, Seuse 1907: 154–5)

Although Jeffrey Hamburger suggests that the displacement of wounds from the human body to cloth badges serves simply as a critique of Henry's early asceticism, the value of the badges depends on their contact with Suso's sanctified flesh.[22] Here we see a male saintly body replace the female body as the site of holiness. Women's role is now the dissemination of physical objects sanctified, not by their own actions or bodies, but by those of the male saint. Thus we can see the ways in which prescriptions for bodily and meditative practice can both depend on and shape gender ideologies.

My examples, like Asad's, come from the Christian Middle Ages, a period in which the centrality of liturgical and paraliturgical practices is largely unquestioned (although the role of these practices in inculcating religious experience and belief is only beginning to be studied). What of modern Protestantism, however, often understood as a religious tradition determined by its insistence on the centrality of faith – and hence of belief – alone? My contention that Kant's conception of practical reason depends on a particular form of askesis, one partially masked by its association with a putatively universal reason, suggests that similar forms of practice can be uncovered within Protestant Christianity. Again, I only have room here for a single example, one suggestive of the intense gendering of many Christian traditions of practice as well as of the limitations of studies of religion focused primarily on belief.

R. Marie Griffith's *God's Daughters: Evangelical Women and the Power of Submission* (1997) studies the Women's Aglow Fellowship, an interdenominational organization of charismatic Christian women founded in 1972 (although with roots in a smaller organization started in 1967). Women's Aglow meetings center on testimonials, singing, public prayer, tears, prophecy, exorcisms, and ecstatic transformation by the Holy Spirit. Griffith provides a fascinating account of the movement through analysis of the central themes articulated in oral testimonials and those printed in Women's Aglow Fellowship periodicals. She demonstrates the ways in which the Aglow women's stories of powerlessness, abuse, secrecy, and shame parallel those found in second wave feminist literature, even as the two groups' strategies for coping with these issues fundamentally differ.[23] Her focus on narrative enables these comparisons and provides a useful locus for attempting to undermine the sharp divide between explicitly anti-feminist evangelical Christian women and US feminists. From the perspective of my analysis of practice, ritual, and belief, however, Griffith too readily allows the Aglow women's self-understanding of the relationship between "spontaneity" and "ritual" to shape her telling of their story.

Griffith briefly describes a regular chapter meeting's fairly uniform schedule. Usually held in hotel conference rooms or other non-religious public spaces, meetings begin with music, followed by announcements, testimonies, an offering, a talk by a special speaker, and ending with more music and the reception of "prayers from specially trained prayer counselors or coordinators." Griffith argues that despite these formalized elements, "the women continue to value and emphasize 'spontaneity' over 'ritual,' believing the former to maintain openness to the spirit of God while the latter effectively hinders or even closes off such a possibility" (Griffith 1997: 27). Hidden by this account is the way in which the formalized movement from music and prayer to testimonials and then back to music and individualized prayer works to generate the tears, prophecies, and effusions of the spirit experienced by the Aglow women. In other words, their practice, more carefully observed and described, might be understood as itself strengthening belief in and engendering an experience of a judging, yet also munificent and forgiving God.

Attention to the constitutive power of practice might also help elucidate the seeming intractability of debates between non-feminist evangelical women and feminists. These differences are not simply the result of conflicting propositions about the world and women's place within it, but reflect deeply embodied dispositions, emotions, and beliefs. Appeals to reason will never be able fully to overcome the divide – a divide that tends toward an absolute refusal of debate – between the two groups. Recognition of the learned nature of one's *habitus* can begin to open spaces for understanding, yet it is the very nature of the *habitus* to cover over its own learned status. Belief successfully inculcated through bodily practice renders itself "natural" and hence resistant to critique and change (see Bourdieu 1977). (Hence the insistence of the Aglow women that God engenders their experience rather than that their experience engenders God or an encounter with God.) Even if we begin to recognize the learned nature of many of our most deeply embedded dispositions and beliefs, new practices that enable a re-formation of the self will be required for their transformation. And as Feuerbach reminds us, religion appeals not only to reason, but to the body, emotion, and desire. This marks what is arguably the most crucial divide between the Aglow women and their secular feminist critics. Although the latter are also shaped by learned dispositions and beliefs grounded in emotion and desire, the epistemological and political assumptions of liberalism refuse to recognize the embodied nature of the *habitus*. From the standpoint of the religious believer, moreover, the consolations of liberalism are weak, insufficient to the desires satisfied, at least in part, by religion (see also Mahmood 2001a).

Anderson and Jantzen both argue that we need not settle for a choice between forms of political liberalism cut off from the body, emotion, and desire and a wholesale relativism in which any claims to adjudication between competing practices and beliefs are eschewed. Desire and emotion themselves are shaped both by bodily practices and by reason (now no longer so easily differentiated), making it possible that new conceptions of practical reason and of the practices that inculcate it can be articulated and enacted. Yet without attention to bodily, mental, and spiritual practices and rituals and their powerful shaping of the *habitus*, the transformation of practical reason and of religiosity demanded by feminist philosophers like Anderson and Jantzen will necessarily fall short.

Notes

1 See Anderson (1998) and Jantzen (1999). See also Anderson (2001, 2002a, 2002b). Philosopher Luce Irigaray's work is crucial to both Anderson and Jantzen. See, among other texts, Irigaray (1985, 1993a, 1993b, and 1996). For other recent work on feminist philosophy of religion, much of it also influenced by Irigaray, see Frankenberry and Thie (1994); Hampson (1996); Hollywood (2002a); and Coakley (2002).

   A question that remains unanswered in this literature is that of the relationship between philosophy of religion, philosophical theology, and theology. Like much contemporary analytic philosophy and, arguably, like the work of Irigaray, Anderson and Jantzen are engaged in philosophical theology, a point to which I will return in the paper.

2 Most introductions to the philosophy of religion define the field in terms of the clarification and justification of religious belief. This is also the case with

anthologies for classroom use, which rarely, if ever, include sections on practice or ritual. Even the widespread interest in religious experience and mysticism ultimately reverts to questions of belief and justification, for the central philosophical dispute – the one to which all other questions lead – concerns whether religious experience can provide a means of justification for religious belief. See, for example, Proudfoot (1985); Alston (1991); and Bagger (1999).

3 Jantzen argues that her work does not focus on belief, yet given the centrality to her work of religious discourse and the symbolic, however broadly conceived, and the absence of any extended discussion of practice or ritual, it is difficult to see how she fully escapes the confines of more traditional forms of analytic philosophy of religion.

4 Anderson distinguishes fiction, myth, and illusion in the following ways. Fiction she defines, rather flatly, as something that "has been made up." Illusions are defined in a quasi-Freudian way as ideas unconsciously generated "from fear of the contingencies and losses in life." Myths, finally, are complex configurations of narratives and concepts that "constitute a people's meaningful, qualitative identity." Anderson gives considerable attention to myth, articulating its relationship to embodiment, desire, and mimesis. Although I think these distinctions require more adequate conceptions of fiction and illusion to be fully convincing, the issue lies beyond the scope of my argument here. See Anderson (1998: 118, 127–64).

5 Hence they are not illusions, as defined by Anderson.

6 Essential for Jantzen are the "criteria of trustworthiness and mutual accountability by which aspects of the symbolic can be tested against its fruitfulness in creating a space for the woman subject." Such criteria arguably do not respond to all the problems raised by critics of moral and epistemological relativism, but this issue will have to wait for exploration in another paper.

7 See Jantzen (1991: 306–8).

8 For more on this issue as it applies to Irigaray's writings on religion and the ambivalent responses to them by feminists, see Hollywood (2002a: 234–5).

9 Or perhaps better, of differently taught bodies.

10 On the medieval reception of Aristotle and the doctrine of *habitus*, see Nederman (1989–90).

11 Put in another way, without claims to the primacy of belief over action and hence to the necessarily symbolic nature of ritual action, the distinction between ritual action and instrumental action breaks down and with it the need for a distinction between bodily practices and ritual. All that remains is the distinction between those actions that use the body as the instrument for transforming the body and those actions that use other instruments toward other ends.

12 For more on bodily practices and ritual as performative, see Hollywood (2002b).

13 Asad cites phrases from Mary Douglas's interpretation of Mauss's essay (Douglas 1970). Asad disagrees deeply with Douglas's account of Mauss and asks how, given his own reading of Mauss's essay, it has been understood as a founding document for symbolic anthropology. "Was it," Asad wonders, "because 'ritual' was already so powerfully in place as symbolic action – that is, as visible behavioral form requiring decoding?" (Asad 1993: 77)

14 For an extremely influential proponent of this view, see Scarry (1985).

15 From this standpoint, Mauss and Asad seem closer to an Aristotelian conception of practical reason. A longer version of my argument will require attention to both Aristotle's account of *habitus* and its deployment within medieval moral and sacramental theology. See Nederman (1989–90) and Colish (1993).

16 In the case of Benedictine monasticism, bodily practices and rituals are elaborately codified in a text; in other instances, prescribed modes of action are passed down through person-to-person interactions (and of course this kind of interaction also plays an essential role in monastic discipline, as the *Rule of Benedict* continually emphasizes).

17 For the kiss of the heart and drinking blood from Christ's side wound/heart, see Hollywood (forthcoming).
18 On this point and the important corrective it provides to the work of Pierre Bourdieu, see Mahmood 2001b.
19 On the salvific power of Christ's blood and the centrality of blood in representations of the Passion, see Hollywood (forthcoming), and Hamburger (1998).
20 For the fluidity of gender in the later Middle Ages, see Bynum (1987, 1991), and Hollywood (1995).
21 The Franciscan authored *Meditations on the Life of Christ*, for example, addressed to women, most often calls for readers to identify with Mary. As Robin O'Sullivan argues, Angela of Foligno, like Ebner, refuses this identification instead insisting on her oneness with Christ on the cross. See O'Sullivan (2002) and Hollywood (2002a: 69–74).
22 Hamburger writes, "the way in which the young – that is, spiritually immature – Suso so literally imitates Christ's passion bears an uncanny resemblance to the self-inflicted sufferings of numerous nuns." (Hamburger here cites only Elsbeth von Oye, although further examples are readily available from the hagiographical literature.) "By contrast," Hamburger continues, "in Part II of the Life, Suso deliberately distances himself from the extreme asceticism in which he indulged as a novice. The *imitatio Christi* is recast in ritualized, institutionalized forms, governed by texts and enacted through images. Instead of drawing blood, Stagel embroiders in red silk; rather than mortifying her flesh, she emulates her advisor's asceticism by adorning her body in his image." Although I agree with Hamburger that this movement between Books I and II of the *Life* is decisive, it is crucial also to note that Suso's body remains the source of sanctification. Stagel adorns her flesh, but her flesh never gains the power evinced, still in Book II, by Suso's, a power gained precisely through the ascetic action against which he advises Stagel and his other followers. See Hamburger 1998: 263–6.
23 I follow Griffith here in generalizing about US second-wave feminism, but with full recognition of the enormous variety of positions and practices that exist within it. Griffith emphasizes the mainstream traditions of liberal feminism most visible to evangelical women and, arguably, most critical of fundamentalist Christian women.

Bibliography

Alston, W. (1991) *Perceiving God: The Epistemology of Religious Experience*, Ithaca: Cornell University Press.
Anderson, P. S. (1998) *A Feminist Philosophy of Religion*, Oxford: Basil Blackwell.
—— (2001) "Gender and the Infinite: On the aspiration to be all there is," *International Journal for Philosophy of Religion* 50: 191–212.
—— (2002a) "Myth and Feminist Philosophy," in K. Schilbrack (ed.), *Thinking Through Myths: Philosophical Perspectives*, 101–22, New York: Routledge.
—— (2002b) "Feminist Theology as Philosophy of Religion," in S. F. Parsons (ed.), *The Cambridge Companion to Feminist Theology*, 40–59, Cambridge: Cambridge University Press.
Asad, T. (1993) *Genealogies of Religion: Disciplines and Reasons of Power in Christianity and Islam*, Baltimore: The Johns Hopkins University Press.
Bagger, M. (1999) *Religious Experience, Justification, and History*, Cambridge: Cambridge University Press.
Bourdieu, P. (1977) *Outline of a Theory of Practice*, trans. R. Nice, Cambridge: Cambridge University Press.

Bynum, C. W. (1987) *Holy Feast and Holy Fast: The Religious Significance of Food to Medieval Women*, Berkeley: University of California Press.

—— (1991) *Fragmentation and Redemption: Essays on Gender and the Body in the Later Middle Ages*, New York: Zone Books.

Coakley, S. (2002) *Powers and Submissions: Spirituality, Philosophy, and Gender*, Oxford: Blackwell.

Colish, M. (1993) "*Habitus* Revisited," *Traditio* 48: 77–92.

Douglas, M. (1970) *Natural Symbols*, London: Barrie and Rockliff.

Ebner, M. (1993) *The Major Works*, trans. and ed. L. Hindsley, New York: Paulist Press.

Foucault, M. (1985) "Sexuality and Solitude," in M. Blonsky (ed.), *On Signs*, Baltimore: The Johns Hopkins University Press.

—— (1986) *The Use of Pleasure*, trans. R. Hurley, New York: Vintage.

Frankenberry, N. and Thie, M. (eds) (1994) "Special Issue: Feminist Philosophy of Religion," *Hypatia* 9.

Griffith, R. M. (1997) *God's Daughters: Evangelical Women and the Power of Submission*, Berkeley: University of California Press.

Hamburger, J. (1998) *The Visual and the Visionary: Art and Female Spirituality in Late Medieval Germany*, New York: Zone Books.

Hampson, D. (1996) *After Christianity*, London: SCM Press.

Harvey, V. (1995) *Feuerbach and the Interpretation of Religion*, Cambridge: Cambridge University Press.

Hollywood, A. (1995) *The Soul as Virgin Wife: Mechthild of Magdeburg, Marguerite Porete, and Meister Eckhart*, Notre Dame: Notre Dame University Press.

—— (2002a) *Sensible Ecstasy: Mysticism, Sexual Difference, and the Demands of History*, Chicago: University of Chicago Press.

—— (2002b) "Performativity, Citationality, Ritualization," *History of Religions* 42: 93–115.

—— (forthcoming) "Sexual Desire, Divine Desire; Or, Queering the Beguines," in G. Loughlin (ed.) *Queer Theology: New Perspectives on Sex and Gender*, Oxford: Basil Blackwell.

Irigaray, L. (1985) *Speculum of the Other Woman*, trans. G. Gill, Ithaca: Cornell University Press.

—— (1993a) *An Ethics of Sexual Difference*, trans. C. Burke and G. Gill, Ithaca: Cornell University Press.

—— (1993b) *Sexes and Genealogies*, trans. G. Gill, New York: Columbia University Press.

—— (1996) *I Love to You*, trans. A. Martin, New York: Routledge.

Jantzen, G. (1991) "Do We Need Immortality?" in A. Loades and L. D. Rue (eds) *Contemporary Classics in Philosophy of Religion*, La Salle, Illinois: Open Court Press.

—— (1999) *Becoming Divine: Towards a Feminist Philosophy of Religion*, Bloomington: Indiana University Press.

Kant, I. (1950) *Critique of Pure Reason*, trans. N. K. Smith, London: Macmillan.

—— (1956) *Critique of Practical Reason*, trans. L. W. Beck, Indianapolis: Bobbs-Merrill.

Mahmood, S. (2001a) "Feminist Theory, Embodiment, and the Docile Subject: Some Reflections on the Egyptian Islamic Revival," *Cultural Anthropology* 16: 202–36.

—— (2001b) "Rehearsed Spontaneity and the Conventionality of Ritual: Disciplines of Ṣalāt," *American Ethnologist* 28: 837–8.

Mauss, M. (1979) "Body Techniques," in *Sociology and Psychology: Essays*, trans. B. Brewster, London: Routledge.

Nederman, C. (1989–90) "Nature, Ethics, and the Doctrine of 'Habitus': Aristotelian Moral Psychology in the Twelfth Century," *Traditio* 45: 87–110.

O'Sullivan, R. (2002) *Model, Mirror and Memorial: Imitation of the Passion and the Annihilation of the Imagination in Angela da Foligno's Liber and Marguerite Porete's Mirouer des simples âmes*, Ph. D. Dissertation, University of Chicago Divinity School.

Preus, J. S. (1987) *Explaining Religion: Criticism and Theory from Bodin to Freud*, New Haven: Yale University Press.

Proudfoot, W. (1985) *Religious Experience*, Berkeley: University of California Press.

Scarry, E. (1985) *The Body in Pain: The Making and Unmaking of the World*, Oxford: Oxford University Press.

Seuse, H. (1907) *Deutsche Schriften*, Stuttgart: Kohlhammer.

Strauch, P. (ed.) (1882) *Margaretha Ebner und Heinrich von Nördlingen: Ein Beitrag zur Geschichte der Deutschen Mystik*, Freiburg and Tubingen, Mohr.

Suso, H. (1989) *The Exemplar, With Two German Sermons*, trans. F. Tobin, New York: Paulist Press.

3 Rites of passing

Foucault, power, and same-sex commitment ceremonies

Ladelle McWhorter

I. The alleged decline of ritual in modern life

According to Catherine Bell, "The popular contention that ritual and religion decline in proportion to modernization has been something of a sociological truism since the mid-19th century" (Bell 1997: 254). Conventional wisdom maintains that ritual practices just don't hold central importance in the lives of those raised in the industrialized world as compared with the importance such things had for our distant ancestors or for our contemporaries in non-industrial societies. Some have contended that this is because ritual tends to be strongly correlated with pre-scientific cosmological beliefs that our society has for the most part outgrown.[1] But for whatever reason, "[c]omparatively speaking," writes Ronald Grimes, "Western industrial societies spend less time and energy on rites than do people living in more traditional, small-scale societies and less than Asian, Middle Eastern, and African peoples" (Grimes 2000: 111).[2]

Bell traces this "sociological truism" back to Herbert Spencer,[3] who believed that societies evolve over time from a state of primitive existence wherein ritual activities are frequent, elaborate, and of central importance, through more sophisticated forms of social, economic, and technological organization wherein ritual begins to decline in importance, to modern industrialization where ritual has little if any significant place. The decline comes about naturally as societies become better adapted to environments where resources are scarce – the presumption being that ritual has no real practical value.[4] Spencer's view is intimately bound to his Social Darwinism, but, as Bell points out, its assumptions about and prognosis for ritual are hardly peculiar to Spencer or to the late nineteenth century. A generation later, Max Weber too claimed that modernization and industrialization bring along with them what he called a "disenchantment of the world" (Bell 1997: 198, 254), a radical secularization of life with a concomitant reduction in ritual practices; as our lives become more focused on material production and more rationalized (to use Weber's term), there is virtually no place for rites and ceremonies that appeal to mythical entities, expend resources without material return, or poeticize processes (e.g. birth, sexual maturation) that we have come to see as simply biological. Frequently, as Bell shows, in both the nineteenth and early twentieth centuries, ritual was set in opposition to reason itself: while primitive minds need ritual to calm their fears and make "sense" of what was not really understood, with the maturation of reason and the development of modern science we have naturally dropped those practices.

In the second half of the twentieth century, Bell acknowledges, there are notable challenges to the so-called "secularization thesis."[5] Nevertheless, she contends, much recent work in anthropology still relies on the idea that ritual is somehow opposed to modernization. She cites Victor Turner and Clifford Geertz, who, she claims, see modern manifestations of ritual as attempts at psychological compensation for what some people experience as the harsher aspects of modern life (Bell 1997: 25); hence, despite their less condescending attitude toward ritual practitioners, these scholars, like their predecessors, assume that where transition to modernization is complete, ritual could be expected to be of little importance.

There are, of course, increasing numbers of people who view ritual positively – not as reversion to primitivism, but as a healthy aspect of any human life, including the modern.[6] Unlike Weber or his secularist successors, these people lament that Westerners don't engage in ritual very often and fear that when we do we don't get much satisfaction from the experience.[7] What rituals remain in our cultural repertoire – church worship, marriage rites, funerals – are typically brief, market-conscious, commercialized to a distracting or even corrupting degree, and often experienced as ordeals to be endured rather than as means of enriching our lives, bringing communities together, or connecting with a larger world or transcendent purpose. They argue that we need more ritual to offset the rationalization and industrialization that have contributed to our disaffection with nature and community as well as to ritual's decline. Ronald Grimes writes,

> There is a growing suspicion that the so-called Western way of life has reached a precipice. In a few hundred short years it has done untold damage to the planet and to indigenous peoples. Extraordinarily long-lived cultures such as the Hopi and the !Kung have an enduring commitment to ritual. Ritual is their way of attuning themselves to one another and to the land; ritual is their means of maintaining a sustainable culture. "Their" ritual practices may, in the long run, be more practical than "our" practicality. Psychologists and anthropologists are suggesting that the "spiritual technology" of ritual has survival value for the human species as well as beneficial ecological consequences.
>
> (Grimes 2000: 13)[8]

Writers like Grimes claim that ritual is not merely a protective measure taken in reaction to the hardships of industrialization (a kind of cultural "comfort food") but that it has a constructive role to play in creating and maintaining a good, healthy modern society.

The fact remains, though, that whether ritual is seen as a primitive form of behavior that has faded in importance as Westerners have become more

scientifically enlightened or it is seen as a healthy, reasonable way to nego-
tiate and perhaps overcome the difficulties and dangers that lurk in so many
aspects of modern life, the majority opinion still holds that we latter-day
Westerners engage in ritual activity less often than do our counterparts in
localized, tribal societies. As Grimes puts it, ours is "an increasingly deritu-
alized environment" (Grimes 2000: 111).

There is a minority view, as Peter Burke notes (without espousing it).
Some scholars have begun to hold

> that all societies are equally ritualized; they merely practice different
> rituals. If most people in industrial societies no longer go to church regu-
> larly or practice elaborate rituals of initiation, this does not mean that
> ritual has declined. All that has happened is that new types of ritual –
> political, sporting, musical, medical, academic and so on – have taken
> the place of the traditional ones.
>
> (Burke 1987: 223; cited and paraphrased in Bell 1997: 254)

According to this minority view, says Burke, "If we think that another society
. . . is more highly ritualised than ours, that – so the argument goes – only
reveals our own ethnocentrism" (Burke 1987: 223–4). Because we think of
ritual as primitive, irrational, or otherwise bad – because to us moderns
ritual is a dirty word, as Mary Douglas has suggested[9] – we refuse to see it
in our own lives.

Robert Bocock is a proponent of the view that ritual is significant in
modern life. In his *Ritual in Industrial Society*, he writes:

> once one starts looking for ritual action it is amazing how much there
> is – hand-shaking, teeth cleaning, taking medicines, car riding, eating,
> entertaining guests, drinking tea, or coffee, beer, sherry, whisky, etc.,
> taking a dog for a walk, watching television, going to the cinema, listening
> to records, visiting relatives, routines at work, singing at work, children's
> street games, hunting and so on. One can go on adding activities *ad
> infinitum* and still stretch the definition of ritual to include them all.
>
> (Bocock 1974: 15)

But this passage reveals an obvious problem. As critic Jack Goody points
out, once the concept *ritual* is allowed to include activities that have no
connection to religion or the supernatural, it is quickly reduced to mere
routinization or repetition (which as Bocock acknowledges can encompass
just about everything) and so is no longer a useful analytic category (Goody
1977: 25). Goody suggests that Victor Turner's definition of *ritual* – "formal
behaviour for occasions not given over to technological routine, having reference to beliefs in mystical beings or powers" – is preferable in that it carves
out a specific object domain for the discipline of Ritual Studies (Goody 1977:
27).[10] But, Goody contends, Turner's definition perpetuates Western arro-
gance by implying that societies in which ritual (thus defined) is central are
more superstitious, irrational, and scientifically backward than our own.

I don't want to take sides here on the value of Turner's definition or Goody's charge of ethnocentrism. I simply want to point out that if we insist, as Turner does, that ritual has an essential relation to belief in the supernatural and is unconnected to technological production, it will appear that ritual has declined significantly in the West since industrialization.[11] In what follows I want to sketch out a different way of looking at this issue of ritual's alleged decline in our society, one that will involve a challenge to Turner's definition but that will avoid rendering the term *ritual* so broadly that its utility is compromised. I don't intend to define *ritual* or present a theory of ritual; I leave that work to experts with broad field experience on which to draw. Instead, I only want to show that if we reject Turner's contention that ritual is non-technological – in other words, if we view ritual as a kind of technology – we will see not a decline in ritual with industrialization but rather a major shift in the focus and uses of ritualization in the modern West.

II. Another perspective: Michel Foucault and the rituals of power

Michel Foucault documents a dramatic change in Western societies' use of ritual dating from the late eighteenth century, a date that coincides with the latter years of Europe's various Enlightenments and its widespread secularization and industrialization. Prior to that time, spectacular public rituals – like the ostentatious public execution of the attempted regicide Damiens in 1757 – are quite frequent. After that time, there is a sharp decrease in their frequency coupled with a sharp increase in attention to economy, rationality, and appropriate measure in the administration of justice and other affairs of state and daily life. It is this change that some scholars have interpreted as the West's turn away from ritual.

Foucault does not, however, attribute this decline in ritual spectacle to intellectual maturation as Enlightenment, Neo-Kantian, or Social Darwinist thinkers might, nor does he suggest that the more bureaucratic and economic methods of punishment and social control that displace public execution and similar spectacles are necessarily less ritualistic in nature. He maintains instead that through the eighteenth century secular institutions, in an effort to deal with unprecedented population growth among other things, began to implement means of more careful monitoring of individuals. Under such circumstances and with such bureaucratic imperatives and objectives, large public spectacles became more difficult to organize and control and so declined in frequency and official favor.

Foucault's study *Discipline and Punish* begins with eyewitness descriptions of the highly ritualized (and by our standards extravagant) execution of an attempted assassin:

> On 2 March 1757 Damiens the regicide was condemned "to make the *amende honorable* before the main door of the Church of Paris," where

he was to be "taken and conveyed in a cart, wearing nothing but a shirt, holding a torch of burning wax weighing two pounds"; then, "in the said cart, to the Place de Greve, where, on a scaffold that will be erected there, the flesh will be torn from his breasts, arms, thighs and calves with red-hot pincers, his right hand, holding the knife with which he committed the said parricide, burnt with sulphur, and, on those places where the flesh will be torn away, poured molten lead, boiling oil, burning resin, wax and sulphur melted together and then his body drawn and quartered by four horses and his limbs and body consumed by fire, reduced to ashes and his ashes thrown to the winds."

(Foucault 1979: 3)[12]

Damiens had attacked the king; hence, although he had not done any bodily harm, it was considered necessary and appropriate that the king retaliate. The would-be usurper had to be both symbolically and literally annihilated in an overwhelming display of sovereign might; his punishment had to bespeak the terrible power that his crime had challenged – a power ordained by God and reflective of a supernatural as well as a natural hierarchy. The manner in which he was to die, therefore, was carefully ritualized as a public spectacle in which every word, every object, and every gesture was meaningful, in which everything pointed to the majesty and might of the monarchy. Damiens' execution was both a symbolic and a literal enactment of royal power.

Western nations sponsor no such displays anymore – as the expression of either a divinely ordained king or a sovereign body politic. Executions – where they occur at all – may be and in fact in most cases *must* be witnessed by some specified number of citizens, but spectators are carefully selected, and media coverage is brief. Indeed, executions themselves are brief, relatively clean, technologically managed, and not particularly symbol-laden. They are intended to be efficient, not meaningful. Legal execution is not a site of lavish ritualization in modern society.

In fact, there appear to be very few sites of lavish ritual expenditure in modern life. Westerners rarely spend huge amounts of money, time, and energy on projects or events that yield no profit. So if we assume, à la Turner, that ritual is essentially symbolic action without material results, we will not see much ritual in industrial societies.

However, even for ritual prior to 1757, Turner's definition is inadequate. The execution of Damiens was not *merely* symbolic; a real man died, horribly, and no doubt thousands of people were frightened or awed into renewed submission to their king. The execution of Damiens was not just a *representation* of power; it was an *exercise* of power that reinforced a certain kind of relation between subjects and king.

Up through the mid-eighteenth century, the staging of such public spectacles was one of the ways in which power was exercised and institutionalized. It was one of the technologies of power.[13] What changes in modernity is not so much the degree to which societies ritualize; what changes, Foucault's work suggests, is the way in which institutions of power in Western societies manifest and sustain themselves. This set of changes brings about not a decline but a shift in the focus of ritual. Ritual is no longer lavish, but it is pervasive, and increasingly so as new configurations of power extend themselves. To see how changes in power networks resulted in ritual change and also how new and newly adapted rituals made extension of new power networks possible, we must examine Foucault's analysis of disciplinary power.

One of the clearest accounts of modern re-configurations of power occurs in Foucault's discussion of French military discipline. At the beginning of the seventeenth century, the soldier was taken to be something like a natural kind:

> . . . the soldier was someone who could be recognized from afar; he bore signs: the natural signs of his strength and courage, the marks, too, of his pride; his body was the blazon of his strength and valour; and although it is true that he had to learn the profession of arms little by little – generally in actual fighting – movements like marching and attitudes like the bearing of the head belonged for the most part to a bodily rhetoric of honour. . . .
>
> (Foucault 1979: 135)

A soldier's skill was developed on the foundation of virtue and comportment that was not the product of training. However, by the late eighteenth century, virtually any man could be turned into a soldier; virtually any male body – no matter how inept or out of shape – could be re-formed into a tool of military might. The soldier had become a product, the outcome of management strategies, of exercises of disciplinary power.

What had happened? Populations had grown; new technologies had been introduced (such as the rifle, which increased the distance at which targets could be hit and greatly shortened the time needed for reloading, thus dramatically changing the tactics of battle). And new institutions and forms of wealth had begun to emerge (the factory and its valuable, but vulnerable, machinery). Military leaders were confronting a changed situation, and they gradually altered their theories and techniques to deal with it. In this process, human bodies came to be thought of – as René Descartes thought of them – as machines, collections of parts interacting in space. Techniques were developed for rendering those interactions more efficient, for realigning those parts relative to one another and adapting them to the parts of other machines – weapons, or in other institutional contexts looms, turbines, etc.

This notion of bodies as machines, which became widespread in late seventeenth-century Europe, opened up all sorts of possibilities for managing large groups of people and training them to do jobs that were more complicated and required more precision of movement than ever before. New techniques for disciplining bodies sprang up in all sorts of settings, particularly in institutions such as factories and schools. There was no over-arching mandate and certainly no conspiracy at work, but at virtually every level power relations became infused with techniques of training designed to render mechanically conceived bodies both productive and obedient to authority. Foucault writes:

> It was certainly not the first time that the body had become the object of such imperious and pressing investments; in every society, the body was in the grip of very strict powers. . . . However, there were several new things in these techniques. To begin with, there was the scale of control: it was a question not of treating the body *en masse*, "wholesale," as if it were an indissociable unity, but of working it "retail," individually; of exercising upon it a subtle coercion, of obtaining holds upon it at the level of the mechanism itself – movements, gestures, attitudes, rapidity: an infinitesimal power over the active body. Then there was the object of control: it was not or was no longer the signifying elements of behaviour or the language of the body, but the economy, the efficiency of movements, their internal organization; constraint bears upon the forces rather than upon the signs. . . . Lastly, there is the modality: it implies an uninterrupted, constant coercion, supervising the processes of activity rather than its result. . . . Thus discipline produces subjected and practised bodies, "docile" bodies. Discipline increases the forces of the body (in economic terms of utility) and diminishes these same forces (in political terms of obedience). . . . [D]isciplinary coercion establishes in the body the constricting link between an increased aptitude and an increased domination.
> (Foucault 1979: 136–8)

This was the first phase of power's reconfiguration in modernity. A second soon began. As the eighteenth century wore on and such disciplinary techniques grew more sophisticated, some disciplinarians began to reformulate their conceptions of the bodies on which they acted. Such a technician was J. A. de Guibert, who posited that the body is not simply a machine, a collection of parts driven by physical forces external to them; rather, each body has a force of its own, a natural developmental force that drives it to grow and change. This natural force, a temporal dimension of physical life rather than a purely spatial one, is what we run up against when bodies simply do not respond as we would like to mechanical disciplinary techniques. Guibert and his successors wanted to study these developmental forces to harness their power to create the sort of soldiers (and eventually workers, parents, and citizens) that they required. According to Foucault, Guibert stands at the beginning of a long process of refiguring human bodies not as machines but as organisms, as beings whose essence is temporal development, not Cartesian extendedness and motion (Foucault 1979: 155). Over the next few decades, as the idea of the body as developing organism came to be more widely and carefully articulated, disciplinary possibilities never before imagined arose. Observation of development recorded in careful detail allowed statistical study of whole segments of the population. Development could be "normed" and predicted, and techniques for re-directing developmental forces could be devised. Foucault labels this new way of seeing *normalization.* "To normalize," in Foucault's parlance, is not to make normal (which would be to homogenize); it is to understand and know individuals *in their individuality* as beings appropriately identified in relation to developmental norms. This way of understanding human beings – ourselves – is now so widespread that we can hardly imagine any alternative.

According to Foucault, ritual is an absolutely indispensable tool in modern configurations of power – but not the spectacular rituals that made sovereignty so splendidly visible while it humbled, silenced, and even annihilated lowly subjects; rather, a newly adapted form of ritual that shifts visibility away from those at the top of the hierarchy and onto those at the bottom. This new form of ritual is thoroughly secular, unlike the spectacles of sovereignty, but – as Foucault demonstrates and I will argue below – it is historically connected with religious practices. Hence, we can deem these new practices *ritual* without thereby engaging in a reductivism that would render the category meaningless.

Absolute sovereignty had no interest in the details of lowly subjects' individual existences. The sovereign was the supreme individual; he (or she) was unique, unlike all others, almost unimaginably greater than they. The body of the sovereign was sacred and was symbolically merged with territory and nationality or race. Authority radiated from this point, and obedience to that authority consisted principally in surrendering one's material goods and producing words and gestures of fealty. But – in a changing economy and a growing population – governmental administrators came to understand that they could not manage resources well enough to make wealth and war without detailed knowledge of those very subjects. Hence, what had to be made visible was each individual – each soldier, each schoolchild, each potential or actual childbearer, each petty criminal. Each one must be counted, observed, interrogated, monitored, known. Thus the exercise of power was no longer an attempt to overwhelm into submission; it was now an attempt to cajole (or coerce) into self-exposure, confession. Authorities remained relatively quiet, relatively hidden, while they encouraged their subjects to reveal the details of their existence. Individuality was no longer a matter of splendor and transcendence but of norm and deviation, identification and subjection. Thus new – or, as I will argue, not so new – rituals were devised, rituals calculated first of all to *promote* the visibility of the lowly subject, to display his or her individuality, to bring it to light, and, second, to *remake* that lowly subject to produce a soldier, a skilled laborer, a proficient engineer, an attentive mother of robust babies, or – if nothing else – a docile, manageable, useful petty criminal or madman.

To expose and to transform – these were the imperatives modern regimes formulated in relation to their subjects. It was necessary first to know as precisely as possible the current state of each subject's development. Only so could officials prescribe the most effective forms of training for each individual. Then, through each stage of training, it was necessary to know the state of the individual's "soul." Thus, the first ritualized aspect of modern disciplinary practice was what Foucault calls "the examination":

The examination combines the techniques of an observing hierarchy and those of a normalizing judgment. It is a normalizing gaze, a surveillance that makes it possible to qualify, to classify and to punish. It establishes over individuals a visibility through which one differentiates and judges them. That is why, in all the mechanisms of discipline, the examination is highly ritualized. In it are combined the ceremony of power and the form of the experiment, the deployment of force and the establishment of truth.

(Foucault 1979: 184)[14]

Foucault offers rich descriptions of these ceremonies and rituals – school examinations, military reviews and parades (Foucault 1979: 188),[15] even medical rounds (Foucault 1979: 185), all intended to bring to light the current stage of development of the subject examined – in terms of the level of academic achievement, military or technical skill, progress toward a certain standard of health, etc. These ceremonies of examination produce valuable information for the examiners, which ultimately enables them to devise disciplinary means for further transforming their examinees. But they also, in themselves, have a direct effect upon those examinees:

The examination as the fixing, at once ritual and "scientific," of individual differences, as the pinning down of each individual in his own particularity (in contrast with the ceremony in which status, birth, privilege, function are manifested with all the spectacle of their marks) clearly indicates the appearance of a new modality of power in which each individual receives as his status his own individuality, and in which he is linked by his status to the features, the measurements, the gaps, the "marks" that characterize him and make him a "case."

(Foucault 1979: 192)

Ritual examinations individuate and identify, and thus they instill a sense of self in the one who must reveal him or herself; at the same time, by compelling self-disclosure, they stage an habitual submission to the demand to be accessible to figures of authority, officials of all kinds, just as in previous generations one would, by confession, make one's heart open to God.[16]

The similarity to Christian religious practices is no accident, for these new rituals were derived from the monastic disciplines developed in previous centuries. Monastic discipline had been used successfully by the Catholic Church to transform individuals for hundreds of years. Talal Asad writes, "Hugh of St. Victor's conception of ritual gesture and speech as the discipline of the body that is aimed at the proper ordering of the soul expresses very well the central purpose of the monastic program" (Asad 1993: 139). The purpose of monastic life as a whole, with its rigid schedules and meticulous prescriptions, was to re-organize the soul; in other words, it aimed to re-make the person. As Asad puts it,

The formation/transformation of moral dispositions (Christian virtues) depended on more than the capacity to imagine, to perceive, to imitate – which, after all, are abilities everyone possesses in varying degree. It required a particular program of disciplinary practices. The rites that were prescribed by that program did not simply evoke or release universal emotions, they aimed to construct and reorganize distinctive emotions – desire (*cupiditas/caritas*), humility (*humilitas*), remorse (*contritio*) – on which the central Christian virtue of obedience to God depended. This point must be stressed, because the emotions mentioned here are not universal human feelings, not "powerful drives and emotions associated with human physiology," such as those referred to [by Victor] Turner. They are historically specific emotions that are structured internally and related to each other in historically determined ways. And they are the product not of mere readings of symbols but of processes of power.

(Asad 1993: 134)[17]

There is nothing natural about a well-ordered Christian soul. It is an achievement, even if religious disciplinarians believed that it was not achievable by human means alone. Monastic discipline is the method by which a human being participates in and contributes to this achievement.

Asad argues that monastic ritual strictly construed – praying or singing the liturgy – cannot be separated from monastic life as a whole, the purpose of which was to develop Christian virtues. Citing the *Rule* of Saint Benedict, Asad writes, "[A]ll prescribed practices, whether they had to do with the proper ways of eating, sleeping, working, and praying or with proper moral dispositions and spiritual aptitudes, are aimed at developing virtues that are put 'to the service of God' " (Asad 1993: 63). Thus,

[t]he liturgy is not a species of enacted symbolism to be classified separately from activities defined as technical but is a practice among others essential to the acquisition of Christian virtues. In other words, the liturgy can be isolated only conceptually, for pedagogic reasons, not in practice, from the entire monastic program.

(Asad 1993: 63)

He argues that theorists who have seen ritual as symbolic expression rather than as productive process have failed to understand the extreme degree to which the ritualized discipline of monasticism was designed to produce new selves – and thus they have also failed to understand how completely ritual pervaded monastic life.

If monastic discipline could produce human subjects with Christian virtues, dispositions, desires, and capacities, it could also – in some modified form – produce other sorts of selves with other sorts of virtues, dispositions, desires, and capacities. And so it was put to use. Foucault writes, "The new disciplines [first mechanical, then normalizing disciplines] had no difficulty taking up their place in the old forms; the schools and poorhouses extended the life and the regularity of the monastic communities to which they were often attached" (Foucault 1979: 149). Even as late as the nineteenth century, factory work and mining were organized along religious lines; "when rural populations were needed in industry, they were sometimes formed into 'congregations,' in an attempt to inure them to work in the workshops . . ." (Foucault 1979: 149). And even military training long retained a monastic flavor. "In the Protestant armies of Maurice of Orange and Gustavus Adolphus, military discipline was achieved through a rhythmics of time punctuated by pious exercises; army life, Boussanelle was later to say, should have some of the 'perfections of the cloister itself . . .'" (Foucault 1979: 150). These disciplines, exercises, and rites now no longer had as their ultimate purpose the creation of a Christian soul; their purposes were much more mundane: the creation of highly skilled individuals completely controlled and readily deployed even in very large numbers by small cadres of administrators and military elite.

Beyond the various adaptations of examinations, then, normalizing discipline employs all sorts of ritualized procedures for shaping subjects (although most of those are thoroughly integrated with ongoing surveillance and examination). Once normed models of development were in place, procedures for cultivating allegedly inherent developmental forces and training individuals in the skills desired were implemented. We have only to remember the very stylized and graduated exercises of elementary school pedagogy, coupled with standardized tests and rehabilitative punishments, to get a sense of the sorts of disciplinary strategies modern regimes of power began to employ on a massive scale. Life in secular training and therapeutic institutions is at least as scheduled, programmed, regulated, and routinized as life in monasteries ever was. And most of us spend much of our lives in such institutions.

In sum, then, even through great historical changes, ritual helped to impose order upon the societies that Foucault studies. It is a means, therefore, of exercising power. In the past, rituals of public execution, for example, produced power relations in which sovereignty was highly visible and magnificent in its potency and in which subjects were either awed and frightened into obedience or made to signify its greatness even while being crushed beneath its weight. As these older regimes of power passed away, so too did many of the ritualistic techniques that characterized them. The pageantry and myth of grand monarchy is no longer a significant part of the modern world. A similar story of political decline could be told about other institutions in Western history known for grand ritual. It makes sense, then, that social observers might believe they were witnessing a decline in ritual *per se*. But if we refuse Turner's separation between ritual and technology and adopt Asad's view that ritual is a kind of technology of the self and, further, if we characterize the relationship between ritual and the supernatural as a matter of historical contingency, it makes sense – I would argue it makes much more sense – to maintain that ritual in modern society is no less present and compelling than it was in the age of Christian monarchies.

III. Rituals of power/practices of freedom

Ritual, as we have construed it in Foucault's text, is a technology of power, a highly versatile tool for imposing hierarchy and order, for managing populations, and for producing docile and useful types of human selves. In various forms it has aided kings and clerics in controlling the masses. Nowadays, in somewhat muted disciplinary form, it shapes our lives from cradle to grave, rendering us compliant and ever more accessible for official scrutiny and use. Childhood and adolescence are a series of examinations, recitals, and graduations, hundreds of more or less public displays of our status and occasions for judgments regarding our progress in relation to developmental norms, charted throughout in physicians' files and school computers if not also in records of social psychologists and juvenile courts. By adulthood we are so deeply informed by these rites of self-presentation and official pronouncement that we can hardly imagine how life could go on in their absence, who we would be without them, or how our own children could feel attended and loved without subjection to them – for to be loved is to be known and accepted as precisely what we are, with our own unique set of percentiles and deviations from the norms. We have virtually no other concept of personhood, no other account of individuality. We are normalized through and through, and we normalize those in our charge, primarily by means of the repeated exercise of disciplinary surveillance and assessment through the medium of ritualized examination. As Ronald Grimes asserts, "Effective ritual knowledge lodges in the bone, in its very marrow" (Grimes 2000: 7). Who and what we are is what the rituals of normalizing power have made us to be.

Foucault's analysis of normalizing power should make us very suspicious of ritualized disciplinary practices that fix our identities in relation to norms (mental and physical health, intellectual development, sexual orientation, acquisition of "marketable skills") and of practices that aim to channel our future development in relation to such norms. In fact, it should make us suspicious of any ritualized process of identification, even supposedly liberatory ones such as "coming out of the closet" or "owning" one's addictions. These practices subject us to institutionalized control even while they subjectify us, making us into the type of individual that normally bears such an identity. Perhaps, given the specificity of Western industrial society, ritual examination and self-disclosure inevitably increases the docility of participants and therefore diminishes freedom. Perhaps in our society any ritual that emphasizes confession of self-identity or profession of one's emotional state, convictions, or beliefs will reinforce rather than oppose normalizing regimes. Perhaps any ritualized disciplinary regime will end up doing nothing more than eliminating whatever in us is unpredictable or spontaneous or creative or open to the new.

When we stop to consider this state of affairs, we may be appalled. We may look at the sites Foucault points out where rigid schedules, highly routinized action, and strict hierarchy are standard – sites such as hospitals, schools, military installations, and prisons – and imagine that if we could disrupt their ritual practices, we could put an end to the ways in which they control lives and infringe on freedom. Ritual itself looks like a potentially effective point of counter-attack. If we could eliminate ritual, perhaps we could disable powerful institutions and regain a lost measure of human liberty.

For all his criticism of normalizing ritual, however, this is not Foucault's response.[18] In his last works Foucault explores ritual activity precisely as a means of practicing freedom, especially for those whom our society tends to oppress – homosexuals, for example. He proposes disciplined self-cultivation – what he calls *askeses* – as a counter to contemporary Western regimes of normalizing power, in particular the regime of power he calls the *dispositif de sexualité* (Foucault 1976: 30), which subjects each one of us to a supposedly essential sexual identity and truth. In a 1981 interview with the French gay magazine *La gai pied*, he stated,

> Asceticism as the renunciation of pleasure has bad connotations. But the *askesis* is something else: it's the work that one performs on oneself in order to transform oneself. . . . [I]t's up to us to advance into a homosexual *askesis* that would make us work on ourselves and invent, I do not say discover, a manner of being that is still improbable.
>
> (Foucault 1989: 206)[19]

Foucault calls the process of creating and sustaining a way of life "ethics." Ethical practice is a kind of self-stylization, an attempt at transforming oneself and one's life. Sometimes it has a telos – such as personal purification, salvation, or attunement with the unchanging Logos – but even when there is a set goal, processes of self-transformation, undertaken by oneself, are always open-ended, never fully under anyone's control. Ethics tends, therefore, to open up new possibilities, to render the future a bit less predictable, and so to introduce an element of risk and play into the world. Because of this opening toward the unknown and the unmanageable, Foucault characterizes ethics as "a practice of freedom." It is inherently resistant to the totalization and identification that characterizes normalizing regimes. The task for those who would oppose the power of normalization is to maximize ethics' tendencies to resist identification – in other words, to place the emphasis on ethical practice as self-transformation rather than on whatever outcome such practices might be hoped to have. The task is to find ways of living, exercises, *askeses* that unsettle us, move us, change us in ways that keep us perpetually open to some degree of unsettlement, movement, and change, rather than tie us firmly to one identity, one truth, and one life trajectory.

We know that ritual practices have the power to transform. In fact, Victor Turner seems to hold the view that all genuine ritual is transformative and that liminality is ritual's very essence.[20] We do not have to go that far, though, to affirm the value of ritual in any project of self-transformation and even to view ritual as a key aspect of a way of life that maintains an openness to unprogramed possibility. Nor do we have to valorize ritual and deny its role in maintaining a sometimes oppressive status quo; it may be that most ritual practices have been instituted as a way of managing passage and confining liminality so that order could be enforced through what might otherwise be disruptive change. We need only affirm that there is no necessary connection between ritual and rigid control. The point of ritual might not be successful pass*age* but rather perpetual pass*ing*, transformation without an ultimate telos. Ritual might, then, be a part of an anti-normalizing ethical way of life. It might be a practice of freedom.

IV. A queer rite of passage/ing

As a way of putting Foucault's assertion to the test, I want to examine a ritual practice that has become important in recent years in the gay/lesbian/bisexual/transgendered community of Richmond, Virginia, namely, that of the commitment ceremony.[21] The purpose of my examination is to consider both the risks and dangers of such rites in light of ritual's involvement with normalizing regimes and the transformational potential and possibility for resistance that may lie within them. The question is whether such ritual practices, as techniques or exercises of power, are or can be *askeses* that would help invent a homosexual ethics or way of life.

First it is necessary to provide some context. Richmond, together with its suburbs, is a city of about 600,000 people. It is one of the oldest cities in the US, only a few miles up river from Jamestown, with a history that dates back to the early seventeenth century. Its downtown streets are paved with cobblestone ballast from British tobacco ships; on the hill above those streets stands St John's Church, where Patrick Henry made his famous speech in support of raising a militia to fight King George III: "Give me liberty, or give me death!" Virginians are very proud of their history, and that pride shows in the way that historic monuments, museums, and battle sites are preserved and maintained. Richmond itself boasts over twenty museums and numerous historic districts. Monument Avenue, stretching through several blocks of the Victorian neighborhood known as The Fan, displays a collection of enormous effigies of Confederate generals and statesmen (Robert E. Lee and his horse tower over a circular green as large as a small city block) and one highly controversial statue of native son Arthur Ashe, an African-American tennis champion and city benefactor who died of AIDS.

As the 1996 controversy surrounding erection of the Ashe statue demonstrated, that history is not without blemish. And Virginians' – particularly white Virginians' – dedication to it is not without oppressive effects. It must be remembered that, while Virginia had no George Wallace and Richmond had no Bull Connor, the state and city put up an amazingly stubborn if relatively non-violent resistance to integration from the 1950s through the 1970s. Several counties simply canceled public school altogether for several semesters rather than educate blacks alongside whites. Richmond schools did not finally integrate until the mid-1970s. While many private colleges and universities in the Deep South rushed to integrate early on in protest of their local governments' recalcitrance, Richmond's largest private institution, the University of Richmond, refused to integrate until after the city schools did, in 1978.

The state (which prefers to be called the Commonwealth, although its wealth is concentrated in few and quite uncommon hands) holds a special place in the history of the regulation of marriage. Like many Southern states, it long claimed the right to refuse marriage licenses to interracial couples, a right the Supreme Court finally took away in *Loving v. Virginia* (1968), the case that invalidated all anti-miscegenation laws across the country. But in 1975, twenty-one years before Congress decided to protect heterosexual marriage against the allegedly corrupting effects of same-sex unions by passing the Defense of Marriage Act (DOMA), the Virginia General Assembly enacted a law restricting the issuance of marriage licenses to heterosexual couples only. It followed up in 1995 (again, a year before the federal government's DOMA) with a law that gave the state the right to disregard the Full Faith and Credit Clause so as not to afford recognition to same sex marriages that might be performed elsewhere.

Devotion to tradition has not prevented the Commonwealth from setting a number of legal precedents, especially regarding homosexuals. It has been as innovative in child custody as it has been in marriage law. In 1993, a circuit court denied Sharon Bottoms custody of her son on the grounds that as a lesbian she is a felon under the state's Crimes Against Nature Law, despite having never been charged with such a crime.[22] While denial of custody to homosexual parents is not unusual in itself,[23] this was the first case in which custody was granted not to the child's other biological parent but to the child's grandmother, thus opening the door for any relative to sue a homosexual parent for custody. Ms Bottoms' visitation rights were also severely restricted, and the boy was not permitted to see his mother's life partner at all. All these provisions were substantially upheld in appeals in 1995 and 1998.[24]

Given the lengths to which the state has gone to control its citizens' sexual and affectional expression and living arrangements, it makes sense that Richmond's gay, lesbian, bisexual, and transgendered residents tend to keep a low profile. Any public revelation of homosexual status (and all of the above would be considered a homosexual status) is risky. Homosexuals have no job protection, no right to equal treatment in housing, and no right to use public facilities. Under these circumstances, making a public declaration of life commitment to someone of the same sex in a church, park, or hotel ballroom might be seen as an act of great courage and resistance to oppression. But, given Foucault's disturbing analyses, we cannot reach such a conclusion without further inquiry. Defying repression, as he shows very clearly in *The History of Sexuality, Volume 1*, is simply playing into the larger networks of power that regulate sexuality in our society (Foucault 1980: Part IV). So we must ask: is such a ritualized profession of one's commitment, which is automatically also a declaration of one's homosexual status or identity, a way of opposing normalization – or of playing into it? And to the extent that these rites *are* marriage ceremonies,[25] do they simply affirm and reinforce the state's right to regulate so-called private life?

Marriage, as both a rite and an institution, has been critiqued extensively in feminist literature from the eighteenth century to the present. Feminists have been extremely wary of the ways in which government aids individual men in dominating women by giving them rights over women's property, labor, sexuality, and reproductive capacity. Marriage in British common law was the union of a man and a woman which resulted in the legal disappearance of the woman – she lost her property rights, could not determine her own domicile, and could be subject to severe beatings without recourse; if she ran away, she could be forcibly returned or lose her means of support and her children. For centuries, marriage laws in both Europe and the US made women virtual slaves. Accordingly, Frances Wright's abolitionist utopian community Nashoba, founded in 1825, refused to recognize marriage. Wright declared, "[N]o woman can forfeit her individual rights or independent existence, and no man can assert over her any rights or power whatsoever beyond what he may exercise over her free and voluntary affection" (Rossi 1973: 93). In 1851, feminist utilitarian J. S. Mill expressed extreme distaste for the institution even while entering into it with Harriet Taylor,

> the whole character of the marriage relation as constituted by law being such as both she and I entirely and conscientiously disapprove, for this among other reasons, that it confers upon one of the parties to the contract, legal power and control over the person, property, and freedom of action of the other party, independent of her own wishes and will.
>
> (Rossi 1973: 191)

In the twentieth century, feminists often drew on the work of Friedrich Engels, who identified marriage as "the first class oppression" in human prehistory. Marriage, he asserts, "is based on the supremacy of the man," its "express purpose being to produce children of undisputed paternity" (Rossi 1973: 479). For this purpose, women's sexual and economic liberty was eliminated and their right to defend themselves against their husbands' physical and sexual assaults denied. Simone de Beauvoir writes,

> In primitive societies the paternal clan, the gens, disposed of woman almost like a thing: she was included in deals agreed upon by two groups. The situation is not much modified when marriage assumes a contractual form in the course of its evolution; when dowered or having her share in inheritance, woman would seem to have civil standing as a person, but dowry and inheritance still enslave her to her family. During a long period the contracts were made between father-in-law and son-in-law, not between husband and wife. . . .
>
> (de Beauvoir 1952: 426–7)

Marriage laws were modified in the industrialized West over the course of the twentieth century, with women gaining some property rights and some rights to divorce, child custody, and self-defense, but long after mid-century marriage was far from egalitarian. In 1969, a group called The Feminists staged a protest at the New York City Marriage License Bureau. They distributed a leaflet entitled "Women: Do You Know the Facts About Marriage?" in which they listed a number of legalized inequities enshrined in marriage law. These included the legality of marital rape and differential grounds for divorce for husbands and wives. The leaflet proclaimed: "We can't destroy the inequalities between men and women until we destroy marriage" (Morgan 1970: 602).

More recently, Claudia Card has argued that marriage is essentially licensed access to another human being. Such unbridled access, which the state does not grant to parties in any other type of contractual relationship, makes it impossible to protect people from abuse, stalking, and even murder. She writes, "Although many states now recognize on paper the crimes of marital rape and stalking and are better educated than before about marital battering, the progress has been mostly on paper. Wives continue to die daily at a dizzying rate" (Card 1996: 15). She contends that since intimacy is the essence of marriage, access will never be regulated sufficiently to make marriage safe.

Whether one is feminist or not, one has to acknowledge that historically the institution of marriage has been catastrophic for women, a governmental means of controlling their labor, sexuality, and reproductive lives, generally to their detriment. Much has changed in recent years. Some feminists now maintain that marriage under current US law is an egalitarian institution.[26] But given its history as a tool of oppression and exploitation, we still might wonder if it has any merit, egalitarian or not. We might well be suspicious of marriage still, and therefore of marriage rites as well, as part of a disciplinary system designed to give bureaucrats information about and normalizing control over the sexual, affectional, domestic, and reproductive lives of citizens. One might still wonder (as have many Canadians since the Ontario Supreme Court ruled on July 12 2002, that refusing recognition of same sex marriage violates the Charter of Rights and Freedoms) why government should play any role in legitimizing (and illegitimizing) any life partnership at all (Tibbetts 2002). Perhaps the best way of reducing the power of normalizing discipline in our lives, regardless of who we are, is simply to eliminate government's authority to issue (or withhold) marriage licenses and thus to abolish the legal institution of marriage altogether as some Canadian governmental officials have suggested.

I am not going to take a position on that issue here. Instead, I am simply going to point out that same sex commitment ceremonies are *not* initiation into the legal institution of marriage, and they need not be interpreted as an expression of desire for initiation into that institution. A couple may have no wish to invite state regulation of their relationship and yet may still want to have a ritual through which they acknowledge, announce, solidify, or somehow transform their relationship and themselves.

That granted, we must explore what the positive – that is, non-normalizing, freeing – effects of such rites might be. Can they serve as *askeses*, ethical practices, a mode of transformation that emphasizes pass*ing* rather than pass*age*, open possibility rather than finality, completion, or static goal?

No purely theoretical answer to this question will be conclusive, for we can only know what difference such rites make if we or someone we know undergoes them. On this point, Ronald Grimes is surely right (and is perhaps surprisingly in agreement with Talal Asad) that the differences that ritual makes are bodily, physical, emotional, and life-shaping. To know the difference they make may require not just thinking about but living them. Therefore, I will depart from academic decorum and describe my own experience.

My partner Carol Anderson and I had a commitment ceremony in the summer of 2002. For almost a year in advance we planned the ceremony as well as the reception and trip that would follow it. I entered into the project with some apprehension, not about the decision to spend my life with Carol (which I had made two years before), but about how we would frame the event and what meaning it would take on in the Richmond GLBT community and among our heterosexual families and friends. What would they think we were doing, I wondered; and what *were* we doing?[27] What would a ritual do that a simple announcement of our love and commitment would not do? These questions weighed on me, which is one reason why in the spring of 2002 I accepted the invitation to write this essay, to spend some time reading and thinking about ritual practices in relation to my philosophical work. I welcomed the opportunity to make the research and writing of this essay part of the preparatory process.

Here are some of my fears and worries over the course of that year:

1 How would our straight friends and family perceive what we were doing? Would they think we were just play-acting and thus view this expression of our love as something vaguely juvenile or pity us because we could not manage to pull off "the real thing"? How could we make this ceremony something they would recognize and respect – a powerful "rite of passage" like marriage ceremonies are – when there is no legal institution of marriage that we could pass into? How would we communicate to others, especially others to whom GLBT communities are foreign, what new state or phase of life we felt we were entering?

2 Why were we inviting people to watch us express our commitment? What was the role of the witnesses physically present at this event? In legal ceremonies, the witnesses' job is simply to vouch for the identities of the two parties joined, but we had no need of that. More troubling, in conventional weddings, guests form an audience of spectators often eager to critique the proceedings. The last thing we wanted was for people – especially straight people – to assume the role of detached and critical spectator, as if Carol and I were just actors in some kind of play.

3 How could our ceremony honor both Carol's religious beliefs and my virtual lack of them? This is a concern any couple with differing beliefs would have, but my concern went further than simply how could we integrate two different traditions or creeds. Christian marriage ceremonies

typically invoke – in fact justify themselves with reference to – some sort of metaphysical timelessness; the couple is entering into an eternal bond blessed by an eternal being. Transformation, therefore, is ideally highly contained and severely limited. Of course, some of what finds its way into Christian ceremonies is not particularly Christian; it comes out of a tradition of romanticism that embraces not only timelessness but also quite often the fusion of identities and metaphysical pre-destination, leaving room for little or no open possibility at all. But whatever the source, if our ceremony was to be a rite that emphasized the transformational power of ritual and celebrated the transforming of each of us, we needed to minimize that kind of language. Yet at the same time, of course, I did want to speak in superlatives and celebrate the senses in which Carol and I are fused together, and I did want to make a lasting commitment. Furthermore, I knew the people we invited would expect those things. Why else have a commitment ceremony?

Gradually, over several months, some answers to these questions evolved through conversation between Carol and me and also with other members of our community and through reading books on same-sex commitment ceremonies.[28] We were able to write a ceremony that reflected both our differing religious views and our common spirituality. Throughout the ceremony, both in visual symbols and in words and music, we invoked natural cycles of transformation – birth, growth, seasonal renewal, passage – and natural, mortal images of strength, endurance, and fidelity, while at the same time repeatedly acknowledging that the forces of life of which we are a part always transcend us and are never completely under human control. We decided that the role of the guests was to pledge their support of our relationship and to promise to bear witness in the larger community and world to the reality of our love and commitment, so we had the minister charge the congregation with this responsibility and solicit their oral acceptance of it. Given the hostility to same-sex relationships that exists in that larger world, our witnesses (unlike mere spectators) were thus taking on a serious political responsibility.

The process of creating our ceremony together and with our friends was a deeply transforming one for me. I had to confront my fears about whether my straight friends would take our relationship seriously. I had to talk with Carol about our differences and work to establish common ground. I had to deal with vendors and service providers who might be hostile to me when they realized my "intended" was a woman. Doing these hard things had some important effects on me, both my thoughts and feelings *and* my physical comportment, bearing, self-presentation. But most importantly, Carol and I together created something – something I would call a work of art – that expressed our love and our selves in ways I doubt I would ever have been able to articulate otherwise. I came to understand her and myself and our relationship differently than I had understood it before, to live an awareness of its dimensions that I did not have before.

I would not say this was a process of identifying what already existed. I don't feel that that year was a process of discovery of who we really are together; there were elements of discovery, but it felt much more creative than that. Just as artists suddenly see in ordinary things around them a solution to some aspect of a project they are working on, at times we suddenly saw something in an entirely new way, in new relation to other things. And consequently the world we live in changed. Further, friends volunteered to work on parts of the ceremony and accompanying celebrations independently of us, so the event as a whole was not under any one person's direction. It became a large, cooperative enterprise to which many people brought their talents and imaginations. It was a community project; our community was building something together.

In retrospect, I realize that initially I had thought of the ceremony as something like a formal public announcement of a relationship that already existed, not really as what Arnold van Gennep called a "rite of passage."[29] I wanted public recognition of a relationship that many people with whom I have daily contact refuse to respect. In other words, I wanted to change the behavior of some of the people around me. But I didn't anticipate changing my*self* in any deep way. As we and our friends planned and prepared, however, I began to realize that changes were occurring and that the ceremony might turn out to be a rite of passage in van Gennep's sense after all – *except*, not only the movement of passing through but also the space to be passed into was evolving as we prepared. We would be initiated not into a pre-fabricated institution of marriage but into something that had not existed before, something unique that we, our close friends, a few members of our families, and our community would make for us and that we would continue to make and sustain throughout our lives.

When that thought occurred to me, I began to feel more deeply attended and cared for than I have ever felt. Carol and I had each put ourselves into the ceremony – we had exposed some of the most vulnerable and precious parts of ourselves – and those selves were being taken up and affirmed and given place in a larger world. That was not something my life as a lesbian had led me to expect from anybody anywhere at any time. How could that experience fail to change me?

It wasn't just thoughts that affected me, however, and not even just thoughts about actions we were taking. I believe the practice of standing before eighty people, including many straight people, and more or less commanding them to pay attention to an aspect of myself and my life that even still I have an instinct to shield and protect from any scrutiny was a way of unlearning and re-learning how to comport myself in the world. It was a way of embodying my sexuality that made it something to celebrate and share rather than something to keep out of other people's (and therefore harm's) way. For as long as I can remember, being the center of attention in any context has meant being categorized and evaluated – usually with negative consequences. To walk the thirty feet from door to altar holding

Carol's hand, therefore, to be looked at by all those people, was not easy. That I stood up to do it at all is a testament to my hope – actually it was a living enactment of my hope – that not all relations have to be normalizing relations. For that hope to be reinforced – for me to be able to take those steps – required every one of the smiles I saw and every pair of shining eyes. I needed every ear to hear what Carol and I had to say. I needed every tongue and every set of lips and lungs to exclaim loudly in affirmative response to the minister's charge to support us and bear witness on our behalf. The process of creating the ceremony enabled me to arrive at the site and present myself, my happiness and conviction, to our friends and loved ones, but the ceremony itself produced new happiness and new conviction. It was not simply the final enactment of what we had planned; it exceeded its design in the transformative effects that it had. It was an embodiment, however brief, of a community of love and joy assembled around and encompassing Carol and me.

Even though Carol and I had already shared a home and a life for three years, the ceremony marked a beginning for us. We both have the sense that we are embarked on something new together, with the support of people around us. Our ceremony was not just an announcement, a way of symbolizing or representing for an audience what we already knew to exist. It wasn't just a "confession" of love or a self-declaration. Its primary purpose and effect was not the fixing of our identities. It created something new and set in motion a joint, perhaps communal, creative process. And in doing so, it challenged fixed identities and enabled us to claim some power to re-create ourselves.

Based on my own experience, I can endorse same-sex commitment ceremonies as potential practices of freedom in Foucault's sense. I believe that because of this experience – because of the discipline, if you will, of creating and going through the ceremony (as well as the accompanying parties and honeymoon trip and the rather strange and wonderful process of researching and writing this essay at the same time) – my life is more open to possibility now than it was a year ago. I am a little less sure what the future will be like and a little more willing both to throw myself into it come what may and to take some responsibility for shaping it. For I know, in my marrow, as Grimes would say, that all is not set and unchangeable. There *is* something new under the sun, and there are neither identity categories nor norms nor statistics to predict what it will become. Therefore I firmly believe that ritual can be an *askesis*, an ethical practice of freedom.

On second thought, then, I *would* like to take a position on the question of the abolition of marriage. The whole thing should be done away with – no more government licensing but also no more standardized liturgies and no assumptions about vows or rings or clothes or cakes or clergy. Let it all be gone, so that heterosexual people, too, can have the kind of experience that I have had – so that they too can invent their own places within their own communities to love each other and to create themselves.

V. Summation

In this essay, I have considered the widespread belief that Western industrial societies are less characterized by ritual than are non-Western
non-industrialized societies. I have suggested that whether that belief is true
depends on how the word *ritual* is defined. If ritual is held to be primarily
representational (symbolic or expressive) rather than materially productive,
it might well appear that Western society has become increasingly less ritualized since the Renaissance. The grand pageantry of monarchy and
pre-Reformation Catholicism has been largely lost, and most rites that recall
those traditions have been streamlined, truncated, marginalized, or reduced
to mere formality or elegant diversion.

However, if we understand ritualization as a means of exercising power
– as not merely symbolic but more importantly economically and/or politi-
cally productive – the allegation of a decline in ritual since industrialization
is dubious. As Foucault's work indicates, ritual – a technology historically
continuous with though different from religious monasticism – operates at
the very heart of contemporary power networks to produce the types of
human subjects needed by dominant institutions (industry, including medical
and other therapeutic industries, the military, the bureaucratic state with its
welfare system and police force). What has happened, then, might be best
described not as a decline of ritual but as a shift of focus from the top of
the political hierarchy (the sovereign) to the bottom (the individual normalized subject). Our society's rituals both reflect and enable and sustain that
shift.

This way of approaching the question of the place of ritual in modern
society may lead to cynicism. Viewing ritual as a technology of management
or social control certainly de-romanticizes it, to say the least. So our first
response might be to advocate what our predecessors have already falsely
proclaimed: a reduction of ritual practice, perhaps an end to it altogether.

That is not what Foucault himself recommends. Ritual, like any technology
of power, is dangerous; it can be put to oppressive and exploitative uses
and can produce obedient, uncritical human selves proficient in furthering
projects of oppression and exploitation. But if we are to oppose such projects and their stultifying effects, we must exercise a counter-power. We
must employ technologies of power to re-shape our world and the selves we
have become. Foucault has asserted that ritual, as a technology of self- and
community-shaping, can be part of an ethical *askesis*, part of a transformative
discipline; ritual can be a practice of freedom.

We cannot know whether Foucault is correct in his assertion, I have maintained, unless we experiment with ritual practices to undergo whatever freeing
effects they might have. I have reported that my own experience of a same-
sex commitment ceremony confirms my belief that Foucault is right. My
experience has shown me that careful, deliberate, thoughtful ritualization is
one way in which to live more creatively and more ethically.[30]

Notes

1 Peter Burke notes several hypotheses in his essay "The Repudiation of Ritual in Early Modern Europe," where he writes, "It is often said that ritual has declined in modern societies, as a result of the rise of rationalism or technology or of the increasing value placed on individualism, privacy, spontaneity, authenticity and sincerity, 'the true voice of feeling,' as Keats called it" (Burke 1987: 223).

2 Grimes cites Schlegel and Barry (1980: 696–715), as evidence for this claim. One might also cite Shils (1975). Shils asserts, "It is very probable that there are fewer ritual acts per capita practised nowadays than several centuries ago."

3 Bell may be relying here on the work of Peter Burke, who also attributes this view first of all to Herbert Spencer (Burke 1987: 223).

4 Rain dances, for example, are an ill-adaptive use of energy and time as compared to development of technologies for water storage and irrigation.

5 David Martin was one of those scholars. He also lists Peter Berger, Bryan Wilson, Karel Dobbelaere, Rodney Stark, Thomas Luckmann, Richard Fenn, and Steve Bruce as contributors to the debate over the secularization thesis (Martin 1995: 295).

6 As an example of this view, Bell offers the statements of Rev. Deborah A. McKinley, spokesperson for the Presbyterian Church (USA), who says members of her denomination "are discovering the importance of ritual action and its ability to draw us beyond the cerebral" (Bell 1997: 257). Here is her gloss on McKinley: "Reverend McKinley's comment reflects the attitude, popular since the early 1970s, that ritual is basically good for you."

7 Grimes offers numerous examples of the hollowness of contemporary North American ritual practice. One such example is that of a young girl's confirmation (Grimes 2000: 96–7).

8 To be fair to Grimes, his position is much more complex than this quotation indicates. As was clear in the first quotation above, he notes that in some areas of the industrialized world, ritual has increased. For example, in Japan "modernization does not necessarily imply a reduced place for ritual" (Grimes 2000: 177). Furthermore, even in the US some types of ritual have increased with modernization; in relation to funeral rites, he notes, "The shift from the Puritan era to the present is in the direction of increasing, not decreasing, ritual" (Grimes 2000: 267).

9 Burke cites Douglas (1982: 34). A similar impatience with historical denunciations of ritual practices is evident in Douglas's better known work *Purity and Danger: An Analysis of the Concepts of Pollution and Taboo* (Douglas 1966: 63ff.).

10 According to Goody, this definition is from Turner (1967: 19).

11 Bocock actually focuses on religious ritual in his book, not teeth cleaning and sherry drinking, and argues that ritual still must be seen as much more central in the lives of twentieth-century British citizens than most anthropologists suppose. He does, however, retain the view that ritual – however widespread it might still be – is non-rational action (Bocock 1974: 17).

12 This passage can be found in the French in Foucault 1975: 8.

13 I take it that Catherine Bell would concur in this characterization of ritualization. In *Ritual Theory, Ritual Practice* (Bell 1992: 204), she writes, "Ritualization is a strategic play of power, of domination and resistance, within the arena of the social body." This comment occurs in the midst of a discussion of Foucault's work.

14 This can be found in the French in Foucault 1975: 187. The French terms are almost identical to the English – *ritueliser, rituel.*

15 This latter he calls "an ostentatious form of the examination" (Foucault 1979: 188).

16 Bell insists on the point that what I have here loosely referred to as staging a habit is a practice not of communicating submission to a subject but of infusing his or her body with submissiveness (Bell 1992: 99). She cites Bourdieu 1977: 94, where Bourdieu discusses the process of the embodiment of principles. He writes, "If all societies and, significantly, all the 'totalitarian institutions,' in Goffman's phrase, that seek to produce a new man through a process of 'deculturation' and 'reculturation' set such store on the seemingly most insignificant details of *dress, bearing,* physical and verbal *manners,* the reason is that, treating the body as a memory, they entrust to it in abbreviated and practical, i.e. mnemonic, form the fundamental principles of the arbitrary content of culture."

17 The statement from Victor Turner is quoted at length in Asad (1993: 128), and comes from Turner (1969: 52–3).

18 Nor would it be Bell's response. She insists that despite how ritual might at times have been used to exercise social control, it can be a way for individuals to empower themselves. See Bell (1992: 116).

19 This can be found in the French in Foucault (1994: 165).

20 This is Ronald Grimes' interpretation of Turner's work (Grimes 2000: 121). There he refers only to Victor Turner, *The Ritual Process,* but he implies that this view develops through Turner's work into the 1980s. In *The Ritual Process,* Turner does not make such a sweeping claim, but it is implied, especially in Chapter 5 where he discusses liminality in relation to several very different types of ritual, applying the idea well beyond van Gennep's use of it to understand rites of passage.

21 Many of these occur under the auspices of the Richmond Metropolitan Community Church and in such cases they are also called Rites of Holy Union.

22 *Bottoms v. Bottoms* (1993), Circuit Court of Henrico County, Virginia. Judge Buford Parsons opined, "I will tell you first that the mother's conduct is illegal. It is a Class 6 felony in the Commonwealth of Virginia. It will tell you that it is the opinion of this Court that her conduct is immoral. And it is the opinion of this Court that the conduct of Sharon Bottoms renders her an unfit parent."

23 Other cases through the 1990s were infamous, but probably most infamous among them was the Florida case in which an 11-year-old girl was placed in the custody of her father, a convicted murderer, rather than her lesbian mother. Escambia Circuit Court Judge Joseph Tarbuck said, "This child should be given the opportunity and the option to live in a non-lesbian world" (Davey 1996: A–1). The father, John Ward, had shot his first wife Judy twelve times during a dispute over the custody of their children. Although the lesbian mother, Mary Ward, was shown to be an attentive and responsible parent, an appeals court in Pensacola upheld Tarbuck's decision in August of 1996 (Epstein 1996: 1). Mary Ward later died of a heart attack. The child, Cassey Ward, is 18 years old at the time of this writing and therefore no longer in anyone's custody. She recently took part in the 25th anniversary celebration of the National Council for Lesbian Rights, the organization that provided attorneys for Mary Ward's unsuccessful custody battle. At that event, she spoke in defense of her mother, saying, "Being a lesbian did not make my mother, or any mother, unfit" (National Council for Lesbian Rights 2002).

24 See *Bottoms v. Bottoms,* No. 1930–93–2 (Va. Cir. Ct. (Henrico) September 7, 1993), "Judge rules against Lesbian mom," *The Washington Blade,* March 13, 1998, p. 14.

25 And they certainly can be construed that way, despite refusal of legal recognition. As Ronald Grimes writes, "although the legal and moral status of same sex marriage is currently debated, their social reality cannot be denied" (Grimes 2000: 171).

26 Calhoun writes, "Heterosexual marriages have largely been *de*-gendered under the law. All of the nineteenth- and early twentieth-century laws have been eliminated that made married women legally dead on the assumption that man and

wife are one and that that one is the husband. The law no longer compels married women to adopt their husband's name, to share his domicile wherever he chooses it to be, to provide domestic services, and to submit to marital rape. The elimination of long-term alimony and the introduction of alimony for needy ex-husbands both resulted from abandoning the assumption that only husbands are economic providers within marriage. Repeated court refusal to employ sex-based classifications in family law has meant that all that is left of gender in marriage laws are the constructs 'husband' and 'wife,' evacuated of substantive content" (Calhoun 2000: 118).

27 This question was explicitly asked on the questionnaire Carol and I had to fill in for Rev. Gillian Storey of the Metropolitan Community Church of Richmond. It took me several weeks to answer.

28 We happened upon three books, although there are others: Butler (1990), Sherman (1992), and Ayers and Brown (1994).

29 See van Gennep (1960), in which the phrase *rites de passage* was first introduced. This book was originally published in French in 1908.

30 I would like to extend special thanks to my life partner Carol Anderson for her painstaking critiques of several versions of this essay and to my student assistant Martin Hewett for his helpful research and careful editorial work on parts one through three.

Bibliography

Asad, T. (1993) *Genealogies of Religion: Discipline and Reasons of Power in Christianity and Islam*, Baltimore: The Johns Hopkins University Press.

Ayers, T. and Brown, P. (eds) (1994) *The Essential Guide to Lesbian and Gay Weddings*, San Francisco: Alyson Books.

Bell, C. (1992) *Ritual Theory, Ritual Practice*, New York: Oxford University Press.

—— (1997) *Ritual: Perspectives and Dimensions*, New York: Oxford University Press.

Bocock, R. (1974) *Ritual in Industrial Society*, London: George Allen and Unwin, Ltd.

Bourdieu, P. (1977) *An Outline of a Theory of Practice*, trans. R. Nice, Cambridge: Cambridge University Press.

Burke, P. (1987) *The Historical Anthropology of Early Modern Italy*, Cambridge: Cambridge University Press.

Butler, B. (ed.) (1990) *Ceremonies of the Heart: Celebrating Lesbian Unions*, Seattle: The Seal Press.

Calhoun, C. (2000) *Feminism, the Family, and the Politics of the Closet*, New York: Oxford University Press.

Card, C. (1996) "Against Marriage and Motherhood," *Hypatia* 11: 1–23.

Davey, M. (1996) "Lesbian or killer: Who gets daughter?" *St. Petersburg Times*, 31 Jan., p. A–1.

de Beauvoir, S. (1952) *The Second Sex*, trans. H. M. Parshley, New York: Vintage Press.

Douglas, M. (1966) *Purity and Danger: An Analysis of the Concepts of Ritual and Taboo*, New York: Routledge.

—— (1982) *In the Active Voice*, London: Routledge and Kegan Paul.

Epstein, G. (1996) "Judge rules against lesbian mom," *The Tampa Tribune*, 31 Aug, p. 1.

Foucault, M. (1975) *Surveiller et punir: Naissance de la prison*, Paris: Editions Gallimard.

—— (1976) *La volonté de savoir*, Paris: Editions Gallimard.

—— (1979) *Discipline and Punish: The Birth of the Prison*, trans. A. Sheridan, New York: Vintage Press.

—— (1980) *The History of Sexuality, Vol. 1*, trans. R. Hurley, New York: Vintage Books.

—— (1989) "Friendship as a Way of Life," in S. Lotringer (ed.), *Foucault Live: Interviews 1966–1984*, trans. J. Johnston, New York: Semiotext(e).

—— (1994) *Dits et écrits, Vol. IV*, Paris: Editions Gallimard.

Goody, J. (1977) "Against 'Ritual': Loosely Structured Thoughts on a Loosely Defined Topic," in S. Moore and B. Myerhoff (eds), *Secular Ritual*, Amsterdam: Van Gorum.

Grimes, R. (2000) *Deeply Into the Bone: Re-Inventing Rites of Passage*, Berkeley: University of California Press.

Martin, D. (1995) "Sociology, Religion and Secularization: an Orientation," *Religion* 25: 295–303.

Morgan, R. (ed.) (1970) *Sisterhood is Powerful*, New York: Vintage Books.

National Council for Lesbian Rights (2002) *NCLR Newsletter*, July, San Francisco.

Rossi, A. (ed.) (1973) *The Feminist Papers*, Boston: Northeastern University Press.

Schlegel, A., and Barry, H. (1980) "The Evolutionary Significance of Adolescent Initiation Ceremonies," *American Ethnologist* 7: 696–715.

Sherman, S. (ed.) (1992) *Lesbian and Gay Marriage: Private Commitments, Public Ceremonies*, Philadelphia: Temple University Press.

Shils, E. (1975) "Ritual and Crisis," in *Center and Periphery: Essays in Macro-sociology. Selected Papers of Edward Shils, Vol. 2*, Chicago: University of Chicago Press.

Tibbetts, J. (2002) "Feds may leave marriages to the church," *The Ottowa Citizen*, 28 July. Online. Available HTTP: http://www.canada.com/national/ (accessed 28 July 2002).

Turner, V. (1967) *The Forest of Symbols: Aspects of Ndembu Ritual*, Ithaca: Cornell University Press.

Turner, V. (1969) *The Ritual Process*, London: Routledge and Kegan Paul.

van Gennep, A. (1960) *The Rites of Passage*, trans. M. Vizedom and G. Caffee, Chicago: University of Chicago Press.

The Washington Blade (1998) "Judge rules against lesbian mom," 13 March, p. 1.

4   Scapegoat rituals in Wittgensteinian perspective

Brian R. Clack

I

Perhaps the first thing that strikes the reader of Wittgenstein's *Remarks on Frazer's Golden Bough* is Wittgenstein's insistence that Frazer is wrong – crucially wrong – in holding that magical beliefs and practices have the character of *mistakes*. This contention is certainly uppermost in Frazer's thoughts, as can be seen by considering his account of the nature of homoeopathic magic. The practice of magic is grounded in the ritualist's acceptance of a law, the Law of Similarity, which states simply that "like produces like, or that an effect resembles its cause" (Frazer 1922: 11). On the principles of homoeopathic magic, a magician wishing to harm his enemy may fashion a small model of that person and then proceed to damage the model by running a needle through it, or by burning it, or by breaking it into pieces. As an example of such a practice, Frazer describes a Malay charm, in which one makes

> a corpse of wax from an empty bees' comb and of the length of a footstep; then pierce the eye of the image, and your enemy is blind; pierce the stomach, and he is sick; pierce the head, and his head aches; pierce the breast, and his breast will suffer.
>
> (Frazer 1922: 13)

The intention of such acts of effigy-mutilation seems to be to effect a corresponding injury in the person represented by the effigy. But no such injury can result thus, so, as attempted homicide, effigy-mutilation is patently futile. It is therefore mistaken to believe that by means of magic one's enemy can be incapacitated or killed. And this applies to the whole field of homoeopathic magic, not just to its nefarious branches: attempts to bring rain by sprinkling water on parched soil, and attempts to hasten the onset of summer by burning large fires are likewise abortive. Such actions just *do not work*. They cannot hope to achieve what they set out to do. The mistake of magic, according to Frazer, is of a particular type, arising from a misapplication of the association of ideas: "Homoeopathic magic commits the mistake of assuming that things which resemble each other are the same" (Frazer 1922: 12). And the mistakes of magic are not just incidental to its nature, as though some magical acts *might* be effective. No, for Frazer, magic is *by definition* mistaken: "It is . . . a truism, almost a tautology, to say that all magic is necessarily false and barren; for were it ever to become true and fruitful, it would no longer be magic but science" (Frazer 1922: 50). Frazer is not so explicit about the erroneous nature of *religion* (distinguished from magic by its belief in gods rather than in the impersonal laws postulated by magic), but the implication is there nonetheless: just as spells and magical rites do not work, the central religious practices of prayer and sacrifice are likewise ineffective. As Frazer sees the development of human thought, history presents us with the story of one erroneous theory (magic) being usurped by another erroneous theory (religion), which in turn is gradually replaced by a valid and true theory of the universe (science). All these three seek to do the same thing (understand, explain and control the natural world), but science is the only one which can arouse in us a "cheerful confidence in the soundness of its method" (Frazer 1922: 712).

Wittgenstein's own articulation of the nature of ritual actions can be seen to emerge from his rejection of this view that magic is in some manner mistaken. That Frazer's verdict is perverse is said to be shown by an observation of the numerous practical skills that members of primitive societies possess: "The same savage who, apparently in order to kill his enemy, sticks his knife through a picture of him, really does build his hut of wood and cuts his arrow with skill and not in effigy" (Wittgenstein 1979: 4). The lesson is clear: if "savages" employ magical techniques because of their lack of scientific or technical knowledge, then we should expect them to build in effigy, hunt in effigy, cook in effigy, fish in effigy, and so on. But they do not. Indeed, the technical competence of primitive peoples suggests, at least to Wittgenstein, that magic is of a different order altogether than simply failed science. Likewise, if magic is a mistake, and so obvious a mistake at that, then why is it not detected sooner?

> Frazer says it is very difficult to discover the error in magic and this is why it persists for so long – because, for example, a ceremony which is supposed to bring rain is sure to appear effective sooner or later.
>   But then it is queer that people do not notice sooner that it does rain sooner or later anyway.
>
> (Wittgenstein 1979: 2)

Wittgenstein's argument here is, in truth, not particularly compelling. If the efficacy of a rain-making ritual is never tested (by, say, performing the ritual one year, refraining from performing it the next, and then comparing the results), then how could people ever know that "it does rain sooner or later anyway?"

A better argument against the characterization of magical acts as mistakes can be found by comparing a magical act and its apparent inefficacy with an act patently exhibiting the character of a blunder. A failed assassination attempt may be due to a bungled action: the assassin may mistakenly have loaded his gun with blank cartridges. But what if the assassin failed because, instead of shooting his intended victim, he stuck pins into an effigy of him? Could it really make sense in this latter context to claim that the assassin had merely bungled the attempt on his intended victim's life, that he had committed an error? Here one might wish to say, as Wittgenstein did in another context: "For a blunder, that's too big" (Wittgenstein 1966: 62).

If Wittgenstein wants to say that magical acts are not mistakes then he must, of course, be committed to a view of their nature which runs contrary to that offered by Frazer. For, to recall, Frazer wants to say that magical acts are *instrumental* acts, attempts to achieve some desired concrete end (the death of an enemy, the coming of the rains). Conceived thus, magical acts surely *are* mistakes, for such ends cannot be attained by homoeopathic methods. So, if magical acts are not mistakes, they must be other than instrumental. And Wittgenstein does indeed appear to contend this, for it seems (at least at first glance) that he wishes to locate the character of magical acts within the category of the *expressive*. We may note, first of all, how he effects this change of aspect from the instrumental to the expressive in his reflections on effigy-destruction:

> Burning in effigy. Kissing the picture of a loved one. This is obviously *not* based on a belief that it will have a definite effect on the object which the picture represents. It aims at some satisfaction and it achieves it. Or rather, it does not *aim* at anything; we act in this way and then feel satisfied.
>
> (Wittgenstein 1979: 4)

Wittgenstein's technique here might be called *introspective hermeneutics*. He compares an exotic rite (effigy-burning) with a practice with which he is himself personally familiar (kissing a photograph of a loved one); he detects the lack of an instrumental motive in his own case (Wittgenstein does not expect the loved one to feel the effect of his kiss); he discerns instead an overridingly expressive dimension in the act (in the absence of the loved one, satisfaction is attained from kissing his or her picture); and consequently he imputes a comparable expressive meaning to the exotic practice (the magician is not trying to kill his enemy: his hatred takes the form of destroying an image of the foe). If such a case makes ritual activity appear a little too individualistic and idiosyncratic, Wittgenstein also provides examples of communal rites which are likewise expressive rather than instrumental. For example: "If the adoption of a child is carried out by the mother pulling the child from beneath her clothes, then it is crazy to think that there is an *error* in this and that she believes she has borne the child" (Wittgenstein 1979: 4). This runs counter to Frazer's suggestion that

> if you pretend to give birth to a boy, or even to a great bearded man who has not a drop of your blood in his veins, then, in the eyes of

primitive law and philosophy, that boy or man is really your son to all intents and purposes.

(Frazer 1922: 14)

Wittgenstein is contending that no such homoeopathic mistake takes place here: the purpose of the rite is to declare dramatically to the assembled crowd that the mother is going to treat this adopted child just as she treats her other children, that she will love and cherish the child as one of her own. Similarly, rituals regarding the onset of rain are to be regarded as dramatic ceremonies whereby a community expresses its desire for the coming of rain, rather than as pitiful and futile attempts to bend nature's will to the hopes of that community (Wittgenstein 1979: 12; cf. Beattie 1966: 203). In all these cases, then, we see a movement from consideration of rituals as ineffective instrumental actions (mistakes) to seeing them as satisfying expressive actions. As M. O'C. Drury summarizes Wittgenstein's position: "They were not mistaken beliefs that produced the rites but the need to *express* something" (Drury 1973: x).[1]

II

Frazer is disdainful of magic; that much is certain. The information gathered together in *The Golden Bough* is not presented in an entirely disinterested way, but rather forms part of a narrative demonstrating the pre-scientific history of humanity to have been a monstrous farrago of folly and suffering. In the face of this vociferous assault, Wittgenstein appears to have been coming to the defense of magic and religion. As we have seen, he rejects the view that magical acts are blunders, he berates Frazer for being "more savage" than the peoples he is studying, and he resists any attempt to explain ritual practices. His tendency in this respect chimes with the perceived character of the Wittgensteinian view of religion in general, which is frequently seen as having distinctly fideistic motives. This perception is largely due to the somewhat reckless application of Wittgenstein's idea of the "language-game" to religion by some of his followers in their earliest writings on religion, and Wittgensteinian philosophers have had to work very hard to try to refute the claim that they are simply trying to protect religion from criticism and skeptical attack (see Phillips 1986: 1–16). One standard manoeuvre has been to suggest that, while ritual beliefs and practices are not the kind of thing that can be regarded as being "mistaken," certain such beliefs and practices may in fact harbor deep "confusions." A confused practice could certainly be criticized, and the production of such a practice would refute the charge that Wittgensteinianism is wholly (and perhaps unthinkingly) uncritical of magic and religion. Fortunately, such a practice was located, and located indeed by Wittgenstein himself. The practice deemed to be a prime example of a confused ritual was the scapegoat rite as described in the book of Leviticus.

In the ritual of atonement, two goats would be brought before the high-priest. One would be offered as a sin-offering to Yahweh (Leviticus 16: 9), sacrificed and its blood sprinkled upon the mercy seat (16: 15). The other (the scapegoat) would then be sent away into the wilderness to Azazel, an obscure term referring either to a demon of the waste, or, more probably, to a geographical region.[2] Leviticus tells how the high-priest

> shall lay both his hands upon the head of the live goat, and confess over him all the iniquities of the people of Israel, and all their transgressions, all their sins; and he shall put them upon the head of the goat, and send him away into the wilderness by the hand of a man who is in readiness. The goat shall bear all their iniquities upon him to a solitary land; and he shall let the goat go in the wilderness.
>
> (16: 20–2, *Revised Standard Version*)

And now Wittgenstein's judgment on this practice:

> The scapegoat, on which one lays one's sins, and who runs away into the desert with them – a false picture, similar to those that cause errors in philosophy.
>
> (Wittgenstein 1993a: 197)[3]

Here we have, then, a denunciation of a particular ritual. The scapegoat rite embodies a "false picture." But what exactly is wrong with this ritual, and what is its connection with "errors in philosophy"?

One answer to (at least the first of) these questions has been put forward by both Rush Rhees and D. Z. Phillips. It is worth quoting Rhees at length:

> In the rite of the scapegoat (Leviticus 16: 20–22) several analogies come together. It would be natural in a tribal society to speak of "bearing the sins of others": of a family sharing the sin committed by any member of it, or of children bearing the sins of their forefathers. The sins of the people come between them and God. But purification was possible through sacrifice, and then the people could turn to God again for help. Here there are metaphors enough, but they need not mislead anyone. Suppose then: "If the people assembled here do bear the sins of their fathers, and of their brothers now living, then why should not the priest bring in some animal to be made one of them in this sense only – that it bears their sins – and then, after laying his hands on it, send it with their sins away from them into the wilderness?" When Wittgenstein calls this rite a misleading picture, he may mean something like this: consider
>   1 "Children carry the sins of their fathers."
>   2 "A goat, when consecrated, carries the sins of the people."
> In the first sentence "carry" is used in the sense of the whole sentence. In the second sentence "carry" seems to mean what it does in "The goat carries on his back the basket in which we put our firewood"; and yet it *cannot* mean that.
>
> (Rhees 1982: 81–2)

Why can it not mean that? Rhees' answer is that it is something to do with the nature of a *goat*:

> Perhaps we should not find it incongruous – we should not find the picture jars in symbolizing what is intended for it – if you said that a *man* might take on himself the sins the people have had to bear, and offer himself in atonement for them. But a goat? What would it mean to say that a goat has to bear its *own* sins, let alone that it has to bear the sins of *people*?
>
> (Rhees 1982: 82)

Phillips concurs with Rhees' analysis, stressing that while "it is not too diffi-cult to understand the common enough conception in tribal societies of one man taking on himself the sins of another" (Phillips 1993: 90), the use of an animal for such a purpose is bewildering and unintelligible: "What does it mean to speak of an animal feeling remorse for his own misdeeds, let alone being able to remove the sins of a people?" (Phillips 1993: 90).

According to Rhees and Phillips, then, the confusion inherent in the scape-goat ritual concerns consciousness of sin. As a human being, I can experience consciousness of wrongdoing; I can feel guilt; I can feel the weight of my sins on my shoulders. And if I can bear my own sins, then the idea of me taking the sins of others onto my back and bearing those likewise is at least an intelligible notion. Contrariwise, a goat can never feel guilt or responsi-bility for what it has done, so it cannot make sense to expect the goat to remove the burden of guilt from our shoulders.

As an analysis of the "false picture" embodied in the scapegoat ritual, these ideas are superficially plausible but are in fact deeply problematic. Berel Dov Lerner has shown how, in their treatment of this ancient Israelite prac-tice, Rhees and Phillips betray both a prejudice in favor of the Christian religion and its doctrines, and an unhelpful tendency to explicate and analyze the rituals of other religions by means of Christian notions. By confessing that he finds no problem in the idea that a man might take upon himself the people's sins, Rhees, Lerner writes,

> has let the cat out of the bag. The notion of a man taking on the sins of others and offering himself (or should I write Himself) in atonement for them is all too familiar. Rhees has been misled by the application of a picture – the Christ idea – to a culture in which it simply had no application ... By modelling his interpretation of the scapegoat ritual on the crucifixion, Rhees reduces it to a kind of confused religious farce.
>
> (Lerner 1994: 609)

Phillips is perhaps even more guilty than Rhees of this Christianizing tendency. In his treatment of the issue, he quotes from *The Interpreter's Bible*, in which we find the statement that it "is obvious that sins could not really be trans-ferred to a goat." That assertion is then followed by this passage:

Christ, as identified with man in his shame and sin, rejected by men and driven away bearing their sins and done to death for their forgiveness, is symbolically depicted, crudely and inadequately yet really, in the scapegoat.

(Phillips 1986: 31)

One may wonder which is preferable: to describe ancient rituals as embodying false and confused proto-scientific notions (as Frazer does) or to describe them (as Phillips and Rhees do) as embodying false and confused proto-*Christian* notions.

It is somewhat ironic to accuse someone of being unfair to a scapegoat, but it is undeniably puzzling as to why the Wittgensteinian finds this particular rite worthy of censure above all others. And this is particularly so when the technique employed in so much Wittgensteinian analysis of ritual practices exhibits a notable sense of interpretational charity, trying to maximize the intelligibility of a practice against those who would describe it as essentially ludicrous and mistaken. Because presenting effigy-mutilation as a failed attempt at homicide is uncharitable to the ritualist, Wittgenstein rejects Frazer's account and replaces it with his own expressivist, symbolic version. Phillips likewise does this with Tylor's comments on the primitive conception of the soul (see Phillips 1988: 314–15), and goes so far as to suggest, rightly, that to understand a ritual we must "take account of the role played by the ritual in the details of the lives of the people who celebrate it" (Phillips 1988: 328). If by such a method we can in general move away from accounts which present ancient and exotic practices as flawed, mistaken, or barbarous, towards accounts which see them as intelligible expressions of perfectly understandable human feelings and values, then why is it impossible to do this in the case of the scapegoat?

Rhees is plainly not unaware of this possibility, for he actually toys with it: "We may think first that the picture set out in the scapegoat ritual is a form of symbolism or form of expression: the way in which those people expressed their longing for release from the burden of sin" (Rhees 1982: 83). Well, that seems satisfactory enough. At the very least, it coheres with much Wittgensteinian analysis of ritual. Rhees' reason for rejecting it as anything other than a "first" thought about the meaning of the rite is interesting:

But suppose someone asked, "Do they *get* the purification for which they have longed, when the scapegoat is sent into the wilderness?" Would this be all a misunderstanding? Or is there not something that does make us want to ask it?

(Rhees 1982: 83)

The question is not "Did that ritual work, then? Did it take away the sins?" (We all know what the answer to *that* question would be.) No, Rhees' question is different, and arises from consideration of Wittgenstein's suggestion that magic functions to bring wishes to representation: "The representation of a wish is, *eo ipso*, the representation of its realization" (Wittgenstein 1993b: 125). Hence, the question to be asked about the scapegoat rite is: "Is the performance of the ritual itself the experience of purification? Is what they long for taking place in this portrayal [representation] of it?" (Rhees 1982: 83). But this, Rhees thinks, commits us to holding that "the scapegoat shows a confusion of what belongs to the symbolism or phraseology with what is portrayed or described in this phraseology" (Rhees 1982: 83), thus illustrating that what we have in this rite is a misunderstanding of the logic of language.

It is, however, hard to see that such a criticism could be leveled at the scapegoat without implicating many other (if not all) ritual actions. Can it not, for instance, function as a censure of effigy-burning, even as that is described by Wittgensteinians? Does not the mutilation of an effigy, conceived as the expression of a wish, confuse "what belongs to the phraseology with what is portrayed in this phraseology?" The mess that both Rhees and Phillips end up in when trying to explicate the problem of the scapegoat is due to an inherited Christian sensibility and to a rather unedifying acceptance of all that Wittgenstein has to say. For, ultimately, their reason for singling out the scapegoat as an especially confused practice is that *Wittgenstein said* it was confused.

III

What is striking about comparing Wittgenstein's (very brief) comment on the scapegoat with the amplifications given by Rhees and Phillips is that Wittgenstein never even suggests that the problem with the rite is the presence in it of an *animal* for whom the consciousness of sin and responsibility is absent. If the scapegoat ritual is "a false picture, similar to those that cause errors in philosophy," then we surely have to ask how many errors in philosophy are caused by a process analogous to thinking confusedly that an animal can feel responsibility of sin. Very few, if any, and certainly none of the kind that Wittgenstein was especially interested in. And it is, of course, well known that Wittgenstein, throughout all the other changes in his philosophical outlook, held that philosophical problems arose as a result of misunderstanding the workings of *language*. It would appear, therefore, that Wittgenstein is detecting something comparable to a language-generated confusion in the scapegoat rite. That this *is* the case becomes clear when we turn to the context of Wittgenstein's comment on the Leviticus practice, a context which is twofold: his passages on the nature of philosophy in the so-called "Big Typescript," in which the scapegoat remark is located; and the *Remarks on Frazer's Golden Bough*, which isolates other, comparable "false pictures" in magic and religion. It is only by ignoring this context, and by approaching Wittgenstein's scapegoat comment with a misplaced Christian sensibility, that one could have reached the conclusions arrived at by Rhees and Phillips.

The section of the Big Typescript in which the remark on the scapegoat appears is principally concerned with how traditional philosophical problems arise out of what Wittgenstein calls "traps of language." "People are deeply imbedded in philosophical, i.e. grammatical confusions" (Wittgenstein 1993a: 185), he writes, continuing:

> Language contains the same traps for everyone; the immense network of well-kept false paths. And thus we see one person after another walking the same paths and we know already where he will make a turn, where he will keep on going straight ahead without noticing the turn, etc., etc. ... As long as there is a verb "to be" which seems to function like "to eat" and "to drink", as long as there are adjectives like "identical", "true", "false", "possible", as long as one talks about a flow of time and an expanse of space, etc., etc., humans will continue to bump up against the same mysterious difficulties.
>
> (Wittgenstein 1993a: 185–7)

One of the problems of language which generates philosophical confusions is its apparent uniformity, a uniformity suggested by the written or spoken appearance of words and sentences, by the fact that "the clothing of our language makes everything alike" (Wittgenstein 1958: 224). Because paradigm examples of verbs, such as "to eat," "to drink," and "to run," suggest an activity or process, we have a tendency to think that all verbs function likewise, and then find ourselves in difficulties with verbs like "to be" or "to mean." The philosophical difficulties thus arising are the product of attending only to what Wittgenstein would call "surface grammar," which gives us an oversimplified conception of language, a conception which does not recognize and respect its complex and motley character:

> Teaching philosophy involves the same immense difficulty as instruction in geography would have if a pupil brought with him a mass of false and far too simple ideas about the course and connections of the routes of rivers and mountain chains.
>
> (Wittgenstein 1993a: 185)[4]

So: the "false pictures" that Wittgenstein is alerting us to in the Big Typescript, the false pictures that "cause errors in philosophy," are those resulting from a primitive and simplistic view of language.

When we turn to the *Remarks on Frazer's Golden Bough*, written just two years before the construction of the Big Typescript, we find remarkably similar views about the pitfalls of language, but this time connected with how these traps give rise to ritual practices rather than to abstruse philosophical problems. Here Wittgenstein suggests that certain practices might arise from the kind of surface grammar bewitchment we encounter in philosophy. And he employs the same term he used to describe the scapegoat – "a false picture" (*ein falsches Bild*) – to characterize these practices:

> We should distinguish between magical operations and those operations which rest on a false, over-simplified notion of things and processes. For

instance, if someone says that the illness is moving from one part of the body into another, or if he takes measures to draw off the illness as though it were a liquid or a temperature. He is then using a false picture, a picture that doesn't fit [*ein falsches, das heißt hier, unzutreffendes Bild*].

(Wittgenstein 1979: 5)

It is debatable whether the distinction Wittgenstein wishes to draw here between "magical operations" and those operations involving false pictures is a workable one, and I have discussed this elsewhere (Clack 1999: 112–25). The point is, however, that in a lot of his comments on ritual, Wittgenstein is detecting the same over-simplified application of concepts that he highlighted in the Big Typescript.

For example, he discusses Frazer's account of the custom of "Carrying out Death." This European Lenten observance involves the making of an effigy of Death – sometimes out of straw and fastened to a pole; in other places, a doll covered by a shroud and carried in a tiny coffin – which is paraded around the village of the celebrants, while the people chant "We carry death out of the village." At the close of the celebration, the effigy of Death is ritually slaughtered, and the celebrating children return to the village declaring that Death has left and that Life has returned. Consideration of this case leads Wittgenstein to reflect on the similarity of this custom to certain misleading philosophical notions:

> To cast out death or to slay death; but he is also represented as a skeleton, as in some sense dead himself. "As dead as death." "Nothing is so dead as death; nothing is so beautiful as beauty itself." Here the image which we use in thinking of reality is that beauty, death, &c. are the pure (concentrated) substances, and that they are found in the beautiful object as added ingredients of the mixture.
>
> (Wittgenstein 1979: 10; cf Wittgenstein 1993a: 199)

Wittgenstein wants here to connect this Lenten observance with the Platonic doctrine that properties are ingredients of things. In the *Blue Book*, Wittgenstein speaks of this doctrine as being one of the confused philosophical tendencies which leads one into the "complete darkness" of metaphysics. He says:

> The idea of a general concept being a common property of its particular instances connects up with other primitive, too simple, ideas of the structure of language. It is comparable to the idea that *properties* are the *ingredients* of the things which have the properties; e.g. that beauty is an ingredient of all beautiful things as alcohol is of beer and wine, and that we therefore could have pure beauty, unadulterated by anything that is beautiful.
>
> (Wittgenstein 1969: 17)

What Wittgenstein sees in the custom of "Carrying out Death," then, is the application of an over-simplified language in which words and concepts such as "death" and "life" are seen as pure qualities, or reified forms, existing in abstraction from objects exhibiting signs of life and death. By reifying an abstract noun, the peasants in the European custom have been misled by the substantive "death." Friedrich Waismann's warning with regard to the language-generated problems of metaphysics is pertinent here:

> When we deal with a substantive, we involuntarily think of the case in which the word is correlated with an object, in the same way that the name of a person is connected with the person . . . We look for a "being" which will fit the word in question, we people the world with aetherial beings to be the shadow-like companions of substantives.
>
> (Waismann 1965: 90)

We have here, therefore, in the origination of certain rituals, just as we have in metaphysics as it is viewed by Wittgenstein, a misunderstanding of the logic of language.[5]

Given this background, we should say that Wittgenstein considers the scapegoat ritual to be simply another example of a ritual involving a linguistic or conceptual confusion. Just as we have in certain primitive ritual operations a false and over-simplified picture of things and processes; and just as we have in the custom of "Carrying out Death" a ritual born of the reification of abstract substantives, a confusion of an identifiability-dependent characteristic with a substance (cf. Baker and Hacker 1984: 273); so we have in the scapegoat rite, in Wittgenstein's eyes, a combination of both of these problems. Here, sin is reified, treated, not as offensive and immoral *action*, but as an aetherial substance which can, by means of a primitively-conceived act of transference, be passed from one being to another, loaded onto the back of one who can take away the sinner's burden. It is irrelevant in this context whether the recipient of the sins is a goat or a human being. We might accordingly rephrase Wittgenstein's remark thus: "The idea that one's sins can be transferred to another – a false picture, similar to those that cause errors in philosophy."

IV

Given the perceived rejection by Wittgenstein of all that Frazer had to say about ritual, it might come as something of a surprise to discover that Frazer's conclusions about the scapegoat mirror exactly those suggested in the foregoing analysis. But while the Wittgensteinian's "ethnographic naïveté" (Pitkin 1972: 102) results in treating the Leviticus rite in isolation, as though it were an anomaly in the ritual life of humanity, Frazer's more extensive knowledge allows him to place and to consider the rite within the much larger context of those comparable practices centered on what he calls "the transference of evil." Indeed, in the ninth volume of the thirteen-volume edition of *The*

Golden Bough, entitled "The Scapegoat" (a volume which runs to 453 pages), the Jewish use of a scapegoat is dealt with in only one sentence:

> On the Day of Atonement, which was the tenth day of the seventh month, the Jewish high-priest laid both his hands on the head of a live goat, confessed over it all the iniquities of the Children of Israel, and, having thereby transferred the sins of the people to the beast, sent it away into the wilderness.
>
> (Frazer 1913: 210)

That the Jewish rite is only a particular instance of an extraordinarily widespread custom will entail that Wittgenstein's diagnosis of conceptual confusion will apply to vast swathes of ritual life. To establish this we need to take a brief look at Frazer's description and explanation of rites involving the transference of evil.

Frazer explains first of all the principle on which rituals centered on the transference of evil rest:

> The notion that we can transfer our guilt and sufferings to some other being who will bear them for us is familiar to the savage mind. It arises from a very obvious confusion between the physical and the mental, between the material and the immaterial. Because it is possible to shift a load of wood, stones, or what not, from our own back to the back of another, the savage fancies that it is equally possible to shift the burden of his pains and sorrows to another, who will suffer them in his stead.
>
> (Frazer 1913: 1)

The confusion isolated by Frazer as the root cause of all manner of scape-goat expulsions has great affinities with the confusion detected by Wittgenstein, though the latter sees this as a more linguistic confusion; one, moreover, which is present, not just in the "savage mind" but in the minds of philosophers who consider words to function uniformly as the names of objects or things (he is, of course, thinking of the theory contained in his own *Tractatus Logico-Philosophicus*). From this confusion, Frazer states, there flows "an endless number of very unamiable devices for palming off upon some one else the trouble which a man shrinks from bearing himself" (Frazer 1913: 1). Sometimes the "trouble" palmed off is an illness, and the practice of transference of ailments perhaps springs from the observation that illnesses can indeed be transferred. An example:

> In some of the East Indian islands they think that epilepsy can be cured by striking the patient on the face with the leaves of certain trees and then throwing them away. The disease is believed to have passed into the leaves, and to have been thrown away with them.
>
> (Frazer 1913: 2)

It may be on the model of transference of illness that practices concerning the transference of sin or guilt arose. Perhaps guilt was viewed as some kind of moral illness, which, like influenza, could be transferred to someone else. Frazer documents examples where sins are transferred to inanimate objects, animals, men, and man-gods. Of the first kind:

> When an Atkhan of the Aleutian Islands had committed a grave sin and desired to unburden himself of his guilt, he proceeded as follows. Having chosen a time when the sun was clear and unclouded, he picked up certain weeds and carried them about his person. Then he laid them down, and calling the sun to witness, cast his sins upon them, after which, having eased his heart of all that weighed upon it, he threw the weeds into the fire, and fancied thus that he had cleansed himself of his guilt.
>
> (Frazer 1913: 3)

With regard to sins being transferred to animals, Leviticus provides us with a prime example, but it is by no means an isolated instance (Frazer 1913: 31–7); sins have also commonly been transferred to human scapegoats. This was sometimes done in times of catastrophe (during a plague, say), or periodically, in order to rid a community of its accumulated guilt. For example: "The city of Abdera in Thrace was publicly purified once a year, and one of the burghers, set apart for the purpose, was stoned to death as a scapegoat or vicarious sacrifice for the life of all the others" (Frazer 1913: 254). As can be seen from these examples, sometimes these transference rituals are individually performed, at other times communally; sometimes occasional, at other times periodic. And when communal and periodic, such a rite might be combined with another ceremony commonly encountered in ancient societies: the sacrifice of a man who impersonated a god. Frazer writes:

> If it occurred to people to combine these two customs, the result would be the employment of the dying god as a scapegoat. He was killed, not originally to take away sin, but to save the divine life from the degeneracy of old age; but, since he had to be killed at any rate, people may have thought that they might as well seize the opportunity to lay upon him the burden of their sufferings and sins, in order that he might bear it away with him to the unknown world beyond the grave.
>
> (Frazer 1913: 227)

One of these ancient dying gods who also performed a scapegoat function was, according to Frazer, Christ. Combining the separate functions of the two goats in Leviticus, the Christian doctrine of atonement presented Jesus as the perfect sin-offering (Hebrews 9: 13–14), the shedding of whose blood has sanctified and cleansed humanity (Hebrews 13: 12); and he also, like a scapegoat, was the suffering servant, "wounded for our transgressions" (Isaiah 53: 5): "the Lord has laid on him the iniquity of us all" (53: 6). So

impressed was Frazer with the similarities between the barbarous circumstances of Jesus' death, the classical doctrine of the atonement, and the savage
transferences of evil he encountered, that the ninth volume of *The Golden
Bough* was originally to have been titled, not "The Scapegoat," but "The
Man of Sorrows."

V

The foregoing digression is intended to demonstrate two things. First,
Wittgenstein's analysis of the confusions inherent in the scapegoat is not
radically dissimilar to Frazer's diagnosis. Second, given the widespread nature
of practices involving the notion of transference of evil and sin, Wittgenstein's
analysis, if persuasive, has to be extended to countless other rituals, extended
even to the foundations of Christianity itself. And if such a conclusion does
indeed follow, there will need to be a reassessment of Wittgenstein's perceived
relation to religious belief and practice. For instead of producing an expressivist defense of religious belief against intellectualist and skeptical censure,
Wittgenstein's account of numerous central ritual practices is itself somewhat critical, seeing such practices as arising from linguistic and conceptual
confusions. Indeed, in his "Lecture on Ethics" Wittgenstein even went so far
as to generalize totally this lesson with regard to the linguistic misunder-
standings inherent in religious thinking: "I want to impress on you that a
certain characteristic misuse of our language runs through *all* ethical and
religious statements" (Wittgenstein 1965: 9). The apparently throwaway
remark about the scapegoat, seized on by the Wittgensteinian to evade the
charge of fideism, is, as we have seen, in fact deeply subversive of humanity's
religious life; it reveals Wittgenstein to be no great friend and defender of
faith, and if pressed strongly, as we have here done, it shakes the very foundations of the Christian faith. For just as one might raise moral objections
to the classical account of atonement (why should an innocent man bear the
sins of others?); and just as one might come to see it as illustrative of savage
and barbarous thinking ("without the shedding of blood there is no forgiveness of sins" [Hebrews 9: 22]); so Wittgenstein's diagnosis of the problems
inherent in the scapegoat ritual suggests that the idea of Christ taking on
himself the sins of the world is a confused one. In Wittgensteinian perspective, the atoning death of Christ, no less than the poor old scapegoat in
Leviticus, comes to be seen as "a false picture, similar to those that cause
errors in philosophy."

   There is a difference between detecting confusions in an idea and finding
an idea laughable. Though Wittgenstein thought that metaphysics was
confused, he never ridiculed it, and instead stressed constantly the depth of
metaphysical questions, remarking to Drury, for example, that he regarded
past philosophical systems as "among the noblest productions of the human
mind" (Drury 1984: 105). We might effect a similar move with regard to
the ritual actions and events under consideration here. Though confusions
may be present in scapegoat rituals, these ceremonies deal with such important

matters – guilt, death, forgiveness – that they never can appear ludicrous, they are never just mistakes. And this is surely true of the atonement. The idea that we are forgiven and that new life is held out to us *as the result of the death of a man*; that the shedding of blood has washed away our human guilt; and that great cathedrals have been built, great art and music composed, because of this event and our beliefs about it – is there not "something deep and sinister" at work here?[6] When we think of the crucifixion of Christ and the idea of atonement associated with it, our judgment might well echo Wittgenstein's haunting comment on the terrible death of the King of the Wood described in the opening pages of *The Golden Bough*: "This is what took place here; laugh if you can" (Wittgenstein 1979: 3).[7]

Notes

1 For an argument against both this expressivist interpretation of Wittgenstein's account of ritual and the adequacy of introspective hermeneutics, see Clack (1999).
2 Azazel seems originally to have referred to the place to which the scapegoat was sent, for the word means "jagged rocks, precipice" (Black and Rowley 1962: 248). Perhaps the scapegoat would have been driven over a precipice onto jagged rocks, taking the sins with it. Only later did the word come to refer to some demonic being (the tenth in order of the Fallen Angels, according to 1 Enoch), so it is wrong of D. Z. Phillips (1986: 29) to state so emphatically that Leviticus tells us how the scapegoat is "driven into the wilderness, the abode of Azazel, leader of the evil angels." Leviticus provides Phillips with no warrant for such an assertion and, at the very least, the scapegoat should not be regarded as a sacrifice offered to a being named Azazel.
3 It is worth noting the version of this remark quoted by Rhees (1982: 81): "The scapegoat, on which sins are laid and which goes out into the wilderness with them, is a false picture, like all the false pictures of philosophy. Philosophy might be said to purify thought from a misleading mythology."
4 In transcribing this passage, I have omitted all the variant expressions included in Wittgenstein's manuscript.
5 See Clack (1999: 107–34) for a fuller consideration of the connections Wittgenstein draws between magic and metaphysics.
6 Wittgenstein (1979: 16) detects "something deep and sinister" in the fire-festivals of Europe as these are described by Frazer.
7 I am grateful to Colin Crowder, Tom Hamilton, Jonathan Herapath, and Helen O'Sullivan for their helpful comments on an earlier version of this paper.

Bibliography

Baker, G. P. and Hacker, P. M. S. (1984) *Wittgenstein: Meaning and Understanding*, Oxford: Basil Blackwell.

Beattie, J. (1966) *Other Cultures*, London: Routledge & Kegan Paul.

Black, M. and Rowley, H. H. (1962) *Peake's Commentary on the Bible*, London: Thomas Nelson.

Clack, B. R. (1999) *Wittgenstein, Frazer and Religion*, London and Basingstoke: Macmillan.

Drury, M. O'C. (1973) *The Danger of Words*, London: Routledge and Kegan Paul.

—— (1984) "Conversations with Wittgenstein," in R. Rhees (ed.), *Recollections of Wittgenstein*, Oxford: Oxford University Press.

Frazer, J. G. (1913) *The Scapegoat* (volume 9 of *The Golden Bough*), London: Macmillan.

—— (1922) *The Golden Bough*, Abridged edn, London: Macmillan.

Lerner, B. D. (1994) "Wittgenstein's Scapegoat," *Philosophical Investigations* 17: 4.

Phillips, D. Z. (1986) *Belief, Change and Forms of Life*, London and Basingstoke: Macmillan.

—— (1988) *Faith after Foundationalism*, London: Routledge.

—— (1993) *Wittgenstein and Religion*, London and Basingstoke: Macmillan.

Pitkin, H. F. (1972) *Wittgenstein and Justice*, Berkeley: University of California Press.

Rhees, R. (1982) "Wittgenstein on Language and Ritual," in B. McGuinness (ed.), *Wittgenstein and His Times*, Oxford: Basil Blackwell.

Waismann, F. (1965) *The Principles of Linguistic Philosophy*, London: Macmillan.

Wittgenstein, L. (1958) *Philosophical Investigations*, Oxford: Basil Blackwell.

—— (1965) "A Lecture on Ethics," *Philosophical Review,* 74: 3–12.

—— (1966) *Lectures and Conversations on Aesthetics, Psychology and Religious Belief*, Oxford: Basil Blackwell.

—— (1969) *The Blue and Brown Books*, Oxford: Basil Blackwell.

—— (1979) *Remarks on Frazer's Golden Bough*, Doncaster: Brynmill Press.

—— (1993a) "Philosophy," in *Philosophical Occasions, 1912–1951*, Indianapolis: Hackett.

—— (1993b) "Remarks on Frazer's *Golden Bough*," in *Philosophical Occasions, 1912–1951*, Indianapolis: Hackett.

5 Ritual inquiry

The pragmatic logic of religious practice

Michael L. Raposa

I

The American philosopher, Charles S. Peirce, conceived and articulated a theory of inquiry that underscores the continuity between belief and conduct, while describing human reasoning in terms of the deliberate modification of habits, the exercise of a type of self-control. Here I explore the hypothesis that something like the logic of Peirce's pragmatism (or "pragmaticism" as he came to prefer) is embodied in various forms of ritual activity. Religious rituals are designed for no single purpose, serve multiple and sometimes widely disparate purposes. Nevertheless, they often consist of practices intended to inculcate, reinforce or transform specific beliefs and habits, and thereby to shape human conduct in deliberate ways.[1]

This exploration is limited to an initial foray; the full explication of such a hypothesis would require a much more extended analysis. I want, at least, to sketch a map of the territory, to mark those features of ritual activity that can readily be understood from a pragmatic perspective or be perceived as displaying pragmatic principles. The more playful aspects of ritual behavior, for example, both presuppose and stand in tension with the regular, redundant elements of ritual in a way that mirrors the relationship between abduction and induction in Peirce's logic. These same redundancies often facilitate religious insight, a phenomenon that might be illumined by the pragmatist's account of the efficacy of experimental method. Students of religious ritual have much to learn from Peirce's investigation of the interrelationship between attention, emotion, and habit formation. Moreover, Peirce's insistence that inquiry is an essentially communal activity may be relevant to the task of evaluating the significance of ritual performances for those religious communities that prescribe and sponsor them.

Within the context of pragmaticism, logic is best conceived as semiotic; that is, all human inquiry can be analyzed as a process of sign interpretation. Ritual, also, can be perceived as a symbolic process and the characteristic vagueness of its symbolism might best be understood in terms of the logical theory that Peirce supplied. That theory is doubly useful, suggesting not only how rituals might be interpreted, but also that ritual itself can be a complex form of interpretive behavior, neither mute nor pre-cognitive, but rather an eloquent expression of religious ideas and meanings.

II

From the perspective of pragmatism, a belief constitutes a program for action and is not to be regarded as some sort of abstract principle. Peirce's position differs from that of some of the other pragmatists in that, on his account, the meaning of any given belief is never completely determined by individual actions already performed. Rather, what a belief means is defined in terms of how one would be disposed to behave under specific circumstances, whether those circumstances obtain or not. In other words, a belief is a "rule" for action, a "habit" of conduct. In Peirce's view, "our beliefs guide our desires and shape our actions."[2] Their meaning is displayed in tendencies to feel or to act in certain ways, in general patterns of conduct. Nevertheless, for Peirce as for all of the pragmatists, the connection between thought and action, between belief and conduct, was an explicit one. To act deliberately in a manner consistent with one's beliefs represents the actual embodiment in conduct of specific rules of thought. In fact, the more well-entrenched a particular belief becomes, the less conscious one may be of its actual operation, despite its increased power as a disposition to produce observable behavioral effects.

What a person believes, then, is not likely to be revealed, episodically, in an isolated action or event. A person's genuine or "living" beliefs may only be discernible over time, through the observation of a whole series of events, allowing for the determination of a specific pattern of conduct. This is true, on Peirce's account, for a first-person as well as a third-person judgment about matters of belief. That is to say, I have no privileged access, through the power of introspection, to the beliefs that actually guide my desires and shape my actions.[3] It is possible for someone to convince me, for example, that I have sexist beliefs that I had previously denied possessing, or for me to come to the same sort of conclusion about myself, by means of a careful examination of my behavior, of the shape that it assumes under various relevant circumstances.

Now, much of religious ritual is characterized by the fact that some precise pattern of behavior is predetermined for those individuals who engage in its performance. Here the patterns that emerge seem less properly descriptive of what any given participant actually believes than prescriptive, specifying the sort of conduct that is appropriate. If the connection between belief and conduct is conceived as a weak one (or if the gap between thought and action is maintained to be wide), then the idea that prescribing conduct can also shape belief must lose a good deal of its force. But from the pragmatist's perspective, just the opposite is the case. Thought is embodied in action so that the deliberate shaping of conduct in ritual is designed to have a real effect on belief. Beliefs are habits for Peirce, and habits typically become entrenched over time. And so, to return to the example just presented, if I am not a sexist but I deliberately choose to behave in a consistently sexist fashion (perhaps because of peer pressure), then I certainly run the risk of transforming myself into one.

Consequently, one of the first contributions of the philosophy of pragmatism to a general understanding of ritual is the support that it lends to the critique of any theory of ritual as thoughtless action.[4] A number of historically prominent theories would fit this type, perhaps the most extreme examples being those psychoanalytic accounts that portray religious ritual as a form of neurotically compulsive behavior. This is not to deny that there might be a kind of activity for which such theories supply an adequate description. But not all or even most of religious ritual can be reduced to activity of that kind. A richer, more complex account is required. Ritual is less appropriately conceived as thoughtless action than as a thinking through and with the body. The gestures, movements, utterances, and other actions that comprise religious ritual represent a kind of deliberate behavior, one of the purposes of which is habit formation. To regard ritual as such is to conceive of it as a form of spiritual exercise. Moreover, these exercises are governed by a logic that Peirce's pragmatism can help to describe.

III

I want to suggest that religious ritual is very much about the way that human beings pay attention. Ritual organizes and directs the attention of its participants, supplying a distinctive frame for human experience.[5] At the same time, the repeated engagement in ritual activity can be a discipline of attention, allowing participants gradually to develop certain habits or powers of perception.

Peirce considered the formation of habits to be an essentially inductive process. In one of his earliest published articles, he concluded that "the formation of a habit is an induction, and is therefore necessarily connected with attention" (5.297). This observation is important not only because it describes habituation as a matter of induction, but also because that same process is characterized as being linked to specific acts of attention. Yet it is a potentially misleading characterization if it is taken to suggest that this relationship (between induction and attention) is an exclusive one. In fact, every form of conscious inference involves the exercise of attention, albeit in different ways. Peirce identified deduction with the act of attending selectively to one of the facts represented in a given premise, for purposes of explication; in this respect, deduction was to "be considered as the logical formula for paying attention" (2.643). Moreover, hypothetical or abductive reasoning is rooted in careful observation, a practiced attentiveness to phenomena as they appear. Induction is distinctive, then, not simply because the attention is engaged (since this is true in all forms of deliberation), but because of how it is directed in a special way to the similarities among things, leading to the establishment of certain habits of expectation.

Habits formed inductively play an important role in shaping the kind of thinking that occurs both in deductive and abductive reasoning. But it is the relationship between induction and abduction that seems especially crucial for an understanding of ritual.[6] The regular, redundant features of ritual behavior generate a whole pattern of expectations. These expectations have a complex function with respect to the religious objectives of ritual participants or of the sponsoring community. In part, such behavior is designed to be confirmatory, that is, to confirm by embodying in practice (gestures, utterances, etc.) those religious beliefs that are shared by members of the community. These may range from quite general perspectives on the nature of reality to beliefs that are of particular relevance to some special occasion or celebration. Here, induction is a process of strengthening belief-habits, perhaps of inculcating ("inducing") them in persons who are marginal to the community, for example, religious initiates or novices, young children, or the spiritually lukewarm.[7]

At the same time, the redundancies characteristic of much of ritual distinguish its performance sharply from the ordinary activities and experiences of participants. This "distancing" effect combines with a heightened sense of security (at least for persons practiced in the ritual, who have established comfortable habits of expectation about how the ritual unfolds) to produce an environment and a frame of mind conducive for play behavior, a "license" to play. Inductively established beliefs define the space and provide the rules for playing. Being unfamiliar with and nervous about the rules of a game can ruin a play experience. When these rules have become ingrained as second nature, however, even while their liveliness may be diminished to the point of slipping out of consciousness, their power to shape play behavior will increase proportionately. Repetitive behaviors require less and less attention from ritual participants, increasing the risk of boredom, but nevertheless liberating attention so that it can be directed in novel and creative ways. Redundancy can also effect a reduction in the level of "noise" in the environment, dramatically decreasing the risk of distraction (Raposa 1999: 105–35).

In his 1908 essay, "A Neglected Argument for the Reality of God," Peirce portrayed a type of abductive reasoning that takes the form of "pure play" or "musement" (6.452–93). The upshot of this discussion was Peirce's conclusion that, in certain instances, musement can "flower" into religious meditation, can acquire a religious significance. I am suggesting here that ritual represents an invitation to musement, and further, that it can guide the path of musement into distinctively religious territory. This is most likely to occur to the extent that the symbols employed and the beliefs embodied in ritual practices have powerful religious connotations (just as my cognitive play is more apt to become religiously meaningful when I am engaged in the meditative reading of a scriptural text than when I am enjoying a mystery novel). But there is no iron law of necessity determining that this must be the case; if there were, the kind of thinking that results could not be characterized as genuinely playful. Abductive inferences are never bound by the same laws of logical necessity that govern deduction. Rules or habits of thought are engaged in musement, brought "into play." In the process, they tend to be suggestive of certain related ideas and feelings, whether they operate as vague dispositions lurking just below the threshold of conscious thought or whether they themselves become the subject matter for playful inquiry. The carefully designed rubrics for ritual may gently influence how musement unfolds, but can never guarantee its precise course or results. That is why an hour spent in a church, temple, mosque, or synagogue can just as readily supply the environment for daydreaming about entirely secular matters as it can offer the occasion for lively religious reflection.

Peirce regarded belief-habits as constituting both the stopping place and starting point of inquiry (5.397). That is to say, beliefs are both the established result of inductive reasoning and the guiding premises for abductive inferences. Insofar as ritual displays the same pragmatic logic as scientific experimentation, it not only embodies and confirms particular religious beliefs, but also deploys them as rules for framing religiously meaningful play behavior. Now, experimentation can be characterized as both a test and a discipline. The scientist places hypotheses on trial in the laboratory, gathering evidence relevant to their verification or falsification. Continued testing will typically result in the formation of some reasonably secure beliefs. Subsequently, these beliefs will operate as powerful habits of thought to guide the scientist's inquiries concerning related phenomena, helping to mold a distinctive perspective. These habits represent a type of cognitive skill developed in the laboratory, a skill that facilitates scientific insight and discovery. Regarded as such, they are the fruits of experimentation conceived primarily as a discipline or exercise, rather than simply as a testing procedure.

There is an ongoing and often serendipitous experimentation with religious beliefs that occurs in the everyday activities of religious persons. Insofar as these beliefs determine actual conduct (in the making of moral choices, for example), actions deliberately undertaken with the expectation of achieving specific results (either in the short or long run), they are continuously being put to the test. Religious ritual represents a special type of conduct and so a special kind of test. The prescribed ritual drama supplies the opportunity for participants to experiment with a variety of thoughts and feelings. The repetitive elements in ritual allow participants to test the same ideas and emotions under conditions that remain relatively stable over time, or playfully to substitute alternatives, trying out or "trying on" other possibilities. Repeated engagement in ritual behavior can result in the acquisition of skill, comparable to that developed in laboratory investigation, the sort of skill that generates religious awareness and insight.

Experimental and ritual situations are both distinguished from ordinary experience by their artificial quality, the highly artful abstracting of particular beliefs and behaviors for emphasis, along with the deliberate suppressing of a massive variety of information deemed irrelevant for present purposes. Ritual selects from an infinite number of possible actions only those few that fit the pattern it supplies or might be regarded as necessary for producing its intended effects. Such action is circumscribed by ritual space, its duration measured in ritual time. Within this ritual framework, attention is directed to particular objects of contemplation rather than being allowed to wander uncontrolled and vulnerable to capture by whatever happens to arouse interest. It is for this reason, once again, that ritual can be appropriately characterized as a strategy for paying attention, a type of practice that consists both in the organizing and the exercising of attention.

IV

Attention increases the "subjectivity intensity" or "liveliness" of our awareness of a thing (7.396ff., 7.555). In Peirce's view, "objectivity intensity" is the characteristic of a phenomenon that tends to capture our interest *willy nilly*. A loud noise, a brilliant flash of light, a violent altercation – these are all the sorts of things that tend to intrude on consciousness and demand attention. On the other hand, our interest in anything can be increased simply by the deliberate act of our choosing to pay attention to it. The same is true for phenomena imagined or remembered rather than presently experienced. Peirce noted that not only will a thought be "remembered for a longer time the greater the attention originally paid to it," but additionally that "by attention a thought may be recovered which has been forgotten" (5.295).

This increase in subjective intensity is temporary since an idea, as soon as it becomes the object of attention, begins to suggest other, related ideas. The original idea will either drop out of consciousness altogether as it is replaced by these related notions or the awareness of it will be gradually diminished as it becomes linked to complex sets of ideas in a process of generalization (7.398). This loss of liveliness is compensated for by an increase in the power of such complex sets to excite reactions and bring new ideas to the center of attention (6.104ff.). Once again, inductively established habits, themselves the product of deliberate acts of attention, can be conceived as capacities for channeling the attention in new directions, generating fresh insight.

Peirce observed that "attention is roused when the same phenomenon presents itself repeatedly on different occasions" (5.296). The redundant elements of ritual direct attention in just this fashion. But ritual action embodies a great variety of framing strategies, using gesture and song, for example, to mark off certain elements of experience as being of special significance. Objective and subjective intensity, on Peirce's account, typically correspond to one another. That is why a sharp whistle or loud clap of the hands is a generally effective means for attracting attention. Yet they need not always correspond, so that a person deeply immersed in some train of thought might very well fail to hear a loud noise and later be unable to recall its occurrence.

Peirce explained that subjectively intense thoughts are most especially subject to self-control. Precisely as the objects of our attention, their combinations and transformations are more readily affected by volition.

> The action of thought is all the time going on, not merely in that part of consciousness which thrusts itself on the attention and is most under discipline, but also in its deeply shaded parts, of which we are in some measure conscious but not sufficiently so to be strongly affected by what is there. But when in the uncontrolled play of that part of thought, an

interesting combination occurs, its subjective intensity increases for a short time with great rapidity. This is what constitutes the fixation of attention. Contemplation consists in using our self-control to remove us from the forcible intrusion of other thoughts, and in considering the interesting bearings of what may lie hidden in the icon, so as to cause the subjective intensity of it to increase.

(7.555)

The strategy of much of religious ritual is "to remove us from the forcible intrusion of other thoughts" and so to bring consciousness "under discipline." To observe this strategy is not suddenly to deny the playful quality of much ritual behavior. Although the distinction is a subtle one, it was important for Peirce to distinguish between the activity of musement as he prescribed it in the Neglected Argument and any state of mind that could be characterized as "dreaminess" (6.458). The relevant distinction here is not between non-playful and playful behavior, but between a form of cognitive play that is self-controlled and one that is largely uncontrolled or undisciplined. Self-control implies that the attention is engaged in such a fashion as eventually to result in the formation of a habit, thus shaping subsequent behavior. Such control does not require that the object of attention must be determined rigidly in advance. It implies, rather, the necessity of achieving a certain state of mindfulness; the muser will always have "eyes open, awake to what is about or within." This is what it means to exercise one's freedom on Peirce's view.[8] The act of choosing deliberately the objects and the quality of one's attention in the present moment has a gentle but powerful influence (by means of a process of habit formation) over future versions of the self, gradually transforming beliefs and inclinations. Precisely because self-transformation is gradual, freedom is something both realized and manifested in the Peircean "long run."

Clearly, ritual is a discipline of self-transformation, as well as an act of confirmation. Such is the logic of all inquiry, as new beliefs and perspectives can only be established against the background supplied by those commitments and dispositions that remain secure. (For the pragmatists, evolution rather than revolution served as the primary model for understanding human inquiry.)

The analogy between ritual and inquiry may appear problematic to anyone who rightly perceives the former as being something other than a purely intellectual exercise. Ritual engages the body as well as and sometimes more decisively than the mind. The most powerful effects of religious ritual may be experienced primarily as emotional rather than intellectual. Within the context of Peirce's pragmaticism (and his objective idealism), however, these kinds of sharp distinctions or dichotomies (mind/body or thought/feeling) lose some of their typical force. Feelings *are* vague thoughts on his account and physical movements, insofar as they are meaningful, represent thoughts embodied in and thus signified by actions. The logic of induction can be physiologically explicated in terms of habit formation. And the logic of abduction supplied the basis for Peirce's understanding of emotion as a peculiar form of cognition:

Hypothesis substitutes, for a complicated tangle of predicates attached to one subject, a single conception. Now, there is a peculiar sensation belonging to the act of thinking that each of these predicates inheres in the subject. In hypothetic inference this complicated feeling so produced is replaced by a single feeling of greater intensity, that belonging to the act of thinking the hypothetic conclusion ... which I call an emotion. Thus, the various sounds made by the instruments of an orchestra strike upon the ear, and the result is a peculiar musical emotion, quite distinct from the sounds themselves. This emotion is essentially the same thing as an hypothetic inference, and every hypothetic inference involves the formation of such an emotion. We may say, therefore, that hypothesis produces the *sensuous* element of thought, and induction the *habitual* element.

(2.643)

Hypothetical or abductive inferences range from the most complex acts of judgment involved in the classification of phenomena to the simplest acts of perceiving "x as y." In every such case, inference is a matter of paying attention. Attention increases the subjective intensity of our awareness of a thing, that is, raises our interest.

Everything in which we take the least interest creates in us its own particular emotion. This emotion is a sign and a predicate of the thing. Now, when a thing resembling this thing is presented to us, a similar emotion arises; hence, we immediately infer that the latter is like the former.

(5.308)

Here, Peirce's technical discussion of the interdependence of induction and abduction as forms of logical inference (or as "stages of inquiry") has been translated into a new idiom, one describing the dialectical interplay of habit and emotion. Emotion is governed by the same logic that shapes acts of recognition or the generation of fresh insight. Habit is a product of the same redundant patterns that ground the inductive formulation of general rules of thought. The latter supplies a grid or a pattern for the former, as the attaching of a predicate to something is a process always gently "ruled" by existing beliefs about the typical characteristics of things of that kind. But it is the act of paying attention, in each case, that determines the extent to which these processes can be portrayed as deliberate or self-controlled.

Since self-control was understood by Peirce to operate primarily at a distance, as volition exerted over future conduct, the tangible effects of ritual behavior cannot be measured simply in terms of actions, emotions, or insights that occur within the immediate context of the ritual itself. Both the redundant and the playful behaviors that constitute ritual action are a form of training or practice, an exercise in the gradual development of certain capacities. The extended testing of those capacities may occur in various locations, not only in ritual space, but also in the perceptions and choices that color our everyday experience of the world. Scientific testing takes place in the laboratory, but observations and experiences bearing on the results of such inquiry can occur in a great variety of settings and situations. In addition, these results can have a broad practical significance when applied to problems and activities outside of the laboratory. Similarly, the testing of religious belief in ritual is a process that can be extended beyond the ritual domain. Insofar as ritual is transformative, it is designed to have a real effect on the future conduct and experiences of practitioners, not only or even primarily in the narrowly circumscribed arena of ritual itself.

This emphasis on the future is linked to another feature of pragmatism, salient among those characteristics that explain its relevance to the task of understanding religious ritual. Within the context of pragmatism, the "self" is conceived as social, essentially, rather than accidentally inter-subjective in character and constitution.[9] Peirce's careful analysis of the logic of scientific inquiry exposed the fact that such inquiry is a communal activity. Those observations and experiences bearing on the results of inquiry or shaping its future development, need not be *my* experiences. Nor do my experiences have any particular scientific value if they cannot be duplicated numerous times by numerous others. Peirce consistently argued that "logic is rooted in the social principle" and he was blithe to describe that logic, at least on some occasions, in distinctively theological terms (2.654–5).

The primary locus of ritual's transformative effects has been identified here as the individual person's habits or capacities and these effects accumulate over time. For Peirce, "our power of self-control certainly does not result in the smallest bits of our conduct, but is an effect of building up a character" (4.611). Now, not only are the ritual practices that shape character typically public and social, but even rituals designed for private practice, exercises in solitude, are communal in origin, often prescribed by communal authorities. Moreover, the habits inculcated in ritual are social in their consequences as well as in their origin. That is to say, they are frequently intended to strengthen the bonds of "communitas," to foster an awareness of the level and significance of one's relationship to others that extends powerfully beyond a more mundane recognition of basic social connections and responsibilities.[10]

The ritual community exists in time. It has a communal memory formed in the repeated acts of attention directed by members to significant episodes in its sacred history. Ritual participants develop the capacity to extend in memory and in hope their bonds of connectedness to various individuals and events, many located in an ancient past or a distant future that they as individuals have never experienced. Nevertheless, the meaning of their own lived experience is in great measure shaped by this sacred past and future, in much the same way that any given scientific experiment presupposes a complex history of investigation and defines its immediate purpose in terms of inquiry's long-term objectives. Habits of conduct fueled by narrowly egoistic impulses are as infelicitous for the purposes of religious ritual as they are ineffective in the laboratory. Ritual may be all about the self, about "building up a character," about how the self deliberately directs its attention and shapes its capacities. But the logic that it embodies is a logic of relations and of self-transcendence, in such respects directly comparable to, if not identical with, the logic of Peirce's pragmatism.

V

The territory being surveyed here is vaster than these remarks can suggest, the domain of religious ritual more complex and its logic frequently a bit more convoluted. I can only gesture toward further regions of this territory, pointing out some important landmarks at a distance but not offering here the close inspection that they deserve. These correspond to philosophical terrain that Peirce himself did explore with great care and in considerable detail, so that the groundwork has at least been laid for the application of his researches to the problem of religious ritual. I refer in particular, first, to Peirce's formulation of a theory of logic as semiotic and, second, to the potential understanding of ritual as a complex process of semiosis.

The assertion that ritual is a symbolic process, incorporating a great variety of different kinds of signs in its performance, seems relatively commonplace even if not altogether unproblematic.[11] The special contribution of pragmatism to an understanding of ritual symbolism consists, once again, in its explication of the logic that governs such a process. In the first place, that logic is especially well-equipped, at least in Peirce's articulation of it, for the task of evaluating the inherent vagueness of religious symbols. On Peirce's account, every sign is necessarily vague to a greater or lesser extent, "leaving its interpretation more or less indeterminate" (5.505). Something is determinate only with respect to those characters that can be predicated of it universally; in every other respect, it is indeterminate. Peirce argued that no sign can be completely determinate in all respects, so that perfect precision in the use of signs is impossible. In every communication, some level of vagueness will invariably persist, not least of all "because no man's interpretation of words is based on exactly the same experience as any other man's" (5.506).

Such considerations enable a preliminary mapping of those characteristics of religious symbolism that might usefully be understood in the terms established by Peirce's logic of vagueness. In the first place, religious symbols are sufficiently vague so as gently to shape but not completely to determine their possible interpretations. This creates an opportunity for the kind of play behavior frequently observed in ritual contexts. Symbols marked by a high degree of precision, like those utilized in performing certain mathematical calculations or giving carefully detailed practical instructions, direct the attention of the interpreter to a radically delimited field of possible meanings. As already noted, the power of attention is also deliberately engaged in the sort of abductive reasoning embodied in ritual play; but here the range of candidate interpretations is not rigidly determined, so that the ritual participants can play with a variety of alternative possibilities, in effect, experimenting with them.

Peirce conceived of the vague as that to which the principle of contradiction does not apply. "For it is false neither that an animal (in a vague sense) is male, nor that an animal is female" (5.505). The vagueness of religious symbolism, then, is a factor that might help to explain not only the ludic but also the "liminal" quality of much ritual behavior.

Liminal entities are neither here nor there; they are betwixt and between the positions assigned and arrayed by law, custom, convention, and ceremonial. As such, their ambiguous and indeterminate attributes are expressed by a rich variety of symbols in the many societies that ritualize social and cultural transitions. Thus, liminality is frequently likened to death, to being in the womb, to invisibility, to darkness, to bisexuality, to the wilderness, and to an eclipse of the sun or moon.

(Turner 1969: 95)

Recall that emotions are also hypotheses from a Peircean perspective, thought-signs that are distinguished by their high degree of vagueness. It should not be surprising to observe, then, that the typical response to religious symbols often consists in emotions rather than more determinate cognitions. Indeed, what participants actually feel when they engage in ritual behavior is a significant part of their *interpretation* of what the ritual means. These interpretations may not, in any given case, be neatly translatable into words, unless it be the sort of figurative language characteristic of poetry or the lyrics in song. Every interpretation, on Peirce's view, is of the nature of a sign, thus itself subject to further interpretation (and determination). But interpretations can be rendered excessively precise to a point where they distort the meaning of their objects. If this were not a real danger, then poems, songs, and ritual performances could all be replaced, without the risk of loss of meaning, by analytical accounts of their significance. Kissing or embracing would never be more powerfully symbolic than a simple verbal declaration of one's affection. And such verbal declarations would serve as perfectly adequate representations of the very deepest feelings of love, awe, or fear.

Insofar as religious ritual can be portrayed as a deliberate form of spiritual practice, its objective will not be to elicit from participants random emotions or flashes of feeling, but rather, to cultivate certain habits of thought and feeling, as well as of conduct. The real meaning of any sign, for Peirce, always consisted in such a habit, the sign's "logical interpretant."[12] "Moreover ... every man [*sic*] exercises more or less control over himself by means of modifying his own habits." Ritual semiosis, as a self-controlled process, involves the continuous production of signs. Every act of interpretation is also the creation of a new sign. Meaning is constantly being deferred to the future, to be embodied in a subsequent sign, to be revealed in an emerging pattern of significance. This is another way of pointing out that rituals are designed not only for the strengthening or confirmation of beliefs, but for the ongoing task of renewal and self-transformation.

VI

Ritual action is neither thoughtless nor simply a vehicle for the expression or communication of ideas. Rather, ritual is itself a type of inquiry, a kind of thinking embodied in conduct, behavior that can be conceived as a deliberate process of semiosis. I have not argued that this is the only correct way to understand ritual behavior. But the obvious objection to such an argument would consist in the claim that ritual participants are doing much more than thinking or inquiring when they engage in ritual activity, that their practices are not solely or even primarily intellectual exercises. And this objection could be construed as damaging to the account of ritual articulated here even in the absence of arguments for its exclusive truth or adequacy. Such an account would seem, at best, to offer a highly distorted picture of what religious ritual is all about.

The force of such an objection is compelling only to the extent that one ignores or repudiates the theory of inquiry defended by Peirce and other pragmatists. That is to say, understanding ritual *as* inquiry already presupposes a dramatic transformation of commonplace perspectives on thought and thinking. It requires that one employ the generously expanded sense of what it means to "engage in inquiry" or to "give an interpretation" that Peirce's philosophy supplies. On his account, inquiry is a deliberate process of habit formation and habits are signs that can be embodied in patterns of feeling and conduct, as well as formulated in speech as beliefs.

It may be useful to conclude my sketch of the pragmatic logic of ritual with the very brief consideration of an example. The Roman Catholic liturgical celebration of the Mass is a practice that is perceived to be central in its significance to the spiritual lives of Catholic Christians; it is also a practice complex enough to embody many of the features that are regarded by scholars as characteristic of religious ritual. At the same time, the Mass would not commonly be described – by participants, by theologians, or by scholars of religion – as constituting a type or form of *inquiry*, so that the example chosen is not immediately biased in favor of the account that I have supplied.

One readily observable feature of the Mass is the element of redundancy that is incorporated into its practice. While allowing for some variation – in biblical texts read, prayers said, hymns sung, color of priestly vestments worn, etc. – there is nevertheless a remarkable continuity, both throughout history and across a diverse geographical terrain, in the nature of its performance. The basic structure of the Mass is fixed, organized around the twin foci supplied by the scripture and by the Eucharist. Its entire framework is designed to focus the *attention* of participants, first on the word preached and then on the bread and wine consumed. Beliefs about the special significance of these elements of the ritual are embodied in the prescribed behavior of the ritual participants: they preface the reading of the gospel with the *singing* of an alleluia; they *stand* attentively as it is being read; they *kneel* in adoration at the consecration of the Eucharist, etc. This behavior is repeated during every celebration of the Mass so as to become habitual. It is an essentially inductive process of the sort that Peirce described as being involved in the formation of any habit through repeated acts of attention. Even many of the variations in liturgical practice are designed for the purpose of establishing or strengthening belief-habits, as the changes themselves are rule-governed rather than purely random, reflecting significant patterns in the liturgical calendar, for example, the movement from "ordinary time" into special seasons like Advent and Lent.

This observation of redundancies should not obscure but rather helps to expose the fact that the celebration of the Mass is intended to be precisely that, a communal "celebration"; the spirit of the Mass is essentially playful.[13] (I do not intend this to be an accurate description of the actual attitudes and behavior of all participants in the Mass on every occasion of its performance; for any number of reasons such participants might be bored and disinterested rather than fully engaged and playful.) Like the rules of a game, the liturgical rubrics create an appropriate framework for play behavior. The Mass unfolds within the sacred space around the altar, in a place (church) especially designated for such activity. Its beginning and end are clearly marked by precise ritual gestures and utterances. The regularities and redundancies in the Mass, both distinguish its performance from other, "ordinary" activities and establish a meaningful form as well as parameters for play. This ludic activity might consist in the sort of cognitive play that characterizes the meditative listening to a scriptural reading or a homily; in the raising of voices together in prayer or song; in the play of images and emotions that arise in the felt encounter with a sacred presence or in interaction with other persons in the ritual community.

Such play behavior is "abductive" even to the extent that it is manifested in physical movement or in emotion rather than in the precise verbal articulation of some hypothesis. Feelings of love or awe or gratitude, within the context of the ritual action, can all be construed as part of the interpretation of what that ritual means. The "taking and eating" of the Eucharistic bread, or the gesturing with arms outstretched in acts of praise and thanksgiving, are physical signs that represent a kind of thinking through and with the body.[14] Meaning is a complex semiotic phenomenon. No mere act of taking, eating, or gesturing is in itself necessarily meaningful, just as explicitly sexual acts need not signify genuine relations or feelings of love. Yet neither are the gestures or acts irrelevant to the generation of meaning in semiosis, as if the meaning were something entirely extrinsic, attached to them like a code.

Inquiry is typically understood as a deliberate, purposeful activity. Religious ritual has been characterized here as just such a deliberate activity, designed for the purpose of transforming habits and capacities, shaping human conduct in the long run. And this portrayal of ritual as purposeful may seem to contrast somewhat with the identification of the spirit of the Mass as playful. Precisely as play behavior, the liturgy has no ends beyond itself, is not a form of "training" for anything in particular.[15] Indeed, to paraphrase Peirce's prescription for musement in the Neglected Argument, its only purpose is the temporary casting aside of all of those purposes that typically dominate our practical lives.

Despite the nature of Peirce's prescription, he regarded musement as a form of abduction, continuous with other modes or types of human inquiry. Moreover, the cognitive dispositions potentially developed in musement were perceived by Peirce as facilitating religious insight, so that musement can be considered both as an experiment and as a kind of training or practice.[16] The key to resolving this apparent contradiction, I would suggest, is Peirce's idea of a "developmental teleology"; "this teleology is more than a mere purposive pursuit of a predeterminate end" (6.156). That is to say, any activity that is guided by the purpose of "casting aside all specific purposes" is still to be considered, in a vague but nevertheless important sense, as *purposeful*. Such an activity involves the cultivation of a certain habit of disinterestedness or of detachment, similar to the sort of disposition required of anyone who wishes to enter into the spirit of play. It is not that play is an activity completely without purpose, but rather, that it is bound in advance to no particular end.

It was in just this fashion that Peirce understood the spirit of all genuine inquiry, a type of activity that achieves its end "without directly striving for it." The fruits of inquiry are not defined by any individual, not to be considered as *mine* or limited to that toward which my "endeavors are directed"; rather, they consist in the "achievement of the whole people." Recall Peirce's insistence that the sole principle of logic was "social" and that inquiry was an essentially communal activity. Interestingly, it was not the Mass or any other specific religious ritual, but inquiry in general that Peirce was describing when he wrote about a process by means of which persons become "gradually more and more imbued with the Spirit of God" (5.402 note 2). Yet participation in the Mass, like all inquiry, involves the deliberate but gradual shaping of various capacities, prominent among them, a certain habit of detachment. This habit is developed, for example, in the continuous fostering through practice of an attitude of receptivity (arms outstretched) to whatever might occur and, correspondingly, a sense of gratitude (in the taking and eating of the bread) for gifts as they are received. Here, again, meaning is constantly being deferred to the future, something awaited rather than simply achieved, and something always shared rather than the product of any one person's deliberations.

Notes

1 I am not articulating a "theory of ritual" in this paper of any sort that proposes the application of a single conception to all ritual performances. It is sufficient for my purposes to be able to make the more modest case that *some* religious rituals can be portrayed as forms of inquiry, usefully described as embodying a pragmatic logic of inquiry.

2 Charles S. Peirce, from his famous 1877 essay on "The Fixation of Belief." See Peirce (1935–58, volume 5, paragraph 371) (subsequent references to Peirce's eight volume *Collected Papers* will be abbreviated in the conventional form, e.g. "5.371").

3 For Peirce's critique of claims alleging any such powers of intuition or introspection, see his early article on "Questions Concerning Certain Faculties Claimed for Man" (5.213–63).

4 Catherine Bell supplies an extended discussion of various theoretical attempts to construe ritual in terms of a sharp dichotomy between thought and action (1992).

5 As general background for this claim, consult Goffman (1974).

6 On the relationship between induction and abduction in Peirce's thought, see Raposa (1989: 134ff). and Raposa (1999: 144–48, 156–59).

7 Consider Pascal's brilliant meditations on the relationship between habit and conversion, in Pascal (1966: 152–3 and 274–6).

8 Here Peirce agreed with his good friend William James that freedom is a matter of the deliberate control of one's power of attention. See my discussion of both pragmatists in the final chapter of Raposa (2003).

9 This is certainly true for Peirce's pragmatism, and for other thinkers partially influenced by him, particularly John Dewey and George Herbert Mead.
10 Review Victor Turner's development of the idea of "communitas" in Turner (1969), especially ch. 3.
11 Not every theorist of ritual would agree that ritual behavior ought to be construed as symbolic behavior. See, for example, Staal (1975).
12 On habits as logical interpretants, see the account in Peirce 5.470ff., including his definition of "semiosis" in 5.484, and his portrayal of semiosis as self-controlled in 5.487.
13 Perhaps the two most influential theological meditations on the playfulness of the liturgy are Guardini (1998), especially chapter five on "The Playfulness of the Liturgy," and Rahner (1967). Johan Huizinga referred to and developed Guardini's insights about the liturgy in his own classic, Huizinga (1955: 19).
14 For two very different but equally interesting perspectives on the meaning of bodily gesture in ritual performance, consider Erik Erikson's extraordinary insights linking children's play to ritual behavior among adults, in Erikson (1977), and Joseph Ratzinger's theological explication of the meaning of postures and gestures in the liturgy, in Ratzinger (2000: 184–207).
15 Guardini makes such a claim explicitly (1998: 65–6), contrasting the Mass in this regard with the goal directed practice of St Ignatius of Loyola's spiritual exercises. But Ratzinger, in his own work bearing the same title, is not reluctant to identify the liturgy as a form of *askesis*, a "training for love, a training to help us accept the Wholly Other, to be shaped and used by him" (176).
16 On musement as both an "experiment" and a type of spiritual practice, see Raposa 1989: 134–41.

Bibliography

Bell, C. (1992) *Ritual Theory, Ritual Practice*, New York: Oxford University Press.

Erikson, E. (1977) *Toys and Reasons: Stages in the Ritualization of Experience*, New York: W. W. Norton & Co.

Goffman, E. (1974) *Frame Analysis: An Essay on the Organization of Human Experience*, New York: Harper & Row.

Guardini, R. (1998) *The Spirit of the Liturgy*, trans. A. Lane, New York: The Crossroad Publishing Company.

Huizinga, J. (1955) *Homo Ludens: A Study of the Play Element in Culture*, Boston: Beacon Press.

Pascal, B. (1966) *Pensées*, trans. A. J. Krailsheimer, Baltimore: Penguin Books.

Peirce, C. S. (1935–58) *Collected Papers of Charles Sanders Peirce*, (eds) C. Hartshorne, P. Weiss, and A. Burks, Cambridge, MA: Harvard University Press.

Rahner, H. (1967) *Man At Play*, New York: Herder and Herder.

Raposa, M. (1989) *Peirce's Philosophy of Religion*, Bloomington: Indiana University Press.

—— (1999) *Boredom and The Religious Imagination*, Charlottesville: University Press of Virginia.

—— (2003) *Meditation and the Martial Arts*, Charlottesville: University of Virginia Press.

Ratzinger, J. (2000) *The Spirit of the Liturgy*, San Francisco: Ignatius Press.

Staal, F. (1975) "The Meaninglessness of Ritual," *Numen* 26: 2–22.

Turner, V. (1969) *The Ritual Process: Structure and Anti-Structure*, Ithaca, NY: Cornell University Press.

6 Ritual metaphysics

Kevin Schilbrack

I. Introduction

Clifford Geertz famously defines religion as a system of symbols that functions to unite a certain way of life or ethos with a certain world view or metaphysics (1973: 87–141). In his view, religion by definition involves metaphysics, its understanding of the structure of reality. Moreover, of the different features in any religion, Geertz says that it is primarily ritual that instills in religious people how their recommended way of life is connected to the way things are.

> It is in some sort of ceremonial form – even if that form be hardly more than the recitation of a myth, the consultation of an oracle, or the decoration of a grave – that the moods and motivations which sacred symbols induce in [people] and the general conceptions of the order of existence which they formulate for [people] meet and reinforce one another. In a ritual, the world as lived and the world as imagined fused under the agency of a single set of symbolic forms, turn out to be the same world.
>
> (1973: 112)

I find Geertz's metaphysical interpretation of rituals valuable as a starting place for thinking about a philosophy of ritual because it explicitly ties ritual not merely to a people's understanding of its social environment, but also to its understanding of an even more inclusive environment, reality itself.[1] "Metaphysics" is a term that is often used in divergent or even incompatible ways, and some deny that any form of metaphysics is intelligible. But if one takes metaphysics in the roughly Aristotelian sense, as Geertz and I do, as inquiry into the generic or necessary features of human existence, then one has a definition of metaphysics that is, I contend, both defensible and fruitful.[2] Studies of religious rituals, however, do not always give attention to metaphysics. The real subject matter of ritual, it is often said, is not reality as such but one's social or political categorization. This turn from metaphysics is a widespread trend with deep philosophical roots. I am persuaded by the recent text by Nancy Frankenberry and Hans Penner who argue that twentieth-century studies of religion operate under the legacy of positivism (Frankenberry and Penner 1999). They argue that though the positivists' identification of meaningfulness with verifiability and their rejection of metaphysics have been discredited in principle, they continue to be presupposed by those theories of religion (and I would add by those theories of ritual) that envision no way in which religious metaphysical views about the nature of things might be meaningful. Many accounts of ritual therefore proceed as if a religion's metaphysics is not relevant to what people are up to in their rituals. In this context, it is worth noting that in his own analyses of religious rituals (as opposed to his definition), Geertz himself largely ignores metaphysics. As Henry Munson has shown, Geertz in his analyses of cases tends to reduce religion to the overt appearance of behavior and personality traits – that is, to a culture's style or ethos – and to give inadequate attention to how practices are informed by a worldview (Munson 1986). So perhaps even Geertz hesitates to speak of religious metaphysics in this era of what Jürgen Habermas calls postmetaphysical thinking. The question that inspires this paper, then, is this: if one were to pursue an interpretation of ritual that included metaphysics, what would it look like?

Pursuing this question reflects my view that the discipline of philosophy of religion ought to include philosophical reflection not only on religious beliefs, its traditional focus, but also on the other features of religion as it is lived. Such growth will require philosophers to develop the tools for reflection on religious storytelling, sacrifice, pilgrimage, spiritual discipline, rites of passage, and other religious practices. This paper seeks to contribute to this project by tracing two lines of development in recent conversations regarding the body and suggesting how philosophers of religion might contribute to them and thereby to the study of rituals. My proposal consequently has two complementary parts, which I have subtitled "ritual bodies as philosophical objects" and "ritual bodies as philosophical subjects." I close with a discussion of what it means to speak of metaphysics as embodied, so that those interested in this dimension of ritual action do not assume that speculative thinking is limited to what goes on in texts or in minds.

II. Ritual bodies as philosophical objects

The study of religion, like the study of culture generally, has for the most part ignored the body and has treated religious meanings as the product of minds. When the body was present at all, it has usually been as a natural body, a body without history or culture. Nevertheless, there is a tradition in social theory and philosophy, increasingly sophisticated over the twentieth century, and pouring forth like water from a fire hose in the last generation, which sees the body as a social construction and therefore as an important medium of expression (for overviews, see Shilling 1993: ch. 4; Turner 1996).

The different approaches that have been labeled social constructionist – for example, those of Marcel Mauss, Mary Douglas, Erving Goffman, Pierre Bourdieu, and Michel Foucault – espouse a variety of positions on the relation of the body to its social meanings. Douglas, for example, interprets the body as a vehicle for social symbolism, whereas Foucault argues more radically that the body is an effect of discourse. But if one may generalize, the social constructionist tradition rejects the idea that anatomy is destiny and provides tools for understanding the meanings of body parts, sensations, and activities as the products of specific social forces. Here bodies are systems of signs that stand for or express social relations. Consequently, engagement with this tradition gives one the possibility of seeing a religious ritual as an act of social inscription, as writing on bodies.

Where does metaphysics fit on this approach? Sometimes, it doesn't. Sometimes, the social constructionist view seems to be that if the body itself is a social construction, culturally and historically variant, then all bodily knowledge is local knowledge, and there is no place left for metaphysical claims that allege to be true "always and everywhere." But such an argument is flimsy. Just because the speaker comes from a particular cultural and linguistic context, it does not follow that what she is talking about is also local. Thus, given the value of the work that social constructionists have done to show the ways in which bodies are culturally inscribed, here is an important but rarely asked question which one might ask: what can these cultural inscriptions be *about*? In other words, if the body is a text, what is the subject matter of that text? When one asks this question, one sees that the overwhelming tendency has been to study how bodies are inscribed with social or political categories. As Edmund Leach says in a classical statement of this view, "rituals are to be understood as forms of symbolic statement about the social order" (1954: 62). Roy Rappaport summarizes: "one of the important functionalist theories of ritual is based upon ... an assumption of empirical independence between ritual and the world external to the congregation" (1984: 2). Such approaches tend to study, above all, the means by which race, gender, and class are socially constructed and inscribed on people's bodies.[3] As a consequence, when social constructionist approaches have focused on religious rituals and practices, the focus has primarily been on how religion legitimates social categories, and rarely on the religion's metaphysical speculations. Relatively little attention has been given to how bodies are inscribed with a religion's "most comprehensive ideas."

If one is interested in seeing how ritual practices are informed by a metaphysical ideology, then one ought to make a distinction between two kinds of markings that rituals and other cultural practices might seek to inscribe on the body. First, rituals can seek to inscribe the marks of *contingent* characteristics. Contingent characteristics are those that one may or may not exhibit, characteristics that permit of an alternative. For example, some rituals may aim explicitly to mark their participants as adult and no longer children, dead and no longer among the living, or married and no longer single. And such rituals may at the same time aim tacitly to mark the participants with other contingent characteristics of identity and social location: as masculine (as opposed to feminine), heterosexual (as opposed to homosexual), African American (as opposed to Caucasian), Catholic, American, healthy, bourgeois, or sexy, and so on, as opposed to their alternatives. All these inscriptions mark one as a member of one class rather than another and so by definition these inscriptions refer to contingent characteristics. Yet it is also possible that a ritual might seek to inscribe marks or inculcate attributes that represent what are taken to be *necessary* characteristics. Necessary characteristics would be characteristics that a person cannot fail to exhibit, characteristics that apply to human existence as such and which therefore do not permit of an alternative.[4] To present or to acknowledge such bodily characteristics through a ritual would be to present or acknowledge features that those inscribed share in some way with every other human being, or every other sentient being, or perhaps even everything else that exists. Insofar as a ritual seeks to inscribe this kind of mark, it makes sense to speak of the inscription of ritual metaphysics.[5]

Making this distinction between contingent and necessary marks permits one to see rituals as a process through which a religion makes their most abstract teachings concrete, giving facticity to their ideology. It is true that if a characteristic really is a necessary feature of the human condition, then an individual is always already characterized by it; one would be characterized by it, that is, even before inscription. For this reason, one can expect that such rituals will not present themselves as *making* people X nor training them to *become* X, but will present themselves rather as training people to "realize" or "acknowledge" that they are X. Ritual leaders may assert that though one falsely believes or appears to be Y, one's "true self" is X. But the goal in any case is to provide visible, tactile instantiation to teachings that might otherwise seem merely conceptual. The goal is to have the ritual participants perceive metaphysical truths "in the flesh." Such metaphysical knowledge, inscribed on bodies through ritual, is also practical knowledge. This ritual knowledge of reality is used to shape conduct, to get people to act "properly," as "we" act, as "true humans" act, or as the Gods act. In this way, ritual metaphysics is used to alienate a range of possible behaviors as not in accord with ultimate reality, and thereby to fabricate *authentic* human beings, authentic in the sense that their behavior is authorized by the very nature of things.

Consider an example. In the *Satipaṭṭhāna Sutta*, the Buddha recommends the practice of cremation ground meditation or contemplation of foulness (*asubhāvanā*). In order to develop mindfulness of the repulsiveness of the body, the monk might visit cremation grounds and contemplate the corpses decomposing there. The Buddha advises that the monk who engages in this form of meditation should explicitly think to himself that his own body has the same nature as that dead body, that it will become the same as that dead body. One is studying one's own inescapable end. In *The Path of Purification*, his encyclopedic commentary on the Theravāda path, Buddhaghosa provides a detailed discussion of how to prepare for and carry out this method of meditation (Buddhaghosa 1976: 185–203). The monk should first find a teacher who can explain the method: how to approach the cremation grounds, how to be attentive to what surrounds the corpse, and how to apprehend and absorb what one sees. The monk should inform a senior elder of the Community, but then should go to the cemetery alone. Buddhaghosa describes in some detail the different kinds of bodies: lucky the monk who finds a bloated corpse, he writes, but there are also corpses that are livid and discolored, festering and oozing pus, cut up, gnawed by animals, scattered, hacked up, bleeding, worm- and maggot-infested, and merely skeletal. The monk should avoid contemplating the corpse of someone of the opposite sex. One meditative device is to reconstruct the separated parts of a corpse (for example, of an executed criminal or the victim of an animal attack), but one who does this should do it with a walking stick or a staff so that he does not become so familiar with the bodies that they lose their repulsiveness. In all these cases, Buddhaghosa presents the bodies precisely as text-like, sign-bearing objects:

> The meditator should apprehend the sign [of foulness] thoroughly in that body. ... He should advert to it in well-established mindfulness. He should see that it is properly remembered, properly defined, by doing that again and again. Standing in a place not too far from and not too near to the body, he should open his eyes, look and apprehend the sign. He should open his eyes and look a hundred times, a thousand times, [thinking], 'Repulsiveness of the bloated, repulsiveness of the bloated', and he should close his eyes and advert to it.
>
> (1976: 192)

The aim is to transform how one perceives living bodies. The lesson to be learned is that "a living body is just as a dead one, only the characteristic of foulness is not evident in a living body, being hidden by adventitious embellishments" (201). This brand of meditation is practiced less often today, since cremation grounds are lacking, but Mathieu Boisvert reports that some contemporary monks in Sri Lanka pursue this form of meditation by visiting autopsy rooms (Boisvert 1996).

How should one understand this practice? Certainly, it can be interpreted in terms of the psychic transformation it pursues. Aiming at the restraint and eventual elimination of sexual desire, this practice, though not common, forms part of the ascetic dimension of Theravāda discipline. Buddhaghosa clearly praises cremation ground meditation for its ability to help one overcome lust and achieve tranquility of mind (196).[6] But on a metaphysical interpretation of this practice, the elimination of lust should not be divorced from a more comprehensive understanding of the nature of persons and the nature of reality. In Buddhism, a characteristic that is often alleged to be necessary in the sense of being shared by everything that exists is that of "being impermanent." Out of attachment to their lives, human beings may want to see themselves as eternal, as having some part of themselves which is not transient, but impermanence is nevertheless (along with suffering and the lack of selfhood) one of the unavoidable "marks of existence." Attention to the metaphysical dimension of Buddhist rituals, then, looks to see whether

Buddhist rituals seek to inscribe on bodies this kind of attribute. From this perspective, the contemplation of foulness may be a psychological technique, but it gets its sense from a more inclusive vision: one should eliminate one's lustful attachment to bodies because bodies, like all other compound things, are impermanent.

There are some who wish to distinguish a religion's "metapraxis," its justification of its practices, from its metaphysics, its justification of its beliefs (Kasulis 1992). Such a distinction may have its uses. But in this example at least, the Theravāda practice seems to find its justification precisely in Theravāda metaphysics. If this idea that religious rituals are typically couched in metaphysical systems is right, this returns us to Geertz, who theorizes that religious practices and religious metaphysics mutually support each other in a circular relationship (1973: 141):

> Religious belief and ritual confront each other and mutually confirm one another; the ethos is made intellectually reasonable by being shown to represent a way of life implied by the actual state of affairs which the world view describes, and the world view is made emotionally acceptable by being presented as an image of an actual state of affairs of which such a way of life is an authentic expression.
>
> (Geertz 1973: 127)

To interpret this activity apart from Buddhist metaphysics is possible, and for some purposes it may be valuable, but one should keep in mind that, in so doing, one is abstracting the actions from the context that provides their justification as wisdom. In other words, recognizing that rituals can involve themselves in this kind of concern therefore resists putting a wall between the concepts of orthopraxy and orthodoxy.

On a metaphysical interpretation, then, rituals like cremation grounds meditation can be described as the "social construction" of the body; they do inscribe bodies as texts. But the point being made here is that these are metaphysical texts. A proper Buddhist body is a metaphysically informed body. Thus the point of the ritual is to represent the body in the light of a Buddhist metaphysics of impermanence, and thereby to train those who undergo the ritual in a Buddhist discipline of detachment and the restraint of desire. The ritual construction of Buddhist bodies is at the same time the construction of a metaphysically informed understanding of subjectivity. One can put this process in a Foucauldian way. For Foucault, as one shapes the way that one perceives bodies, one also polices oneself and shapes oneself as a subject. As Steven Collins suggests:

> the *Vinaya* rules, the meditations on the body, and the effort to eradicate desire for material and sexual existence, serve to create in the body of the Buddhist monastic practitioner the space for an individualized or "subjectivized" analysis. In so far as salvation is conceived as a spiritual state manifested in both mind and body, the attempt wholly to

inhibit (or perhaps, exorcise) all sexual drives and thoughts, and not merely to prevent overt sexual activity, necessarily induces psychic conflict, a conflict which opens up the interior terrain for which texts and doctrines provide the map. In this private zone of operations the de-sexualized and thus in one sense the de-socialized individual can embody in imagination the immateriality posited in the doctrines of Buddhism, and in this way "touch the deathless with the body."

(Collins 2000: 200–1)

The bodies of monks and nuns "embody in time and matter the eternal and immaterial Truth – they actualize, we might say, the ideology" (Collins 2000: 188).

To be sure, what is taken as a necessary characteristic of reality may differ from one religion to the next. For example, those Muslims who undertake the *hajj* traditionally wear the white *ihrām* attire that sets them apart as pilgrims. "Pilgrim" is in this respect a contingent characteristic. Some people at some times are pilgrims, but this is not true of all people at all times, let alone all of reality at all times. But one might say that in Islam a characteristic that an individual cannot fail to exhibit, a characteristic that permits no alternative, is the attribute of "being a creation of God." Islam teaches that whether one knows it or not – indeed, even if out of idolatry one wants to deny it – it is necessarily true that one is a creation of God. This characteristic applies to every thing in every context, and therefore one's body can be read as a sign with this message on it. This theistic metaphysics serves then to justify the Islamic ethos of submission. The question regarding Islamic rituals like the clothing, gestures, and activities one performs during the *hajj*, then, is whether they inscribe Muslims with this characteristic of creatureliness, and if so, how. Put otherwise, a metaphysical interpretation of Islamic rituals would pursue the hypothesis that, whatever other categories they inscribe, Islamic rituals train bodies to display metaphysical attributes.

This ritual interest in the metaphysical conditions of life is typically not pursued for its own sake. Rather, ritual knowledge of the nature of things typically serves to put the ritualists (back) into accord with that necessary truth, to train their emotions and appetites and comportment according to its patterns, so that they become microcosms of the cosmic order. Thus, according to the Qur'an, in the ritual prostration that symbolizes and constitutes one's submission, one not only marks oneself as an obedient Muslim (as opposed to a non-Muslim); one also resembles the stars and the trees which, without human recalcitrance, submit to God's will and worship Him (55.5). In replicating the behavior that the rest of reality does "naturally," then, observant Muslims are "doers of the truth" (Denny 1994: 113). Similarly, Buddhist meditation on at least some accounts also aims at the actualization of a truth that the rest of reality already embodies. As the Zen teacher Dōgen puts it, it is not correct that all beings exist *in* time but rather that all beings *are* time. The rat and the tiger are times; the pine tree and the bamboo are times. Thus to an audience not of philosophers of religion but practicing monks, Dōgen says, metaphysically, "You must see all the various things of the whole world as so many times" (Dōgen 1985: 77; cf. Schilbrack 2000).

To make this distinction I am recommending between necessary and contingent ritual inscriptions is not to deny that ritual metaphysics have social functions. On the contrary, metaphysical teachings may primarily serve precisely to mark social boundaries, to reinforce political stratification, and to justify cultural hierarchies and differentiation. There is typically an intimate connection between ritual metaphysics and religious authority. The relationship between the sacrifice of Purusha to the varna system (*Rig Veda* 10.90) is an apposite example. In fact, to present contingencies as necessities is perhaps the primary way that religions have this effect, and to embed this metaphysical view in one's perception of and experience of one's very body is perhaps the primary way that religious rituals accomplish this. Liz Wilson argues that the cremation ground meditation has had this very effect (Wilson 1996). In post-Aśokan (third century) accounts of Buddhist saints, stories of cremation ground meditation recurs as a common theme, but in these stories the one who comes to realize the foulness of bodies is typically a male monk, and the dead, decaying, or disfigured body that represents the impermanence of things is typically the body of a woman. Consequently, these representations of the body privilege the androcentric perspective of the male renouncer. Women are present in the stories not as subjects in their own right, but primarily as nameless and voiceless objects of the male gaze. Women are thus subordinated to men by this very representational practice. Men who reflect on these representations of the women's body progress toward liberation through aversion to the feminine body as a trap; but women who reflect on these stories lose their sense of agency.

Nevertheless, to assume that because bodily codes locate one sociologically they therefore must always be *about* one's social location is to confuse the function of inscriptions with their content. The question of religious metaphysics and its role in socialization may not be separable, but they are distinguishable – as distinguishable, in fact, as metaphysics and sociology are generally. In other words, ritual activities, gestures, and clothes provide the emblems that create and express religious identity. It is undeniable that such emblems, whether metaphysical or non-metaphysical, have a social dimension. Nevertheless, it is a valuable interpretive strategy to ask whether a given ritual reflects an interest in metaphysics, in my judgment, because this strategy protects the study of rituals from divorcing these practices from the extra-social reality as it is perceived by the participants. In fact, this strategy connects ritual participation to a reality that, from the perspective of the participants, does not perish. A metaphysical reality by definition exists necessarily and under all conditions and therefore it can have the power to save or redeem or liberate.

III. Ritual bodies as philosophical subjects

In the previous section, I recommend that those who study rituals as the social construction of bodies should appreciate the distinction between metaphysical and non-metaphysical inscriptions. In turning to part III, however, I want to insist that if the study of bodies as sites for or products of cultural inscription were the entirety of the study of rituals, it would be distortedly one-sided. Religious rituals should be seen not simply as a means for transmitting values and teachings, not simply a set of actions during which religions inscribe certain marks on the bodies of the practitioners. Though it is true that rituals do this, on such an approach the ritual body is solely a passive medium of knowledge gained elsewhere. This is the impoverished sense in which the phrase "ritual knowledge" is often used, but in my judgment, ritual can be seen in some cases at least as a form of inquiry itself, a source of knowledge in its own right. From this perspective, complementary to the first, the ritual body is an active subject of experience.[7]

This idea of bodily knowledge is new in philosophy and its application to ritual activities is still largely undeveloped. Those interested in exploring how rituals bodies can be the subjects of experience can profit from philosophical work on the idea of the body-as-subject, especially by existential phenomenologists, and on embodied ways of knowing, especially by cognitive scientists and feminist philosophers.[8] Those interested in approaching ritual in this way can draw on this work in order to pursue two more-focused questions: what does it mean to speak of ritual knowledge? And what does it mean to say that there is ritual knowledge that is metaphysical?

To address both of these questions, I want to build upon a seminal article by Theodore Jennings (Jennings 1982). Jennings argues that ritual is not primarily an illustration or dramatization of knowledge gained through other means, such as myth or speculation. Ritual can also be a symbolic structure that performs noetic functions in ways peculiar to itself, a distinctive mode of "coming to know." As Jennings puts it, "ritual action is not only the product but is also the means of a noetic quest, an exploration which seeks to discover the right action or sequence of actions" (Jennings 1982: 114). Ritual knowledge is for Jennings a form of practical wisdom. It is gained not by detached observation or contemplation but through action. When engaged in ritual, Jennings says, "[m]y hand 'discovers' the fitting gesture (or my feet the fitting step) which I may then 'cerebrally' *re*-cognize as appropriate or right" (Jennings 1982: 115).[9]

How, exactly, does a person or a community explore the world and discover knowledge through a ritual? Jennings's theory works like this: a repeated action, such as cutting with an axe, is an *exploratory* or knowledge-*producing* action, in that through trial and error one discovers what to do and how to do it. In the practice of using the axe, the axe itself wordlessly teaches me through my hands, arms, and shoulders how it is to be used. Analogously, then, ritual involves discovery because it too involves altering one's environment. Especially in the liminal phase, Jennings says, a ritual provides a structured openness to novelty that is the condition for the possibility of exploration and discovery. Even if the ritual does not engage with wood or tools or anything other than its own ritual objects, "even then we must say that the exploratory 'doing' is a doing which alters the ritual complex or its constituent parts in some way" – for example, one learns the right thing to do with the chalice (Jennings 1982: 116). In this way, rituals are truth-pursuing activities: they manipulate objects and, like scientific theories, develop over time in order to test hypotheses. Once a community has learned something through its ritual inquiries, the often-noted repetition of ritual actions is then pedagogically valuable to transmit this knowledge to future inquirers. "This relatively stable repertoire provides the necessary framework for exploration in much the same way that a mastery of relevant data and theoretical construction is indispensable for 'scientific' exploration and discovery" (Jennings 1982: 115).

In my judgment, Jennings is persuasive both that rituals can be a source of knowledge and that the primary object of ritual knowledge is "how to act" or "the fitting action." But Jennings underestimates, I suggest, the extent to which ritual knowledge of action also involves descriptive beliefs. He claims, for example, that "[r]itual knowledge is not so much descriptive as it is prescriptive and ascriptive" because "the object of ritual knowledge is an action or a set of actions (or rhythm of actions) rather than a state or condition" (116, 112; cf. also 120). "Ritual action does not primarily teach us to see differently but to act differently. It does not provide a point of view so much as a pattern of doing" (117). Jennings is right that ritual action may not involve "*detached* observation" (116; emphasis added), but surely acting typically involves seeing; knowing how involves knowing that. An action is not recognized as appropriate or "fitting" simply in itself, as a set of gestures, apart from the beliefs about the world that inform it.[10] Thus to interpret ritual knowledge with Jennings as knowledge of what to do should not preclude one from recognizing that rituals can also involve disciplining one's powers of attention. Rituals often involve training ritualists how to see. In fact, if one understands beliefs as habit of conduct, as the pragmatists do, then by shaping one's habits, ritual also shapes one's beliefs; the two tasks are not separate, as Michael Raposa argues in this volume. Certainly, providing a point of view is central to meditative practices like visiting cremation grounds. Buddhaghosa is explicit that the purpose of the practice is to gain knowledge (*jnana*) and to achieve non-delusion (Buddhaghosa 1976: 193).

If this idea that ritual activities can be a form of inquiry and so a source of knowledge is plausible, I now turn to the possibility of seeing a ritual specifically as a form of metaphysical inquiry, that is, as a source of knowledge about the most general contexts of human existence. The possibility of metaphysical knowledge is needlessly confused, in my opinion, when metaphysics is identified solely with an investigation of claims about noumenal or supernatural realities. This paper focuses on metaphysics not as an inquiry into a world beyond human experience, but rather as an inquiry into the character of experienced things in general. Can a ritual lead to this kind of knowledge?

To begin to answer this question, it is worth pointing out that, on the noetic view of ritual above, since ritual knowledge is knowledge gained by being engaged in activity, the knowledge it produces is not insulated from the world. For example, when one learns to chop wood, one learns not only about oneself (for instance, where the limits of one's abilities can be found), but also that this wood is harder to cut than that is, this axe is sharper than that one, that one can trust this other worker. As Jennings puts it, participants in a ritual learn not only who they are in the world or what they are capable of, but also "how it is" with the world (Jennings 1982: 113).[11] One can put this point in existential-phenomenological terms, so that ritual knowledge is knowledge of being-in-the-world, or in pragmatist terms, so that ritual knowledge is an activity in which an organism transforms its environment to pursue its purposes.

If one accepts the interpretation of ritual knowledge as world-connected in this way, then ritual can be, in part, an inquiry into the way things are. Ritual knowledge is metaphysical, then, to the extent that the ritualists inquire into the way things are in general or under all circumstances. Rituals provide a structured corporeal engagement with some particular aspect of human life, such as health, dreams, song, house building, dance, childbirth, voice, or eating. Insofar as a ritual induces one to pursue metaphysical knowledge, however, it offers an invitation to understand these particular aspects of life as emblematic of the nature of human experience or things more broadly. The hypothesis of a metaphysical interpretation of rituals is that rituals focus on part of the world as revealing a wider reality. For example, it may be that the Muslim comes to appreciate that it is not just the trip to Mecca that is a pilgrimage; life itself is a pilgrimage. The human condition as such is that of a pilgrim, and all people are in the same situation. In the Buddhist example, the cremation grounds practice shows that the physical objects of sexual desire are impermanent, but the monk may come to understand by extrapolation that his own body is also impermanent – and that in fact every existing thing is impermanent. Thus rituals give rise to metaphysical thinking when they induce participants to experience features of the ritual as features of the human condition generally.

This focus on the necessary aspects of the human world points to another difference between this approach and that of Jennings. Jennings holds that rituals involve altering the world and, for this reason, "that to which the ritual action corresponds" will not be an "immutable state of affairs" (120). According to Jennings, what a ritual reveals is a "world in act" and "[t]he ritual … intends to transform this world in act" (120). But on a metaphysical interpretation, that to which the ritual action corresponds may well be an aspect of the world that is immutable, something to which the ritualists have no intention of changing. On the contrary, by seeking to put their actions in accord with this necessary aspect of their world, it is often themselves that ritualists seek to transform by means of ritual. Jennings's approach to ritual knowledge has received sustained critical reflection on this point from Ron Williams and James Boyd (Williams and Boyd 1994: 59–155). Williams and Boyd agree that rituals can have a noetic function, but they argue that this function arises not from its adaptability, but precisely from its repetitiveness. Like a stable artistic masterpiece whose metaphors lure people to transformation, a ritual teaches not by assuming a stable self who changes the ritual in order to experiment on the world, but by providing a stable ideal which can serve to help transform the practitioner. In their words, precisely because it is repetitive or (for the most part) invariant, ritual serves as "both stabilizing horizon and lure to new insight" (Williams and Boyd 1994: 83). Whereas for Jennings, then, a ritual is like a theory which the investigators will refine so as to better accord with the object of their investigation, for Williams and Boyd, a ritual is an already perfect instrument and if it is to serve its purpose as a noetic tool, it is the practitioner who must change.

Insofar as a ritual seeks this kind of speculative knowledge of the comprehensive context for life, it makes sense to speak of ritual as a metaphysical inquiry. Moreover, insofar as ritual seeks knowledge of the fitting acts – that is, insofar as it seeks *practical* wisdom – ritual metaphysics includes knowledge of what one should always and everywhere *do*. Ritual metaphysics would thereby identify a general form of acting (detached from impermanent things, perhaps, or submissive to the Creator) that is alleged to be appropriate always and everywhere, under all conditions. The product of such inquiry, then, would be a wisdom that puts one's bodily activities in accord with the nature of things, a wisdom that is always pragmatic. Jennings himself recognizes this practical value of ritual metaphysics in his notion of "ontological praxis." Some acts, he says, are more comprehensive in the scope of their object and aim at exhibiting the very action or rhythm of reality as such. Jennings uses the idea of ontological praxis to make the following hypothesis regarding the centrality of ritual metaphysics to the behavior that the religion generally prescribes:

> To the extent to which the originative act or ontological rhythm which is known by the ritual performance is comprehensive in character, it may be taken to be paradigmatic for a correspondingly wide variety of behavior by its participants. If this is true we would expect to find a correlation between the ontological radicality [or comprehensiveness] of a ritual and its importance as a model of, or paradigm for, other actions. The expectation of such a correlation would serve as an important heuristic tool in the investigation of ritual.
>
> (Jennings 1982: 122)

A ritual is a metaphysical inquiry, then, to the extent that it aims at increased knowledge of being in the world authentically, that is, being in the world in the way authorized by the very nature of things.

IV. Metaphysics embodied

There may be some readers who are willing to accept the idea of body knowledge, and even the idea that such knowledge can be gained through ritual activity, but who remain skeptical of this paper's interest in metaphysics. This paper's agenda may strike some readers as implausible, perhaps because it seeks to connect ritual practices, a cultural product usually seen as everyday and shared in common among the humblest participants, and metaphysical speculations about the nature of reality in general, a cultural product usually seen as reserved to the literate, leisured representative intellectuals of a religious community. The study of a religion's metaphysics, an objection might run, will be limited to those (few) religions that include a speculative or scholastic tradition, and only of such religions will it make sense to speak of ritual metaphysics.

But this objection requires one to make an invidious distinction between those religions interested in the environment in the most inclusive sense and those that are not, a distinction that does not hold up. To weaken the plausibility of that distinction, I want to close by spelling out how a religion's metaphysical views need not be explicit at all but can be both explored and taught through the ritual body. To make this case, I use the approach to ritual of Catherine Bell, who develops her account of the ritual body from Pierre Bourdieu (and though she does not cite him, I think also from Peter Berger).

According to Bell, ritual activities aim at generating a socialized agent with a "ritualized body," which is to say that the participation in rituals structures one's senses, including one's very "sense of reality" (1992: 80, 221).[12] The ritual generates this sense by bringing the individual body, the community, and "the largest image of reality" into a felt continuity (1992: 115). The ritually informed body can then be understood as a microcosm of a more inclusive whole, reflecting both the structure of one's society and also the structure of reality itself (1992: 94).[13] On this understanding, ritual metaphysics is a matter not (or not just) of giving participants a mental *image* of a larger world, but of giving them the experience of participating in the very patterns and forces of the cosmos (1992: 160 n.206).

How do rituals accomplish this work? Ritual activity produces the ritualized body as the participants come to engage with the structured and structuring environment of the ritual (1992: 98). Through the deployment of certain oppositional structures – such as the opposition between what is divine and what is human, what is masculine and what is feminine, what is above and what is below – the ritual shapes the understanding and the experience of the participants. As the participants come to master the ritual and internalize these schemes, their bodies come to appropriate that ritual world in their habits, dispositions, and gestures. Ritual participation serves to "impress these schemes upon the bodies of participants" (1992: 98–9).

Participation in the ritual structure is thus to discipline oneself by putting one's body structure and actions in accord with the (ritually given) nature of reality. It is experienced as saving or liberating the participants from ways of living that are not authorized by the true nature of things. This is what Bell means by her term "redemptive hegemony" (1992: 83–8, 114–17). Ritual is redemptive in that it is experienced as empowering, as putting oneself in congruence with "the ultimate organization of the cosmos" and thereby gaining "the sense of integrated totality and embracing holism" (1992: 207). It is hegemonic in that the world displayed in ritual is experienced as natural, as commonsensical, and as without an alternative – in short, as reality.[14] Ritual does not create ritual bodies coercively, like a cookie cutter, but rather gives people a sense of mastery or empowerment by providing them with schemes with which they are capable of re-interpreting reality in such a way as to experience the world as in accord with their own goals. For my purposes, however, the important point is that since this process of internalization is performed through the body, the idea of ritual metaphysics is not restricted to literate traditions. In other words, Bell's account enables one to see ritual activities as embodying metaphysics.

Philosophers may be interested in the question whether the ritual inter-pretations of reality – the embodied metaphysics – are in any sense accurate. Bell does not permit such questions, however, but presupposes that ritual metaphysics are never true. Like Peter Berger, Bell holds that the ritually taught nature of the world is always arbitrary, generated and projected by the ritualists onto the plane of human experience. Though she does not argue for this position, it follows from her theory, and she considers it obvious. "Of course," she says, "the redemptive hegemony of practice does not reflect reality more or less effectively; it creates it more or less effectively" (1992: 85). In other words, the world revealed in ritual action is nothing but the creation of the ritualizing itself. Ritualists first construct the ritual world, then objectify it so that they perceive it as if it were not artificial (this is why she calls it "hegemony"), and then they reappropriate it under the mistaken assumption that the values and experiences found in the ritual come from sources outside the ritual (1992: 99, 1997: 139). On Bell's account, then, if one wishes to speak of ritual "knowledge," it is not knowledge of the real world in any sense, but is a confused perception of the ritualists' own projections. By definition, ritual participants misrecognize their world (1992: 82–3, 108–10, 114–17, 220; 1998: 216).[15]

In the above quote (1992: 85), one can see that Bell is willing to speak of rituals as more or less "effective." And so it may be that her theory means to reject a correspondence theory of truth while retaining some other – perhaps neo-pragmatist – understanding of truth. She has written that "I do consider most [rituals] fairly effective responses to the nature of reality as that reality is experienced by the participants. The ineffective ones fade away rather quickly. No ritual can simply write on the body of the participants without giving them useful resources that work in the larger world."[16] But it remains the case that on Bell's account, rituals are not more or less effec-tive responses to a world that exists independently of the ritualists. Rituals generate, create, and constitute a world; they do not reflect, respond to, nor

interact with a world. (For this reason, her work does not embody a pragmatist sense of truth found in Peirce, James, or Dewey, for whom truth was
what helped one deal with a world not of one's own creation.) For Bell,
ritual experiences lack any receptive or passive element, and as a consequence, they are insular. In thinking otherwise, the ritualists are always
mistaken.

Bell's a priori assumption that all ritual senses of reality are arbitrary and
confused is problematic, not least in its tacitly Kantian assumptions about
seeing the world through schemes. A central problem with this account is
that it is one-sided and not fully dialectical, in the sense that it begins with
the projection of schemes onto the world, but it does not explain where the
projecting agent comes from. In this respect, her approach reveals an unwill-
ingness to be fully naturalistic in that it sees "reality" as a projection of human
agency but does not likewise see human agency itself as a product of natural
forces. It is because on her account human schemes of reality are completely
the product of human agency and are not in any respect a response to the
natural world that Bell's approach does not permit one to ask about the truth
of such schemes. I take it that this is why she describes philosophy of religion
as "fading," perhaps to be replaced by approaches to the study of religion that
are grounded in science rather than theology (Bell 2000: 9).

Those like me who are attracted to Bell's account of the creation of ritual
bodies need not accept her one-sided view of human agency. To reject that
view, one need not deny that ritual metaphysics are the product of the human
imagination and reflect the linguistic and cultural context from which they
are projected; from the fact that metaphysical knowledge involves imaginative projection it does not follow that no metaphysical understandings of
reality are possibly true (a totalizing claim if ever there was one). One solution open to those interested in the possible truth of embodied metaphysics
is to join with those who see human involvement with the natural environment as fundamentally circular, and human agency and cognition as always
a form of interaction with one's perceived situation. On such an approach,
ritualizing is a process embedded in and emergent from interactions between
people and their environments.

If Bell were open to seeing ritualizing in this interactive and world-
embedded way, it would create a sizeable number of allies. It would connect
her work to that of cognitive scientists like Francisco Varela and his colleagues
who contend that all thinking is "enactive" in that it is "not the representation of pregiven world by a pregiven mind but . . . rather the enactment of a
world and a mind on the basis of a history of the variety of actions that
a being in the world performs" (Varela *et al.* 1991: 9) and to that of philosophers of mind like Mark Johnson who argues that "[cognitive] patterns emerge
as meaningful structures for us chiefly at the level of our bodily movements
through space, our manipulation of objects, and our perceptual interactions"
(Johnson 1987: 29).[17] It would also connect her to phenomenologists like
Maurice Merleau-Ponty who says that one's embodied dispositions and senses
are acquired through one's interaction with things and situations, and that

these dispositions then in turn determine how things and situations appear to us. In Merleau-Ponty's words, "The world is inseparable from the subject but from a subject which is nothing but a project of the world, and the subject is inseparable from the world, but from a world which the subject itself projects" (1962: 430). And it would also connect her to pragmatists like John Dewey and G. H. Mead who see human knowledge as a "transaction" between an organism and its environment. For Dewey, since it "is obvious without argument that when [people] inquire they employ their eyes and ears, their hands and their brains . . . biological functions and structures prepare the way for deliberate inquiry and . . . they foreshadow its pattern" (1938: 23).

In short, seeing ritual values as connected to the world does not require one to identify a pre-cultural experience, nor even to endorse a representationalist view of knowledge. It only requires one to see the mind and nature as interacting, that is, only a naturalist view of the subject as always already physically embodied and embedded in the world (see Haugeland 1995).

V. Conclusion

This paper aims to sketch one way of seeing ritual activities as forms of thinking, specifically, a form of metaphysical thinking. In so doing, it opposes those who deny that rituals can be world-embedded and truth-pursuing activities. It opposes, in other words, those approaches to the study of ritual that treat rituals as necessarily confused, illusory, or out of touch with reality. It aims in particular to rehabilitate the cosmic dimension of ritual.

The benefits of the idea of ritual metaphysics, as I see it, are double. On the one hand, a recognition of the possibility of speaking of ritual metaphysics should remind those who study rituals that the teachings at work in ritual practices are not limited in their references to the minds of the participants, or even to the society of the participants. There can be bodily inscriptions or ritual knowledge – even though its function may be to socialize – that is not about the social. Consequently, those who study ritual should not exclude metaphysics as a legitimate tool for the interpretation of ritual. Second, those who study religious philosophy or religious metaphysics should also appreciate the truth that religion, whatever else it is, is a set of embodied practices. Specifically, they should include rituals as legitimate objects of philosophical study. On the one hand, therefore, this approach can be seen as antireductionist, and on the other hand, it is anti-Cartesian.[18]

Notes

1 This paper therefore forms part of my larger project seeking to defend the cogency of religious metaphysics and its value for the study of religions. Those interested in this project may look to Schilbrack (2000, 2002a, and 2002b).
2 The term "worldview" is also often used loosely – to refer, for example, to religious views of any matters and not only to generic or non-restrictive statements about what exists. But Geertz clearly uses the term as I do, in this stricter sense,

to refer to the "most comprehensive ideas" or "most general contexts of human existence," "the essential conditions in terms of which life must, of necessity, be lived" (1973: 127, 126, 129; for a defense of Geertz's understanding of religious models of reality, see Schilbrack 2004).

3 To give just one example, Elizabeth Grosz writes: "in our culture as much as in others, there is a form of body writing and various techniques of social inscription that bind all subjects, often in quite different ways according to sex, class, race, cultural and age codifications, to social positions and relations" (1994: 141).

4 To be even more precise, one can distinguish between broader and stricter senses of "necessary," namely, between claims about features alleged to be common to human existence as such (call this metaphysics in the broad sense) and claims about features alleged to be necessary in the sense that they characterize not only human existence, but the existence of anything whatsoever or reality as such (call this metaphysics in the strict sense). See Ogden (1975).

5 Of course, whether a "text" is a body or a book, to be able to "read" it presupposes enough knowledge of the native's worldview to make sense of the text. There is no reason to assume that because interpreters have bodies that they have any privileged access to that to which a ritual refers, and this is true even if the referent of the text is metaphysical. Moreover, to speak of the body as a text is to say that it carries a semantic message, but like a written message it can be either understood by those who display it or not. Thus it is possible to come to an interpretation of ritual bodies that says that, as public "documents," the bodies are inscribed with messages about metaphysics, even though these messages are ignored by the ritualists. In other words, those who interpret bodies as texts find themselves in the usual hermeneutic position in which one must always argue that one's interpretation makes the best sense of the text.

6 Buddhaghosa also says that one realizes that "there is no distinction between a king's body and an outcaste's in so far as its impure stinking nauseating repulsiveness is concerned" (202), and so one might interpret the practice in social terms.

7 It may be worthwhile here to note explicitly a critique of what might be called a thoroughgoing social constructionist position. Several have pointed out that to ignore the body as a material and lived phenomenon and to argue (for example, for Foucauldian or deconstructionist reasons) that the body is not only interpreted but is actually *constituted* through discourse leads to problems and paradoxes (see Shilling 1993: esp. 79–81; T. Turner 1994; and McNay 1991). My paper does not explicitly argue for, though it aims to exemplify, the need for a "both/and" approach that sees the body both as the product of culture and as an existential reality in its own right, both as a system of representation and as a lived experience, both as object and as subject. In this I mean to follow the lead of Bryan Turner (1992, 1996) and Thomas Csordas (1994).

8 The locus classicus for the existentialist phenomenological view is Merleau-Ponty (1962), though needlessly slighted is Sartre (1956: 303–59) (and on Sartre's view of the body as subject, see also Wider 1997). For what is in my judgment an important feminist development of Merleau-Ponty, see Young (1990: 141–209); for an important feminist critique, see Sullivan (2001). For a perspective on embodied knowledge from cognitive science, see Lakoff and Johnson (1999); for one feminist approach, see Grosz (1994, 1995).

9 Seeking to avoid dualism, Jennings resists calling this "embodied" knowledge, however, noting that it "is not so much that the mind 'embodies' itself in ritual action but rather that the body 'minds' itself or attends through itself in ritual action" (Jennings 1982: 115).

10 Barry Barnes has a nice discussion of practices that supports this point. Speaking of acupuncture as an example, he says: "The practice should be treated as involving thought and action together, and in so far as this is the case, embodied theory, as it were, is a part of the practice itself" (2001: 20).

11 Contrast this with Rebecca J. Slough who limits ritual knowledge to the human: "Fundamentally, [ritual] knowing leads to knowledge of the self (its character, competencies, and weaknesses), of others, and the relationship between the experience of the self and the experience of the others" (Slough 1996: 184).

12 Bell is explicit that this dialectical process shapes one's perceptions of the very structure of reality: "a focus on the [ritualizing] acts themselves illuminates a critical circularity to the body's interaction with this environment: generating it, it is molded by it in turn. By virtue of this circularity, space and time are redefined through the physical movements of bodies projecting organizing schemes on the space-time environment on the one hand while reabsorbing these schemes as the nature of reality on the other" (1992: 99).

13 Bell sometimes uses Geertzian language of "models of reality that render one's world coherent and viable" (1998: 206). Hence "ritual practices are a type of sociocultural medium that is capable of grounding human attitudes, worldviews, and institutions in a vision of the nature of things in general" (1997: 190).

14 "Ritualization always aligns one within a series of relationship[s] linked to the ultimate sources of power. Whether ritual empowers or disempowers one in some practical sense, it always suggests the ultimate coherence of a cosmos in which one takes a particular place. This cosmos is experienced as a chain of states or an order of existence that places one securely in a field of action and in alignment with the ultimate goals of all action" (Bell 1992: 141).

15 Elaine Combs-Schilling, who like Bell draws on Foucault and Bourdieu in her studies of rituals, also treats ritual knowledge of reality as completely constructed and so by definition confused: in rituals, "reality has been constructed in such a way that [people's] own hopes, dreams, and accessible pathways of self-worth are tied to it" (1991: 660). Calling this process "culture's sleight of hand," she says, "Culture can make its elaborations appear true by embedding them within the body's most biological truths," thereby making "cultural inventions [into] . . . the best founded of collective illusions" (1991: 678). This view also surfaces in Crossley's use of Bourdieu, in section V of Chapter 1.

16 Email communication, December 12 2002.

17 Like me, Tamar Frankiel suggests that Bell's approach can be helpfully combined with Johnson's, but like Bell herself (1992: 157–8), Frankiel does not seem to recognize the ways in which statements like the following contradict Bell's post-structuralist assumptions: "Image schemata are not imposed by our minds on some malleable stuff out there, but are, he [Johnson] says, 'definite, recurring patterns in an interaction of an organism with its environment. Thus our experience and our understanding partake of the reality of both our bodily organism and our environment . . .'" (Frankiel 2001: 82).

18 For helpful criticisms of earlier drafts of this paper, I would like to appreciatively thank Lawrence E. Sullivan, Catherine Bell, and two anonymous readers for the *Journal of Ritual Studies*.

Bibliography

Barnes, B. (2001) "Practice as Collective Action," in T. Schatzki, K. K. Cetina, and E. von Savigny (eds), *The Practice Turn in Contemporary Theory*, London: Routledge.

Bell, C. (1992) *Ritual Theory, Ritual Practice*, New York: Oxford University Press.

—— (1997) *Ritual: Perspectives and Dimensions*, New York: Oxford University Press.

—— (1998) "Performance," in M. C. Taylor (ed.), *Critical Terms in Religious Studies*, Chicago: University of Chicago Press.

—— (2000) "Pragmatic Theory," in T. Jensen and M. Rothstein (eds), *Secular Theories on Religion: Current Perspectives*, Copenhagen: Museum Tusculanum Press.

Boisvert, M. (1996) "Death as Meditation Subject in the Theravāda Tradition," *Buddhist Studies Review* 13: 37–54.

Buddhaghosa, B. (1976) *The Path of Purification (Visuddhimagga)*, 2 vols, trans. B. Ñyāṇamoli, Boulder: Shambhala.

Clark, A. (1997) *Being There: Putting Brain, Body, and World Together Again*, Cambridge, Mass.: MIT Press.

Collins, S. (2000) "The Body in Theravada Buddhist Monasticism," in S. Coakley (ed.), *Religion and the Body*, Cambridge: Cambridge University Press.

Combs-Schilling, M. E. (1991) "Etching Patriarchal Rule: Ritual Dye, Erotic Potency, and the Moroccan Monarchy," *Journal of the History of Sexuality* 1: 658–81.

Csordas, T. (1994) "Introduction: The Body as Representation and as Being-in-the-world," in T. Csordas (ed.), *Embodiment and Experience: The Existential Ground of Culture and Self*, 1–24, Cambridge: Cambridge University Press.

Denny, F. M. (1994) *Introduction to Islam,* 2nd edn, New York: Macmillan.

Dewey, J. (1938) *Logic: The Theory of Inquiry*, New York: H. Holt.

Dōgen (1985) *Moon in a Dewdrop: Writings of Zen Master Dōgen*, ed. K. Tanahashi, San Francisco: North Point Press.

Frankenberry, N. K. and Penner, H. H. (eds) (1999) *Language, Truth, and Religious Belief: Studies in Twentieth-Century Theory and Method in Religion*, Atlanta: Scholars Press.

Frankiel, T. (2001) "Prospects in Ritual Studies," *Religion* 31: 75–87.

Geertz, C. (1973) *The Interpretation of Cultures*, New York: Basic Books.

Grosz, E. (1994) *Volatile Bodies: Toward a Corporeal Feminism*, Bloomington: Indiana University Press.

—— (1995) *Space, Time and Perversion: Essays on the Politics of Bodies*, London: Routledge.

Haugeland, J. (1995) "Mind Embodied and Embedded," in Y.-H. Houng and J.-C. Ho (eds), *Mind and Cognition*, Taipai: Institute of European and American Studies, Academica Sinica.

Jennings, T. W. (1982) "On Ritual Knowledge," *Journal of Religion* 62: 111–27.

Johnson, M. (1987) *The Body in the Mind: The Bodily Basis of Meaning, Imagination, and Reason*, Chicago: The University of Chicago Press.

Kasulis, T. P. (1992) "Philosophy as Metapraxis," in F. Reynolds and D. Tracy (eds), *Discourse and Practice*, Albany, NY: SUNY Press.

Lakoff, G. and Johnson, M. (1999) *Philosophy in the Flesh: The Embodied Mind and its Challenge to Western Thought*, New York: Basic Books.

Leach, E. (1954) *Political Systems of Highland Burma*, London: Bell and Sons.

McNay, L. (1991) "The Foucauldian Body and the Exclusion of Experience," *Hypatia* 6: 125–39.

Merleau-Ponty, M. (1962) *Phenomenology of Perception*, London: Routledge & Kegan Paul.

Munson, H. (1986) "Geertz on Religion: The Theory and the Practice," *Religion* 16: 19–32.

Ogden, S. (1975) "The Criterion of Metaphysical Truth and the Senses of 'Metaphysics'" *Process Studies* 5: 47–8.

Raposa, M. (2003) "Ritual Inquiry: The Pragmatic Logic of Religious Practice," in K. Schilbrack (ed.), *Thinking through Rituals: Philosophical Perspectives*, London: Routledge.

Rappaport, R. A. (1984) *Pigs for the Ancestors: Ritual in the Ecology of a New Guinea People,* new, enlarged edn, New Haven: Yale University Press.

Sartre, J.-P. (1956) *Being and Nothingness*, trans. H. E. Barnes, New York: Philosophical Library.

Schilbrack, K. (2000) "Metaphysics in Dōgen," *Philosophy East and West* 50: 34–55.

—— (2002a) "Myth and Metaphysics," in K. Schilbrack (ed.), *Thinking through Myths: Philosophical Perspectives*, London: Routledge.

—— (2002b) "The Study of Religious Belief after Donald Davidson," *Method and Theory in the Study of Religion* 14: 334–49.

—— (2004) "Religion, Models of, and Reality: Are We Through With Geertz?" *Journal of the American Academy of Religion* 72(1), March.

Shilling, C. (1993) *The Body and Social Theory*, London: Sage.

Slough, R. J. (1996) "'Let Every Tongue, by Art Refined, Mingle its Softest Notes with Mine': An Exploration of Hymn-Singing Events and Dimensions of Knowing," in M. B. Aune and V. DeMarinis (eds), *Religious and Social Ritual: Interdisciplinary Explorations*, Albany: State University of New York Press.

Sullivan, S. (2001) *Living across and through Skins: Transactional Bodies, Pragmatism, and Feminism*, Bloomington: Indiana University Press.

Turner, B. (1992) *Regulating Bodies*, London: Routledge.

—— (1996) *The Body and Society*, 2nd edn, London: Sage.

Turner, T. (1994) "Bodies and Antibodies: Flesh and Fetish in Contemporary Social Theory," in T. Csordas (ed.), *Embodiment and Experience: The Existential Ground of Culture and Self*, 27–47, Cambridge: Cambridge University Press.

Varela, F. J., Thompson, E. and Rosch, E. (1991) *The Embodied Mind: Cognitive Science and Human Experience*, Cambridge, Mass.: MIT Press.

Wider, K. (1997) *The Bodily Nature of Consciousness: Sartre and Contemporary Philosophy of Mind*, Ithaca: Cornell University Press.

Williams, R. G. and Boyd, J. W. (1994) *Ritual Art and Knowledge*, Columbia, S.C.: University of South Carolina Press.

Wilson, L. (1996) *Charming Cadavers: Horrific Figurations of the Feminine in Indian Buddhist Hagiographic Literature*, Chicago: University of Chicago Press.

Young, I. M. (1990) *Throwing like a Girl and Other Essays*, Bloomington: Indiana University Press.

7 Philosophical naturalism and the cognitive approach to ritual

Robert N. McCauley

I. Introduction

Naturalism in philosophy demands that philosophical proposals exhibit a healthy respect for the methods and findings of the empirical sciences, especially when those proposals address the same domains those sciences do. In the twentieth century, philosophers became a good deal more circumspect about their physical and biological speculations. If philosophy of science has not largely overshadowed metaphysics, then certainly science itself has become a fundamental constraint on credible metaphysical proposals. Instead of advancing grand metaphysical programs, many twentieth century philosophers have chosen to explore the broader implications of prevailing scientific theories and attempted to disentangle apparent conceptual snarls some seem to contain.

The number of domains where philosophers must heed scientific developments has only increased as modern science has progressed. At the outset of the twenty-first century, philosophers who pronounce about matters of mind and language without regard to the cognitive sciences do so at their peril. Some philosophical naturalists suspect that Kripke's pronouncements about the necessary properties of pains may suffer the same fate as Kant's assurances about the a priori truth of Newtonian mechanics, Fichte's insistence about the number of planets in our solar system, and Bergson's presumptions about the basis of life. When scientific research generates innovative schemes that both systematically organize the pertinent phenomena and supply new explanatory and predictive insights, philosophers' declarations about what is imaginable or about what our concepts demand often appear quaint in retrospect.

For the philosophical naturalist, little, if anything, distinguishes some legitimate philosophical endeavors from the theoretical speculations of scientists. Naturalists hold that philosophy enjoys no privilege. Typically, philosophers' only advantages arise from their wider views of things and their increased sensitivities to the structures and strengths of arguments. Certainly, philosophers' guesses are as good as anyone's, and, given that they are a comparatively intelligent lot, often their guesses are better. Too often, though, the flipside of having wider views of things is insufficient knowledge of the details, and the suggestiveness of their guesses does not obviate in the least the advantages for philosophical proposals that manifest familiarity with the sciences.

Philosophical discussions of ritual might follow various paths. To the extent that religious ritual (on which I will focus) involves what appears to be repetitive transactions with agents who allegedly possess counter-intuitive properties, traditional projects in metaphysics, epistemology, and the philosophy of religion offer familiar means for handling such materials. They address questions about the properties of such agents, the plausibility of such configurations of properties in agents, the evidence for the existence of agents with such properties, and the status of linguistic usage pertaining to all of this. But, finally, most of these philosophical undertakings address some of the conceptual infrastructure of rituals rather than anything very directly connected with the performances of the rituals themselves.

Largely in response to the work of Peter Winch (1958), the most popular philosophical approach over the past four decades to what seems to be so transparently irrational conduct and belief is a broadly interpretive approach. On this approach, the crucial task is to figure out what these peculiar actions and anomalous utterances mean and, in the process, to clarify the forms of life they constitute. Ritual is just one symbolic form among many, but one that presents special problems, since it usually involves more than just beliefs and utterances about them. Rituals are actions. What do people – often large groups of people – take themselves to be doing, not only when they carry out such rituals but repeat them over and over again? And what do such actions mean when they do not seem to serve their alleged purpose? Rituals in which participants prepare and present foods daily to the ancestors end not with the ancestors consuming those meals but rather the people who presented those foods in the first place doing so (Whitehouse 1995: 66–78). What do such descriptions of actions mean when they stray so far from what is manifest? Why do people carry out actions that all of the empirical evidence suggests are thoroughly incapable of achieving the aims in mind? What is accomplished, for example, when baseball players move one of their hands vertically and then horizontally across their upper-bodies before they step into the batter's box?

Such questions not only invite interpretations of rituals, they reliably provoke additional conundrums. If the ancestors' survival and welfare no longer depends upon their consuming food, then why pretend that they have any interest in the food in the first place? Why must Muslim pilgrims scale Mt Safā and Mt Marwah? And if they must, then why more than once? And if more than once, then why seven times, not five? What is the meaning of all of this? Because of the special problems rituals present and because religions' conceptual schemes present plenty enough problems for them on their own, ritual has usually been something of a sideshow among theologians and philosophers of religion out to explicate religious meanings.

Clifford Geertz (1973) proposed that scholars simply focus on carefully portraying, i.e. thickly describing, participants' conduct and comments and ascertaining what can be made of them *in context* about how they hold together. Philosophers and social anthropologists explored how adjudicating such questions of meaning and evaluating the truth of the resulting symbolic claims are connected with the conceptions of reason we deploy (see, for example, Wilson 1970 and Hollis and Lukes 1982). The emerging recognition of their intimate connections bestowed particular prominence on a set of approaches that suggested, in effect, that since the meanings of symbols turn on thick descriptions of their details and the details of their surroundings, the appropriate standards for assessing these special claims and conduct are always temporally and spatially *local* too. The most extreme relativists did not despair so much as celebrate the resulting renunciation of all-encompassing standards of rationality. By contrast, their critics saw such takes on these matters for the discussion-stoppers that they are. They reduce all inquiry about different cultural arrangements to travelogues.

In contrast to the prevailing interpretive mode of analysis, the philosophical naturalist's approach to ritual focuses on our explanatory and predictive interests. They consider such questions as why people perform rituals (especially in light of all the fuss and bother), why people repeat the rituals they perform, and why various rituals have the features that they do. This approach welcomes the interpretivists' thick descriptions, but since the naturalists' principal interests are in ascertaining causes rather than explicating meanings or reasons, those thick descriptions only provide data for explanatory theories to organize rather than touchstones for appraising conceptions of rationality. For science to proceed, causal theories must exhibit a good deal of stability in order for researchers to formulate empirical tests. Science cannot afford the conceptual luxury of thick description in which the semantic commitments of analytical frameworks can shift as often as do those frameworks' contexts of application. Consequently, for the philosophical naturalist a reasonable place to begin examining ritual is with scientific treatments.

Prima facie, ritual looks like a topic for which the social sciences and cultural anthropology, in particular, are most appropriately suited, and dominant explanatory theories in these disciplines would serve as perfectly proper points of departure for the philosophical naturalist. The problem, though, is that for the past thirty years cultural anthropology has been dominated by cultural interpreters and, more recently, by their post-modern descendants. Suffice it to say that formulating empirically testable theories that address such explanatory questions has not been a high priority within this discipline over the past few decades. So, it should come as no surprise that those cultural anthropologists who have retained a vision of the discipline's scientific mission (e.g. Sperber 1975 and 1996) have suggested that students of culture look to its psychological foundations, where explanatory theorizing and experimental testing have undergone an explosion of activity during exactly the same period. Subsequent research along these lines has indicated that the cognitive and psychological sciences offer valuable resources for explaining components of culture, including ritual.

The central assumption of what Dan Sperber calls an "epidemiological" approach to culture is that culture is constituted in part through distributions of beliefs in populations of human minds. Humans have lots of beliefs. Every human mind contains various idiosyncratic beliefs. Human minds also probably come automatically equipped with some intuitive beliefs in common. (Recently, many scholars – e.g. Tooby and Cosmides [1992] – have suggested that the range and variety of this kind of intuitive belief may be far greater than previously suspected.) But human minds also contain other beliefs (both intuitive and reflective) that manifest striking similarities across individuals but that have arisen not as a part of our built-in equipment but rather on the basis of communication with other human beings. Cultures change, in large part, because the frequencies of those communicated beliefs change within populations of human minds.

That such regularities across individual minds should exist at all among these communicated beliefs is surprising at one level, according to Sperber, in light of the vagueness and the vagaries of human communication and the tendencies of human minds to misunderstand, to misremember, and – often just for the fun of it – to mess around with ideas. Sperber insists that communication usually does *not* result in the replication of beliefs but rather in their alteration. Consequently, among other things, this new psychologically grounded account of culture must explore the cognitive variables that influence the shape of these beliefs as well as their persistence, their proliferation, and their resulting distributions. The shift to the cognitive level is vital, since detecting such distributions of beliefs is not the same thing as explaining them. A pivotal question is how cognitive processes constrain both the forms of these beliefs and their transmission (see Sperber 1996: 106–12).

Nonetheless, the position entails no drastic psychological reductionism. That is because, first of all, it is not out to explain everything about culture. Second, these widespread, enduring, communicated beliefs are only a subset of the class of "cultural representations" (Sperber 1996: 25). An epidemiological approach to culture highlights the causal interactions between these beliefs and a second sort of cultural representation, which Sperber (1996: 61–2) calls "public representations." Public representations of culture basically come in two forms: objects and practices. The former are artifacts and include everything from clothing, icons, and architecture to tools, texts, and voting booths. They are the parts of the natural world that humans have intentionally altered to serve their own purposes. In and of themselves, these objects are not topics of psychological investigation, though, of course, human beings have plenty of states of mind and mental representations (that cognitive scientists may study) pertaining to such objects.

In fact, humans *must* have these mental representations for these objects to exist as public representations of culture. As Sperber (1996: 81) notes, public representations of culture "have meaning only through being associated with mental representations." At least currently, such mental representations are only readily accessible to the individuals who have them. By contrast, public representations of culture are accessible to anyone possessing the right communicated beliefs (i.e. the right mental representations about those public representations).

Typically, the mental representations and states of mind about objects that are public representations of culture are tied up with various *practices* associated with those objects. Such practices concern language, education, agriculture, politics, religion, art, science, and more. The connection between practices and mental representations is, perhaps, more transparent than it is in the case of objects. That practices are practices and that they are the specific practices that they are clearly depend at least as much upon people's mental representations as they do upon their publicly available properties. That the practices that constitute a wedding are the practices that constitute a wedding depends crucially upon the participants' beliefs about those practices.

Of course, prominent among such practices are the performances of rituals. The cognitive approach to the study of ritual concentrates (a) on the similarities among the mental representations that people possess about ritual actions, (b) on cognitive explanations of those similarities, and (c) on the implications of those cognitive theories for explaining a variety of rituals and ritual systems' features (see Lawson and McCauley 1990 and McCauley and Lawson 2002).

The strategy of attending to the mental representations that accompany cultural practices offers some important advantages. Approaching ritual or any other cultural phenomenon in this way increases the prospects for testing hypotheses experimentally, since the cognitive sciences generally and psychology especially have developed far more extensive and sophisticated experimental means for testing theories than have the social sciences. Moreover, minds and brains (even more so) are far more discrete, localized systems than cultural systems are. No area of scientific inquiry has undergone any more exciting developments over the last third of the twentieth century than have the cognitive sciences. These disciplines contribute both methodological and substantive assets to the project of explaining culture.

Further philosophical advantages of such an approach are that it can preserve as much of both a materialist account of culture and an ontological unity to science as can be had in tandem with a healthy respect for the multiple levels of explanation currently pursued in science (see McCauley 1986 and 2001a). Those positions rely on no more than the wholly plausible presumptions (1) that socio-cultural phenomena and, more specifically, the systems for interpreting public representations of culture, can be described and, in part, explained in psychological terms, i.e. in terms of individual participants' cognitive processing, and (2) that that cognitive processing, in turn, can be described and, in part, explained in terms of those participants' brain processes.

The next part of this paper briefly surveys the emergence of philosophical naturalism, pointing at the end to the crucial role that the development of the cognitive sciences has played in its contemporary incarnations. The final part examines the cognitive approaches to culture and to ritual in greater detail. In addition to reviewing some of their philosophically interesting implications, it will also examine some of the latter's salient explanatory achievements.

II. Philosophical naturalism

One way to characterize the history of modern epistemology and metaphysics is to recount the penchant of philosophical speculation to spawn empirical sciences, which, as they mature, return to commandeer intellectual domains on which philosophy had previously presumed to possess a proprietary claim. The growth of modern science over the past four centuries has been marked by groups of researchers explicitly adopting new terms ("physics," "chemistry," "biology," "psychology," "sociology," etc.) for designating the specialized inquiries that have resulted and for distinguishing those sub-fields from the whole of natural philosophy – a term which has, not coincidentally, fallen (except in historical discussions) into nearly total disuse.

Ironically, this process by which philosophy has managed to limit its own purview is a direct consequence of philosophers' insistence on rational, disciplined inquiry. We ask philosophical proposals for greater precision and detail, and in that process of pressing their conceptual resources, we expect them both to organize, illuminate, and square with our new discoveries about the world. What the birth of modern science brought were means for meeting such demands that are far more systematic, more efficient, and more penetrating than any devised before. The collective accomplishments of communities of scientific experts fostering theoretical competition, discovering empirical evidence, and constantly monitoring the credibility of that evidence has proved far more effective at producing fruitful accounts of the world than isolated speculations in philosophy where assessments rely far too often on nothing more than common sense, available anecdotes, and the canons of logic. Scientific standards encompass these considerations (at least if the common sense and the anecdotes can withstand critical scrutiny and theoretical progress) as well as the far more exacting demand that theories meet and pass empirical tests that scientists have developed systematically, employing experimental techniques of increasing sophistication.

In less guarded moments, some naturalists' enthusiasms about scientific progress have enticed them into entertaining the possibility of completely eliminating normative epistemology and the metaphysics that presently facilitates it (e.g. Churchland 1979: chapter 5). There are two problems here.

First, the metaphysics behind presumptions about our possessing (mental) attitudes toward contents that informs normative epistemology substantially overlaps, at least currently, with the metaphysical commitments of the psychological and socio-cultural sciences. Consequently, this especially fervent version of naturalism generates a paradox, since fulfilling its goals would – exclusively on the basis of its philosophical projections – jeopardize the status of entire sciences that have been up and running now for more than a century. This is paradoxical to the extent that all versions of naturalism aim, instead, to foster scientific initiatives and to restrain philosophical hubris.

Ultimately, this first problem of these fervent versions of naturalism is a function of their adopting an insufficiently fine-grained model of intertheoretic relations in science. Their models (e.g. Bickle 1998) are coarse grained, because they handle all cases of intertheoretic relations the same way. More specifically, they treat cases of theoretical succession *within a science* and cases of relations of theories *across different sciences* at the same time as if they were the same (McCauley 1986 and forthcoming). Theory succession within a science sometimes does result in the sort of fell-swoop eliminations of theory and ontology that this fervent naturalism envisions. Lavoisier's explanation of combustion in terms of chemical reactions involving oxygen brought about the elimination of both Stahl's phlogiston based account and of phlogiston itself. By contrast, intertheoretic relations in cross-scientific settings, at least when the sciences in question have achieved much momentum at all, do not involve the eradication of theories and their ontologies. There the sorts of conceptual and ontological incompatibilities that provoke scientific revolutions within particular sciences over time, instead, elicit inquiries about how adjusting the theories in question might achieve some measure of theoretical reconciliation across explanatory levels. Patricia Churchland (1986: 374) has termed this "the co-evolution of theories" in science. The co-evolution of theories and research in cognitive psychology and computational modeling in neuroscience has not led to the elimination of either enterprise. On the contrary, scientists working at each level have readily exploited the conceptual, experimental, and evidential resources available at the other (McCauley 2001a). This is not to deny that eliminations of theories and their ontologies do not occur in either psychology or neuroscience, but rather to submit that such outcomes are the results of developing *within* each of those sciences superior alternatives that are overwhelmingly incompatible with the currently reigning frameworks.

The second problem with such fervent forms of naturalism is their failure to recognize that because the current conceptual framework in terms of which normative issues are formulated may not persist in the face of scientific progress in the cognitive and psychological sciences, it does not follow that the underlying normative concerns will disappear with them.[1] Philosophers may be able to distinguish facts and values easily enough in the abstract (and think that they can dispense with the latter), but on the hoof all forms of inquiry involve a swirl of both at every turn. If the pursuit of science enables us to devise increasingly better accounts of the way the world is or, at least, to manage things better than our predecessors, then philosophers' normative proposals risk irrelevance, if not irresponsibility, if they insist on employing categories that have become obsolete from the standpoints of explanation and prediction. Naturalists, however, must understand that those same sciences are basically mute about the implicit norms that pervade them and their associated practices. If naturalism is to include a robust picture of the scientific enterprise, then those norms are not just legitimate, but obligatory, targets for philosophical reflection. Although naturalists insist, contrary to traditional epistemology, that the sciences must rigorously constrain the categories from which we should expect to fashion our most compelling metaphysical and epistemological pictures, we can never create those pictures by simply doing more science. Getting better theories about the facts alone will not make those implicit norms explicit. Naturalism as a *philosophical* position becomes both implausible and self-defeating, if its aim is simply to cheer the total usurpation of philosophy by science. Naturalism is not scientism. Its goal is not to put philosophy out of business. Philosophy still has plenty of jobs to do.

Questions remain, though, about how those jobs are best done. In the broadly transcendental tradition of Kant, philosophers such as Husserl (1970) and Thomas Nagel (1986) hold that some philosophical tool or insight provides philosophy with a unique form of analytical leverage with which it can explore such things as the very possibility of doing science. Other philosophers (e.g. Searle 1992) eschew the trappings of transcendental perspectives in favor of ordinary language and common sense (and even lay claim to a naturalistic orientation) but, nonetheless, pronounce no less confidently about the ways some things must be, either because our current concepts say so or – what is nearly the same thing – because common sense clearly shows that some scientific reductions are unthinkable (see Churchland and Churchland 1998: chapters 8 and 9).

But the history of science has, of course, quite regularly been a history of achieving what was once the unthinkable – prevailing conceptual commitments to the contrary, notwithstanding. As Popper argued, Kant, in effect, made two mistakes. First, he incorrectly concluded from the fact that many of our expectations about the world are both genetically a priori and (even) logically prior to observation that they are, therefore, a priori valid. Although many of his transcendentally oriented successors have hedged on Kant's full-blown ambitions for a priori validity, they persist in committing his second, lesser, but more subtle error. They, like Kant, presume that because we automatically find (our experience of) the world to be a certain way that we must be *successful* in our imposition upon nature of the constitutive expectations in question. Popper demurs: "When Kant said, 'Our intellect does not draw its laws from nature but imposes its laws upon nature,' he was right. But in thinking that . . . we necessarily succeed in imposing them upon nature, he was wrong. Nature very often resists quite successfully . . ." (Popper 1963: 48). That such cognitive dispositions come so naturally to us and that our presumptions about such dispositions do too, do not warrant any conclusions about their successful application to the world. They only possess a passable probability of success (as measured, ultimately, by our reproductive success) in our species' environment-of-evolutionary-adaptedness (Tooby and Cosmides 1992).

More often than not, in the last century the privileged expectations under debate have concerned our *inner* natures, i.e. our mental lives, rather than the external world. These include everything from traditional phenomenology's presumptions about pure, mental exercises gaining access to the contents and character of the mental representation undistorted by any theoretical commitments, to Nagel (1974) drawing epistemological conclusions about the character and limits of scientific objectivity on the basis of what he takes to be inescapable presuppositions about human subjectivity, to proposed reductions of consciousness bemusing Searle, because he finds the proposed psycho-neural identities so obviously implausible on what are, basically, common sense grounds.[2,3]

For the naturalist, traditional philosophical tools and insights and attention to ordinary language and common sense are perfectly legitimate means for initiating inquiry and valuable propaedeutics to the formulation of more *systematic* theories. Moreover, the sheer inertia these means enjoy on the basis of their widespread appeal, their intuitive charm, and their long-standing philosophical service indicates that their counsel and influence should not be discounted nor even curtailed unless it is fairly clear how each of those apparent virtues can be explained away (on a case by case basis).

Even if they cannot be explained away, though, for naturalists these considerations neither guarantee anything nor are they always the whole story. The first sticking point is simply the relentlessness of human fallibility in the development and application of even what have proved to be our best tools and insights up to now (including those of science). Second, the interpretivists are right to affirm the thoroughly contingent character of even our most familiar conceptual commitments as they are embedded in our ordinary language, in our common sense, and in our everyday assumptions about both the world and its workings. On this count, naturalists simply highlight two related considerations: first, that those conceptual commitments' contingency is the best possible evidence that they are only speculations and, second, that those everyday assumptions about the world and its workings include assumptions about our minds and their workings.[4]

Finally, these standard philosophical tools neither supersede nor diminish our obligations as inquirers to press those more systematic theories – as rigorously as we can – for greater precision, for greater detail, and for a continuing ability to make sense of new features of the world. Why should simply sifting through the intuitions – even the intuitions of particularly thoughtful, intelligent people – that dominate at a particular time and place and checking them against what is, in effect, a comparatively casual project in the sociology of language exhaust the methods of philosophy? Not only do they not provide the whole story, in domains where means for systematic empirical inquiry have emerged, they no longer even provide the whole of the introduction to the story.

Suggestions that one of philosophy's most valuable contributions to human knowledge is its penchant for spawning sciences and that philosophers are obliged to square their proposals with the facts and, more specifically, with the scientific facts (where we have them) go back at least as far as Hume, arguably as far as Descartes, and even as far, perhaps, as the thirteenth century (Grant 1996). It was Quine, however, who was principally responsible for naturalism's revitalization in epistemology over the last few decades. Noting logical empiricism's inability to provide a compelling reconstruction of scientific rationality, Quine asked "why all this creative reconstruction, all this make believe? ... why not settle for psychology?" arguing that it is "[b]etter to discover how science is in fact developed and learned than to fabricate a fictitious structure to a similar effect" (1969: 75, 78). Developing a useful philosophical account of scientific rationality will turn, in part, on gaining "an understanding of science as an institution or a process in the world . . ." (Quine 1969: 84). Therefore, pursuing the sciences of science at *multiple* analytical levels will prove a fundamental ingredient in the new, naturalized epistemology that Quine anticipated. A naturalized epistemology amounts to the sciences of science and normative epistemology standing in a relationship of "reciprocal containment" (Quine 1969: 83).

Consonant with his rigorous empiricism, however, Quine unfortunately restricted his own speculations to a pinched and narrow form of psychological investigation, namely, behaviorism. Of course, the crucial development since Quine sketched his account has been the emergence of the cognitive sciences, which have generated a much broader set of investigative techniques and yielded a far deeper and richer picture of the structure and operations of the human mind. It is also a picture that offers much greater promise of achieving fruitful integration with related sciences at adjoining analytical levels in science, both above and below.

III. The cognitive approach to ritual

As Quine hoped, one of the most carefully studied topics of the new sciences of the mind is scientific reasoning itself.[5] Cognitive scientists' research on scientific thinking and practice has simultaneously revealed

- well worn methods for provoking creative, promising solutions to scientific questions (e.g. Dunbar 1995 and 1997),
- recurring limitations and fallibility of individual scientific reasoners (e.g. Mynatt *et al.* 1981), and
- effective strategies that scientific communities have devised for compensating for those individuals' limitations and, as a result, for making sound global judgments, given the evidence available at the time (e.g. Thagard 1992).

Such scientific research on science has encouraged the development of more sophisticated and detailed epistemological proposals concerning the reasonableness of the sciences. Instead of advancing disembodied philosophical ideals formulated in isolation from actual scientific activity, naturalists' proposals aim to identify patterns and practices that underlie exemplary scientific achievements in order to understand just what humans are capable of doing (if not very often individually in the short run, then at least collectively over the longer run in a surprising number of cases). For the naturalist, though, even these newly proposed epistemological ideals must themselves inevitably undergo overhaul and revision in the light of both new empirical findings in the sciences of science and the emergence of new forms and methods of scientific research that invariably accompany theoretical innovations, especially in new domains.

The sciences of science and particularly the cognitive science of science are flourishing enterprises (see, for example, Keil and Wilson 2000 and Carruthers *et al.* 2002). But, as with most contemporary intellectuals, most cognitive scientists, until quite recently, have simply found topics like religion and ritual embarrassments. At one level this is no surprise. No topic – not sex, death, taxes, nor terrorism – can elicit any more quirky, unpredictable responses from intellectuals than can the topic of religion and its accoutrements such as ritual. On this front, cognitive scientists generally fly with the flock.

That they do so, though, is, at another level, a puzzlement. The cognitive processing that undergirds science is of interest to cognitive scientists, because it has proven reasonable and largely explicable. But on some fronts the cognitive processes involved in science are also comparatively unusual. Some of the cognitive tasks that doing good science requires are ones that humans usually find extremely difficult to do. This is one of the major reasons why, in the long expanse of human history, lasting traditions of empirical science are comparatively rare (McCauley 2000). By contrast, the cognitive processing that undergirds religion and ritual seems *less obviously explicable* (since it is much less obviously rational) yet far more *widespread*. Cognitive science has had a great deal to say about the generally rational, largely tractable, easily isolable, but comparatively uncommon forms of cognition associated with science, but, with a few welcome exceptions, next to nothing to say (until recently) about the unreasonable, sprawling, but ubiquitous forms of cognition associated with things like ritual and religion.

Happily, a small group of cognitive scientists (e.g. Barrett 2000) have turned to these topics over the past decade or so and advanced proposals that aim to substantially demystify religion and ritual – by no means the least for their fellow cognitive scientists![6] As is true with any scientific pursuit, these researchers advance diverging views about a dozen different matters, but their mutual subscription to at least two positions unites them. The first is that many recurrent features of religion and ritual turn, primarily, on the proclivities of the human mind, and that scholarship during the twentieth century, especially within cultural anthropology, has overestimated the contributions of culture – certainly, "culture" conceived as some super-individual force – to these patterns. Consequently, these researchers agree that the theories, methods, and findings of the cognitive sciences over the past three decades offer the study of symbolic forms (such as ritual) a wealth of resources. Their second joint commitment is that, appearances to the contrary notwithstanding, religion generally and religious ritual in particular involve relatively modest variations on everyday cognitive processing – variations that are themselves commonplace and not at all unique to religion. In the remainder of this section, I will explore some of the implications of this second commitment for a cognitive account of religious ritual.

All of these cognitive theorists maintain that, in large part, what makes religion what it is turns on perfectly ordinary variations arising and persisting in the course of the operations of comparably ordinary mental machinery.

Thus, contrary to the dominant assumptions of mainstream religious studies, accounting for religious belief and conduct requires neither employing special methods nor postulating distinctively religious or "spiritual" faculties or sensibilities (Lawson and McCauley 1993). Whether the modestly counter-intuitive representations characteristic of religion and religious ritual arise and persist in human minds

1   because of a need to explain anomalous (i.e. counter-intuitive) phenomena and various feelings associated with experiencing them, or
2   because of an overly sensitive agent detection device, convincing us, for example, that agents possessing counter-intuitive properties are what are always going-bump-in-the-night, or
3   because, however they arise, they prove particularly recognizable, attention grabbing, memorable, communicable, and motivating,

they certainly do not differ drastically from our intuitive understandings of the world. Reliably, these representations involve small irregularities in our standard assumptions about the world. So, although the gods, goddesses, and ghosts as well as the demons, angels, and ancestors, who populate religious ontologies and with whom the religious interact in rituals, possess abnormal physical, biological, or psychological properties (so that they can be everywhere at once, born of virgins, or capable of knowing our thoughts), they are otherwise perfectly normal agents with all of the standard sorts of interests, motivations, and states of mind we acknowledge in our conspecifics. Their few peculiarities make these representations easily recognizable, attention grabbing, and memorable (Jesus walked on water!), while their conformity with virtually all of our default assumptions about psychologies and social relations enable even the most naive participants to reason about them effortlessly. We can deploy the same folk psychology that we utilize in human commerce to understand, explain, and predict the gods' states of mind and behaviors. Most particularly, so far as ritual is concerned, they have the same sorts of interests and understandings of transactions with other agents that characterize the wide range of interactions that arise in every human society (Boyer 2001).

To describe these representations as *"modestly"* counter-intuitive presumes a contrast not only *with our standard assumptions* about the world (that, in fact, agents have bodies and cannot be everywhere at once, that members of sexually reproducing species arise as the results of the standard procreative acts, and that only the mentally ill think that they hear others' thoughts), but also *with far more radically counter-intuitive representations* that humans have proven capable of entertaining. The overwhelming majority of these sorts of representations have arisen not in fiction or in fantasy but rather in science. Over the history of science these have included representations of such things as the earth spinning at roughly a thousand miles an hour, of "solid" matter as mostly empty space, of light as both like particles and like waves, and of the contents of human consciousness as often largely disconnected with the actual causes of human behavior. Sooner or later, traditions of scientific investigation reliably generate radically counter-intuitive representations. That it inevitably involves radically counter-intuitive representations is one of the reasons why science is so difficult to learn and so difficult to do (McCauley 2000). Most prominently, it is no coincidence that one way of describing the progress of science in human history is to note its increasing restriction over the centuries of those domains in which it is any longer legitimate to employ that ever-so-intuitively-appealing mode of explanation that relies on the concept of *agent causality* (Churchland 1989).

Nor has religion even cornered the market on modestly counter-intuitive representations. Representations of agents of similar sorts are the currency of folklore, fairy tales, comic books, cartoons, and, of course, mental illness. When the same sorts of counter-intuitive properties in which religions traffic are attributed to Superman, Mighty Mouse, or the Big Bad Wolf, we regard them as fantastical amusements that are childish, laughable, or silly. People who seriously claim to be able to interact first hand with such counter-intuitive agents (as most religious people do when they participate in ritual or in prayer) but who, crucially, are *unable* to enlist others in these speculations are quite regularly confined by their families, their friends, or the state.

These similarities among these various sorts of modestly counter-intuitive representations notwithstanding, religious representations clearly do present additional explanatory problems, since, unlike Superman, Mighty Mouse, and the Big Bad Wolf and unlike the imagined interlocutors of the mentally ill, religious representations elicit all sorts of special attitudes and behaviors from large numbers of individuals that give every indication of their seriousness and convictions about these matters. Even scholars of religion, no matter how cultivated their sensitivities, inevitably confront claims about particular features of someone else's deities – especially those of small religious groups that have yet to garner widespread followings – that they find nothing short of hilarious. Yet comparably incredible claims about the counter-intuitive properties of their own cultures' gods regularly elicit acquiescence, if not outright reverence and ritual participation.

Human beings' proclivities to carry out individual and collective rituals associated with their religious representations present further explanatory tasks. But, of course, religion is not unique on this front either. Some of what we commonly regard as non-religious representations are capable of generating such behaviors as well. Not only are representations of Santa Claus and the Tooth Fairy capable of eliciting such conduct from human beings too, but both representations of nation states (such as flags) and representations of Elvis do as well. In light of the number of domains in which representations of modestly counter-intuitive agents arise and on the assumption that veneration neither of the Tooth Fairy, nor of the state, nor of Elvis (Santa Claus may be a much closer call) should count as paradigmatic cases of religious ritual,[7] it seems fairly clear, at least from a cognitive standpoint, that religiosity exploits a variety of human cognitive endowments that have no logical or psychological unity. Cognitively speaking, religion is an exceedingly complicated contraption calling on all sorts of psychological propensities that are, otherwise, usually unconnected. The standard features of religious mentality and conduct are cobbled together from the susceptibilities of a disparate compilation of evolved psychological dispositions[8] that typically develop in normal human minds for very different reasons – both from one another and from anything having to do with religion.

Religious ritual exploits at least one such disposition, namely, our possession of a cognitive system for the representation of agents and their actions. It is critical to humans' survival (and, surely, to many other animals' survival as well) that they are able to distinguish agents from other things in the world and actions from other events. (It is also critical to entertaining narrative accounts of the succession of events over time.) The key suggestion is that an inability, in species' environments-of-evolutionary-adaptedness, to make these distinctions reliably would guarantee them far too many opportunities to serve as their various predators' lunch (Tooby and Cosmides 1992). Psychologists (e.g. Leslie 1995) have offered a variety of proposals about the various features that cue agent-detection in human beings, attaching prominence to such considerations as some things' abilities not only to move themselves but to move themselves in irregular paths in the pursuit of various goals.

For comparatively sophisticated social creatures such as ourselves, the issue is not only one of detecting and avoiding predators. We also recognize a relevant class of agents in the world with whom we can interact and whose aid we might be able to recruit.[9] For most of us most of the time, some subset of our conspecifics exhaust this class of recruitable agents. Human goals and our abilities to communicate them are sufficiently complex that we develop and deploy what has become known in the literature (e.g. Wellman 1990) as "theory of mind" in calculating our own behaviors, others' reactions to our behaviors, and their calculations about both as well as about our own calculations. In order to manage in our complicated network of social relations, allowing not only for our own but other agents' goals and interests as well, we quickly develop the ability to "read" those agents' minds, a capacity that seems firmly in place by middle childhood.[10]

Tom Lawson and I have argued that participants' representations and knowledge of their religious rituals rely on garden variety cognitive capacities concerning the representation of agents and their actions, which develop quite naturally in every normal human being (Lawson and McCauley 1990 and McCauley and Lawson 2002). A wide range of evidence from developmental psychology indicates that human beings readily distinguish agents and actions at a very early age (see Rochat *et al.* 1997). At ages as early as nine months, children seem capable not merely of recognizing agents but of attributing goals to them (Rochat and Striano 1999). This cognitive machinery seems task specific, and it is – with only a few exceptions – pervasive among human beings (Baron-Cohen 1995).

These cognitive capacities are parts of what we have referred to as the human "action representation system" (Lawson and McCauley 1990: 87–95; McCauley and Lawson 2002: 10–26). Our cognitive system for the representation of action imposes fundamental, though commonplace, constraints on ritual form. Attention to these constraints enables us to look beyond the variability of religious rituals' culturally specific details to some of their most general underlying features. The point, in short, is that religious rituals (despite what often seem to be their bizarre, inexplicable qualities) are conceived as actions too, and human beings bring the same representational apparatus to bear on them as they do with all other actions. Thus, our general system for the representation of action is also responsible for participants' representations of their religious rituals' forms. Postulating special machinery to account for the representation of religious rituals is unnecessary. That normal human beings readily grasp such features of actions intuitively is the first line of evidence that they possess such a system of representation. That these simple, basic distinctions about actions and, therefore, about rituals will provide a framework for systematically explaining and predicting many of religious rituals' recurrent features is an additional consideration suggesting that the human brain possesses such representational machinery.

Agents and their agency are clearly central concepts for the representation of action, but they are not the whole story. A representational framework for characterizing this special sort of event must also capture familiar presumptions about the internal structures and external relations of actions. Our theory of religious ritual begins with what have proven to be some relatively uncontroversial assumptions about that representational system. Specifically – without pretending to capture all of the nuances of action representation of which human beings are capable – it will suffice to note that the representation of actions will include slots for agents and for the acts they carry out as well as for the patients of those actions, and for the various qualities, properties, and conditions sufficient to distinguish them. Agents with particular properties do things, and, more often than not, they do things to other things (including other agents).

Rituals' basic structures are no different. They comprise the roles (agents, acts, instruments, and patients) that distinguish actions (and rituals) both from other events and happenings and from one another. They permit – as ritual elements – the various entities and acts, as well as their properties, qualities, and conditions, that can fulfill these roles in religious rituals.

The representations of ritual actions also manifest routine points of variability in actions, such as whether they involve the use of instruments as a condition for their success, and they accommodate the enabling relationships between actions, such as whether the performance of one act presupposes the performance of another. Rituals' action representations conform to the constraint that although any item filling the role of the agent may also serve as a patient, not all items that serve as patients may also fill the agent role. So, agents can do things to other agents, and agents can act on objects, but objects – except for some exceptional objects in religious ritual contexts – are not agents capable of action.

That last qualification provides a significant clue about what is distinctive about religious rituals. First, to reiterate, note, that from the standpoint of basic action structure *nothing* is distinctive about religious rituals. It is not any transformation of the operations or the structures of the outputs of the human action representation system that sets religious rituals apart. Their distinctiveness, instead, turns exclusively on introducing entities with counter-intuitive properties into at least one of the slots of their basic action structures. So, when some inanimate object (e.g. a statue of a saint) is presumed to possess counter-intuitive psychological properties, such as the ability to hear prayers and, perhaps, the ability to refer them to other unseen agents for immediate action, the possibility arises of what we would otherwise regard as an inanimate object possibly serving in the role of an agent in religious ritual contexts.

The representations of religious rituals are no different from the representations of normal actions. Inanimate objects are incapable of agency. Within the conceptual schemes of religious systems, however, some things that we normally regard as inanimate objects (statues, paintings, mountains, the sun, etc.) are *not* classified that way. It is the insertion of these and other modestly counter-intuitive representations into the slots of religious rituals' action structures that is both distinctive and determinative.

Rituals' basic action structures and the roles attributed to agents with counter-intuitive properties, in particular, are the key considerations in the theory that Lawson and I have proposed for predicting a number of those rituals' features that recur across the wide array of religious ritual systems. Assuming our theory's principles describe, albeit quite abstractly, capacities that are psychologically real, they also constitute a first pass at an empirically testable, explanatory hypothesis about the cognitive mechanisms behind participants' facility at generating comparatively stable judgments about those features – both across subjects and within subjects over time (see, for example, Barrett and Lawson 2001).

Most participants' knowledge of their ritual systems is overwhelmingly implicit (Reber 1993). It is like their grammatical knowledge of the language that they speak or their knowledge of the basic etiquette and social conventions of their culture (concerning, for example, the constraints on appropriate bodily contact in various social settings). To call such knowledge "implicit" is to highlight the fact that under most circumstances, it is knowledge to which people have little, if any, direct, conscious access. So, although native speakers of a language have little difficulty understanding well-formed utterances of no more than moderate complexity and, usually, only slightly more difficulty producing such utterances themselves, they are often incapable of articulating even a single principle underlying those competences.

Their instant sensitivity to violations suggests that people have a mastery over these domains and a mastery that, in fact, involves both considerable knowledge and knowledge that is considerably detailed. If a lecturer chooses to position his or her face three inches from the face of someone sitting in the first row of the audience, everyone will immediately recognize the breach of etiquette involved. Moreover, they will be clear about the relevant variables, namely, that this is primarily a matter of a violation of personal space, that it may be complicated somewhat by the genders of the lecturer and the unfortunate audience member, but that between the two inappropriate extremes the volume of the lecturer's voice is of relatively minor importance in this embarrassing and uncomfortable situation. In short, not only do participants in such symbolic-cultural systems immediately detect such violations, they are usually clear about the particular features of the violations that render them problematic.

Typically, participants in such symbolic-cultural systems (language, etiquette, religious ritual, etc.) do not receive explicit instruction about the principles underlying such competences, or, if they do, such *explicit* instruction is often partial, occasional, and not fully consistent. Participants appear to acquire their knowledge of these systems spontaneously on the basis of mere exposure. Whether this is the result of minds *innately* prepared to detect such patterns in the social environment, as Chomsky has so famously and so controversially maintained, or not, the necessary sensitivities to stimuli in the environment always presume the possession of tacit hypotheses that determine what count as *relevant* phenomena (see Elman *et al.* 1996).

Religious ritual is no different. The overwhelming majority of religious ritual participants in human history have acquired their knowledge of their rituals in just this way. Note that that overwhelming majority was either illiterate or non-literate, so any explicit instruction they had was delivered orally and, usually, itself retrieved from all too fallible human memories (as opposed to being retrieved from somewhat less variable texts) (McCauley 1999). It is not a coincidence that so much explicit religious instruction, even in *literate* settings, puts such a premium on *memorization*.

Similarly, participants in religious ritual systems are just as thoroughly and just as systematically sensitive to violations. Although they are normally incapable of laying out explicitly any principles that might organize the constraints on their religious rituals, let alone any mechanisms that might generate them, they possess powerful intuitions about those constraints on the acceptability and effectiveness of religious rituals when either confronted with violations or probed by experimentalists on the topic (Barrett and Lawson 2001). Participants in religious ritual systems have extensive implicit knowledge about their rituals that – on virtually all important theoretical fronts – is four-square with the implicit knowledge that native speakers have about utterances in their natural languages.

The decisive variable for predicting and explaining a wide array of religious rituals' properties concerns precisely where in participants' ritual representations, i.e. in which slots, they presume entry of agents that possess counter-intuitive properties. So, whether, through intermediaries or directly, they are implicated as the agents or the patients in the ritual at hand will determine many of a ritual's properties. When these counter-intuitive agents arise first in (or in connection with) the agent-slot of a ritual representation (e.g. in Christian baptism[11]), resulting in what Lawson and I (2002: 26) have dubbed a "special agent ritual," the ritual in question will typically be performed on each individual patient only once. This is the sense in which we describe these rituals as (normally) *non-repeated*. These rituals may permit substitutions for their instruments or patients, but rarely, if ever, for their agents.

Under most circumstances, participants will intuitively recognize the sufficiency of these special agent rituals to effect important, lasting changes in the ritual patients. Within any particular religious community, no rituals that participants undergo individually will involve any higher levels of sensory stimulation than these. The sensory pageantry associated within a particular religious community with such special agent rituals as initiations and weddings will reliably exceed that characteristic of rituals of purification, blessings, and sacrifices. Around the world, these special agent rituals regularly include such stimulants as music, dance, flowers, incense, and special foods and clothing, and, if these are not enough to reliably get the patients' attention, they often resort to more extreme forms of sensory arousal, such as torture. These rituals tend to produce critical moments in patients' lives that generate salient episodic memories,[12] especially when people throughout the patients' in-group continue to corroborate these rituals' importance, after the fact.

Oddly, their cultural significance notwithstanding, the effects of these rituals can be reversed. Sometimes, couples get divorced, priests get defrocked, and participants can be excommunicated. (Such reversals result in one of the few circumstances in which the original special agent rituals can be repeated with the same patient.) Although sometimes religious systems allow for the possibility of achieving some of these reversals ritually, it seems that at least as often the procedures are juridical. In any event, the procedures reliably involve no elevated levels of sensory pageantry, even though by parity of reasoning their effects would seem to be of comparable religious and cultural significance.

If, on the other hand, an agent with counter-intuitive properties first arises in a ritual's basic action structure in connection with that ritual's instrument or patient, it occasions a contrasting constellation of properties. These "special instrument" and "special patient" rituals, unlike their special agent counterparts, are capable of repetition (with the same instrument or patient) and can sometimes even involve what can seem like incessant repetition. So, for example, Christians celebrate the Eucharist time and time again, even though they are typically baptized only once. Many Jews participate in regular ritual baths, though they have but a single wedding ceremony.

Participants usually do not have memories for specific performances of these special instrument and special patient rituals (except, perhaps, for the very most recent ones), in contrast to their often quite salient memories for their performances of special agent rituals. Their knowledge of these rituals takes the form of what cognitive scientists call a "script" (Schank and Abelson 1977). Most special instrument and special patient rituals are the ones that participants perform so often that they become routine. Under such circumstances, their command of these rituals arises from the familiarity anyone gains with actions they carry out regularly. Their ritual performance becomes the exercise of a well-rehearsed skill in the way that driving does for experienced drivers. Consequently, participants are often said to perform these rituals "mindlessly."

Normally, the routine performance of skilled behaviors does not tend to be particularly arousing emotionally. Nor do special instrument and special patient rituals contain high levels of sensory stimulation, compared with the performances of special agent rituals within the same religious communities. This is true, even when participants do not perform these special instrument and special patient rituals often. This is perfectly possible, since participants may repeat these rituals but they are not usually obligated to do so. An example would be the hajj, the pilgrimage to Mecca that all Muslims are expected to make at least once in their lifetimes. Muslims are free to go on this pilgrimage more than once, if they choose and can afford to do so, but it is not necessary. Special instrument and special patient rituals with low performance frequencies are (like the hajj) often long, complicated, busy, and expensive to undertake, but any emotional stimulation they may involve is typically not a direct function of anything about their forms (McCauley 2001b).

Why are these rituals repeatable and, usually, so often repeated? Special patient rituals make this particularly easy to see. In these rituals, it is the ritual element in the patient slot of the ritual's action structure that, *ex hypothesi,* if not an agent with counter-intuitive properties itself, at least enjoys the most direct ritual connection to an agent with counter-intuitive properties. These are rituals, such as sacrifices, where humans do things to or for the gods (or ancestors or saints, etc.), usually for the purpose of influencing their states of mind and, consequently, of increasing the probabilities of favorable views of the participants and benign behaviors toward them. But humans' abilities and resources are limited, while (for example) the appetites of agents with counter-intuitive properties can be insatiable. Or, in the case of special instrument rituals, since humans' failures are unending, they are always in need of further help. Another blessing never hurts. Therefore, religious participants must perform most of these rituals time and time again. Because such obligations can consume considerable time and resources, many religious ritual systems permit substitutions for a wider range of ritual elements in these rituals in comparison to the allowable substitutions in special agent rituals. Specifically, since human beings are the agents in these rituals, these special instrument and special patient rituals can permit substitutes for these human agents. So, although because of their special, ritually established relationship with the relevant counter-intuitive agent, appropriate members of the church's ecclesiastical hierarchy are the only human agents capable of performing rituals of ordination, Roman Catholicism now permits lay substitutes to *administer* the Eucharist.

By contrast, in the case of special agent rituals (such as ordinations), where agents with counter-intuitive properties are most directly connected ritually with the proximal ritual's agent, it is the agents possessing modestly counter-intuitive properties who act – at least indirectly via their priestly intermediaries. In contrast to humans, the gods (usually) need do things only once. Since that is so often true, these special agent rituals need to incorporate features that will convince their patients that something profoundly important has transpired. This is why, comparatively speaking, these are the rituals within any particular religious community that will come to include lots of sensory pageantry aimed at seizing the patient's attention and arousing his or her emotions. Religious systems around the world regularly manipulate these and additional variables to heighten the salience of these rituals and to increase the probabilities that they will constitute benchmarks in the participants' life histories. Other means range from performing the rituals on all of the members of an entire age cohort, to the revelation of *secret* knowledge, to direct confrontations with the counter-intuitive agents themselves (for example, as masked dancers or as skulls illuminated in caves or as entire mountains). These ritual episodes contribute fundamentally to participants' understandings of themselves. They become integral to participants' identities.

Needless to say, this is not the whole story. Whatever social, cultural, emotional, and motivational dynamics impinge on and are occasioned by religious ritual proceedings, participants' action representation systems automatically deploy to frame ritual arrangements. Participants' competence with their religious ritual systems turns on their abilities to represent agents, actions, and the relationships between them. What distinguishes religious rituals is the introduction of representations of agents possessing counter-intuitive properties into slots in the representations of these actions or of actions they directly presuppose that render such actions obligatory for the participant. I have outlined in this section some of the consequences of all of this for religious rituals' properties and participants' implicit knowledge about these properties. Not only has this outline inevitably involved appeal to other forms of tacit knowledge most human beings possess – beyond their bare abilities to entertain distinctive representations of actions and to operate with folk psychology – but so too will useful extensions of our theory.

Any fuller explication of those consequences will invariably traverse the terrain of human beings' intuitive understandings of their *social* relations. Sooner or later, religious rituals always involve presumptions about some very special agents – but the fundamental point is that simply construing them as *agents* is every bit as important to grasping the structure and character of religious ritual systems as anything about their special counter-intuitive properties. Religious ritual systems allow *transactions* with such agents that have import for participants' *quasi-social* relationships with those agents.

Religious rituals activate other sorts of automatic, instant, and mostly intuitive systems that pertain to human beings' knowledge of their *social* worlds. Normal human cognitive development results, again by middle childhood, in a sophisticated command – even if in little explicit knowledge – of a host of patterns and principles that constrain humans' social relations. The resulting implicit knowledge is capable, in the right circumstances, of generating strong intuitions and powerful emotions in those who possess it, yet they are often startlingly inarticulate about its underlying standards and contours. What they do know about unhesitatingly, most of the time, are such things as how social hierarchies are structured and what they require, how material and social exchange works and the implications of reciprocity, and how they can lay claim in a socially acceptable fashion to their "share" of available resources.

Religious ritual participants' transactions with the gods activate these systems too. They automatically enable participants to enlist all of these insights and more into their understandings of their religious ritual conduct and of their religious ritual systems overall. Religious ritual practices constitute social transactions with the gods that involve much of the same give and take that characterizes our relationships with our conspecifics.

Such forms of knowledge are remarkable in the light of our instantaneous, intuitive access to them, their psychologically compelling authority, and humans' comparative inability to articulate either their foundations or even their superstructures. It is precisely because these are the kinds of knowledge that the tools of traditional analytic philosophy have been hard pressed to illuminate that naturalism in philosophy was born. Over the past two decades, cognitive scientists have turned to the exploration of the natural history of such dispositions in our species (e.g. Tooby and Cosmides 1992) and the mechanisms underlying them (e.g. Elman *et al.* 1996). Advocates of a cognitive approach to religious ritual see promise in these inquiries for gaining insight not only about ritual but about a wide array of recurrent religious and cultural patterns.[13]

Notes

1 Paul Churchland's account (1989: 223) of "a virtuous mode of explanatory understanding" in terms of parallel distributed processing models of cognition signals growing moderation in his own version of philosophical naturalism about our interests in normative epistemology.
2 Searle fatally underestimates just how counter-intuitive scientific achievements can be (Churchland and Churchland 1998: 128; see also McCauley 2000).
3 For an account of the considerations that contribute to the plausibility of psychoneural identities, see Bechtel and McCauley (1999) and McCauley and Bechtel (2001).
4 The mistake that tempted so many interpretivists was to conclude that such sweeping contingency requires that we surrender our hopes for characterizing a compelling account of reasonableness. Pervasive contingency, however, requires no more than construing rationality as carrying out the best search we can for the most effective set of conjectures possible and recognizing that, in fact, we typically must settle for small improvements here and there (see Thagard 1992).
5 As but one illustration, consider the work of Paul Thagard and his collaborators. See, for example, Thagard (1988, 1992, and 1999); Holland *et al.* (1986); and Holyoak and Thagard (1995).
6 See, for example, Lawson and McCauley (1990) and McCauley and Lawson (2002); Whitehouse (1992 and 2000); Guthrie, (1993); Boyer (1994 and 2001); Hinde (1999); Pyysiäinen (2001); Pyysiäinen and Anttonen (2002); Andresen (2001) and Atran (2002).
7 I defend that assumption at length in McCauley 2003.
8 For a discussion of the relation between adaptive cognitive dispositions and their various latent susceptibilities, see Sperber (1996: 66–7).
9 We are, however, not the only species capable of such discriminations. See de Waal (1996).
10 Barrett *et al.* (2001), in effect, argue that children are able to represent (and read) the minds of agents with counter-intuitive properties at an even earlier age.
11 I will confine myself here to illustrations from religious systems with which, I presume, the majority of my readers have some familiarity. See Lawson and

McCauley (1990) and McCauley and Lawson (2002) for discussions of Muslim, Hindu, Jain, Taoist, Zulu, Baktaman, Pomio Kivung, and Latter Day Saints' rituals and more.

12 See Tulving (1983) for an extended, systematic treatment of the distinction between episodic and semantic memory.

13 I wish to express my gratitude to Kevin Schilbrack for his helpful comments on an earlier draft of this paper.

Bibliography

Andresen, J. (2001) *Religion in Mind: Cognitive Perspectives on Religious Belief, Ritual, and Experience*, Cambridge: Cambridge University Press.

Atran, S. (2002) *In Gods We Trust*, Oxford: Oxford University Press.

Baron-Cohen, S. (1995) *Mindblindness: An Essay on Autism and Theory of Mind*, Cambridge: MIT Press.

Barrett, J. L. (2000) "Exploring the Natural Foundations of Religion," *Trends in Cognitive Science* 4: 29–34.

—— and Lawson, E. T. (2001) "Ritual Intuitions: Cognitive Contributions to Judgements of Ritual Efficacy," *Journal of Cognition and Culture* 1: 183–201.

——, Richert, R. A. and Driesenga, A. (2001) "God's Beliefs versus Mom's: The Development of Natural and Non-Natural Agent Concepts," *Child Development* 72: 50–65.

Bechtel, W. and McCauley, R. N. (1999) "Heuristic Identity Theory (or Back to the Future): The Mind-Body Problem Against the Background of Research Strategies in Cognitive Neuroscience," in M. Hahn and S. C. Stones (eds), *Proceedings of the Twenty-First Meeting of the Cognitive Science Society*, 67–72, Mahway, NJ: Lawrence Erlbaum Associates.

Bickle, J. (1998) *Psychoneural Reduction: The New Wave*, Cambridge, MA: MIT Press.

Boyer, P. (1994) *The Naturalness of Religious Ideas*, Berkeley: University of California Press.

—— (2001) *Religion Explained*, New York: Basic Books.

Carruthers, P., Stich, S., and Siegal, M. (2002) *The Cognitive Basis of Science*, Cambridge: Cambridge University Press.

Churchland, P. M. (1979) *Scientific Realism and the Plasticity of Mind*, Cambridge: Cambridge University Press.

—— (1989) *A Neurocomputational Perspective: The Nature of Mind and the Structure of Science*, Cambridge: MIT Press.

—— and Churchland, P. S. (1998) *On the Contrary*, Cambridge, MA: MIT Press.

Churchland, P. S. (1986) *Neurophilosophy*, Cambridge, MA: MIT Press.

de Waal, F. (1996) *Good Natured: The Origins of Right and Wrong in Humans and Other Animals*, Cambridge: Harvard University Press.

Dunbar, K. (1995) "How Scientists Really Reason: Scientific Reasoning in Real-World Laboratories," in R. J. Sternberg and J. Davidson (eds), *The Nature of Insight*, 365–95, Cambridge: MIT Press.

—— (1997) "How Scientists Think: On-Line Creativity and Conceptual Change in Science," in T. Ward, S. Smith, and S. Vaid (eds), *Creative Thought: An Investigation of Conceptual Structures and Processes*, 461–93, Washington: APA Press.

Elman, J. L., Bates, E. A., Johnson, M. H., Karmiloff-Smith, A., Parisi, D., and Plunkett, K. (1996) *Rethinking Innateness: A Connectionist Perspective on Development*, Cambridge: MIT Press.

Geertz, C. (1973) *The Interpretation of Cultures*, New York: Basic Books.

Grant, E. (1996) *The Foundations of Modern Science in the Middle Ages: Their Religious, Institutional, and Intellectual Contexts*, Cambridge: Cambridge University Press.

Guthrie, S. (1993) *Faces in the Clouds*, New York: Oxford University Press.

Hinde, R. (1999) *Why Gods Persist*, New York: Routledge.

Holland, J., Holyoak, K., Nisbett, R., and Thagard, P. (1986) *Induction: Processes of Inference, Learning, and Discovery*, Cambridge: MIT Press.

Hollis, M. and Lukes, S. (eds) (1982) *Rationality and Relativism*, Cambridge: MIT Press.

Holyoak, K. and Thagard, P. (1995) *Mental Leaps: Analogy in Creative Thought*, Cambridge: MIT Press.

Husserl, E. (1970) *The Crisis of European Sciences and Transcendental Phenomenology: An Introduction to Phenomenological Philosophy*, trans. D. Carr, Evanston: Northwestern University Press.

Keil, F. and Wilson, R. (eds) (2000) *Explanation and Cognition*, Cambridge: MIT Press.

Lawson, E. T. and McCauley, R. N. (1990) *Rethinking Religion: Connecting Cognition and Culture*, Cambridge: Cambridge University Press.

—— (1993) "Crisis of Conscience, Riddle of Identity: Making Space for a Cognitive Approach to Religious Phenomena," *Journal of the American Academy of Religion* 61: 201–23.

Leslie, A. (1995) "A Theory of Agency," in D. Sperber, D. Premack, and A. J. Premack (eds), *Causal Cognition: A Multidisciplinary Debate*, 121–47, New York: Oxford University Press.

McCauley, R. N. (1986) "Intertheoretic Relations and the Future of Psychology," *Philosophy of Science* 53: 179–99.

—— (1999) "Bringing Ritual to Mind," in E. Winograd, R. Fivush, and W. Hirst (eds), *Ecological Approaches to Cognition: Essays in Honor of Ulric Neisser*, 285–312, Hillsdale, NJ: Erlbaum.

—— (2000) "The Naturalness of Religion and the Unnaturalness of Science," in F. Keil and R. Wilson (eds), *Explanation and Cognition*, 61–85, Cambridge: MIT Press.

—— (2001a) "Explanatory Pluralism and the Coevolution of Theories in Science," in W. Bechtel, P. Mandik, J. Mundale, and R. Stufflebeam (eds), *Philosophy and the Neurosciences*, 431–56, Oxford: Blackwell Publishers.

—— (2001b) "Ritual, Memory, and Emotion: Comparing Two Cognitive Hypotheses," in J. Andresen (ed.), *Religion in Mind: Cognitive Perspectives on Religious Experience*, 115–40, Cambridge: Cambridge University Press.

—— (2003) "Is Religion a Rube Goldberg Device? Or Oh, What a Difference a Theory Makes!" in B. Wilson and T. Light (eds), *Religion as a Human Capacity: A Festschrift in Honor of E. Thomas Lawson*, Leiden: Brill.

—— (forthcoming) "On Reducing a Science," in L. Faucher, P. Poirier, and E. Ennan (eds), *Des Neurones à la Philosophie: Neurophilosophie et Philosophie des Neurosciences*.

—— and Bechtel, W. (2001) "Explanatory Pluralism and The Heuristic Identity Theory," *Theory and Psychology* 11: 738–61.

—— and Lawson, E. T. (2002) *Bringing Ritual to Mind: Psychological Foundations of Cultural Forms*, Cambridge: Cambridge University Press.

Mynatt, C. R., Doherty, M. E., and Tweney, R. D. (1981) "A Simulated Research Environment," in R. D. Tweney, M. E. Doherty, and C. R. Mynatt (eds), *On Scientific Thinking*, 145–57, New York: Columbia University Press.

Nagel, T. (1974) "What is it Like to Be a Bat?" *Philosophical Review* 83: 435–50.

—— (1986) *The View from Nowhere*, New York: Oxford University Press.

Popper, K. (1963) *Conjectures and Refutations*, New York: Harper and Row.

Pyysiäinen, I. (2001) *How Religion Works*, Leiden: Brill.

—— and Anttonen, V. (2002) *Current Approaches in the Cognitive Science of Religion*, London: Continuum.

Quine, W. V. O. (1969) *Ontological Relativity and Other Essays*, New York: Columbia University Press.

Reber, A. S. (1993) *Implicit Learning and Tacit Knowledge: An Essay on the Cognitive Unconscious*, New York: Oxford University Press.

Rochat, P., Morgan, R., and Carpenter, M. (1997) "Young Infants' Sensitivity to Movement Information Specifying Social Causality," *Cognitive Development* 12: 441–65.

—— and Striano, T. (1999) "Social Cognitive Development in the First Year," in P. Rochat (ed.), *Early Social Cognition*, 3–34, Mahway, NJ: Erlbaum.

Schank, R. C. and Abelson, R. P. (1977) *Scripts, Plans, Goals, and Understanding: An Inquiry into Human Knowledge Structures*, Hillsdale, NJ: Erlbaum.

Searle, J. (1992) *The Rediscovery of the Mind*, Cambridge: MIT Press.

Sperber, D. (1975) *Rethinking Symbolism*, trans. A. Morton, Cambridge: Cambridge University Press.

—— (1996) *Explaining Culture: A Naturalistic Approach*, Oxford: Blackwell Publishers.

Thagard. P. (1988) *Computational Philosophy of Science*, Cambridge: MIT Press.

—— (1992) *Conceptual Revolutions*, Princeton: Princeton University Press.

—— (1999) *How Scientists Explain Disease*, Princeton: Princeton University Press.

Tooby, J. and Cosmides, L. (1992) "The Psychological Foundations of Culture," in J. Barkow, L. Cosmides, and J. Tooby (eds), *The Adapted Mind*, 19–136, New York: Oxford University Press.

Tulving, E. (1983) *Elements of Episodic Memory*, Oxford: Clarendon Press.

Wellman, H. (1990) *The Child's Theory of Mind*, Cambridge: MIT Press.

Whitehouse, H. (1992) "Memorable Religions: Transmission, Codification and Change in Divergent Melanesian Contexts," *Man* 27: 777–97.

—— (1995) *Inside the Cult: Religious Innovation and Transmission in Papua New Guinea*, Oxford: Clarendon Press.

—— (2000) *Arguments and Icons: The Cognitive, Social, and Historical Implications of Divergent Modes of Religiosity*, Oxford: Oxford University Press.

Wilson, B. (ed.) (1970) *Rationality*, New York: Harper and Row.

Winch, P. (1958) *The Idea of a Social Science*, London: Routledge and Kegan Paul.

8 Theories and facts on ritual simultaneities

Frits Staal

Abstract

The use of language primarily displays succession, not simultaneity. It is common for people to talk at the same time or interrupt each other, but such cases are best reduced to cases of succession. Vedic ritual involves not only succession but also simultaneities that are structural. In the "Soma swelling" rite, priests recite two groups of mantras, A and B. First, one priest recites A while touching the bundle of Soma stalks. He then steps aside and recites B without touching Soma. At the same time, the next priest recites A and touches Soma, and so on. Other structural simultaneities may be attributed to a "horror of gaps." A separate class are stage directions. A final comment will be made on multifunctionality in space, a spatial parallel to the concept of simultaneity that relates to time.

I. Theories and facts: by way of introduction

"Thinking through ritual" was imposed upon me by circumstances wholly unforeseen and not of my own making. As a graduate student of philosophy and mathematics, working on logic, I had an opportunity to go to India to study Sanskrit and Indian philosophy. One of my hobbies became the recording of Veda recitation. I knew that bits and pieces of the Veda were recited during marriages and other life cycle rites, but it took a few more years before I discovered that the recitation of long sequences was not only done for me or my tape-recorder, as a rehearsal exercise or even for the sake of their preservation, but did occur also, though very rarely and with extraordinary variations, during performances of the Vedic so-called "solemn" (*srauta*) ritual. A couple of years later I was privileged to witness the 1975 performance, in a remote village in southwest India, of one of the most ancient and venerable of these rituals which had not been performed since 1956: the Agnicayana "ritual of the fire altar", which lasts for twelve days, continues through some of the nights and is replete with acts, chants, and recitations. I was fortunate to obtain the assistance of Robert Gardner who filmed and recorded the ritual together with his staff of photographers and technicians. This put me in possession and control of its physical manifestations on tape, plate, and film – not only in the field but in my Berkeley study, where it became obvious that I ought to write a book about it. What had started as a hobby now became an all-consuming occupation. Since I was mainly interested in establishing the facts, I wrote the first volume of the book, subsequently called *Agni* (Staal 1983) in close collaboration with the chief ritualists and officiants, C. V. Somayajipad and M. Itti Ravi Nambudiri. A second volume included contributions by specialists who wrote about history, archeology, Sanskrit texts, dispersion of elements of the ritual over Southeast, Central and East Asia, the society of the officiants, and other topics. I wrote myself a short essay on "Ritual Structure" which dealt with what I subsequently referred to as "Ritual Syntax." I did not at first call it by that name because, as a logician, I was aware of the relationships between syntax and semantics, but had not found much in the Agnicayana that could be called "ritual semantics" unless it was what the Introduction to the first Volume referred to as "Traditional Interpretations of the Agnicayana." Fortunately, I published the book before setting eyes on Euro-American theories of ritual which would have delayed publication considerably without being of much assistance since all of these theories seemed to be semantic. Was it only then that I started thinking through ritual which would justify my extravagant claim at the beginning of this long and self-indulgent paragraph?

Whatever it is, I published, after *Agni*, a fair amount of theoretical thinking on Vedic ritual (as well as mantras) in relation to Euro-American theories of ritual – or at least the ones I became familiar with (Staal 1984, 1986a, 1988, 1989b). All these theories are semantic because they hold or presuppose that ritual is connected with concepts such as religion, belief, text, myth, or communication. What these categories have in common is meaning. The first three display in addition a monotheist, in particular Protestant, hue. Some of my conclusions were the subjects of discussions (Alper and Padoux in Alper 1988; Grappard *et al.* 1991; Smith 1991; Staal 1993) or included in handbooks or readers. Some were not entirely new to Indology. The most prominent Sanskrit scholar of the twentieth century, Louis Renou, had written: "Vedic religion is first and foremost a liturgy, and only secondarily a mythological or speculative system; we must therefore investigate it as a liturgy" (1953: 29). Equally independent from my writings, though voiced more recently, is the statement by R. N. Dandekar, then the nestor of Indian Vedic scholars: "The Rigvedic mythology can be shown to have hardly any relation to the 'solemn' ritual" (1982: 77).

During the 1990s, when I was thinking about other topics such as the history of science, there occurred a breakthrough in Vedic studies. It was not due to any single work but emerged in professional journals and the proceedings of workshops. I reported on two of the latter (Staal 2000; Witzel 1997; and Bronkhorst and Deshpande 1999). The breakthrough was, at least in part, of a linguistic nature. It was concerned with archeology but focused on the study of Vedic dialects and the fact that some 300 words in the Rigveda, the oldest of the four Vedas, are not of Indo-European origin. I linked those discoveries with the study of Vedic altars and geometry (Staal 1999, 2001c) and the historical development of Vedic ritual in a forthcoming paper. I would like to give a brief account of that long and rather technical article – reducing it to a skeleton that may lack plausibility – because it throws unexpected light on the question why Vedic ritual possesses a syntax but no semantics. I did not discuss whether that result would set the Vedic tradition apart from the other ritual traditions on the planet.

My paper (Staal forthcoming) tried to demonstrate that Vedic srauta ritual developed from an attempt to forge a link between two rival ritual factions: reciters of Rigveda, who are or derive from speakers of Indo-Aryan that entered the subcontinent from the northwest and continued to wander in the eastern direction; and chanters of Samaveda, who belonged to an indigenous South Asian group of ritual specialists and spoke a non-Indo-European language. In the Agnicayana as it is presently known, that ancient stage of development survives in one area where, on several occasions, a row of reciters and a cluster of chanters sit in different places, back to back and facing opposite directions (see Figure 8.3, p. 184). What also survives are the exotic names that both parties use to address certain altars and with which they seem to be already familiar. These names are again non-Indo-European and some of them have been attributed to a Central Asian substrate language. If these reconstructions and demonstrations are correct, there would have been a time that close ritual cooperation took place between people who could not understand or communicate with each other, let alone enquire about each other's myths or speculations (there being no texts in preliterate societies).

An incredible fantasy? Not necessarily, because such a situation is not uncommon today in an international symphony orchestra, especially when there are last minute substitutes or visiting soloists. Musicians are able to cooperate closely without being able to converse with each other, understand or read the same language. The comparison suggests, as I had argued long ago (Staal 1986a, 1989b: ch. 16), that ritual is like music or dance – about which Isadora Duncan said: "If I could tell you what it meant there would be no point in dancing it." In international scientific cooperation, the linguistic situation is similar: experts do not need to know each other's natural language but must be able to understand international artificial languages such as the language of algebra.

I mention this recent article because it supports my theory of meaninglessness, though it was not written for that reason since that conclusion re-emerged only after writing several drafts. It strengthened my conviction, that what thinking-through-ritual needs most is to be steeped in Vedic facts, couched, to be sure, in a little thinking and a bit of theory but not too much. So when I was asked to write on "Thinking through Rituals: Philosophical Perspectives," I was delighted. It is important to pay due attention to facts – though the facts of Vedic ritual are not textual since that ritual tradition is oral, not in the sense of the loose orality paradigm of Milman Perry and A. B. Lord's epics, but in that of the fixed orality of, well, the Vedas (Staal 1986b, 1989a).

The following essay on the simultaneities in Vedic ritual is about facts that, to the best of my knowledge, have not been singled out for description or analysis before. It contrasts ritual with language, the primary and perhaps the only legitimate source of meaning. I think it is unlikely that facts like those that follow are missing from other ritual traditions, but leave that to others to determine and think through.

II. Speakers without hearers?

It is often assumed that ritual expresses or conveys meaning as if it were a kind of language. I believe that this assumption is mistaken, but I shall not argue against it here. However, an indubitable difference between ritual and language is that people who participate or are involved in either, relate to each other differently in the two realms. In the study of language, rules of grammar help explain, among other things, how a speaker produces a sentence and how a hearer decodes or understands it. (The analysis may pay attention to larger or smaller units than sentences – it does not matter in the present context.) For example, in such sentences as English "Peter saw her," grammarians from Panini onwards have made assumptions of the following form: "her" is derived from "she" or from a more abstract underlying form of the third person singular of the feminine pronoun, call it "X." While "X" is a grammarian's creation and never audible or visible in a sentence, the form "she" is visible in other sentences (e.g. "she entered"). It is invisible in "Peter saw her" because the female person referred to is the object of the seeing. Grammarians, psychologists, cognitive scientists, and others assume that somewhere or in some manner in the brain of the speaker, "she" or "X" is replaced by "her" (or something different happens with the same result), because the speaker wishes to convey that the female person referred to is the object of seeing; and similarly, somewhere or in some manner in the brain of the hearer, "her" is decoded or understood as standing for "she" or "X" (or something different happens with the same outcome) so that the hearer understands that the female person referred to is the object of the seeing.

In the study of ritual, there are rules also and there are equivalents or counterparts to speakers but not to hearers. It may be objected that the Gods are hearers, but that has not been the view adopted in classical India. I am not claiming that at the time the Vedic verses were first composed, it was never assumed that Gods hear the phrases or hymns addressed to them. We shall meet with an instance of precisely that assumption which left a trace in the ritual. But both the Srauta Sutras, the earliest works of the "science of ritual" (Staal 1982) that describe and analyze Vedic rituals, and the later ritual philosophy of the Mimamsa are concerned with rules observed by priests, not rules observed by Gods. There is a long prehistory to these developments. After roughly 1000 BCE, ritual began to move to the center stage of attention and become an end and edifice in and for itself from which the Gods obligingly vanished (cf. the quotation from Renou, above). It was followed in due course by a general rejection of the anthropomorphism that had been common in the earlier Vedas, though it had always been more abstract there than in the monotheistic religions of the Near East or the later bhakti religions of India. Around 500 BCE, anthropomorphism was relegated to a popular level of superstition and replaced by *karman*, "(ritual) activity" (in the Srauta Sutras), and *jnana*, "knowledge" (in the Upanishads and also in sciences such as geometry and grammar or linguistics).

If there are no hearers in Vedic ritual, it follows that there are no speakers. The analysis of ritual that we find in the Srauta Sutras and the Mimamsa is accordingly different from the analysis of language in Panini and other Indian grammarians, based as it is upon the notion of a dialogue or conversation between two or more people who assume, in turn, the roles of speaker and hearer. The view that language is used for the expression of knowledge is met with less often (cf. Staal 2001a). The idealized paradigm of a dialogue may be extended without difficulty to a situation in which one person speaks and many are hearing, as in a lecture. The complementary situation, one person hearing and many speaking, is less easy to imagine or construe as a form of communication. I may be able to listen to two people who are trying to engage me in conversation at the same time, but it is annoying; if three or more are talking to me, I am inclined to flee. If, conversely, I am talking to three or more people, they may also run away, but for different reasons, e.g. because they do not want to listen to what I have to say. As for writing, it may be similarly assumed that a writer expects or hopes that many will be reading, but it is hardly relevant to Panini's grammar or the Srauta Sutras which belong to the fifth century BCE (Witzel 1989: 251; 1997: 307–17) since writing did not exist in India before the fourth century BCE (see Salomon 1995 for a critical survey of the recent evidence with further references).

The few remarks I have made and the simplistic cases I have constructed were meant to illustrate no more than that the use of language displays primarily succession, not simultaneity. No doubt, it is not infrequent that people talk at the same time, interrupt each other or simply shoot back without waiting for a speaker to finish, but such cases are probably best analyzed by reducing them to cases of succession.

One of the reasons that Vedic ritual is different from language is that it involves not only succession, but also simultaneities of a kind that are not easily reduced to succession. Nor are they merely due to the fact that priests, during the performance of a Vedic ritual, rarely communicate with each other. It is true that we shall study one instance of simultaneity that is due to the even rarer case of communication between priests having become part of the ritual. But in general, Vedic ritual has nothing to do with communication or the expression of knowledge through language. Though priests are people and therefore familiar with these functions, they do not exercise them when they assume the role of priests. They may not even speak the same language, as we have already seen.

In the Soma rituals that I shall use in most of my illustrations, there are sixteen priests in addition to the Yajamana or patron. Their duties are plentiful and generally taken up successively. Of course, it is not uncommon, if only because there are so many, that different priests engage in different things at the same time: e.g. one priest may clean a vessel while another tends to a fire. Such engagements are more or less haphazard and certainly unstructured. But there are also structured simultaneities and it is primarily to these that I like to call attention.

III. Structural simultaneities

A striking case of simultaneous recitations occurs in the apyayana or Soma swelling rite (Caland and Henry 1906–7 I: 62–3; *Baudhayana Srauta Sutra* 6.19). The original Soma plant was probably a hallucinogenic, but its identity is not known and substitutes have been used for a long time. Along with substitutes, ritualization increased as availability of the original Soma decreased (Staal 2001b). The substitutes resemble the original insofar as they are plants that consist of stalks from which a juice may be extracted by pressing them. Early in the ritual performance and prior to the pressing, these stalks are placed on a stool immediately south of the offering altar. In the Agnicayana, the topic of *Agni*, this happens on the fourth day of a twelve-day performance (Staal 1983 I: 358–9). During the next six days (from the fourth day through the ninth), twice daily, in the morning and afternoon, thirteen priests including the Yajamana touch the Soma bundle and recite mantras. The mantras suggest that Soma was only available in a dried form and that it was attempted to restore its original condition by sprinkling it with water and making it swell. The repeated sprinkling over several days seems to indicate that this swelling was brought about most effectively when it was extended over a period of time. These features of the rites act as constraints on theories about the identity of the original Soma. In our present context, we are concerned with a later stage of ritualization which became the norm and during which Soma was no longer sprinkled with water but with mantras.

Let us begin with the two groups of Soma swelling mantras, A and B:

A   *amsur amsus te deva soma 'pyayatam indrayaikadhanavide*
   a tubhyam indrah pyayatam a tvam indraya pyayasva
   'pyayaya sakhintsanya medhaya
   svasti te deva soma sutyam asiya

   Stalk by stalk may you swell, God Soma, for Indra who possesses
      unique wealth!
   May Indra swell for you; do you swell for Indra!
   Make your friends swell with gain and wisdom!
   With good fortune may I accomplish your pressing, God Soma!
                              (*Taittiriya Samhita* 1.2.11.1 a–b)

B   *yam aditya amsum apyayayanti*
   yam aksitam aksitayah pibanti

tena no raja varuno brhaspatir
apyayayantu bhuvanasya gopah

The stalk that the Adityas make swell,
the imperishable that the imperishable drink,
with that may King Varuna, may Brhaspati,
may the guardians of the world make us swell!
(*Taittiriya Samhita* 2.4.14.1 b)

There are slight variations in the mantras that different priests recite but we need not take them into account. Some priests recite only the mantras of A. Most recite both A and B, in the following manner. First, one priest recites A while touching the Soma bundle. He then steps to the right (or south) and recites B without touching Soma. At the same time, the next priest comes forward to take his turn, reciting A and touching Soma. The result is that A and B are recited simultaneously by two priests, but Soma is touched by one and only once.

This result resembles what we find in music, but it should not be interpreted as a form of harmony, polyphony, or polyphony in the making. There are two voices, but parts and details of the two recitations are not related to each other. There is no counterpoint and only an outsider who is familiar with canons is struck by the similarity of these recitations with "Frère Jacques – Frère Jacques – dormez vous? – dormez vous?" It is a striking feature, and another is equally remarkable. In general, recitations and mantras resemble language more than ritual and for obvious reasons: both are concerned with sound. But in the case of apyayana, the rite (touching Soma) avoids simultaneity, like language, while the recitations display it.

Other cases of simultaneity are simpler and more common. They may involve only recitations, or recitations as well as ritual acts. In the Isti rites – basic rites of which the paradigm occurs in the Full- and New-Moon Ceremonies (Staal 1989b: 79–81) – four priests participate and there is an explicit reference, recognizably ancient because of its linguistic form, to a God who hears. The Adhvaryu priest shouts: *o sravaya* "Make (him) hear!" The Agnidhra responds: *astu srausat* "Be it so! May he hear!" It may be regarded as a kind of ritualized communication between two priests. But two features that have little or nothing to do with communication are that the *a-* of *astu* is made to coincide with the final *-a* of *o sravaya* and that the second syllable *-sat* is shouted loud.

Later in the Isti rite, the Hota priest executes his main recitation called yajya. It ends in the (equally ancient) exclamation *vausat* "may he (i.e. Agni) lead (the offerings to the Gods)!" At the second syllable of *vausat*, also shouted at the top of his voice by the Hota, the Adhvaryu priest makes his oblation into the fire and the Yajamana pronounces his celebrated *tyaga*, "abandon" or "renunciation," e.g. *agnaye idam na mama* "This is for Agni, not for me." The first syllable of *agnaye* is recited at the same time as the exclamation *-sat*. Here, simultaneity pertains not only to recitation but includes the rite of oblation and an expression of renunciation that was destined to have a great future in Indian religion.

IV. The horror of gaps

Unlike the simultaneities of the apyayana sprinkling rites, those of the Isti may be explained by, or are at any rate related to a principle of Vedic recitation referred to as samtatam (Renou 1954: 157 with references and Staal 1983 I: 311, 622). Literally meaning "linked" or "continuous," this term expresses that gaps are avoided in time just as they are avoided in space in the horror vacui of ancient and medieval Europe. More specifically, samtatam means that in long recitations from the *Rgveda* like the sastra recitations, verses are recited without interruption, taking care that the flow of sound is as continuous as possible. Pauses at ends and beginnings are especially avoided. Continuity is effected (cf. *Asvalayana Srauta Sutra* 1.2.20; *Apastamba Srauta Sutra* 24.11.12) by not taking breath at the end of the verse but at the caesura between its second and third quarter. At the end of the verse, only the initial consonant or consonants of the final syllable are retained. The remainder is replaced by a protracted OM, recited with three or four beats (matra), followed immediately and without pause by the next verse. At the gap in the middle of the verse where breath is taken, the final vowel is recited with three beats. For example, the mantra:

> *agna a yahi vitaye / grnano havyadataye / ni hota satsi barhisi*   (1)

> Agni, come to the banquet. Being extolled, come to the gift of offerings!

is recited thrice at the beginning or end of a sastra recitation in the form of (2):

> *agna a yahi vitaye grnano havyadataye-e-e # ni hota satsi barhisom-m-m* *
> *agna a yahi vitaye grnano havyadataye-e-e # ni hota satsi barhisom-m-m* *
> *agna a yahi vitaye grnano havyadataye-e-e # ni hota satsi barhisom-m-m-m* *   (2)

Here, "#" indicates that breath is taken and "*" that there is no pause but that the recitation continues without breathing or interruption. Transformations of this kind are very common. The mantra (1) may be regarded as the underlying form of (2) just as "X" is of "she" or "her" in the example of our introductory paragraph. Meaning is obviously distorted when mantras are recited in this manner; but it is a general feature of mantra recitation that meaning plays no role.

The principle of continuity or linkage accounts for the simultaneities in the ritual exclamations *srausat* and *vausat*. It is not obvious whether it also explains that the acts of Adhvaryu and Yajamana take place at the same time. It certainly throws no light on the case of apyayana which is of a different nature. Apyayana cannot be explained either by assuming that the priests had no time to wait for each other because the ceremony had to be over by a certain time. That happens toward the end of the ritual, from the tenth day onwards when many simultaneities occur but none that are structural: "From now on we are caught in a whirlpool of rites, often overlapping, which continue for three days and two nights through the twelfth and last day" (Staal 1983 I: 598).

Unstructured simultaneities that are due to overactivity, some other business, or lack of time, and structured simultaneities such as the Soma swelling rite or *srausat/vausat* exclamations have to be distinguished from each other and do not affect ritual in the same manner. The former may interfere, the latter allow the ritual to follow its own pace.

V. Stage directions

A separate category of simultaneity consists of stage directions. Each priest must know his own task but also when to perform it and especially: when to start. This has nothing to do with the clock, though it may be related to sunset or sunrise. It pertains to the orderly succession of rites. In relatively simple cases, e.g. during the pastoral rites of the Pravargya, the Samaveda chanter gestures to the Hota that he is about to stop so that the latter may intone his recitation of *Rgveda*. In more complex cases, priests must be familiar with at least some of the rites, chants, or recitations that others perform or execute. A priest who recites *Rgveda* after one or more others have chanted *Samaveda* should know how their chanting ends. That is not a simple matter since Samaveda chanting often consists of long o's and other long vowels that hide the original mantras.

These may be hidden even more confusingly by *stobha*-embellishments such as *hau, hum, bha* that resemble Tantric or *bija*-mantras (Staal 1989b: ch. 20). Most difficult is the Samaveda *aniruktagana* or "unenunciated chant" in which the original words, like the former Gods, have entirely vanished.

Many chants consist of five portions sung by three priests:

1   *Prastota*
2   *Udgata*
3   *Pratiharta*
4   *Udgata*
5   all three.

In these compositions, the *Udgata* starts before the *Prastota* has finished, the *Pratiharta* before the *Udgata* has finished, etc., until the fifth and last portion in which the other two chanters begin before the *Udgata* has finished. Long sequences of such quintuples are very hard to follow and if other priests, who do not know the *Samaveda*, have to excecute their tasks in the middle or at the end of such a sequence, they need help. The *Prastota* provides it by addressing one priest during the middle chant:

> *esa madhyamah*, this is the middle,

and another during the final chant:

esottamah, this is the last one (Staal 1983 I: 604).

There are also chants that consist of repetitions of three basic songs in accordance with a particular pattern, e.g. in three rounds. In the first round, the first song is repeated thrice; in the second, the second song, and in the third, the third. If we refer to the three songs as A, B and C, the resulting "fifteenfold" pattern is:

A A A B C
A B B B C
A B C C C.

Such patterns are referred to by the technical term *vistuti* (Renou 1954: 140–1; Caland and Henry 1906–07 I: 237). They are marked with the help of sticks on a piece of cloth lying on the ground around which the three priests sit. When the Prastota in the above case starts his chant, he puts the first stick down. The three continue placing sticks that refer to chants in the pattern of Figure 8.1, where numbers indicate the order of sticks that are placed on the cloth which corresponds to the succession of chants.

It is much easier to follow the configuration of these sticks than the intricacies of the chants. It helps even the chanters themselves. For though they know their chants already, they also have to know when they have, or no

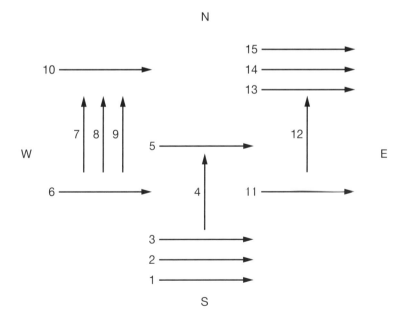

Figure 8.1 Fifteenfold *vistuti* (Staal 1983 I: 627, Figure 48).

longer need, to be repeated. With sticks in front of them, all they have to do is look and, in more complex cases, count. It is only a practical aid but has become part of the ritual – a case of structural simultaneity that does not conflict with the ritual's natural pace.

Musicians all over the world use similar devices. In complex compositions with many instruments or voices, repetitions, and variations, it is not always necessary to memorize what others do. A soloist who has to start long after the beginning of a concerto, may be assisted by the conductor, if there is one, or count bars. Stage directions in Vedic ritual are like hinges on which a door turns. If they are not made or oiled well, the door does not open or close. A ritual performance runs smoothly only when such directions function properly. Since *Samaveda* chanting is the most difficult, most stage directions govern the interaction with Samavedins. There are important practical implications because, all over India, Samavedins are rare. Those who know the ritual chants and how to use them in a ritual performance are even rarer. Most Samaveda ritualists are found in South India. When large Vedic rituals are performed in northern states such as Maharasthra or Uttar Pradesh, Samavedins may be imported from Andhra Pradesh or Tamilnadu in the south.

The cooperation between ritualists from different parts of India is possible provided *Samaveda* chanters belong to the same or almost identical schools. As it happens, two schools of *Samaveda* are available in all the mentioned states and they are very similar: Kauthuma and Ranayaniya. One result of this near-identity of traditions is that stage directions fit.

The Nambudiri Samavedins of Kerala belong to a very different school: Jaiminiya. Their tradition has much weakened but it would be no use to invoke the help of Samavedins from Tamilnadu. The traditions are so different that cooperation would be difficult, rites, chants and recitations would not fit together and stage directions would not work.

VI. Multifunctionality in space

So far I have discussed simultaneity, a concept that relates to time. There is a spatial parallel that may be referred to as multifunctionality in space and on which I will comment briefly. Multifunctionality in space means that one ritual entity, located in one place, performs different functions. A striking example is that of the domestic altar.

The offering altar is an altar on which oblations are poured or thrown. But all oblations, except Soma, are cooked first. Vedic ritual therefore requires another altar, the domestic altar. The fire that is installed on it corresponds to the kitchen fire. In most rituals, the domestic altar is constructed at the western end of the ritual enclosure and the offering altar at its eastern end.

In Soma rituals, the original enclosure is extended in the eastern direction by constructing to the east of the offering altar a new ritual space, the *Mahavedi* (Caland and Henry I: 74; Staal 1983 I: 257–63). At the eastern end of this new space, a new offering altar is constructed. Before that is done, a new domestic altar is constructed in the same place as the old offering altar. The Soma enclosures are depicted in Figure 8.2, where OĀ is the old *ahavaniya* or offering altar which is the same as NG, the new *garhapatya* or domestic altar; and where U = NĀ is the new *ahavaniya* or offering altar.

The new domestic altar is required in most rites that are performed after the new offering altar has been constructed and fire has been carried to and installed on it – i.e. after agnipranayana, "the carrying forth of Agni" (Staal 1983 I: 551–8). Prior to these ceremonies, but after the new domestic altar has been constructed, offerings may continue to be made on the domestic altar as if it were the offering altar. This is in order since fire from the old offering altar has been included in the fire of the new domestic altar. An example of this use of an altar that has become ambiguous or multifunctional is the *prayaniyesti* or "Introductory Offering" (Staal 1983 I: 347). Multifunctionality in space and simultaneity in time interact and intertwine in a remarkable manner inside the Sadas or Hall of Recitation (see Figure 8.2). Within the Sadas, priests sit (*sad-*, whence Sadas) in fixed places, some in front of altars and all facing particular directions (for the priests, especially the Maitravaruna, see Minkowski 1991; for the altars: Staal 2001c). The places of the priests are depicted in Figure 8.3 where arrows show the directions they face.

We need not be concerned with the patron Y (*yajamana*) or his personal priest B (*brahman*). Their location has been marked because they are the chief player and his right hand. Among the others, six priests face east and sit in a row from north to south: Ac: *acchavaka*; Ne: *nesta*; Po: *pota*; Ba: *brahmanacchamsi*; H: *hota*; and M: *maitravaruna*. Most of them recite sastra recitations from the *Rgveda*. Those who face the three remaining directions, west, north and south, are the three *Samaveda* priests Pr: *prastota*; U: *udgata*; and Prat: *pratiharta* who sing *stotra* chants.

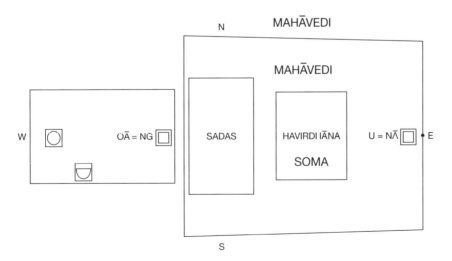

Figure 8.2 Ritual enclosures for the Soma rituals (Staal 1983 I: 53, Figure 4).

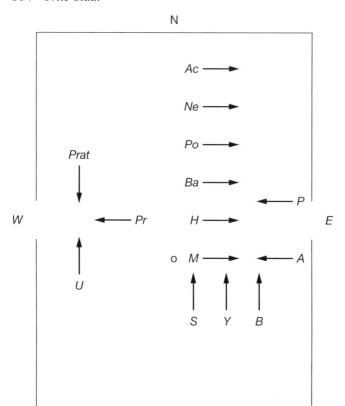

Figure 8.3 Position of priests in the Sadas (Staal 1983 I: 609, Figure 47).

The temporal relationship between *Samaveda* chanters and *Rgveda* reciters has been solved in a regular manner because each Soma sequence starts with a *stotra* chant which is followed by a *sastra* recitation. The spatial arrangement between the priests, however, is awkward. The *Prastota* sits back-to-back to the *Hota* and there is no general or functional relationship in space between Rg- and Samavedins. There are reasons, undoubtedly, for the complexity of these spatial relationships and the interactions between the priests (see Staal 1992: 665–9 and forthcoming), but whatever they are, they clearly show that, within the Sadas, the organization of time is ahead of that of space.

VII. The basic principle: mantras and acts

I now come to the most important, general and characteristic simultaneity of Vedic ritual: that between mantra and act. I have postponed it so far because I wanted to illustrate it first with the help of special cases. The basic simultaneity between mantras and acts is accepted implicitly throughout the ritual and formulated explicitly by the *Srauta Sutras*, e.g. *Apastamba Srauta Sutra* 24.1.38: *ekamantrani karmani* "each act is accompanied by one mantra." This principle has numerous applications. One type of application is exhibited by the simultaneity of the exclamation of the final syllable *-sat* and the acts of Adhvaryu and Yajamana (described above). *Apastamba Srauta Sutra* formulates it in general terms: *mantrantaih karmadin samnipatayet* "one should let the beginning of the acts coincide with the end of the mantras." These metarules of ritual (cf. Staal 1989b: 193–6) are chiefly concerned with structural simultaneities but may also lead to simultaneities that are not structural. When the ritual act is simple but the accompanying recitations or chants last for a long time, the latter may continue after the act has been completed. They may thereby become simultaneous with other acts. An example is the burial of the golden statue of a man underneath the offering altar of the Agnicayana. The *Udgata* bursts into song at precisely that time but his chants continue long thereafter. The *Adhvaryu* priest uses this opportunity to perform a series of silent acts that have little or nothing to do with the golden man (Staal 1983 I: 414–7).

There are other exceptions to the principle that mantras are connected with acts, just as there are exceptions in language to the principle that sounds are connected with meanings. In language, many do – it depends on definitions at least in part – but linguists and logicians, in India and Europe, have long known that words like "of," "that" or "other" do not connect sounds with meanings in any obvious manner. The similarities between ritual, recitations, and language are syntactic, not semantic. Together with the semantic dissimilarities we discussed at the outset, these similarities add fuel to the idea that the syntax of language originated from ritual and chant or recitation, activities that are not confined to humans. Whatever its solution or solutions, the unsolved problem of the origin of language adds interest and spice to the study of the simultaneities and spatial multifunctionalities of Vedic ritual.

Vedic ritual is multidimensional in the literal sense. Its simultaneities and spatial multifunctionalities and other structures that unfold in time and space demand a multidimensional description and analysis. If I were asked how many dimensions would suffice for its adequate description, I would guess it to be a rather large number. However, the subject needs to be studied with greater dispassion and in much greater detail. If I were pressed for a more precise answer at this time, I would say that it is too early.

Note

Diacritics like those in French or German are also used in the transliteration of Sanskrit but have been omitted from this paper.

Bibliography

Translations of Primary Literature

Apastamba Srauta Sutra
Das Srautasutra des Apastamba (1921–28) trans. W. Caland, Vol. I, Göttingen: Vandenhoeck & Ruprecht; Vols II–III, Amsterdam: Koninklijke Akademie van Wetenschappen.

Asvalayana Srauta Sutra
Partly translated by Klaus Mylius, as follows:
"Der erste Adhyaya des Asvalayana-Srautasutra," *Zeitschrift für Missionswissenschaft und Religionswissenschaft* 51 (1967) 245–373.
"Der zweite Adhyaya des Asvalayana-Srautasutra," *Acta Orientalia* 34 (1972) 95–162.
"Der dritte Adhyaya des Asvalayana-Srautasutra, erstmalig vollständig übersetzt und erläutert," *Mitteilungen des Instituts für Orientforschung* 17 (1971) 63–100.
"Der vierte Adhyaya des Asvalayana-Srautasutra, erstmalig vollständig übersetzt, erläutert und mit Indices versehen," *Altorientalische Forschungen* 14 (1987) 108–59.
"Zur Erschliessung der altindischen Ritualliteratur: Asvalayana-Srautasutra V und VI," *Sitzungsberichte der Sächsischen Akademie der Wissenschaften zu Leipzig, Philologisch-historische Klasse* 128/6 (1989) 5–107.
The first six chapters have also been translated by H. G. Ranade (1982). Poona: Veda Vidya Mudranalaya.

Baudhayana Srauta Sutra
The Agnicayana section has been translated by Yasuke Ikari and Harold Arnold in Staal 1983 II: 478–675.

Taittiriya Samhita
The Veda of the Black Yajus School entitled Taittiriya Samhita (1914) trans. A. B. Keith, Cambridge, Mass: Harvard University Press.

Secondary Literature

Alper, H. P. (ed.) (1988) *Understanding Mantras*, New York: State University of New York Press.
Bronkhorst, J. and Deshpande, M. M. (eds) (1999) *Aryan and non-Aryan in South Asia: Evidence, Interpretation and Ideology. Proceedings of the International Seminar on Aryan and Non-Aryan in South Asia, University of Michigan at Ann Arbor, 25–27 October 1996*, Cambridge, Mass.: Harvard University, Dept. of Sanskrit and Indian Studies; Distributed by South Asia Books.
Caillat, C. (ed.) (1989) *Dialectes dans les littératures indo-aryennes*, Paris: Institut de Civilisation Indienne.
Caland, W. and Henry, V. (1906–07) *L'agnistoma: Description complète de la forme normale du sacrifice de Soma dans le culte védique*, I–II, Paris: Ernest Leroux.
Dandekar, R. N. (1982) "Some Aspects of Vedic Exegesis," *Indologica Taurinensia* 10: 71–81.
Grappard, A. G., Mack, B. L., Strenski, I., and Staal. F. (1991) "Symposium: Ritual as Such. Frits Staal's Rules without Meaning," *Religion* 21: 205–34.
Minkowski, C. Z. (1991) *Priesthood in Ancient India: A Study of the Maitravaruna Priest*, Vienna: Sammlung de Nobili.
Renou, L. (1953) *Religions of Ancient India*, London: The Athlone Press.
—— (1954) *Vocabulaire du rituel védique*, Paris: Librarie C. Klincksieck.

Salomon, R. (1995) "On the Origin of the Early Indian Scripts," *Journal of the American Oriental Society* 115: 271–9.

Smith, B. (1991) "Review [of Staal 1989b]," *Journal of Ritual Studies,* 5: 141–3.

Staal, F. (1982) *The Science of Ritual,* Poona: Bhandarkar Oriental Research Institute.

—— (1983) *Agni: The Vedic Ritual of the Fire Altar, Vols 1–2.* In collaboration with C. V. Somayajipad and M. I. R. Nambudiri, Berkeley: Asian Humanities Press. Reprinted (2001) Delhi: Motilal Banarsidass.

—— (1984) "The Search for Meaning: Mathematics, Music and Ritual," *American Journal of Semiotics* 2/4: 1–57; also published as "Ritmo nel rito," *Conoscenza Religiosa* 2: 197–247.

—— (1986a) "The Sound of Religion," *Numen* 33: 33–64, 185–224.

—— (1986b) "The Fidelity of Oral Tradition and the Origins of Science," *Mededelingen der Koninklijke Nederlandse Akademie van Wetenschappen, Afd. Letterkunde,* n.r., 49/8, Amsterdam: North-Holland Publishing Company.

—— (1988) "Vedic Mantras," in H. P. Alper (ed.), *Understanding Mantras,* 48–95, New York: State University of New York Press.

—— (1989a) "The Independence of Rationality from Literacy," *European Journal of Sociology* 30: 301–10.

—— (1989b) *Rules without Meaning: Ritual, Mantras and the Human Sciences,* New York: Peter Lang, 2nd ed. 1993. Reprinted (1999) Delhi: Motilal Banarsidass.

—— (1992) "Agni 1990," in van den Hoek, A. W., Kolff, D. H. A. and Oort, M. S. (eds), *Ritual, State and History in South Asia: Essays in Honour of J. C. Heesterman,* 650–76, Leiden: E. J. Brill.

—— (1993) "From Meanings to Trees," *Journal of Ritual Studies* 7: 11–32.

—— (1999) "Greek and Vedic Geometry," *Journal of Indian Philosophy* 27: 105–27.

—— (2000) "A Breakthrough in Vedic Studies," *The Book Review* (New Delhi), Jan.–Feb. Different version: *Newsletter of the International Journal of Asian Studies* (Leiden), October.

—— (2001a) "Noam Chomsky between the Human and Natural Sciences," *Janus Head (Supplemental) Special Issue: George Washington University 6th Annual Human Sciences Conference* 25–66. Also at http://www.janushead.org/gwu-2001/staal.cfm/.

—— (2001b) "How a Psychoactive Substance becomes a Ritual: The Case of Soma," *Social Research* 68: 745–78.

—— (2001c) "Squares and Oblongs in the Veda," *Journal of Indian Philosophy* 29: 257–73.

—— (forthcoming) "From pranmukham to sarvatomukham. A Thread through the Srauta Maze," *The Vedas: Text, Language and Ritual: Proceedings of the Third International Vedic Workshop,* Leiden, May 29 – June 2 2002.

van den Hoek, A. W., Kolff, D. H. A., and Oort, M. S. (eds) (1992) *Ritual, State and History in South Asia: Essays in Honour of J. C. Heesterman,* Leiden: E. J. Brill.

Witzel, M. (1989) "Tracing the Vedic Dialects," in C. Caillat (ed.), *Dialectes dans les littératures indo-aryennes,* 97–265, Paris: Institut de Civilisation Indienne.

—— (1997) "The Development of the Vedic Canon and its Schools: The Social and Political Milieu," in M. Witzel (ed.), *Inside the Texts/Beyond the Texts: New Approaches to the Study of the Vedas: Proceedings of the International Vedic Workshop,* 257–345, Cambridge, MA: Harvard University Department of Sanskrit and Indian Studies.

9 Moral cultivation through ritual participation

Xunzi's philosophy of ritual

T. C. Kline III

I. Introduction

For the study of ritual, few sources are as rich as the writings of Confucian philosophers. From the beginning of the tradition, Kongzi (Confucius) describes the good human life in terms of ritual practice. He focuses on the ways in which ritual participation enables us to become fully human. From Kongzi onward, the Confucian tradition continued to emphasize and discuss the importance of ritual participation. These discussions of ritual and its significance to the good human life first become fully developed by Xunzi in the fourth century BCE.[1] Xunzi's conception of ritual practice and its connection to moral cultivation prove worthy of examination for several reasons. First, as I have argued elsewhere, Xunzi's conception of ritual and ritual practice is the most sophisticated and compelling defense of ritual practice within the Confucian tradition.[2] The complexity and sophistication of his defense of ritual owes much to the historical moment in which it took shape. Xunzi was the last of the great Confucian philosophers in early China, the period of Chinese history before the unification of the empire under the first emperor of the Qin dynasty in 221 BCE. His writings reveal a thorough grasp of the other philosophical schools of the time – among them Mohists and Daoists – as well as the competing views within his own tradition. Moreover, Xunzi deftly adopts and adapts many of the positions and objections of his intellectual rivals in order to develop and defend his own position. Because of its inherent richness and power, his understanding of ritual participation and its role in moral cultivation had an enduring, profound, and pervasive influence on later Confucian teachings.

Second, as will become clear below, Xunzi's understanding of ritual has much to offer to contemporary discussion of ritual practice and its connection to ethics, not least in terms of the process of moral development. In describing the central role of ritual practice in Confucian moral cultivation, Xunzi makes explicit the connection between ideals of the good human life and the path toward living a good human life. Although many philosophers have been adept at describing and defending a particular form of the good human life, few have given equally compelling explanations of how human beings come to live such lives. Like many early Chinese thinkers, Xunzi focuses attention on describing *how* human beings become good, and Confucian ritual practice plays a central role in his account.

In describing ritual practice and its connection to moral cultivation, Xunzi incorporates somatic and affective aspects that are often overlooked in contemporary philosophical discussions of ethics. He believes that ritual practice shapes, transforms, and orders our cognitive and affective responses to our environment. Ritual practice has this effect because, through ritual participation, we come to embody the rites. Not only do we internalize the conceptual categories and ideals expressed symbolically in the ritual order, but our gestures and movements become ritualized as well. Part of this process of transformation, or ritual cultivation, takes place because of the somatic experience of ritual participation, an experience that enables us concretely to embody the ideals and virtues we find expressed in the ritual order. Xunzi's sensitivity to the various somatic, affective, and cognitive aspects of ritual practice enables him to offer a compelling vision of the life lived fully participating in the Confucian ritual order.

One final reason that Xunzi's theorizing about ritual should interest us is that he engages in a sophisticated form of what Tom Kasulis calls metapraxis. That is to say, Xunzi undertakes a philosophical examination of Confucian ritual practice in order to defend and justify precisely the practices that he examines. As Thomas Kasulis explains, metapraxis

> arises out of questions about the purpose and efficacy of the religious praxes. Religious praxis generally has either a participatory or transformative function. It participates in, to use Rudolph Otto's term, the "numinous." It is transformative in its improving the person or community in some spiritual way (purifying, healing, reconciling, protecting, informing, and so on). Metapractical reflection inquires into the purpose and efficacy of the practice in terms of these participatory and transformative functions.
>
> (Kasulis 1992:178)

Discussions of both the participatory and the transformative functions of Confucian praxis can be found in Xunzi's writings. Through ritual practice, the individual comes to understand and participate in the Dao, the harmonious patterns of individual, social, and cosmic interaction created by the Confucian sages. Simultaneously, the transformative process of moral cultivation occurs. Continuous participation in the numinous order reshapes our nature such that we begin to conform to that order and participate more fully in it. Xunzi explains both participatory and transformative functions of ritual practice in order to justify continued participation in the Confucian ritual order in the face of objections from philosophers who flatly rejected the efficacy of the ritual order and from those who suggested alternative ritual orders.

In his discussion of metapraxis, Kasulis further argues that good metapraxis usually coexists with a complementary metaphysics. When combined, metaphysics and metapraxis produce a coherent vision of the nature of the world and of how participants interact with that world through ritual practice. Xunzi complements his metapractical reflections with a developed metaphysics that describes the original character of the cosmos and human beings. Taken together, his metaphysics and metapraxis provide a compelling vision of life lived within, as opposed to without, the Confucian ritual order. In sum, Xunzi's writings on ritual exemplify philosophy as metapraxis. Careful attention to the elements of his defense of ritual practice yields valuable insight into the ways in which metapraxis was carried out in early Confucianism.

Though our focus will remain on the metapractical aspects of Xunzi's writings, it is necessary to begin with a brief description of his metaphysics. Only with a clear understanding of the context in which ritual activity takes place can we then proceed to consider the central elements of his metapraxis, namely, moral cultivation and its relationship to ritual practice.

II. Metaphysics: human nature, moral psychology, and the cosmos

Xunzi is famous among Chinese philosophers for claiming that human nature is bad (*xing'e*). Yet, this claim, by itself, reveals little about the character of human nature.[3] For a satisfactory explanation, we must further describe the constituent elements of human nature (*renxing*) and determine in what sense they can be construed as bad. Let us begin with Xunzi's formal definition of human nature:

> That which is so from birth is called "human nature." The close connection of response to stimulus, which requires no effort but is so of itself, and which is produced by the harmonious operation of our nature, is also called "human nature." The likes and dislikes, delights and angers, griefs and joys of our nature are called the "dispositions" (*qing*).
> (Watson 139; Knoblock 22.1b; 22/107/22–3)[4]

Human nature is fundamentally immutable and spontaneous. It responds to the environment with feelings of like and dislike, delight and anger, joy and grief. To this list of constituent responses of our nature, Xunzi adds a fondness for our own benefit, the feelings of envy and hatred, as well as the sensory desires of the ear and eye that delight in beautiful sounds and colors (Watson 157; Knoblock 23.1a; 23/113/3–5). Additionally, he mentions the mouth's fondness for good flavors, the mind's fondness of our own benefit, and the body's fondness for relaxation and ease (Watson 160; Knoblock 23.2a; 23/114/12). Closely associated with these responses are common reactions to the external environment. When we are hungry we want to eat, when cold we desire warmth, and when tired we long to rest. Because we are mammals born of other mammals, Xunzi also believes that we have a natural feeling of care and concern for our parents, which manifests itself as love for our parents when they are alive and grief for them when they die (Watson 106; Knoblock 19.9b, 19/96/10–13). All of these spontaneous reactions to the world around us are part of our nature for Xunzi. Moreover, these reactions are the same in every person. "Concerning human nature, the sages Yao and Shun possessed the same nature as the tyrant Jie or Robber Zhi, and the gentleman (*junzi*) possesses the same nature as the petty person (*xiaoren*)" (Watson 164; Knoblock 23.4a; 23/115/22–3). Yao and Shun, the sage rulers of antiquity, had the same set of natural emotional responses as the common people.

Along with these responses of our nature to the environment, Xunzi argues that we have certain innate cognitive and perceptual capacities. For example, our eyes can discriminate between white and black, our ears can discern clear and muddy sounds, and our bodies and skin can distinguish between hot and cold, pain and itching (Knoblock 4.9; 4/15/8–10). Our cognitive capacities include our abilities to make distinctions and to understand things external to us.

According to Xunzi, none of these responses or capacities is inherently bad. He does not, like Augustine, conceive of human nature as immutably evil. Rather, he claims that the elements of human nature, if followed without the direction of ritual and the social roles (*yi*) embodied in the rites, will lead people into chaos and conflict. "All those who follow their nature and indulge their natural inclinations will inevitably become involved in wrangling and strife, will violate the forms and patterns of society, and will end in violence" (Watson 157; Knoblock 23.1a; 23/113/5–6). It is the consequences of following our nature and its natural inclinations that are judged bad. This evaluation holds even though Xunzi includes apparently positive elements in his conception of human nature. Even these supposedly positive traits, when followed without restraint, lead to bad consequences. For example, the natural love and affection between parents and children can become incest if not properly channeled and expressed through participation in the ritual order.

The consequences of simply following our natural inclinations prove harmful partly because of the larger environment in which we find ourselves. The world, Xunzi observes, contains a limited supply of resources that human beings need to survive and to satisfy their desires. If our planet offered unlimited resources, the chance of conflict arising over needed resources would be less. But, even in a world of limitless natural resources, human interaction would need to be shaped through ritual participation. This last point about the larger environment and the need for ritual brings us to Xunzi's vision of the cosmos and its relation to the Dao embodied in the Confucian ritual order.

Xunzi recognizes two other forces in the cosmos besides human beings, namely, Heaven and Earth. Yet, unlike much of the earlier Chinese philosophical tradition, he does not anthropomorphize Heaven and Earth. Instead, he argues that there is a fixed, objective pattern to their workings. Heaven has its patterns of movement (*tianxing*). The stars travel through their yearly journey, the seasons follow one another in sequence, the moon waxes and wanes according to its monthly cycle, the wind and rain follow the cycles of weather, and night follows day. Earth, too, has its natural patterns. Plants and animals follow cycles of birth, maturation, reproduction, and death. The sages looked to these patterns, along with the patterns of human nature, and created the Dao, embodied in the Confucian ritual order, that ordered behavior and brought human beings into harmonious relation with each other and the natural world. It should be emphasized that the Dao was not so much discovered among, as it was inspired by, the patterns of Heaven and Earth. Through careful observation and gradual experiment, the sages created and shaped ritual until it reached the height of perfection in the ritual order of the early Zhou kings.

In creating the human Dao, the sages did more than bring order to human behavior. Prior to the sages, even the natural world admitted of a certain amount of disorder and chaos:

> Heaven gives birth to creatures but it does not order them; Earth can sustain humans but it cannot govern them. All creatures of the cosmos, all who belong to the human race, must await the sage before they can attain their proper places. This is what the *Odes* means when it says: He cherishes and mollifies all the spirits/Even those of the River and the High Mountain.
>
> (Watson 103; Knoblock 19.6; 19/95/3–4)

This passage suggests several important aspects of Xunzi's understanding of the Dao and its relation to the cosmos. First among these, the Dao is distinct from the patterns followed by Heaven and Earth. Xunzi makes this point explicit. "The Dao of which I speak is not the Dao of Heaven or the Dao of Earth, but rather the Dao that guides the actions of mankind and is embodied in the conduct of the gentleman" (Knoblock 8.3, 8/28/15–16). Even in the opening passage of the chapter on Heaven, Xunzi emphasizes the distinct nature of the Dao as opposed to the patterns of Heaven. Heaven and Earth do nothing in particular to make the sage-king Yao prevail, nor to cause the tyrant Jie to perish. They perish or prevail solely on the basis of the ways in which they respond to the patterns of the cosmos.

Since Heaven and Earth operate independently of human beings, responding appropriately to Heaven and Earth becomes one of the central human tasks. We respond in the form of good or bad government. Government, in turn, has at its base the Dao of the Confucian ritual order. "The Dao is the foundation and pattern of good government" (Watson 147; Knoblock 22.3f; 22/110/7). Thus, those who govern respond to Heaven and Earth by either putting into practice the ritual order of the Dao, or by rejecting it and thereby causing chaos. The variation in response demonstrates that while the Dao flourishes or declines, the patterns of Heaven and Earth remain unaffected.

A further part of the proper response to the cosmos involves recognizing the division of activity between Heaven, Earth, and human beings. This division is the second aspect brought out by the above quotation. Xunzi believes we must "distinguish between the activities of Heaven and those of humanity" (Watson 79–80; Knoblock 17.1; 17/79/21). Heaven, Earth, and humanity each have separate tasks to perform. On the social level, Heaven gives birth to human beings, Earth nourishes them, and it is up to human beings to bring order to themselves and much of the rest of the cosmos through creating and participating in the ritual order. On the individual level, Heaven endows us with sensory organs and cognitive capacities, Earth nourishes us, and it is we who must complete the process of becoming fully human by undertaking the project of moral cultivation. "Since a person's nature is bad, he must wait for the ordering power of the sage kings and the transforming power of ritual and social roles (*yi*); only then can he achieve order and conform to goodness" (Watson 164; Knoblock 23.3c; 23/115/17). In general, fully realized human beings, as best represented by the sages, bring the work of Heaven and Earth to completion.

Xunzi recognizes that within this process of completion humans play a vital role. Humans are not simply placed in a helpless and subordinate relationship to Heaven and Earth. Rather, at their best, humans embody the Dao through full ritual participation, taking part in a cooperative relationship with Heaven and Earth. As Xunzi understands this relationship, "Heaven has its seasons; Earth has its riches; man has his governing (*zhi*). Hence, this is what it means for these three to form a triad" (Watson 80; Knoblock 17.2a; 17/80/2–3). By forming a triad with Heaven and Earth, we can be said to be participating in the numinous qualities of the ritual order.

Being part of this triad does not, however, mean that we are capable of the same feats as Heaven and Earth. As humans, we must restrict ourselves to those activities properly within our own power:

> To be refined in purpose, rich in virtuous action, and clear in understanding; to live in the present and remember the past – these are the things which are within your own power. Therefore the gentleman cherishes what is within his power and does not long for what is within the power of Heaven.
>
> (Watson 83; Knoblock 17.6; 17/81/4–6)

Attempting to accomplish what is not within our power leads to disaster. It constitutes a rejection of the ritual order. Xunzi warns against attempting feats not properly within our power by directly arguing against trying to understand too much about the workings of Heaven. Heaven completes activities without acting and obtains without seeking. When we consider the workings of the cosmos, we see only the results and not the forces effecting those outcomes. Because of our inability to observe the forces of Heaven at work, Xunzi calls Heaven's work "numinous" or "godlike" (*shen*), and believes that we should not waste effort on trying to understand it.

Yet, Xunzi does not believe that we cannot understand anything about Heaven and Earth. The sage realizes what knowledge of Heaven and Earth is appropriate for human activities. With regard to Heaven, the cultivated individual "seeks to understand only those phenomena which can be regularly expected." With regard to Earth, "they seek to understand only those aspects which they can put to use" (Watson 81; Knoblock 17.3b; 17/80/17–19). This knowledge is, in effect, the information the sages needed in order to create a ritual order that brought all three members of the hierarchy into harmony. Thus, for a human being, when "his actions are completely ordered; his nourishment of the people is completely appropriate; his life is without injury. This is what it means to truly understand Heaven" (Watson 81; Knoblock 17.3a; 17/80/14–15).

One final point should be noted with regard to the relationship between humans and the cosmos. As a response to Heaven, ritual is not meant to be technological or magical. Xunzi believes we should not attempt to use ritual activity to influence the workings of Heaven, since Heaven will not respond to such attempts at manipulation. Heaven's unresponsiveness reveals the extent to which Xunzi has naturalized his conception of the cosmos. Although his view is not congruent with the natural order assumed by modern science, Xunzi nevertheless distances humankind from Heaven by making any interaction unidirectional. Human beings respond to Heaven; Heaven does not respond to them. Contrary to the prevalent early Chinese understanding of ritual as technology, Xunzi argues that ritual should not constitute a group effort to harness numinous forces to effect our will on Heaven and Earth; instead ritual activity brings order and harmony to the community by recognizing, shaping, and expressing human responses to our situation.

Our situation consists of being born into a disordered cosmos with an innate set of inclinations and capacities that do not naturally and spontaneously lead to harmonious interactions with each other or with the rest of the natural world. Fortunately, Xunzi believes in our ability to use our innate capacities to shape our inclinations such that we can come to live harmoniously with other human beings and our natural surroundings. We transform ourselves through the process of moral cultivation, and ritual practice forms the core of moral cultivation.

III. Metapraxis: moral cultivation and ritual participation

Moral cultivation occupies the central role in Xunzi's philosophy because he uses his view of moral cultivation to connect the various components of his metapractical theory. Moral cultivation concerns the diachronic aspects of moral agency, that is, the development or decline of moral character over time. More specifically, moral cultivation denotes the processes by which we transform, or re-form, our original nature. This original nature, in Xunzi's view, is morally blind and tends toward chaos and conflict. Unlike his Confucian predecessor Mengzi, he does not see moral cultivation as a type of maturation or growth of innate tendencies of human nature. Human nature does not contain innate moral responses that, if properly nurtured, will gradually grow into fully blossoming moral sensibilities. Nevertheless, Xunzi believes, as Mengzi does, that human beings can accomplish the task of becoming fully human only through the process of moral cultivation. "The gentleman knows that what lacks completeness (*quan*) and purity (*cui*) does not deserve to be called beautiful (*mei*)" (Watson 22; Knoblock 1.14; 1/4/16). The recognition that our natures are incomplete motivates us to make up for this lack. Being born a human being constitutes only the beginning of the process of becoming human. We complete that process through moral cultivation. Since being fully human is conceived of in terms of completing the process of moral cultivation, completeness becomes a value in itself. "Heaven manifests its brightness, Earth manifests its breadth, and the gentleman values his own completeness" (Watson 22; Knoblock 1.14; 1/4/20–1).

When Xunzi speaks of moral cultivation in its broadest terms, he refers to it as a process of learning (*xue*). By choosing this term, he rejects an earlier model of Confucian cultivation, espoused by Mengzi, that emphasized self reflection (*si*). Rather than emphasizing the need for reflecting on one's innate responses to situations that elicit a moral reaction, Xunzi advocates learning as the primary activity of moral cultivation. "I once spent an entire day in self reflection, but it was of less value than a moment of study" (Watson 16; Knoblock 1.3; 1/1/12). This shift from reflection to learning has an important consequence for Xunzi's metapraxis. Whereas reflecting involves concentrating on elements of our own motivational structure, learning requires studying texts and participating in ritual activities external to ourselves. With learning, instead of trusting our own moral reactions, we turn to the insights and wisdom of others, especially sages, embodied in external artifacts and activities handed down from the past. This embodied wisdom of the past becomes the guide to moral cultivation.

Xunzi describes cultivation, or learning in terms of craft metaphors, and this choice of metaphors is significant. In their original state, human beings are analogous to the raw materials of the craftsman. The raw material does not grow or mature into a final product. Rather, it is shaped and molded by the intentional activity of the craftsman. This is not a process of working from the inside out, but of the application of external tools and the imposition of external patterns and forms to transform the inner shape. Xunzi clearly describes this process in the opening passages of the first chapter:

> A piece of wood as straight as an ink line may be bent into a circle as true as any drawn with a compass and, even after the wood has dried, it will not straighten out again. The bending process has made it this way. Thus, if wood is pressed against a straightening board, it can be made straight; if metal is put to the grindstone, it can be sharpened.
>
> (Watson 15; Knoblock 1.1; 1/1/3–5)

Using tools, craftsmen steam and bend wood to match the roundness of the compass, and they grind metal to the sharpness of a knife's edge. Only with the active and sustained intervention of the craftsman can the finished product be realized. This process does not imply that the properties of the material itself are irrelevant and may be ignored. To be successful, the craftsman must understand the properties of the raw material, have a keen perception of which methods will produce the desired results, and as much as possible work with the grain as opposed to against it. Likewise, Xunzi believes that the processes of cultivation must take careful account of the natural dispositions of human nature.

Given the analogy between moral cultivation and craft activity, what role does ritual play in this process of crafting oneself? For Xunzi, the role of ritual comes paired with one other element, the teacher. "In learning, nothing is more expedient than to draw close to those who are learned, and of the roads to learning, none is quicker than to love such men. Second to this is to honor ritual" (Watson 20; Knoblock 1.10; 1/3/21–2). In this scheme, the teacher – who may be anyone who has progressed further along the path of cultivation – acts as the master craftsman instructing the apprentice how to work with the tools and materials of their craft. In shaping ourselves, ritual becomes our primary tool. Any student who finds the right teacher and applies himself accordingly, has the capacity to become fully cultivated, achieving even the understanding of a sage.

Given Xunzi's understanding of moral cultivation, the teacher plays a more important role in cultivation than even the rituals themselves:

> Ritual is the means by which to correct your person; the teacher is the means by which to correct your practice of ritual. If you are without ritual, how can you correct your person? If you have no teacher, how will you know your practice of ritual is correct?
>
> (Watson 30; Knoblock 2.11; 2/8/1–2)

Within the context of moral cultivation, the teacher is needed to guide the use of the other tools of cultivation, primarily ritual practice. This need for a human mediator to make ritual an efficacious tool of cultivation for the less fully cultivated has profound implications for Xunzi's conception of tradition and its connection to moral cultivation, but here we turn to focus directly on the role and function of ritual in the process of moral cultivation or learning.

Although teachers act as guides for the process of cultivation, ritual practice constitutes the activity of moral cultivation. "If you want to become like the former kings and seek out benevolence (*ren*) and fulfill proper social roles (*yi*), then ritual is the very road by which you must travel" (Watson 21; Knoblock 1.11; 1/4/1–2). To understand this road, we must begin, as Xunzi does, by considering the origins of ritual. Prior to the emergence of the sages, human society was in chaos. As discussed above, each person was born with a nature characterized by dispositions that recognized no limits. But the world's resources could not satisfy these unlimited desires. Left to their own devices, human beings in the state of nature were inevitably drawn into conflict as they constantly struggled amongst themselves in attempting to satisfy their desires. Escape from this chaotic situation arises through the creation of rituals capable of restraining and transforming the desires of individuals and bringing order to society as a whole. Xunzi succinctly describes this escape from chaos:

> How did ritual arise? I reply: Humans are born with desires. If our desires are not satisfied, we cannot but seek some means to satisfy them for ourselves. If there are no limits and degrees to our seeking satisfaction, then we will inevitably fall to wrangling with others. From wrangling comes disorder and from disorder comes exhaustion. The ancient kings hated such disorder, and therefore they established ritual and social roles (*yi*) in order to allot things to people, to nurture their desires, and to provide for their satisfaction. They saw to it that human desires never ran out of things [to satisfy them] and that these things were not depleted by [the demands of] human desires. Thus both desires and things supported one another and flourished. This is how ritual arose.
>
> (Watson 89; Knoblock 19.1; 19/90/3–5)

The sage kings created ritual in order to eliminate chaos. Ritual effectively allotted things to people, nurtured their desires, and provided for their satisfaction. In another passage, Xunzi also describes how the sage kings created these rituals, "The sage gathers together his thoughts and ideas, practices deliberative and reasoned activities in order to produce rites and social roles (*yi*) and to establish proper models and measures" (Watson 160; Knoblock 23.2a; 23/114/10–11). Humans consciously created rituals to fulfill the purpose of restraining and expressing human nature. This deliberate and creative process, Xunzi believes, led to the unique set of ritual forms that would be capable of transforming and ordering the individual and society. This ritual order embodied the Dao, placing human beings in their proper relationship to each other as well as to Heaven and Earth. In other words, through a process of trial and error, the sages created for us rituals embodying the Dao. In turn, participation in and study of these rituals enables us to cultivate ourselves and become fully human.

How do the rites accomplish these tasks of ordering society and transforming the individual? Recall Xunzi's description of the origin of the rites. There, he isolates the problematic aspect of human nature, the unrestrained pursuit for satisfaction of natural inclinations and desires. Some solutions advocated by other philosophers in early China involved the elimination or a reduction in the numbers of our desires. Xunzi, however, opts for a different solution. Ritual, he argues, addresses desire neither by eliminating or reducing our natural complement of desires. Since our desires constitute an important element of our nature, to eliminate them would be to eliminate our essential nature. As Xunzi describes the situation,

> all those who maintain that desires must be gotten rid of before there can be orderly government fail to consider whether desires can be guided, but merely deplore the fact that they exist at all. All those who maintain that desires must be lessened before there can be orderly government

fail to consider whether desires can be controlled, but merely deplore the fact that they are so numerous. Beings that possess desires and those that do not belong to two different categories. These categories are the living and the dead; they are not the well ordered and the chaotic.

(Watson 150; Knoblock 22.5a; 22/111/4–5)

Rather than eliminating or lessening our desires, Xunzi argues that we must restrain the search for satisfying our desires and, through ritual practice, transform them. It is these two aspects of ritual practice, the restraint and transformation of dispositions and desires, that will serve the focus of the remainder of this essay.

IV. Ritual as Constraint

At its most basic level, ritual constrains the search for satisfaction of and provides appropriate expression for emotions and desires. The constraining aspects of ritual practice are reasonably apparent and should be familiar aspects of any ritual order. Ritual prescribes and proscribes certain forms of behavior. Anthony Yu gives an insightful description of this aspect of ritual in his discussion of desire in *Dream of the Red Chamber*. Discussing Xunzi's understanding of ritual, Yu claims that,

> Consistent with the distinctive topos of classical Chinese philosophy, which construes Dao as a way and a guiding discourse, the prescriptive aspect of the sign delimits the normative locale of the ritual action and specifies its proper content. The prohibitive aspect, on the other hand, cautions against the transgression of its boundary.
>
> (Yu 1997: 64)

We can recognize the importance of this observation for Xunzi's theory if we consider what he believes to be the scope of ritual activity. Ritual, for Xunzi, encompasses almost all forms of human interaction, from lavish court sacrifices for the ancestors of the ruling family to the minutiae of what we would call etiquette. Ritual pervades human activity and provides a prescriptive order for what to wear, how to move, when and how to interact with others in a vast variety of situations. For just about any type of human activity there are proper ritual forms that restrain how someone can seek to satisfy any given desire. One of the simplest examples that Xunzi gives involves hunger. When hungry we desire to eat. Yet, we will refrain from taking food first or taking more than our share when there are others with whom to share. We refrain from performing the action that would lead to the quickest and most direct way of satisfying our hunger because we belong to a ritual order in which eating with others involves an elaborate set of ritual practices, none of which are mere outgrowths of our desire to satisfy hunger.

Xunzi's solution to the problem of the lack of natural resources to satisfy human desires "does not aim so much at the redistribution of economic goods, advocated by so many modern social theories East and West, as it does at a standardized taxonomy of desire itself on the basis of class distinctions" (Yu 1997: 64). The forms for satisfying basic human needs differ according to the different stations of the social order. Within the ritual order, roles and duties as well as material possessions appropriate to our place within the hierarchy are, to a great extent, defined. "Ritual uses material goods for its performance, follows the distinctions of eminent and humble in creating its forms, varies its quantities in accordance with differences of station, and varies its degrees of lavishness in accordance with what is appropriate" (Watson 96; Knoblock 19.3; 19/92/21).

Since we are not born with dispositions naturally suited to harmonious interaction with our surroundings, human and otherwise, it is the constraining aspects of ritual practice that will first be felt when we begin to participate in ritual. In the early stages of moral cultivation, we do not enjoy the reshaping of our original dispositions. We need to be pressured into proper performance of ritual activity. Much like the way crooked wood needs to be steamed and pressed to become straight, ritual practice applies external pressure to our dispositions and desires by restricting how we can seek their satisfaction. The important point to note here is that the restrictions are external to the individual. We begin by learning the boundaries of what is permissible, that is, what we cannot do if we are to uphold ritual prescriptions. In a human life, external constraint begins early and becomes closely connected with shame, something that Xunzi also recognizes. In addition, our learning of the boundaries of ritual activity is closely linked to the distinctions of social status embodied in the rites themselves. "Certainly the system of ritual that Xunzi was familiar with would start from the differences in behavior that corresponded to the fundamental inequalities of parent/child or of ruler/high official/low-ranking official/subject" (Kupperman 2000: 97). The constraints on our behavior correspond to our social roles and aid us in learning how to be a good child, sibling, cousin, and eventually parent, grandparent, subject, and possibly official. Although Xunzi recognizes the efficacy of external constraints in the early stages of moral cultivation, we should eventually internalize these restraints and act spontaneously to fulfill our social roles without transgressing the boundaries of ritual propriety. Yet, not transgressing the boundaries of ritual propriety is a necessary but not a sufficient condition for moral cultivation. It remains to be explained how we concretely inhabit these social roles and transform our dispositions and desires such that they accord with the demands of the ritual order.

V. Ritual as transformative

While ritual functions as a constraining force for Xunzi, it also facilitates the gradual transformation of dispositions and desires and of the methods of seeking their satisfaction. Ritual transforms and channels our originally unshaped desires into more complex and ultimately satisfying forms of expression. The explanation of how this transformation occurs is one of the most interesting aspect of Xunzi's metapraxis. Here we will examine the conceptual shift that occurs when one begins to understand and internalize the ideals embodied in the ritual order, and how the cognitive, affective and somatic aspects of ritual work to transform our original dispositions. Our explanation requires that we first consider Xunzi's conception of moral psychology in more depth.

According to Xunzi, moral psychology begins with elements of our nature. We are born with a nature (*xing*) that reacts to the environment in terms of a set of innate dispositions (*qing*). These dispositions, when activated by our environment, can lead to the creation of a desire (*yu*) for a particular object or outcome in the world. The most direct form of this mechanism involves basic human needs. After a hard day working, we naturally become tired and desire to rest. Yet, as we will see, Xunzi recognizes more complicated forms of desire that arise from more developed dispositions.

In addition to desires and dispositions, Xunzi also describes a separate source of motivation in the heart/mind (*xin*).[5] Our heart/mind has the capacity to understand (*zhi*). Understanding leads to approving (*ke*) and disapproving (*buke*) of things, be they courses of action or people.[6] According to Xunzi, we usually act in accord not with what we desire, but with what we approve (Watson 151; Knoblock 22.5a; 22/111/6–10). Through approval or disapproval, brought about by understanding, the heart/mind controls our actions. Even the strongest desires need not be translated into action; approval and disapproval can control the search for their satisfaction. Furthermore, approval can motivate an action in spite of insufficient or even contrary desire. For example, even though people love life and hate death more than anything else, they can intentionally follow courses of action that lead to their own death. In other words, approval and disapproval are the primary motives of action. Moreover, as judgments of our understanding, approval and disapproval depend on the pre-established categories in which they are formulated. If we understand the world in certain terms, we then approve and disapprove of things in the world in these terms.

Having some grasp of Xunzi's conception of moral psychology enables us to appreciate the changes brought about by ritual participation. Xunzi argues that a shift in conceptual categories takes place through ritual participation. The cultivated – gentleman (*junzi*) – and uncultivated – petty people (*xiaoren*) – see and evaluate the world in fundamentally different ways. At birth we are born as petty people. "If we have no teacher or model to guide us, we can see only benefit (*Li*). . . . If people have no teacher or model to guide them, their heart/mind (*xin*) will be just like their mouth and stomach" (Knoblock 4.10; 4/15/14, 17).[7] A petty person is unable to see the full breadth of the world and is obsessed with benefit and harm. At birth, Xunzi says, we are only able to see benefit and thus actions are good if they bring benefit, bad if they bring harm. This does not imply, however, that we necessarily evaluate actions or persons in terms of benefit and harm *to us*. The possibility remains that we can assess benefit and harm *to others*. Still, assessing people and actions in terms of benefit and harm is, for Xunzi, to reduce our power of approval to the same level as the natural desires of our body, the preferences and aversions of our sensory faculties. To remain in this state is to remain an uncultivated rustic. To become virtuous, to see the world and our actions in terms of virtue and vice – the categories embodied in the ritual order – and thus to see ourselves as moral agents requires moral cultivation, an opening of our evaluations to an alternate source of value.

This point can be made clearer if we consider the origin of desires for Xunzi. We desire something because we recognize that we lack the thing we desire. Recognition that we have a certain lack comes before and is the cause of the desire. Once desires arise, we then begin to seek for their satisfaction:

> Every man who desires to do good does so precisely because his nature is bad. A man whose accomplishments are meager longs for greatness; an ugly man longs for beauty; a man in cramped quarters longs for spaciousness; a poor man longs for wealth; a humble man longs for eminence. *Whatever a man lacks in himself he will seek for outside.* But if a man is already rich, he will not long for wealth, and if he is already eminent, he will not long for greater power. *What a man already possesses in himself he will not bother to look for outside.*
>
> (Watson 161–2; Knoblock 23.2b; 23/114/18–20, italics are mine)

As we are born, with our original nature, we are able to recognize that we lack only those things that can be evaluated in terms of benefit and harm, in terms of the preferences of our sensory desires. If we can only recognize deficiency in these terms, then our desires will only aim at acquiring those things that satisfy this uncultivated sense of lack. We will be completely blind to moral considerations. Even though we will still have the power to approve and disapprove of the ways we seek to satisfy our desires, even this evaluation will be in non-moral, purely instrumental terms. Yet, the psychological mechanism of recognizing deficiency and its motivating force, according to Xunzi, make it possible for us to act for the good and to become virtuous. Teachers who instruct us in ritual practice, models whose behavior embodies the rites, and the conceptual vocabulary that explains the symbolic significance of the rites all present us with examples and guide our recognition such that we begin to see deficiencies in ourselves in terms of moral categories instantiated in ritual practice. Instead of evaluating actions and persons solely in terms of benefit and harm, we now consider virtue and vice.

Given Xunzi's conception of this psychological mechanism, it matters a great deal what examples and categories we use to describe and evaluate actions. If we are not exposed to certain categories, we will be unable to perceive deficiencies in those terms. We will be oblivious to these considerations and, thus, there will be motives inaccessible to us.[8] Without going through the process of cultivation, we remain locked within the categories and preferences of our original nature. We will be left morally blind, unable to participate fully in the numinous qualities of the Confucian ritual order, and outside the individual, social, and cosmic harmony manifest in the Dao.

Ritual practice gives us access to new categories for seeing and evaluating the world both through direct performance of social roles embodied in the ritual order as well as through learning the spoken and symbolic vocabulary and grammar of ritual performance. Consider a relatively simple example, the handshake. As children, we start learning to shake hands. We are instructed to shake hands upon greeting someone as a gesture of openness and friendship. Our performance is gradually shaped through the critique of parents and other teachers. Eventually, we come to understand the significance of a handshake in human interactions – what it means to offer a weak or tentative handshake, a hearty and eager handshake, or to refuse to shake hands. The handshake eventually becomes a potent performative symbol, such as when Yasser Arafat and Yitzhak Rabin shook hands or when an ex-lover offers a handshake in place of a more intimate gesture. At these more developed stages of ritual participation, we literally live within the world of handshakes, evaluating others in terms of the manner, timing, and circumstance in which they shake hands.

For Xunzi, to participate in the ritual order is to live within the world in which gesture, movement, and timing have symbolic value (Neville 2003; Berkson 2003). As he describes learning, "The learning of the gentleman enters his ear, clings to his mind, spreads through his four limbs, and manifests itself in his actions. His smallest word, his slightest movement can serve as a model" (Watson 20; Knoblock 1.9; 1/3/14–5). Learning, through ritual practice guided by the teacher, alters the way in which we understand ourselves and our world. Our speech, gestures, and movements carry symbolic value that when performed accordingly lead to harmonious interactions with others and the cosmos. The conceptual, affective and somatic aspects of ritual practice readily explain Xunzi's claims about the learning of the cultivated person. Yet, there is more to the picture: Xunzi's vision of ritual practice also includes the transformation of one's affective responses and dispositions.

Confucian moral cultivation lasts a lifetime, and we gradually develop a deeper understanding of the ritual order and participate more fully in the Dao. We begin this process equipped with basic human dispositions and desires arising from our nature, approving and disapproving of actions and people in terms of benefit and harm. Given our nature, the path of cultivation begins with a recognition that a life lived outside the ritual order is full of chaos and conflict. According to Xunzi, we begin following the path of moral cultivation because we are motivated either by fear of the alternative, a life of chaos and conflict, or by a prudential choice. Thus, the original motivation for cultivating ourselves is never spontaneous love or reverence for ritual or delight in following the Dao. These motives emerge only later in the process of cultivation. At the beginning, we believe ritual cultivation is a means to other ends: gaining power as a ruler, avoiding harm and conflict, achieving honor and rank, ordering a chaotic situation. With these goals in mind, we find a teacher and embark on our study of the classical texts and practice of ritual.

Once we begin to practice ritual, we immediately involve our affective responses. Ritual requires dramatic re-enactment, and it relies on external symbols to arouse, express, and satisfy our dispositions and desires. As David Wong has observed, Xunzi believes that after being worked upon by the ritual, regulations, music, and learning created by the sages, elements of our psychological makeup can be conscripted into the service of the ritual order (Wong 2000: 148). Xunzi argues that grief and love for one's parents, and the joy and exuberance accompanying victory, while not in themselves moral, lend themselves to being given moral shape and direction.

Furthermore, ritual and music are the most efficacious means for trans-forming these pre-moral affective states. "Rituals are especially effective in shaping and channeling human feelings because they regulate and partially define occasions on which human beings have strong feelings of the sort that can become moral feelings" (Wong 2000: 149). By participating in ritual and music – activities capable of performing this double function of expressing emotion and of defining the occasions for and the forms through which emotion should be expressed – participants transform themselves as well as others. As Xunzi describes this process,

> rites trim what is too long, and stretch out what is too short. They eliminate surplus and repair deficiency, extend the forms of love and reverence, and step by step bring to fulfillment the beauties of proper conduct. Beauty and ugliness, joyful sounds and weeping, happiness and sorrow are opposites, and yet rites make use of them all, bringing forth and employing each in its turn.
>
> (Watson 100; Knoblock 19.5b; 19/94/8–9)

Xunzi's most elaborate example of this process in action is the way that ritual harnesses strong and potentially dangerous emotions of mourning and provides a framework of communal activities for expressing and satisfying these emotions in a harmonious and fulfilling manner. By participating in mourning rituals, we acknowledge the existence of strong desires and dispo-sitions and satisfy them in ways that extend far beyond what we would be capable of without ritual participation.

If we engage in ritual practice long enough, our original dispositions are reshaped into forms that accord with the ritual order, the Dao. When we reach higher levels of cultivation, we come to love ritual practice in itself because it expresses and strengthens elements of our natural dispositions. As we travel further along the path of cultivation, the fit between the internal affective reactions and external ritual forms becomes closer and closer. For sages, there is no divergence between the two.[9] Ritual fully expresses their affective reactions, and it defines the occasions and circumstances in which these reactions arise. The sage has become fully cultivated and sees a life lived within ritual structures as the only one that fully satisfies the need for personal expressions of grief, love, joy, and so forth. At this stage, ritual becomes an end in itself. Sages delight in the practice of ritual. They are at home in the world of ritual gesture and speech. Ritual, thus, makes use of our human nature and transforms it in the process, shaping it in accordance with ritual forms. "Of all the ways to order the temperament and train the heart/mind, none is more direct than to follow ritual" (Watson 26; Knoblock 2.4; 2/6/9–10).

VI. Conclusion

Xunzi's metapraxis justifies Confucian ritual practice because it is the only means by which human beings, born with natural inclinations towards chaos and conflict, transform their original dispositions such that they can harmoniously interact with others and the natural world, thus participating in the numinous qualities of the Dao. Rejecting Confucian ritual practice amounts to refusing to become fully human and to uphold our obligation to cooperate with Heaven and Earth in completing the cosmic order, the Dao. Ritual practice accomplishes these feats because it engages and transforms our natural dispositions and faculties, constraining and shaping forms of expression. Simultaneously, we use our heart/mind to understand the conceptual categories embodied in the ritual order, reenacted through ritual performance. Through repeated performance, we gradually shape our every gesture and word. We eventually perceive the world and react to it, with gestures, movements, and words, all in accord with the Dao. This transformation is possible because ritual makes use of the fact that human movement and demeanor can be given symbolic value. Fundamentally, for Xunzi, we are symbol-creating creatures, and it is through ritual practice that he believes we come to inhabit the symbolic order of the Confucian tradition.

The richness of Xunzi's metapraxis suggests that his insights ought to become part of the contemporary discussion of ritual and moral cultivation. Although no one still engages in the Confucian ritual practices familiar to Xunzi, human beings still find themselves participating in ritual practices that shape how they interact with others and their surroundings. Our possibilities for living a life full of harmonious interactions remain bounded by the ritual order in which we live. In the broadest terms possible, Xunzi highlights for us the fact that we are not simply what we eat, but the ritual we practice. Ethical theory may provide us with compelling visions of the good human life, but it is only through ritual participation that we are capable of living those lives and transforming ourselves into good human beings.[10]

Notes

1 For a concise introduction to both Xunzi and his writings, please see the entries for Xunzi, and *Xunzi* in Yao (2003).
2 See the introductions in both Kline III and Ivanhoe (2000) and Kline III (2003). It might also be argued that Xunzi's ritual theory is one of the most, if not *the* most, sophisticated within the entire Chinese philosophical tradition. As a group, the essays in Kline III (2003) argue for this claim.
3 My description of human nature will be necessarily brief. For a more developed discussion see Hutton (2000), Ivanhoe (2000), and Munro (1996).

4 Quotations from the text of the *Xunzi* are my translations. Often they are adaptations from Hutton (2001), Watson (1963), or Knoblock (1988–94). Following each quotation from or reference to the original Chinese text are the page references for the Watson translation, the chapter and section references for the Knoblock translation, and finally the concordance reference numbers for the Lau and Chen edition of the original text in Chinese given as chapter/page/line number, Lau and Chen (1996).

5 For most early Chinese philosophers, the heart/mind is the seat of both cognitive and affective capacities. Xunzi uses the term in this way as well. Given the combination of cognitive and affective faculties in a single source, it is important to realize that when Xunzi refers to the heart/mind's ability to understand (*zhi*) he is not referring to only a cognitive or conceptual understanding. Understanding for Xunzi must also involve some element of affective response as well.

6 For a more detailed examination of Xunzi's conception of moral reasoning, see Hutton (2002).

7 I have capitalized the romanization for the character meaning "benefit" (*Li*) in order to distinguish it from the homophonous character meaning ritual (*li*).

8 Cora Diamond discusses a very similar insight in two different articles (Diamond 1988, 1991). She too argues that having certain concepts matters for the way in which we live our lives. As she describes, "grasping a concept (even one like that of a human being, which is a descriptive concept if any are) is not a matter of just knowing how to group things under that concept; it is being able to participate in life-with-the-concept. What kinds of descriptive concept there are is a matter of the different shapes life-with-a-concept can have" (Diamond 1988: 266).

9 For an excellent modern example of the type of transformation that Xunzi describes, see Sudnow (2001). In *Ways of the Hand: A Rewritten Account*, Sudnow describes, in meticulous detail, the process of learning to play improvisational jazz piano. Though he never makes any reference to Confucian metapraxis, he provides a beautifully concrete explanation of the stages of development through which he progressed that matches Xunzi's description of the stages of ritual participation. Though the world of jazz piano and the Dao are not congruent, the similarities suggest that Xunzi has identified transformative mechanisms of ritual practice that apply to more than just the Confucian context.

10 I would like to thank all of the contributors to the two anthologies on Xunzi that I have edited – Kline III and Ivanhoe (2000) and Kline III (2003). The insights of this essay owe a great deal to what I have learned from their careful scholarship.

Bibliography

Berkson, M. A. (2003) "Xunzi's Reinterpretation of Ritual: A Hermeneutic Defense of the Confucian Way," in T. C. Kline III (ed.), *Ritual and Religion in the* Xunzi, New York: Seven Bridges Press.

Diamond, C. (1988) "Losing Your Concepts," *Ethics* 98: 255–77.

—— (1991) "The Importance of Being Human," *Philosophy* 30: 35–62.

Hutton, E. L. (2000) "Does Xunzi Have a Consistent Theory of Human Nature?" in T.C. Kline III and P.J. Ivanhoe (eds), *Virtue, Nature, and Moral Agency in the* Xunzi, Indianapolis, IN: Hackett Publishing.

—— (trans.) (2001) "Xunzi," in P. J. Ivanhoe and B. W. Van Norden (eds), *Readings in Classical Chinese Philosophy*, New York: Seven Bridges Press.

—— (2002) "Moral Reasoning in Aristotle and Xunzi," *Journal of Chinese Philosophy* 29: 355–84.

Ivanhoe, P. J. (2000) "Human Nature and Moral Understanding in the *Xunzi*," in T. C. Kline III and P. J. Ivanhoe (eds), *Virtue, Nature, and Moral Agency in the* Xunzi, Indianapolis, IN: Hackett Publishing.

Kasulis, T. P. (1992) "Philosophy as Metapraxis," in F. Reynolds and D. Tracy (eds), *Discourse and Practice*, Albany, NY: SUNY Press.

Kline III, T.C. (ed.) (2003) *Ritual and Religion in the* Xunzi, New York: Seven Bridges Press.

—— and Ivanhoe, P. J. (eds) (2000) *Virtue, Nature, and Moral Agency in the* Xunzi, Indianapolis, IN: Hackett Publishing.

Knoblock, J. (trans.) (1988–94) *Xunzi*, 3 vols, Stanford, CA: Stanford University Press.

Kupperman, J. J. (2000) "Xunzi: Morality as Psychological Constraint," in T. C. Kline III and P. J. Ivanhoe (eds), *Virtue, Nature, and Moral Agency in the* Xunzi, Indianapolis, IN: Hackett Publishing.

Lau, D. C. and Chen, F. C. (1996) *A Concordance to the Xunzi*, Hong Kong: The Commercial Press.

Munro, D. J. (1996) "A Villain in the *Xunzi*," in P. J. Ivanhoe (ed.), *Chinese Language, Thought, and Culture*, Chicago, IL: Open Court.

Neville, R. C. (2003) "Ritual and Religion: A Lesson from Xunzi for Today," in T. C. Kline III (ed.), *Ritual and Religion in the* Xunzi, New York: Seven Bridges Press.

Sudnow, D. (2001) *Ways of the Hand: A Rewritten Account*, Cambridge, Mass.: MIT Press.

Watson, B. (trans.) (1963) *Hsün Tzu: Basic Writings*, New York: Columbia University Press.

Wong, D. B. (2000) "Xunzi on Moral Motivation," in T. C. Kline III and P. J. Ivanhoe (eds), *Virtue, Nature, and Moral Agency in the* Xunzi, Indianapolis, IN: Hackett Publishing.

Yao, X. Z. (ed.) (2003) *The Encyclopedia of Confucianism*, 2 vols, London: Routledge Curzon.

Yu, A. C. (1997) *Rereading the Stone: Desire and the Making of Fiction in* Dream of the Red Chamber, Princeton: Princeton University Press.

10 The ritual roots of moral reason

Lessons from Mīmāṃsā

Jonardon Ganeri

Plutarch said: "At Athens, Lysimache, the priestess of Athene Polias, when asked for a drink by the mule drivers who had transported the sacred vessels, replied, 'No, for I fear it will get into the ritual'" (quoted in Smith 1982: 53–65). There is reason within ritual. Ritual is not the merely mechanical repetition of an act whose form and content is fixed rigidly in advance. When G. K. Chesterton inveighed against "the man of science, [who] not realizing that ceremonial is essentially a thing which is done without a reason, has to find a reason for every sort of ceremonial" (1905: 144), he was wrong to deny reason as such to ritual, although he was of course right in his condemnation of the man of science (for instance, the author of *The Golden Bough*), who seeks to reduce the reason in ritual to that of science, the only kind of reason he knows. Whenever a ritual is performed, there are decisions to be made – about what to leave in, and what to leave out, about how to adapt the model to the circumstances. Ritual acts must "fit" the situation in which they are performed, and ritual acts must "work" (whatever it is for a ritual act to "work," or preserve that which is essential to it qua ritual of a given type). The priestess of Athene Polias had to think about what made her ritual the ritual it was, and be led by this to decide which modifications are, and which are not, consistent with its unity and function.

In this chapter, I will give an account of the reason in ritual. It is an account substantially derived from the ritual theory of the Mīmāṃsā, the Indian interpreters of Vedic ritual. Ritual reason, in the model I want to develop, is governed by relations of substitution and adaptation. It is a matter of deliberation about how a given blueprint or model for a ritual is to be instantiated in an actual ritual action in a particular context. I will then go on to argue that the intellectual virtues associated with ritual reason are precisely those needed for ethical reasoning in general, so that the account of ritual reason becomes a general account of moral reason. Indeed, the process by which this comes about is itself an instance of ritual reasoning at second-order: styles of reasoning about ritual acts are adapted and modified until they become models for practical deliberation outside the ritual sphere. In both these ways, the ritual is a blueprint for the ethical.

I. Ritual and religious duty in the Hindu canon

There are traditionally said to be two parts to the Hindu canon. One is the Veda, which is also called *śruti*, "what is heard." The Vedas are taken to consist essentially in an eternal, authorless body of ritual imperatives of the general schematic form "One who desires heaven ought to perform the agnihotra sacrifice." The Mīmāṃsā school, whose ur-text is the *Mīmāṃsā-sūtra*, is a school of Vedic ritual theory (see Jaimini; henceforth cited parenthetically as MS). It is very difficult to date this text with any accuracy; perhaps in some form it already existed in about 400 BCE and its compilation into the recension as we now have it took place in the following few centuries (see Verpoorten 1987). The best-known of the commentators on Mīmāṃsā are Śabara (*c.*400 CE) and Kumārila (*c.*650 CE). The other part of the Hindu canon is made up of a variety of "lawbooks" or digests on *dharma* – moral, social and religious duty, including duties specific to the "stations" of life. These lawbooks are collectively known as the *dharmaśāstra*, and they are also said to be *smṛti*, "what is remembered." The *Manu-smṛti* – the lawbook of Manu – is the most important and popular of such texts. It dates, again very approximately, from somewhere between 200 BCE and 200 CE (Doniger and Smith 1991, and Lingat 1973). Medhātithi, to whom I shall refer a number of times, is one of several commentators; he lived in the second half of the ninth century or first half of the tenth century CE. From these works on ritual theory and religious duty, what can we learn about the nature of reason? Wilhelm Halbfass has said that "the *varṇāśramadharma* [theory of duty], as understood by the 'orthodox' (*smārta*) core of the tradition and articulated in the *mīmāṃsā* and *dharmaśāstra* literature . . . leaves little room for rational ethical critique," that "attempts from various directions to ethicize and universalize *dharma* . . . are rejected or discarded by the tradition" (Halbfass 1988: 332–3). One of my purposes in this paper is to argue against this analysis of the ethical resources of Hinduism. I will seek to demonstrate instead that a distinctive form of ethical reasoning is centrally located in orthodox Hinduism. My thesis is that a model of ritual reason, introduced and developed in *mīmāṃsā* as a means to reason about the proper way to perform, adapt, and manipulate vedic rituals, is transformed in the *dharmaśāstra* into a model of moral reason, a method of reasoning about "what is to be done" (*dharma*) in a full range of deliberative contexts. The conception of moral reason sustained by the ritual model is particularist and situational, and yet has clear differences from (and merits over) comparable conceptions more familiar to us from Aristotelian ethics (e.g. Nussbaum 1986).

II. Sacred reason

Somewhere in the Vedas, it is reported to be said:

> The gods came down from their world to this world, the ṛṣis followed them, and the people said to them "how then are we going to live?"

To them, the ṛṣis revealed all the proper acts. And so, such reasoning
(*tarka*) as the best of brahmins propound, it alone is sacred (*ārṣa*).[1]

This Vedic passage above is quoted by Medhātithi in his commentary on
Manu's *Manu-smṛti* 12.106. Manu himself is clear about the status of reason
in matters of *dharma* or "what is to be done."[2] The Vedas and *dharmaśāstras*
are beyond question (*amīmāṃsye*), for *dharma* arises out of them, and therefore the use of the art of reasoning (*hetuśāstra*) in disregard of them merits only
expulsion by the virtuous. Nevertheless, he and no other knows "what is to
be done" who, with reasoning (*tarka*) that does not contradict the teachings of
the Veda, inspects the instructions about *dharma* and the ṛṣis' revelations:

> The Veda should be known as the revealed canon, and the teachings of
> dharma as the tradition. These two are beyond criticism in all matters,
> for duty (*dharma*) arose out of the two of them. A twice-born man who
> disregards these two roots because he relies on the arts of reason
> (*hetuśāstra*) should be expelled by virtuous people as an atheist and a
> reviler of the Veda.
>
> (*Manu* 2.10–11)

> The man who uses reason (*tarka*), which does not contradict the teach-
> ings of the Veda, to investigate the sages' (Veda) and the instructions
> about duty – he alone, and no one else, knows duty.
>
> (*Manu* 12.106)

A contrast is made out, partly through the use of two different terms for
"reason" itself (*hetu, tarka*), between two forms of moral deliberation, one
categorically dismissed and the other applauded to the highest degree.
Reasoning of the first sort, which questions the moral standing of actions
enjoined in the Vedas, involves itself in a performative contradiction – or
so argues the commentator Medhātithi – for the Vedas themselves are the
source of the normative criteria against which any action is to be evaluated.
To argue that ritual killing is sinful on the grounds that it is an act of
violence like any other is to forget that the immorality of violence is laid
out only by the Vedas themselves, whose status therefore as a source of
knowledge about *dharma* is presupposed by the criticism of them (Medhātithi,
in Manu 1920–6: 71). What makes an act of violence sinful is not simply
that it is an act of violence, but that it is prohibited by the Vedas, and the
Vedic prohibition cannot without self-reference apply to itself (Medhātithi,
in Manu 1920–6: 62).

Moral deliberation that consists in applying criteria to evaluate actions
involves itself in a performative contradiction when it attempts to criticize
the Veda, for the Veda is, by definition, the means by which such criteria
are tested.[3] The same is true of another part of the religious canon, the
smṛti, the "recalled" traditional writing about *dharma*, a body of texts which,
like the Vedas, consist in rules of proper conduct, but which, unlike the

Vedas, are ascribed to (possibly mythical) human redactors. The relation-ship between the *smṛti* and the *śruti* is fundamental to Hinduism's conception of itself as a religion based on the Vedas. It is in the *smṛti*, the codified tradition of religious instruction, rather than the *śruti*, the "revealed" word describing by-and-large arcane ritual practices, that the actual duties of Hindus are described. How is it, then, that the ethical rules of the *dharmaśāstras*, with their human redactors and group-specific rules, are to be justified, if it is the Veda and the Veda alone which is the foundation of *dharma*? Against the background set by this question, let us consider the nature of that moral reasoning which is so applauded by Manu.

Moral deliberation is in part deliberation about what sort of rules could have a basis in the Veda. The form of reasoning which Manu condemned involved itself in a performative contradiction when it sought critically to evaluate actions enjoined by the Vedas and *dharmaśāstras*, forgetting that it is because of them alone that we know criteria of moral evaluation. What about the style of moral thinking that he praises, even to the point of saying that he alone who employs it knows *dharma*? The commentator Medhātithi identifies Manu's use of the term "reasoning" or tarka here with the kind of reasoning employed by the Mīmāṃsakas in thinking about the right and proper way to perform rituals. It is a form of reasoning that is embedded in a dialectical frame, involving the setting up of a dialogue between a *pūrvapakṣa* or prima facie view, and a *siddhānta* or considered conclusion (Manu 12.106).[4] And Medhātithi goes on to say:

> Reasoning (*tarka*) is an internal (*antarya*) investigation involving adap-tation (*ūha*) and exclusion (*apoha*) – "this is fit to be modified, this to be excluded." When the *mantra* offered in a performance of the Saurya ritual is obtained from the [Āgneya] archetype – *devasya tvā savituḥ prasave 'śvinor bāhubhāṃ pūrṇo hastābhyām agnaye tvā juṣṭam? nirvāmi*" (*Vājasaneya Saṃhitā* 2.11), – the word "*agni*" is excluded as its meaning does not fit, and the word "*sūrya*" is added. This reasoning is not inconsistent with the Veda.
>
> (Medhātithi, in Manu 1920–6: 485)

Medhātithi continues that it would be inconsistent with the Veda either to argue that the whole mantra should be dropped because it fails to fit the new context, or to argue that the mantra should be taken over directly in its unaltered form. The study of the Mīmāṃsā methods of ritual reasoning is therefore commended as the proper way forward in matters of social, ethical, and religious duty.

III. Ritual reason: adaptive reasoning from paradigms

The reference in the above quotation is to a sophisticated theory of reason developed by the Mīmāṃsakas in a particular context. The problem there was this: how ought one to perform ritual acts whose details are only incompletely described in the Vedic texts? It is a species of what we would now call reasoning under uncertainty, working out what to do when we do not have the full facts at our disposal. The method recommended by the Mīmāṃsakas consists in a procedure of transfer (*atideśa*), adaptation (*ūha*), and annulment (*bādha*) of details, from those "model" (*prakṛti*) rituals whose performance is completely specified to those "variant" (*vikṛti*) rituals the details of which are only incompletely given. An appropriate model for the variant ritual is selected according to criteria based on commonality of function, purpose, and structure. A generic metarule for the transfer of details asserts that the variant is to be performed in the same manner as the model,[5] but the blanket rule is subject to caveats permitting the adaptation of transferred details to fit the new context, and the suspension or annulment of the transfer of a detail that has no place in the new ritual. The method of reasoning described here is pragmatic, situational, and informal. Sound judgment and practical wisdom guide the process of selection and adaptation, rather than hard-and-fast rules. That is what makes this the sacred reasoning (*tarka*) of the best of brahmins; they are the ones on whose judgment we can depend (we should see this as the definition of a "best brahmin" rather than as propaganda for an epistemological elite). *Tarka*, sometimes called "suppositional reason," is a style of reasoning that calls upon the reasoner to use skills of imagination, hypothesis, and simulation in thinking through a new situation by means of the adaptation of an old one. It makes a connection between ritual rationality and games of make-believe and pretence (for more on this aspect of the nature of *tarka*, see Ganeri 2001: ch. 6, esp. 158–9).

Although it is developed in a particular context, the Mīmāṃsā theory is clearly a theory of practical reason, a method for deciding what properly is to be done. The pattern exemplified – taking a single instance and transferring its properties to the members of a class of resembling particulars, crops up many times and in many different contexts in the ancient Indian literature. The logicians call it by the nickname "rice-in-the-pan" reasoning (*sthālīpulākanyāya*), for it is nicely illustrated by the reasoning that goes on when we test the firmness of one grain of rice in a cooking vessel, and infer on that basis whether the rest of the rice is cooked. This example is found in texts as diverse as the *Mahābhāṣya* (1.4.23), the *Ts'ing-mu* (a commentary on Nāgārjuna's *Mūlamadhyamakakārikā*), and more especially in the *Mīmāṃsā-sūtra* itself (MS 7.4.12), where it is appealed to in order to resolve a methodological problem about the inferred transfer of ritual procedure to an incompletely specified ritual action.

The question arises as to whether we could transfer the procedural details from ordinary acts, and not just from other Vedic ritual acts. The answer is that they should always be transferred from Vedic ritual acts, for this has been enjoined explicitly in at least one case. Thus MS 7.4.12 says: "As the sign is the prior type (*pūrvavat*), and as the injunctive verb is common to all, it may be indicated even by a single instance, as with the rice in the pan."

Śabara now comments:

> A sign which is prior to the detail (*nyāya*), being seen even in a single case, indicates the propriety of all equivalent (*tulya*) details. Just as one grain of rice cooked equally in a pot, on being pressed, makes known the state of the others too, on the ground that the same cause for this one is present in the case of others too. From all this it follows that in the case of all sacrifices [whose procedure has not been explicitly laid down], the Vedic procedure should be adopted.

The structure of such a pattern of reasoning is now clear: it consists in the transfer of a property from a known instance to relevantly similar other instances. What makes such reasoning possible, as Śabara's comment reveals, is the assumption of a common cause – that whatever it is that has caused the one grain of rice to become soft will similarly have made soft all other grains of rice equivalent in being in the same pan and under the same cooking conditions.[6] Allowances can be made for variation in the place of the rice in the pot and other such situational variables (this is the proper function of the reasoning called *ūha*, "adaptation"). This assumption is a presupposition upon which such patterns of reasoning depend; it is, so to speak, a requirement of reason (the echo of Kant's talk of the requirements of practical reason is intentional). And when the model is extended from rice, through ritual, to moral deliberation more generally, an analogous requirement, this time of practical reason, emerges – that there is a stable moral order, just as there is a stable causal order, in virtue of which actions in one situation may serve as a guide to actions in sufficiently commensurable other situations, and that the actions of one good man may serve as a guide for the actions of others. It is the guarantee that what is good at one time and place is good at others, a guarantee without which moral reasoning based on a method of transfer and modification would collapse. We would be stuck with Aristotle's version of moral particularism, and have to attend to the particular in all its isolated glory, unable to draw upon the rich resources of resemblance and situational adaptation. This presupposition of a stable moral order resonates with another of the many meanings of *dharma*: as that which "upholds" or "supports" people's moral actions.

It is reasoning of precisely this kind that is used to justify those rules of conduct in the *smṛti* to which there corresponds no extant Vedic text. The problem is to explain moral innovation within an ahistorical framework. How can that which does not have a history serve as the basis for that which does? The gauntlet is thrown down in *Mīmāṃsā-sūtra* 1.3.1: if *dharma* is rooted in the Vedas, then whatever is not Vedic cannot be depended on.[7] The reply in 1.3.2 is that reason (*anumāna*) is the proper method (for authenticating the *smṛti*), specifically reasoning from a common cause.[8] One commentator (Śabara) explains that the form of reasoning involved begins with the premise that the persons who compiled the *smṛti*s and acted in accordance with them were people of moral standing whose actions were fully guided by the Veda and who performed all their Vedic duties. It is said then to follow that since some of the rules they followed are Vedic, the others too must be so (the *anumāna*), and from this one may conclude that the authors of the *smṛti* knew of and followed Vedic texts that are now lost to us. The inference is to a mislaid or forgotten Vedic basis for the rules of *smṛti*. A similar strategy is seen at work in the explanation of linguistic change within a model of the fixed and eternal Sanskrit language. New linguistic usages, it is claimed, do not force a revision of the old rules, but are simply new discoveries in an infinite and partly lost reservoir of eternal grammatical rules.[9]

Another commentator, Kumārila, points out that if the conclusion of our inference is the existence of a lost Veda, then it is not an inference from particular to particular on the presumption of a common cause; rather, it takes that inference as a whole as the premise and infers to its presumption, the common cause, as its conclusion. So he reconstructs the argument (of MS 1.3.2) as a sort of inference to the best or only consistent explanation (*arthāpatti*): the only consistent explanation of the claims about *dharma* recorded in the *smṛti* is that they report the contents of now lost Vedas. Both agree, however, that the reasoning in question is not a species of consequential evaluation. We do not look to the consequences of the act, or to the perceived consequences of resembling acts, as we do when we infer that it will rain because the ants are carrying their eggs (Medhātithi, in Manu, 2.6). The reasoning is not from effect to cause (*śeṣavat*) but from cause to effect (*pūrvavat*).

The implication of this argument is that the Vedas are to be regarded not as a limited and specific collection of moral rules, but as an idealized method for moral knowledge. To say of some maxim for action that it is indeed a norm for good conduct is to say that it meets those formal criteria that would entitle us to infer back to a now lost Veda to which it corresponds. In particular, a Vedic injunction mentions no particular, contains no proper name, and so is general in its application. In a discussion about the legitimacy of regional customs (MS 1.3.15–23), a prima facie view is put forward that the Vedic rule that legitimates a regional custom must specify the specific region in which the rule applies.[10] That view is rejected, however, on the grounds that genuinely moral duties must apply in all regions, for that is the nature of such duties.[11] This is not to say that the ritual model of duty is a model of unconditional duty; for there is in the *mīmāṃsā* a well-attested distinction between occasional (*naimittika*) and obligatory (*nitya*) ritual duties. Rather, the point is that geography is not a consideration in the evaluation of moral resemblance. The moral relevance of time, however, is clearly recognized in this model: *when* one performs an action can matter in ways that *where* one performs it never can.[12]

Let us pause and take stock. The general model of reason under consideration is this one: x is F; y resembles x in salient respects; therefore, y is F. The same general model is exemplified in a number of contexts – empirical prediction, ritual practice, and moral deliberation:

Case 1: Rice.   That grain of rice is cooked.
                    This grain is like that one (both have been in the pan for the same time, etc.)
                    Therefore, this grain of rice is cooked too.

Case 2: Ritual.   That ritual is performed thus-&-so.
                    This ritual is like that one (that is the model of which this is a variant).
                    Therefore, this ritual is performed thus-&-so too.

Case 3: Rules.   That rule is Vedic.
                    This rule is like that one (both are followed by a virtuous man).
                    Therefore, this rule is Vedic too.

Case 3 (variant). That rule is Vedic.
                    This rule is like that one (both share certain formal properties, such as generality, impartiality, etc.)
                    Therefore, this rule is Vedic too.

This is the particularist and situational model of reason that is developed in the context of ritual theory and transformed into a general conception of practical reasoning and ethical deliberation. In attaching central importance to resemblances between relevantly similar cases, it is a model at considerable remove from moral particularism of the Aristotelian variety.[13]

IV. The good man as a paradigm of exemplary conduct

Manu lists the Vedas and the *smṛti* as two of his four "roots" of *dharma*:

2.1 Learn the *dharma* that is approved of by the heart, constantly followed by the knowledgeable and the good who have neither hatred nor greed.

2.6 The root of *dharma* is the entire Veda, the *smṛti* and virtue of those who know it, the conduct of the good, and one's own satisfaction.

2.12 The Veda, the *smṛti*, the conduct of the good, and what is dear to oneself – this, they say, is the four-fold manifest mark of *dharma*.

Who is a good man (*sad, sādhu*)? A good man, the commentator explains, is someone who, acting in a manner circumscribed by evidence (*pramāṇa*), directs his efforts towards obtaining what is valuable (*hita*; other meanings possible) and avoiding what has no value – the value of things in the everyday world is well-known, while the value of other things is indicated by the injunctions and prohibitions of the Vedas (Medhātithi, in Manu 1920–6: 51 under Manu 2.1). Such a man must be knowledgeable (*vedavit*; *śiṣṭa*), and indeed be good because knowledgeable. Here, to be knowledgeable is, by definition, to be well-versed in the nature of evidence and the contents of the Vedas. And, moreover, such a man must be free from hatred and greed, since hatred and greed motivate even knowledgeable people to perform improper acts. To free oneself from the base motivations is, indeed, what it is to possess virtue (*śīla*). Virtue consists in directing one's attention away from other things and onto only what is worthy to be done (Medhātithi, in Manu 1920–6: 67 under 2.6).

The good man, then, is a man who tries to instantiate in his actions the *dharma*, the actions that are "to be done." He will use reason to interpret and apply the model actions prescribed in the Vedas, both within and outside the ritual sphere. Manu and the other compilers of the *smṛti* were such persons, and it is for that reason that the *smṛti* is itself a "root" of *dharma*. But how does the good man himself function as a "root" of *dharma*? It is because his conduct is exemplary – in the quite literal sense of being at once an exemplar (an instance) and an example (to be followed). As such, he can play a role in moral reasoning exactly akin to the role played by the archetypal "model" ritual in the Mīmāṃsākas' description of ritual reason.

Kumārila (*c.*650 CE) interprets *Mīmāṃsā-sūtra* 1.3.5–7 as referring to the problem of the conduct of the good. One might think that it is not inconsistent to take the conduct and teachings of leaders of other religions as a moral guide when they are compatible with the Vedas; for example, the Buddha's instructions about the founding of public parks and the practice of meditation, truthfulness, non-violence, and charity. Kumārila's somewhat uncompromising reply is that there is a limit on what can count as sacred (MS 1.3.5–6). In fact, the Buddha and other religious teachers are not "model men," because, although their conduct is sometimes in accordance with the Vedic prescriptions, it is also often not. Their good deeds and teachings, Kumārila says, are mixed up with and dissolve into the rest, just like powdered alum sprinkled on molten gold. More tellingly, Kumārila says that truths about *dharma*, that are so mixed up with untruth, are based on false *reason*, or rather false *uses* of attested patterns of reasoning. The transferential patterns of moral reasoning we have been considering can still lead to truth even if they begin with false paradigms and proceed via false resemblances, just as any invalid argument may happen to have a true conclusion. The invalidity of the argument leaves the conclusion, even if true, unjustified by that argument; likewise here, the good conduct of those who are not "good" men does not carry exemplary weight.

The severity and intolerance of Kumārila's position is partially ameliorated, however, in his discussion of MS 1.3.7, which states that what is found not to have an ulterior motive should be accepted as proper. A condition on a moral rule counting as Vedic, and a stipulation on the conduct of good men, was that the rule was based on no visible ulterior motive such as greed or hatred (MS 1.3.3). So what is ultimately seen to exclude the founding teachers of other religions from the category of "the good" is not that they hold heterodox opinions, bad views mixed in with their apparently good ones, but simply that they reason badly with minds not fully focused on "what is to be done." And that is no argument at all against the possibility of other religions, but simply an *ad hominem*. Kumārila must in any case be careful how heavily he relies on "mixedness" as a disqualifier, for he also has to explain away the various misdeeds of the "good" people in the epics and *purāṇas*, such as the celibate Kṛṣṇa Dvaipāyana, who had children by the wives of his younger brother, and the excessive drinking of Vāsudeva and Arjuna.

In this connection, Kumārila raises a version of the puzzle familiar to us from the *Euthyphro*: "You think those people to be good whose conduct is good; and you hold such conduct to be good as consists in the acts of good people; and thus there being a circularity, neither of the two is established" (Kumārila 1903–24: 183). His answer is that when we take the practices of the good as a guide in our moral conduct, we tend to forget that those practices are themselves good only because the person's actions are a model for good conduct as made known by the Vedas. When a good man engages in new practices, not themselves directly mentioned in the Vedas, using his moral reason in a process of transfer, modification and substitution, our entitlement to regard these new practices as themselves good is derived from an argument – the very same argument indeed that certified the *smṛti* as a proper extension of the *śruti*. The normative grounds of moral conduct spread out from the narrow confines of Vedic ritual through a mechanism of transfer, adaptation, and annulment that is the proper method in moral deliberation.

The same mechanism shows how group-specific forms of moral conduct arise – in the extrapolation of conduct not from one good brahmin to *all* people, but only to all other brahmins, or from one kṣatriya only to others. Relations of resemblance underpin the manufacture of group-specific rules of conduct. The very method by which general maxims are derived as extrapolation from particulars implies that the rules that result will be situational: their scope will be of the form "this and what is similar to it." Yet, as Kumārila astutely points out, we gradually "lose sight of the fact that such rules are only occasional (*naimittika*), and come to think of them as obligatory (*nitya*)" (Kumārila 1903–1924: 186). The ascent of duties specific to caste and social status, one might speculate, is the result of a similar mistake, this time about which aspects of resemblance are relevant to the extrapolation of right and wrong: relations of moral resemblance need not track analogies in social standing. This is not to say that there are no group-specific duties: a daughter has duties that a mother does not have, and vice versa. New rules generalize from historical circumstance, and they strive to do so in a way that will transform them from codes of good conduct into binding moral obligations.

V. Conflicting rules and ethical dilemmas

I have been arguing that the rational methods developed by the Mīmāṃsakas to deal with situations of ritual underspecification found a wider domain of application in ethical deliberation. Something similar is true of the converse, the situation of overspecification or conflict. There is no shortage of examples of Vedic prescriptions that contradict one another ("Pour the libation before the sun has risen." "Pour the libation when the sun has risen." "Hold the *śodaśi* vessels at the *atirātra*." "Do not hold the *śodaśi* vessels at the *atirātra*.") Conflicts arise too within the *dharmaśāstra* as well as between the Veda and *dharmaśāstra*. Yājñavalkya says that "in case of a conflict between two *smṛti*s, reasoning (*nyāya*) guided by practice has the strength."[14] In some cases, it may be possible to diffuse the tension and to argue that no genuine conflict arises. Standard Mīmāṃsā strategies for diffusing the conflict are to argue that one of the prescriptions is not really an injunction (*vidhi*) but rather a commendation (*arthavāda*), or else to show that there is a relation of mutual complementarity (*ākānkṣā*) between the two rules (cf. MS 2.1.46) – that one is a general rule and the other a special case, or that the two rules lack a common subject (see Lingat 1973: 160–1). But there remain many cases of genuine conflict, in which two rules are equally and properly applicable to a given particular. Following André Jolles, let us call such a situation a "case" (Kasus). In his short formalist treatise *Einfache Formen* (1965), Jolles identifies nine basic forms of thought as expressed in language: the legend, the saga, the myth, the riddle, the proverb, the case, the memoir, the tale, and the joke. Unlike the legend, the function of a case is not to illustrate or exemplify a particular moral value in ideal conduct, but to test the norms themselves in a specific instance (a case is *not* an "example" of a norm; an "example" will be called *dṛṣṭānta, udāharaṇa*). A case is a problem in judgment, an exercise in casuistry, in which conflicting sets of norms are balanced one against another, and in the process become themselves the objects of evaluation:

> What is peculiar to the form "case," however, lies in the fact that it asks a question but cannot give an answer, that it leaves the duty of the decision to us but does not contain the decision in itself – what is realised in it is the weighing, but not the result of the weighing. . . . In the case, the temptations and difficulties of balancing lay before us. . . . we could say that in this form is realised the swinging back and forth of the mental activity of weighing and weighing-up.
>
> (Jolles 1965: 191)

Jolles illustrates his idea of the case form with one of the *vetāla* stories from Somadeva's *Ocean of Story-Streams* (*Kathāsaritsāgara*). It is the story of three suitors "all equally virtuous and accomplished," courting the beautiful daughter of a pious brahmin. All of a sudden, she develops a fever and dies. The three suitors respond to this unexpected turn of events in different ways: after she had been cremated, one "made a bed of her ashes and began to live off alms"; the second took her bones to the Gangā. The third became a renunciant and began to wander through the land, and in the course of his wanderings came upon a magical spell, a mantra that could bring the dead back to life. He steals the *mantra*, rushes back, and restores life to his beloved. The three suitors, of course, then begin to squabble. One says, "She is my wife because I brought her back to life with my *mantra*." One says, "She is my wife because I brought her back to life by visiting a sacred pilgrimage spot." The third says, "She is my wife because I looked after her ashes and brought her back to life through my penance." At this point the *vetāla*, a necrophiliac spirit who has been narrating the story, says to King Vikrama, to whom the story is being narrated: "King Vikrama, you be the judge of their dispute. Tell me, whose wife should that girl be? If you know the answer and don't tell me, your head will split open!" The king is asked to adjudicate between three competing norms, three claims to be the one who in his actions most resembles a husband. The king replies, "The one who gave her life is like a father … the one who took her bones to the Gangā is like a son. The one who slept on her ashes and practiced auster- ities in the cremation ground is the one fit to be her husband because his actions were motivated by true love."

The story might remind one of Manu 8.41: "he [the king] who knows *dharma* must inquire into the laws of castes, districts, [mercantile] guilds, and even families and thus settle the particular *dharma* for each." What is the measure, in a "measuring of measure against measure" (Jolles)? When two Vedic injunctions are directly incompatible, the Mīmāṃsakas say that we have the "option" (*vikalpa*), but they do not mean by this that the choice is arbitrary. What about when there is a conflict between *śruti* and *smṛti*, that is, between some known Vedic passage and an inference back to some lost or no longer known Vedic source? The *Mīmāṃsā-sūtra* position is that "in the event of a contradiction, there is no need [for the inference], for it is only when there is no [contradiction] that an inference [is made]" (MS 1.3.3). According to one commentator (Śabara), what this means is that in a conflict between an extant Vedic text and a rule of conduct in the *smṛti*, the inference to a lost Veda that would justify the *smṛti* does not even get off the ground. A rule of *smṛti* contradicted by an extant Vedic text is, on this account, an exception to the inferred general rule that rules of *smṛti* coincide with lost Vedic passages. One might worry that this threatens the justification for the entire body of *smṛti*, for there is an endless number of misplaced Vedic passages. Who is to be sure that among them there is not one that contradicts any given *smṛti* text? Another commentator, Kumārila, is clearly aware of the nature of defeasible evidence (or rather, the defea- sible nature of evidence) – he says that a *smṛti* contradicted by an unknown Veda would be like a fake coin not yet found out; both have currency until the defeater turns up. He redescribes the case as one of preemption: the inference back to a lost Veda that would justify the rule is preempted by the "speedier" extant Vedic passage. The inference would have justified the contradicted norm had it not been preempted (like someone being poisoned and then shot before the poison has a chance to take effect), and the infer- ence does justify a norm just as long as no defeater comes to light. So it is not that contradicted *smṛti*s are exceptions to the general rule, but rather the general rule is suspended (preempted) by a contradicting Vedic passage. Kumārila says that "when two measures are found to contradict each other, ... the point at issue can be decided only by a third measure" (Kumārila 1903–24: 147–8), and he suggests here that the "third measure" is proximity to goal. In this case, the goal is the prescription of an act that ought to be done, and the Vedic injunction, which stipulates an act explicitly, reaches its goal long before the *smṛti* passage, which has to take the back route by way of an inference to some lost Vedic stipulation.

Medhātithi, Manu's commentator, prefers to claim that a contradicted *smṛti* retains its normative force, even if it is over-ridden: "it is only natural that what is directly expressed should over-ride what has been only indirectly indicated, and so is remoter and hence weaker. But from this is does not follow that what has been over-ruled loses its validity" (Medhātithi, in Manu 1920–6: 65). (This might also be Kumārila's final position.) He goes on to compare this with the analogous case that arises when the Mīmāṃsāka reasons from "model" ritual to variant. In such reasoning, the explicit always over-rides the implicit. For a specific injunction pertaining to the variant will always take precedence over the inferential transfer of a detail from the model in accordance with the generic metarule.[15] Here again, "proximity" is the measure against which the conflicting rules are compared, but now it is a method for deciding which of two conflicting norms is the defeator and which the defeated.

Such methods of adjudication work as long as the norms in conflict are of different kinds – one more proximate, more direct, and least dependent – but what if they are, as Kumārila puts it, like two men standing on a step? What if there are two model rituals promoting incompatible modes of performance, or two good men recommending incompatible courses of action? The conflict then is between competing claims of resemblance, just as it was in the case of the three suitors. We will have to choose between norms that do not arrange themselves conveniently along axes of proximity, directness, or logical dependence, and we shall have to bear in mind that choosing one does not deprive the other of its normative pull. When two Vedic injunctions directly contradict one, the Mīmāṃsakas say we have an "option;" but Kumārila reminds us that choosing one does not make the other one go away:

> In the case of the injunctions of the *yava* and the *vrīhi*, at the time that we accept the latter alternative and use the *vrīhi* at the sacrifice, we impose upon the former injunction an invalidity which is altogether foreign to it; and in the same manner, at the time that we accept the other alternative and make use of the *yava*, the extrinsic invalidity that had been imposed upon it is overridden by its own inherent validity; especially is such the case because of both the texts being equal in their authority, both equally forming part of the same Veda, and there being no difference between the two with regard to the proximity or otherwise of their respective goals.
>
> (Kumārila 1903–24: 137)

This is not the only time we meet with the idea of a forced suspension of duty. Manu's theory of the four *yugas* or Ages (Manu 1.84–6) has the duties of man gradually narrowing with each worsening age. The implication is not that there are different duties appropriate to each of the four ages, but that the diminution in man's capacities and longevity renders him capable of performing only some of the duties that befall him; the remainder continue to be duties but ones he is no longer capable of performing (a counter-example to the Kantian dictum "ought implies can"?). The same might be said of the theory of *āpaddharma*, the temporary suspension of duties in times of emergency. The duties remain in force but the times render them impossible to fulfill. And it is the same too in situations of moral conflict. When norms of equal standing are thrown together in a specific case, suspension rather than revision is the preferred model in the resolution of moral conflict.[16]

VI. The heart's approval: moral sentiment

I had said earlier that the choice between competing values with equal claim to validity was not arbitrary. But what are the reasons left to us in choosing how to weigh up competing claims of resemblance? We might feel like Buridan's ass, caught between two bails of straw, but I prefer Kumārila's metaphor of being drawn from both sides by two conflicting Vedic injunctions, as if by two celestial women, and unable to find any difference in their strength or power (Kumārila 1903–24: 134). I return, finally, to the last of Manu's four "roots" of *dharma*: the heart's approval. One suggestion is that the emotions, like inner satisfaction and contentment, are a guide in the evaluation of values: just as the mongoose eats only those herbs that are antidotes to poison, and for that reason we say that whatever the mongoose bites is an antidote to poison, so the learned and good are led by their hearts to choose what is right, and we say that whatever the learned and good do is, for that reason, itself good (Medhātithi, in Manu 1920–6: 68). That is, in perfectly unconflicted cases, the good man has been following his heart all along; so in absence of the usual guides, that is one to be trusted. The poet Kālidāsa has Duṣyanta say: "In matters where doubt intervenes, the inclination of the heart of a good person becomes the best measure." But another idea is that the heart's approval is not merely an indicator – it actually *creates* the measure with which we measure one measure against another. Kumārila puts the idea thus: just as whatever goes into a salt mine turns into salt, so whatever the man learned in the Veda utters, it becomes Vedic (Kumārila 1903–24: 188). Medhātithi expresses the point even more forcefully: the calmness of mind of a good man can turn wrong into right and right into wrong (Medhātithi, in Manu 1920–6: 68).

Can the heart's desire really ever be constitutive of value? The calm king Trivikramasena solved the riddle and closed the case by choosing the suitor whose conduct was most similar to that of a husband, and in doing so he chose to select certain aspects of resemblance over and above others. There was no one right answer: all we can say is that his decision closed the case, and it did so because the decision was made by a man of discernment. The point is that the claims of the other suitors do not disappear; they remain intact but are forced into suspension by the king's decision. When competing norms are in the balance, a choice for one tilts the scales, but the other does not lose its entitlement to make a claim. Still, when the matter is one of competing claims of resemblance, the heart's approval is what judgment consists in. And that suffices, in spite of the contrary, now-suppressed claims. A conflict makes us question the resemblances upon which our norms rest, forces us to decide which are relevant, which less so, and in these matters of resemblance, only the heart can be the judge.

VII. Conclusion

Practical reason or moral deliberation (*tarka*) extracts the norm from the particular and reapplies it to other resembling particulars. The process of extraction presupposes that there is a common cause, a stability in goodness (*dharmanityatā*), in virtue of which what is good here and now can be a guide to what is good somewhere else. Different norms, extracted from different particulars and resting on different judgments of resemblance, will sometimes collide. They are then measured against each other in the to-and-fro of a dialectical process (*vāda*) that first seeks out agreed sites of conflict and then creates a measure with which to adjudicate competing claims of resemblance (this, in fact, is why a logician and a *Mīmāṃsaka* must be present at the *pariṣad*). Norms extracted from particulars will be group-specific (*āśramadharma, svadharma*) to the extent that they are local approximations of more general laws, or if they are descriptive of practice and custom, but must seek to be universal (*sanātanadharma, sādhāranad-harma*) if they are to pass the Vedic test of moral bindingness. And when, for example, the norms of different religions collide, each with its own non-negotiable claim to rest on an ultimate ground of value, one is forced, as in the case (Kasus), to reexamine the derivation of those norms from the ultimate ground, the particulars one has chosen as exemplary, and the judgments one has made about relations of resemblance. The confrontation of incommensurable systems of value is the occasion for a dialectical reevaluation of the relationship between moral deliberation and the stable grounds of goodness. Comparative philosophers of religion create "cases" of their own whenever they juxtapose texts from different religious traditions, and in doing so make explicit the normative frames implicit within those texts. The method of reasoning from cases, the original ritual reasoning of the Mīmāṃsā, is indeed a method for philosophy itself.

Notes

1 *devā asmāl lokād amuṃlokam āyaṃs tānṛṣayo 'nvīyus tānmanuṣyā abruvan katham atho bhaviṣyāmaḥ ebhyaḥ sarvakarmaṛṣayaḥ prāyacchat / tasmād yat brāhmaṇot-tamās tarkayamaty ārṣam eva tadbhavatīti śruteḥ/* (see *Nirukta* 13.11).

2 "*tasya* [*dharmasya*] *kartavyatāsvabhāvatvāt*" (Medhātithi, in Manu 1920–6: 63, 59).
3 On the Vedas as a source of knowledge about *dharma* being a matter of definition, see Medhātithi, in Manu (1920–6: 58): *vyutpādyate ca vedaśabdaḥ / vidanty ananyapramāṇavedyaṃ dharmalakṣaṇaṃ artham asmād iti vedaḥ/*. The Vedas are conceived of, not merely as one body of moral precepts among others, but rather as a set of statements distinguished on formal grounds as that which is capable of testing maxims for action. The Vedas are described in the *Mīmāṃsā-sūtra* (MS 1.1.2) as the 'indicator' (*lakṣaṇa*) of *dharma*, and in the *Manu-smṛti* (2.6) as the 'root' (*mūla*) of *dharma*; but in both cases, the meaning is that they are regulative and not constitutive: they guide the selection of maxims for action but do not themselves create or produce such maxims (cf. Medhātithi, in Manu 1920–6: 59: *kāraṇaṃ mūlam / tac ca vedasmṛtyor dharmapratijñāpakatayaiva, na nirvartakatayā na ca sthitihetutayā, vṛkṣasyeva*). Two of the formal criteria are that the Vedas are "without an author" (*anapekṣa, apauruṣeya*) and "eternal" (*autpattika, nitya*) (MS 1.1.5; 1.1.25–31). These are criteria that apply both to the Vedas as literary objects and as importantly to their contents. The texts themselves are without a history, and their injunctions are law-like, where the lawlikeness of a statement consists in its applying equally and non-arbitrarily, and, in consequence, no particular being mentioned by the law; its content is fully general (MS 1.1.31; 2.4.18: *na caikaṃ prati śiṣyate* 'and no one [person in particular] is enjoined/taught'). A third criterion is that the statement has the form of an injunction or action-prescription (*vidhi*), and a fourth that the action so prescribed has no visible motive for its performance (MS 1.3.4, 7; Manu 2.13). Actions prescribed by the Vedas are actions that "should be done" because they are right to do, as distinct from actions which rest on prudential maxims of self-interest. And also (as Medhātithi makes clear [Medhātithi, in Manu 1920–6: 59]) ordinary acts with detectable effects, such as tilling the land, can be tested by the empirical method of positive and negative concomitance (*anvayavyatireka*). It is only those moral actions without detectable effects which require some other method of testing, and it is for these that Vedic certification is necessary.
4 Medhātithi, in Manu (1920–6: 71) under Manu 2.10: *na punarayamartho vedasyādyaḥ pūrvapakṣa utasvidyaḥ siddhānta ityeṣā mīmāṃsā niṣidhyate / yato vakṣyate 'yattarkeṇānusandhatte sa dharma veda netara iti.*
5 Cf. Śabara under 9.3.1: *yat prakṛtau kartavyaṃ tat vikṛtau iti.* Cf. under 7.1.12.
6 Compare also *Nyāya-sūtra* 1.1.32–6 for a similar model of reasoning.
7 *dharmasya śabdamūlatvād aśadbam anapekṣaṃ syāt.*
8 MS 1.3.2: *api vā kartṛsāmānyāt pramāṇam anumānaṃ syāt.*
9 The point is made well by Madhav Deshpande; see Kahrs (1998: 187).
10 MS 1.3.15: *anumānavyavyasthānāt tatsaṃyuktam pramāṇaṃ syāt.*
11 MS 1.3.16: *api vā sarvadharmaḥ syāt, tannyāyaytvādvidhānasya*; MS 1.3.18: *liṅgābhāvac ca nitasya.*
12 A fact possibly related with the migratory habits of the ancient aryans.
13 See Dancy (1993) for an explicit denial that a particular case's resemblance with other cases is relevant to its moral evaluation.
14 2.1: *smṛtyor virodhe nyāyas tu balavān vyavyahāratạḥ*; see Lingat 1963: 168. cf. (Vācaspatimiśra 1956: 40): *paraspara-virodhe tu nyāya-yuktam pramāṇavat.*
15 Cf. MS 5.1.19–21 – the *sākamedhīya-nyāya*; also 6.5.54.
16 Related ideas can be found in Williams (1973).

Bibliography

Chesterton, G. K. (1905) *Heretics*, New York: John Lane.
Dancy, J. (1993) *Moral Reasons*, Oxford: Oxford University Press.

Doniger, W. and Smith, B. (1991) (trans.) "Introduction," in *Manu, The Laws of Manu*, London: Penguin Books.

Ganeri, J. (2001) *Philosophy in Classical India: The Proper Work of Reason*, London: Routledge.

Halbfass, W. (1988) *India and Europe: An Essay in Understanding*, Albany: SUNY.

Jaimini (1863–77) *Mīmāṃsā-sūtra, with Śabara's Bhāsya*, ed. M. Nyayaratna, Calcutta; trans. as *The Mīmāṃsā-sūtra of Jaimini*, trans. M. L. Sandal, 1925, Allahabad: B. D. Basu.

Jolles, A. (1965) *Einfache Formen*, Tübingen: Max Niemeyer Verlag.

Kahrs, E. (1998) *Indian Semantic Analysis*, Cambridge: Cambridge University Press.

Kumārila (1882–1903) *Tantravārttika*, ed. G. Sastri, Varanasi: Benares Sanskrit Series 2; (1903–24) trans. as *Tantravārttika*, trans. G. Jha, Calcutta: Sri Garib Das Oriental Series 9.

Lingat, R. (1973) *The Classical Law of India*, California: University of California Press.

Manu (1972–84) *Manu-smṛti, with the commentaries of Medhātithi et al*, vols 1–6, ed. J. H. Dave, Bombay: Bharatiya Vidya Bhavan; (1886) trans. as *The Laws of Manu*, trans. G. Bühler, Oxford: Clarendon Press; (1920–6) trans. as *Manusmṛti: The Laws of Manu with the Bhāṣya of Medhātithi*, trans. G. Jha, vols 1–5, Calcutta: University of Calcutta Press.

Nussbaum, M. (1986) *The Fragility of Goodness*, Cambridge: Cambridge University Press.

Smith, J. Z. (1982) *Imagining Religion: From Babylon to Jonestown*, Cambridge: Cambridge University Press.

Vācaspatimiśra (1956) *Vyavahara-cintāmaṇi: A Digest on Hindu Legal Procedure*, ed. and trans L. Rocher, Gent: Gentse Orientalislische Bijdragen.

Verpoorten, J.–M. (1987) *Mīmāṃsā Literature*, Wiesbaden: Otto Harrassowitz.

Williams, B. (1973) *Problems of the Self*, Cambridge: Cambridge University Press.

11 Ritual gives rise to thought
Liturgical reasoning in modern Jewish philosophy

Steven Kepnes

I. Introduction

In his path-breaking study, *Symbolism of Evil* (1969), the French philosopher Paul Ricoeur suggests that symbols are not mere ornamentations to thought, but that they are primal engines for thinking about complex existential issues. At the end of his book, Ricoeur coined the now famous phrase, "symbol gives rise to thought" (Ricoeur 1969: 347). In this essay, I make a similar argument in regard to Jewish rituals. Ritual, especially in the form of synagogue liturgy, plays a crucial function in the expression of Jewish philosophy. Basing myself on modern German Jewish philosophy, I attempt to show how Jewish rituals can give rise to the representation and contemplation of eternal truths, ethical ideals, dimensions of time, and the nature of God. And in addition to modes of representation and contemplation, I argue that ritual plays a uniquely important role in connecting thought to the body, to human action, and to community. In its role of linking thought and action, ritual offers resources to address some of the perennial and contemporary issues of philosophy.

It is fairly easy to see why it is that ritual provides an important focal point for modern Jewish philosophy. Since Jewish law has always been central to Judaism, modern Jewish philosophers concentrate on liturgy as an arena, set apart from public life, in which traditional *halakhic* or legal obligations can be fulfilled. Liturgical observances in synagogues are considered "safe" for modern Jews, because they parallel Christian observances in Churches and therefore are easily accepted by fellow Christian citizens in the modern nation state. These behaviors occur out of public sight and satisfy the modern objective of the separation of church and state.

In my own recent work, I have been struck by the philosophical, ethical, and theological power of ritual for a new movement in Jewish philosophy called "Textual Reasoning."[1] Textual Reasoning grew out of both the traditional Jewish focus on Torah and its interpretation and the recent focus on texts and hermeneutics in philosophy and religion. Textual Reasoning has used Jewish texts as a means to more organically connect Jewish thought to Judaism and Jewish community at the same time that traditional thought could be corrected by critical tools of philosophy and literary criticism. Following the interest in Jewish texts, I have been drawn to the power of ritual and liturgy for the objectives of Textual Reasoning. Like texts, liturgies provide a concrete form of religious expression that stands between thought and practice. Liturgical behaviors provide a kind of middle reality, what Victor Turner (1969) called a "liminal" space, between fantasy and reality. This space allows for the projection of ethical ideals and a unique form of religious and philosophical pedagogy that foster a kind of "training in Judaism" (to paraphrase Soren Kierkegaard). Thus, the title of the book on which I am presently working is *Liturgical Reasoning*. This book will focus on the reflections on liturgy of the German ethical monotheists – modern Jewish philosophers who adapted modern philosophy as a critical tool to draw out the ethical implications of Judaism for modern culture. This movement spans the eighteenth to the twentieth centuries with its leading figures being Moses Mendelssohn, Hermann Cohen, Abraham Geiger, Martin Buber, and Franz Rosenzweig. In this present essay, I review representative sections of Mendelssohn, Cohen, and Rosenzweig's philosophies of liturgy to show just how it is that "ritual gives rise to thought."

II. Liturgy as representation in Mendelssohn's *Jerusalem*

Moses Mendelssohn was the central figure in the Berlin *Haskalah* or Jewish enlightenment of the end of the eighteenth century. He was responsible not only for liberalizing German Jewish religious culture, but also for contributing to the enlightenment of German secular and Christian society. He developed important arguments for the separation of church and state, religious liberty, and tolerance. As both an observant Jew and an avatar of the enlightenment, Mendelssohn was an important public figure who drew attention from politicians, philosophers, and theologians. Immanuel Kant and Johann Georg Hamann criticized his work and Christian theologians tried, unsuccessfully, to convert him to Christianity.[2]

Moses Mendelssohn's *Jerusalem: Or on Religious Power and Judaism* (originally published in Berlin, in 1783) may easily be described as the first work of modern Jewish philosophy and the book that provides the theoretical basis for modern liberal Judaism. *Jerusalem* is built on a division of Jewish revelation in two – into "rational truths" and "revealed legislation" [*göttliche Gesetzgebungen*] (1983a: 97). Mendelssohn argues that the "rational truths," like the existence of God, Providence, and the immortality of the soul, are eternal and available to all humans through observation of nature and pure rational contemplation. They require no religious training or doctrines to discover. "Revealed legislation," on the other hand, includes the laws that are particular to the Jews and that were given at one historical moment and revealed through the miracle of God's speech to Israel. Rational truths are "eternal and immutable" (1983a: 90); revealed legislation is given historically (1983a: 93). Rational truth is revealed through "nature and thing," and the legislation is known through the testimony of "word and script."

Mendelssohn's division of revelation into two forms provides the justification for modern Jews to accept enlightenment notions of truth as revealed to them through science and modern philosophy at the same time that they could give their allegiance to the particular laws and liturgies of Judaism. This allegiance is deserved, Mendelssohn argues, because Jewish laws provide pathways to inspire and forge uniquely Jewish ties to the eternal truths of enlightenment religion. Mendelssohn answers the enlightenment charge that Judaism imposes a heteronomous law on individuals by arguing that the focus on law allows Jews to give their assent to religious truths freely, without any coercion. Unlike Christianity, which demands allegiance to prescribed beliefs, Judaism only demands observance of ritual behaviors. This sets the mind free to discover religious truths through an open process of intellectual and spiritual discovery. Mendelssohn sums this all up with his famous words: "The law . . . did not impel [Jews] to engage in reflection; it prescribed only actions, only doing and not doing. The great maxim of this constitution seems to have been: *Men must be impelled to perform actions and only induced to engage in reflection*" (1983a: 119).

For Mendelssohn, and for most Jewish philosophers that preceded him and for the German Jewish ethical monotheists that followed him, the real threat to monotheism has always been idolatry. Mendelssohn presents idolatry as a freezing of the dynamic process of human discovery of God into fixed images or doctrines. The problem of idolatry for Mendelssohn is thus, largely, a problem of representation. How does one represent the God who transcends all that is material and therefore lies beyond any representation of him? The main strategy of monotheism, as Mendelssohn sees it, is to move from concrete and pictorial representations of the divine to alphabetical, written script. But alphabetical script also suffers from problems. On the one hand, written script is fixed and the fixed word can miss the dynamic spontaneous character of divine presence and religious discovery. And on the other hand, alphabetic script is too abstract and direct and does not foster a process of discovery:

> We have seen how difficult it is to preserve the abstract ideas of religion among men by means of permanent signs. Images and hieroglyphics lead to superstition and idolatry, and our alphabetical script makes man too speculative. It displays the symbolic knowledge of things and their relations too openly on the surface; it spares us the effort of penetrating and searching, and creates too wide a division between doctrine and life.
> (1983a: 119)

Mendelssohn argues that the most creative solution that the Torah offers to the problem of representing God and the process of religious discovery is provided by the "ceremonial law" (1983a: 102). Mendelssohn took this phrase from Spinoza. But where Spinoza saw ceremonies as antithetical to philosophy, Mendelssohn took the opposite position, that the two were intricately related. Mendelssohn believes, as Maimonides puts it, that all laws, including the ceremonial laws, "conform to wisdom."[3] In Mendelssohn's terms, the ceremonial laws prescribe actions that encapsulate and point to the ethical and the divine and also serve to provide stimulants for contemplation of truth and questioning (118).[4] In addition, to this connection to contemplation of God, truth, and morality, Mendelssohn argues that the ceremonies provide answers to the problem of representation of the divine. Mendelssohn suggests that liturgical practices are uniquely suited to avoid idolatry and represent the process of divine discovery because they are, at once, transitory and embodied, social and enacted. He therefore applauds Moses (and God) for the genius of the law:

> In order to remedy these defects, the lawgiver of this nation gave the *ceremonial law*. ... The truths useful for the felicity of the nation as well as each of its individual members were to be utterly removed from all imagery; for this was the main purpose and the fundamental law of the constitution. They were to be connected with actions and practices, and these were to serve them in the place of signs, without which they cannot be preserved. Man's actions are transitory; there is nothing lasting, nothing enduring about them that, like hieroglyphic script, could lead to idolatry through abuse or misunderstanding (1983a: 119–20).

Thus, Mendelssohn develops a penetrating philosophical answer to the question of why Judaism relies so heavily on ceremonial actions that are prescribed by religious law. These actions are tools in the fight against idolatry. They are sophisticated forms of representation that can be seen, themselves, as a special "kind of script or symbolical language."[5] They are a kind of script brought to life through which a series of moral ideas and theological notions are put forth for human contemplation. In Ricoeur's words, liturgies "give rise to thought" about God and ethics.

However, in addition to representing the divine, Mendelssohn suggests that liturgy has other powers. Liturgy presents the philosophical and theological quest for God as a social and communal matter. It puts individuals in touch with elders who provide oral instruction as to the meaning of the liturgies. Liturgies "also have the advantage over alphabetical signs of not isolating man, of not making him to be a solitary creature, poring over writings and books. They impel him rather to social intercourse, to imitation, and to oral, living instruction" (1983a: 120).

In conclusion, Mendelssohn suggests that liturgies are vehicles of mediation that not only connect individuals to the community and the young to the old, but liturgy connects religious teaching to lived life. Thus, as Mendelssohn argues, through liturgy "teaching and life, wisdom and activity, speculation and sociability were most intimately connected" (1983a: 120).

III. Hermann Cohen: Shabbat – festival of universal brotherhood

Almost a century after Mendelssohn's *Jerusalem*, the great Neo-Kantian philosopher, Hermann Cohen, produced the most influential statement of modern Jewish ethics in his posthumously published *Religion of Reason Out of the Sources of Judaism* (1919, 1995). After a stellar career as a proponent of the Neo-Kantian school of critical idealism, Cohen wrote a work of Jewish ethics that at once responded to enlightenment charges of Jewish particularism and established a pattern for modern Judaism as a rational and ethical religion concerned with the alleviation of human suffering of all peoples. As a combination of neo-Kantian philosophy and Jewish philosophy, Cohen's book was destined to remain largely unread by the common Jew, but its philosophical originality and ethical profundity established it as the leading expression of modern Jewish ethics.

One of the central foci of Cohen's book is the argument that a purely rational and philosophical ethics is not fully adequate to the ethical life. Cohen claims that ethics needs religion as its complement and, furthermore, he suggests that liturgy holds the key ingredients that philosophical ethics lacks. In his discussion of liturgy, Cohen provides us with a theory of Jewish liturgy that complements that of Mendelssohn. However, in addition to providing us with a theory, Cohen analyzes the philosophical and ethical power in particular Jewish liturgies. Recent attention to Cohen's interpretation of the festival of Yom Kippur and the philosophical and ethical importance of the liturgies of atonement or *Versöhnung* has been accomplished by the important book by Michael Zank, *The Idea of Atonement in the Philosophy of Hermann Cohen* (2000). Accordingly, we will not dwell on atonement but, instead, look at Cohen's interesting and influential interpretation of the weekly festival of rest, Shabbat. In Cohen's interpretation of this important holiday, we find surprisingly relevant insights into the connection between a particular Jewish set of liturgies and universal notions of brotherhood.

Cohen's discussion of the Shabbat liturgy emerges in *Religion of Reason* in Chapter 9 when he speaks of the philosophical problem of religious love. Cohen tells us that religious love is one of those areas that philosophical ethics is ill-equipped to handle. Religious love is poorly understood by philosophy because religious love is not knowledge, neither is it sexual love, eros, nor aesthetic love. Cohen suggests that religious love begins with love for the stranger. And he argues that this is the key to our understanding of human love of God and God's love for humans (1995: 145). The meaning of God's love is his compassion for the stranger. And as we imitate God, and come to love the stranger, the one who is different and seemingly beyond us, we come to love God who is the very definition of difference and that which transcends us. But how do we love the stranger, the one who is poor, unattractive, often more like a *Untermensch* than a *Nebenmensch*? Cohen provides us with an exegetical answer. "Love the stranger . . ." (Deut. 10:19) "for you were strangers in the land of Egypt" (Lev. 19:34). We learn to love the stranger through a process of compassion (*Mitleid*) for her that is built out of our own experience of suffering. "For you know the heart of the stranger" (Ex. 23:9). Cohen admits that this process, though ruled by reason, emerges as something of a riddle, even as a miracle (1995: 146). For love of the poor occurs not only by reason and will but also by a process of self-reflection on our own suffering and a recognition of the mutual suffering that the poor shares with Israel. But how from here we find ourselves able to love God and to receive God's love for us is somewhat mysterious.

Where this mystery is solved for Cohen is in the Jewish festivals and Jewish liturgy. In the case of the ideal of loving the stranger and the poor, Cohen suggests that we look to the festival of Shabbat, which he calls, the "keystone for social ethics" (1995: 156). Making Shabbat into the festival of social ethics requires Cohen to move the primary associations of the festival from a celebration of the ideal of a perfect natural creation to a celebration of social ideals. To do this, Cohen assumes the role of the "textual reasoner." Jewish exegetes have noticed for centuries that the commandment for Shabbat observance is given in two slightly different ways in Exodus (20:8–11) and in Deuteronomy (5:12–16). Most rabbinic commentaries, however, have focused on the differences in the first words that are used to communicate the commandment. Thus, we have, in Exodus, *Zahor*, "remember" the Sabbath day, and in Deuteronomy we have *Shamor*, "observe" the Sabbath day. What is crucial for Cohen is that in both versions rest is commanded for the Israelite and the servant and the stranger. What this means is that Shabbat "is meant to secure the equality of men in spite of the differences in their social standing" (1995: 157). The difference in the two versions in scripture, however, is the *Taamei ha-Mitsvot*, the reasons for the commandments. The Exodus version gives the creation as the reason for the Shabbat commandment, "for in six days the Lord made heaven and earth, the sea, and all that in them is, and rested on the seventh day; therefore the Lord blessed the seventh day, and hallowed it." Deuteronomy, on the other hand, ties this reason for Shabbat observance to the Israelite experience in slavery and in the Exodus from slavery. "And remember that you were a servant in the land of Egypt, and that the Lord your God brought you out of there with a mighty hand and an outstretched arm: therefore the Lord your God commanded you to keep the Sabbath." Thus, Israel's experience of slavery provides for compassion for her servants and for strangers. Cohen tells us that the ethical reason for Shabbat given in Deuteronomy is "that thy manservant and maidservant may rest as well as you (*kamokhah*)." Cohen underscores the fact that the commandment presents the servant in direct parallel to the Israelite. The servant is *kamokhah*, as yourself. In the word *kamokhah*, Cohen hears resonances of the commandment to love the neighbor (1995: 157). Thus, through Shabbat, the servant becomes a neighbor whom we are commanded to love. As we read in the holiness code of Leviticus, "you shall love him [the servant] as yourself (*v'ahavtah lo kamokha*)" (Lev. 19:34).

Therefore Cohen suggests that love for one's neighbor, God's love for humans, and human love for God, are established through the mediation of the festival of Shabbat. "In the Sabbath the God of love showed himself as the unique God of love for mankind" (1995: 158). Cohen asks the rhetorical question: "What meaning does the love of God have?" and he responds: "The answer is now found to be the compassion for the poor, which God awoke in us through his commandments [to observe Shabbat]" (1995: 158).

In the days of Israelite religion, compassion for the poor was made palpably clear on Shabbat by the fact that servants and strangers rested alongside Israel. In the rabbinic and modern periods, that compassion must be initiated through a liturgical practice in which we recall the situation of the Israelite past, enact an egalitarian situation by inviting guests into our synagogues and homes, and imaginatively project the ideal situation of social equality and harmony into the future. Through its liturgies, Cohen suggests that Shabbat "awakes in us" love for the stranger and humankind. Knowing that that love has its source in God, love for God quite naturally follows.

The series of laws and liturgies that are connected to Shabbat show themselves to be a locus of ideas, feelings, and practices that link the ideal of compassion for the poor, universal love of humanity, and love of God. Therefore, Shabbat stands *between* the abstract ideals of philosophy and monotheism and the concrete realities of social and political life. Shabbat stands as a weekly reminder to Jews of their ethical obligations to their fellow man and the goal of social equality and justice. Shabbat recharges and motivates Jews with love of God and hope for the messianic future. As Cohen suggests, "out of God's social love for men develops God's universal love as presented in Messianism" (1995: 158). Shabbat provides laws and liturgies that provide a living actualization of the ideal situation of social equality in ancient Israelite society and in the contemporary Jewish synagogue community. This is the ideal situation that monotheism hopes to bring about for the entire world.

IV. Rosenzweig and liturgical time

In turning to Franz Rosenzweig and his writings on liturgy, we are brought to consider elements that transcend Mendelssohn and Cohen's mainly rational, ethical, and social interpretations. Rosenzweig wrote at a time in which Hegelian idealism was being challenged by the existentialists and the neo-Romantics. Rosenzweig's thought can be seen as a creative and critical engagement with both the thought of philosophical idealism and with existentialism in an attempt to forge a new relationship between philosophy and theology. Rosenzweig remains an ethical monotheist in his concern to bring the ethical message of monotheism to the world, but like his older colleague Martin Buber, he sought to move the hyper-rational thrust of ethical monotheism toward an appreciation for religious experience. In his *The Star of Redemption* (1985 [1921]), Rosenzweig presents liturgy as the vehicle through which Jews come into intimate relation with fellow Jews, constitute themselves as a sacred community, and build up a spiritual power that works for the redemption of the world. Through liturgy, Jews transcend the limits of profane time and come into contact with sacred time and eternity.

The Star of Redemption begins with a critique of Hegelian philosophy for its failure to deal with the death of the human individual and its presumptuous attempt to place reason before reality and subsume it in the totality of the "All." In his *New Thinking* (1999), which was written four years after the

Star, Rosenzweig identifies the central problem of modern thought as the separation between the subjective realm of individual experience and community and the "objective realm" of rational science, philosophy, and politics. Martin Buber sought to overcome the gap between subjectivity and objectivity in his book *I and Thou* (1987). "I–Thou" describes a realm beyond the subjective feelings of the individual and before the reification of the individual into objectifiable qualities.

For Rosenzweig, the language of the I–Thou realm, the language that is to take over where both idealist and existentialist philosophers left off, is theology, and the practical form of theology is liturgy. Rosenzweig turns to theology and liturgy because the existentialist critique of idealism and rationalism had left the Hegelian "All" in tatters. Rosenzweig's own interpretation of the result of this breakdown is that it yields three separate elements: "God," "world," and "humans." What is positive about this development is that philosophy no longer tries to reduce one or two of the elements to the third and therefore comes to appreciate the unique "essence" of each. What is negative about this separating out of the primal elements is that they appear to human thought as isolated and disconnected. The demise of idealism depletes philosophy's ability to forge the links between the elements. And existentialism, with its elevation of the supra-rational, non-linguistic experience of the individual, also lacks adequate resources. Therefore, Rosenzweig argues that theology can be called upon to step into the breach. Theology can be turned to because it supplies the language and terms through which the connections between God, humans, and world can be understood. And those terms are: "creation," "revelation" and "redemption."

God is intricately related to the world because God created it. He determined its boundaries and nature. And though this appeared to be a past and finished event, as the text of the beginning of the morning prayer service says, God maintains his relationship to the world by renewing it every day. God relates to humans through creation, but the unique character of this relationship is known through revelation. God reveals his love and word to the human and thereby prepares her to be a relational being by awakening her soul. As ensouled beings, humans turn to other humans and the world and thereby help to spark the process of redemption that God will bring to final fruition in the ultimate redemption. Taken together, the elements God, world, and humans, form a triangle which, when configured against the triangle of creation, revelation, and redemption, in opposed position, form the six-pointed Jewish star of David.

We may think of the field in the center of that star as an enlarged field of I–Thou relations. I like to refer to this as a "relational field"[6] – a world of relations, in which humans live not as isolated selves but as human souls who enjoy intimate relations to other humans, the natural world, and God. The notion of a relational field suggests a whole different mode of "being-in-the-world" with possibilities for intimate relations, altered temporal experiences, and encounters with God as not only a source of ethics and morality but what Rudolph Otto called a "mysterium tremendum." What

Rosenzweig's *Star* suggests is that we consider synagogue liturgy as a space within which Jews meet each other as Thous and conceive of nature and the biblical text as speaking to them. Through synagogue liturgy, Jews are able to address God and experience God's presence and address him as their "eternal Thou." While the relational terms – creation, revelation, and redemption – appear somewhat abstract when related in philosophical and theological language, they take on a more concrete shape and reality in liturgy. For example, Rosenzweig argues that Shabbat reviews and celebrates the relational terms in its three major liturgical services. Thus Friday night stresses the theme of creation. For the lighting of the Shabbat candles recalls God's first words of creation: "Let there be light!" and the theme of creation appears in the blessings over wine and in the synagogue service. The theme of revelation is celebrated in the focal ritual of the morning service, the reading of God's revealed word, the Torah. And the theme of redemption is recalled in the final third meal and in the afternoon service where there are repeated calls for the end of exile and the coming of the messiah.

Rosenzweig claims that through participation in Shabbat liturgy our sense of our relations to humans, to God, and to the natural world are intensified to the point that we feel addressed in new ways and open to transformed forms of relationship. For example, Rosenzweig relates an experience he had on Shabbat in which narrative of Balaam's speaking ass was chanted. In the midst of the liturgical reading, Rosenzweig explains, suddenly the ass did speak to him!

> All the days of the year Balaam's talking ass may be a mere fairy tale but not on the Sabbath wherein this portion is read in the synagogue, when it speaks to me out of the open Torah. But if not a fairy tale what then? I cannot say right now; if I should think about it today, when it is past, and try to say what it is, I should probably only utter the platitude that it is a fairy tale. But on that day, in that very hour, it is, well, certainly not a fairy tale, but that which is communicated to me provided I am able to fulfill the command of the hour, namely to open my ears.
>
> (as translated in Glatzer 1970: 246)

Here, we have a concrete example of what it means to relate to God's created beings as Thous able to communicate with us. Thus, I would suggest, in Buber's terms, that we can consider synagogue liturgy a space within which Jews meet each other as Thous and conceive of the spheres of nature and the biblical text as speaking to them.

In part three of the *Star*, Rosenzweig focuses on the ability of liturgy to open up and explore dimensions of time that are not available in the purely secular realm. Here, Rosenzweig moves away from Mendelssohn and Cohen's stress on the ability of liturgy to prepare Jews for the work of justice in historical time to focus on eternal time. The Jews are a "people that are denied a life in time for the sake of life in eternity. ... Its position is always somewhere between the temporal and the holy"(1985: 304). What Rosenzweig suggests is that liturgy preserves this position between the temporal and holy. Liturgy, after all, is itself a kind of "liminal" activity that takes place between fantasy and reality. Liturgy transpires in a kind of pretend or dream space, a space that is set aside from the profane, and designated as holy. Rosenzweig argues that history, for the Jews, never tells the story of events that are lost to the past. Rather, they exist in memory and remain "eternally present." He turns to the liturgy of the Passover Hagaddah: "Every single member of this community is bound to regard the Exodus from Egypt as if he himself had been one of those to go out" (1985: 304). Thus, it is through liturgy that the Jewish people make their way back to their past and are able to re-present their past as present. And it is liturgy that brings the future redemption to the present by presenting images of the redeemed present and experiences of its peaceful and harmonious qualities through rituals of rest and communitas such as those of Shabbat. It is liturgy through which the Jewish people's sense of their eternity unfolds and develops in their consciousness. In one of his most memorable phrases, Rosenzweig puts it this way: liturgy "is the reflector which focuses the sunbeams of eternity in the small circle of the year" (1985: 308).

Liturgy has the ability to transform the secular and the scientific notions of time as one moment after another, moving forward in a linear fashion. Through liturgy, time is bent into a circle in which past moments of revelation are relived and the future redemption is proleptically experienced. Liturgy has the ability to turn past and future time into present. Liturgy has the ability to elongate and even stop time. In doing this, liturgy not only bends time into form and shape, but gives the monotony of clock time, in which every second is the same, a sense of shape and drama. The moment before the candles are lit and Shabbat is ushered in is different than the time in which Shabbat transpires. The time before the beginning of a fast day is different from the time when the fast begins. Each festival carries a theme that gives its time a unique quality that distinguishes it from the time of other festivals. The holiday of Passover heralds the freshness of new beginnings that spring and the birth of the people out of slavery portends. The early autumn festival of booths or Sukkot brings a sense of an ending and accomplishment as the harvest is communally enjoyed and the period of being lead and protected by God in the wilderness is remembered. When all the festivals are taken together, the secular year itself is given a sense of temporal wholeness. Liturgy, Rosenzweig, tells us, transforms the secular year into a "spiritual year" (1985: 310). It is this transformation that opens the Jewish people to the experience of its "eternal life."

While we have already discussed the ways in which Shabbat allows Jews to gain a deeper perception of the relational terms – creation, revelation and redemption – Rosenzweig also suggests that Shabbat plays a crucial role in altering the Jew's perception of time. Rosenzweig presents Shabbat as an opportunity to exit from the challenges and obligations of the historical moment and secular notions of time as a linear progression toward the future. Shabbat, for Rosenzweig, puts the Jew in touch with a sacred time in which the arrow of time moves backward toward an Edenic past before history and jumps forward to eternity. Rosenzweig tells us that in Shabbat the spiritual year finds its foundation, regulation, and sense of wholeness. The Sabbath accomplishes this through its prohibitions against work, its commandments to rest, and its successive liturgical readings from the Torah. These are apportioned to each week so that the entire five books are finished in a year's time.

Through the liturgical reading of portions of the Torah, "the Parashah Ha-Shavuah," the Jew moves through the week with the text and time of the Torah. The Parashah Ha-Shavuah marks each week with the episodes, characters, and laws of the different Torah portion for that week. At the same time, the consistency of the Shabbat ritual and liturgy, which envelops the Parashah with its sameness, provides the year with a regularized spiritual base:

> In the circle of weekly portions, which, in the course of one year, cover all of the Torah, the spiritual year is paced out, and the paces of this course are the Sabbaths. By and large, every Sabbath is just like any other, but the difference in the portions from the Scriptures distinguishes each from each, and this difference shows that they are not final in themselves, but only parts of a higher order of the year. For only in the year do the differentiating elements of the individual parts again fuse into a whole.
>
> (Rosenzweig 1985: 310)

Rosenzweig comments that Shabbat provides a peaceful and stable counterpoint to the other historical festivals like Pesach, which celebrates the Exodus from Egyptian slavery, and Shavuot, which celebrates the giving of the Torah at Mount Sinai. Where these festivals take the Jews back through the "anguish and bliss" (1985: 311) of Jewish historical time, Shabbat provides an "even flow" of peace out of time through which "whirlpools of the soul are created" (1985: 311). These "whirlpools of the soul" provide a constant communal resource for the Jew to receive God's love. Like the created world that Shabbat celebrates, Shabbat itself is "always there, wholly there, before anything at all happens in it" (1985: 311). However, just as God did not create the world once and for all but must renew the creation daily, so Jews cannot observe Shabbat only once a year but must observe and renew Shabbat weekly. This parallel suggests that the "work," the "service," the "*avodah*" which Jews perform to make Shabbat a day of rest, parallels the creative work that God performed in making the world. The work of "making Shabbat" which humans do involves a combination of domestic and liturgical preparations in the profane time before Shabbat that allows Shabbat to be a time of rest. These preparations include domestic chores like preparing meals in advance so cooking is not done on Shabbat, setting out special cutlery and candlesticks, and arranging for lighting. The preparations also include learning the Shabbat Torah *parashah* and studying the exegetes. What these preparations mean is that when Shabbat is ushered in through synagogue prayer and the saying of prayers in the home, secular time can be brought to a stop and life can be lived in a different quality of time. The time of Shabbat foregrounds holiness, family, community, study of Torah, and rest. Participation in liturgical events in the synagogue and home make the field of relations between humans, God, and world come alive and allow for what Mendelssohn called "the contemplation of things holy and divine."

The liturgical time of Shabbat is time unobstructed by secular aims of acquisition and goals of productive work. The liturgical time of Shabbat is a kind of completing or "finishing" (Genesis 2) of creation which Rosenzweig suggests "lends reality to the year" (1985: 310). Rosenzweig does not explain exactly what he means by this reality, but it must be the reality that revelation and the promise of redemption bring to the world. This is very different from Hermann Cohen's view in which "reality" is the real world of politics and work and Shabbat serves the purpose of replenishment and "collecting oneself for more work" (1985: 314). Indeed, Rosenzweig reverses the Cohenian view to suggest that all work is preparation for the reality that occurs in liturgical time. Since the central meaning of Shabbat is the celebration of creation, this means that Shabbat is correlated with the natural world and its rhythms and cycles. Shabbat is the celebration of natural life and the human as creature of nature. Shabbat prescribes the enjoyment of the senses through taste, sight, touch, and hearing. Sexual relations between husband and wife are encouraged as are eating, singing, dancing, and social interactions.

Rosenzweig recognizes that central to Shabbat are the three meals: evening, Shabbat day, and afternoon. These meals, eaten by families and their guests in homes, create a sense of *communitas* by simultaneously satisfying the human bodily need for food and the spiritual need for community. "The sweet and fully ripened fruit of humanity craves the community of man with man in the very act of renewing the life of the body" (1985: 316). Meeting basic bodily needs and celebrating the natural creation, Shabbat has a sensual quality to it. It expresses a sense of satisfaction in the goodness and completeness of God's created world. Shabbat's temporal direction is toward the past when the world was created as good. It recalls images of Eden and of Eve's joy in seeing, touching, and tasting the fruit of the tree in the middle of the Garden. Recalling that "ideal" time, before time, and distinguishing itself sharply from profane time, Shabbat thematizes the "a-historical" dimension of Jewish liturgical time. The time of Shabbat thereby serves Rosenzweig well in his attempt to delineate an a-historical, "eternal" dimension to the Jewish people and to Jewish religion. Thus, he says, "Shabbat is like a preview that can only be realized to the full in other festivals yet to come" (1985: 313) and in the final redemption of the world that is to come. The rest of Shabbat is joyful, and replenishing of the body and soul to make the congregation "feel as if it were already redeemed" (1985: 315). Yet, Shabbat is also incomplete enough and self-contained in the Jewish ritual and liturgical setting as to suggest that it is a "dream of perfection" (1985: 313) not yet fully realized and only to be "anticipated" (1985: 315) in the final redemption of human history and the world.

V. Conclusion

In conclusion, modern Jewish philosophy finds fertile ground and stimulation for thought in the variety of rituals and synagogue liturgies that mark the Jewish festivals. For all the figures we reviewed, ritual and liturgy builds relations between humans and humans, humans and the world, and humans and God. For Mendelssohn, liturgy allows for non-idolatrous representations of the divine and produces a series of human connections that build Jewish community. Cohen also stresses the equalizing effect on the community and the images and motivations that are built to encourage Jews to make larger connections to those that suffer outside of the Jewish community. Rosenzweig builds toward the notion of a relational field built out of the theological terms, creation, revelation, and redemption. In addition, Rosenzweig is concerned to show how liturgy allows Jews to re-experience significant moments from the past and embrace a present reality charged with a sense of eternity.

Notes

1 See Kepnes *et al.* (1998); Kepnes (2001); Ochs and Levene (2002). For the website of the Society of Textual Reasoning see http://www.bu.edu/mzank/STR/general.html. For the chat-line, see TR-list@bu.edu.
2 For a good review of the Christian challenges to Mendelssohn see the "Introduction" to *Jerusalem* (Mendelssohn 1983a) by Alexander Altmann.
3 Maimonides (1963 II: 507). Maimonides (1975) gives something of an Aristotelian argument for the value of the laws as a means to discipline character and inculcate ethical virtues in his "Eight Chapters [*Shemoneh Parakim*]" from his *Commentary on the Mishna.*
4 Mendelssohn has entered into the complex Jewish discussions on the *ta'amei ha-mitsvot*, the reasons for the commandments. As Altmann tells us in his commentary to *Jerusalem*, this tradition does not endeavor to ascertain a utilitarian meaning for the mitsvot and recognizes that attempts to plumb the depths of these reasons brings the searcher into the awe-filled place of "God's sanctuary" (Ps.73:17). Altmann reminds us that for the Jewish mystical tradition, Kabbalah, the depths of the *ta'amei ha-mitsvot* lie in the secrets of God's ten *sefirot*, or ten spheres of emanation. See Altmann in Mendelssohn (1983a: 226).
5 Letter to Herz Homberg (Mendelssohn 1975: 147).
6 I adapt this word from an expanded sense of Buber's notion of the *Die Zwischenmenschlich*, the "interhuman." Buber (1965) described the "interhuman" as a dimension of the lived human world and explained it as a complex web of human interactions and social processes.

Bibliography

Buber, M. (1965) "Elements of the Interhuman," in *The Knowledge of Man*, trans. M. Friedman and R. G. Smith, New York: Harper and Row.

—— (1987) *I and Thou*, trans. R. Smith, New York: Scribners.

Cohen, H. (1919) *Religion der Vernunft aus den Quellen des Judentums*, Leipzig: G. Fock.

—— (1995) *Religion of Reason Out of the Sources of Judaism*, trans. S. Kaplan, Atlanta: Scholars Press.

Glatzer, N. (1970) *Franz Rosenzweig: His Life and Thought*, New York: Schocken.

Kepnes, S. (2001) "Introduction to the Journal of Textual Reasoning," *The Journal of Textual Reasoning: Rereading Judaism after Modernity* 1:1 http://etext.lib. virginia.edu/journals/tr/volume1/index.html.

——, Ochs, P., and Gibbs, R. (1998) *Reasoning After Revelation: Dialogues in Postmodern Jewish Philosophy*, Boulder: Westview.

Maimonides, M. (1963), *The Guide of the Perplexed, Vol I–II*, trans. S. Pines, Chicago: The University of Chicago Press.

—— (1975) "Eight Chapters," in R. Weiss and C. Butterworth (eds), *Ethical Writings of Maimonides*, New York: Dover.

Mendelssohn, M. (1975) *Moses Mendelssohn: Selections From His Writings*, ed. and trans. E. Jospe, New York: Viking.

—— (1983a) *Jerusalem: Or on Religious Power and Judaism*, trans. A. Arkush, Hanover: University Press of New England.

—— (1983b [1783]) *Jerusalem oder über religiöse Macht und Judentum, Gesammelte Schriften Jubiläumsausgabe*, Band 8, Stuttgart: F. Frommann Verlag.

Ochs, P. and Levene, N. (eds) (2002) *Textual Reasonings: Jewish Philosophy and Text Study at the End of the Twentieth Century*, London: SCM.

Ricoeur, P. (1969) *The Symbolism of Evil*, trans. E. Buchanan, Boston: Beacon.

Rosenzweig, F. (1979 [1921]) *Der Stern der Erlösung, Der Mensch und Sein Werk. Gesammelte Schriften II*, Haag: Martinus Nijhoff.

—— (1985 [1921]) *The Star of Redemption*, trans. W. Hallo, Notre Dame: University of Notre Dame Press.

—— (1999) *The New Thinking*, ed. and trans. A. Udoff and B. Galli, Syracuse: Syracuse University Press.

Turner, V. (1969) *The Ritual Process*, Chicago: Aldine.

Zank, M. (2000) *The Idea of Atonement in the Philosophy of Hermann Cohen*, Providence: Brown Judaic Studies.

12 Ritual and Christian philosophy

Charles Taliaferro

"God wishes to be served with both the body and the spirit together."
The Cloud of Unknowing (1957: 172)

I. Introduction

It is regrettable that mainstream, contemporary philosophy of religion has largely ignored the role of ritual in Christian life and practice. Very few standard anthologies today in philosophy of religion contain any material on prayer, the sacraments, meditation, fasting, vigils, religious hymns, icons, pilgrimages, the sacredness of places or times, and so on, and yet these play different roles in much religious life. A neglect of this terrain results in an excessively intellectual or detached portrait of religion.[1] In this paper, I seek to articulate some of the virtues involved in Christian ritual and their role in an individual's religious identity. The integration of human and divine virtues forms part of what is involved in what Christians believe about the Church, namely, that it is the Body of Christ. Due to constraints on space, the position I advance should be read as programmatic, an effort to set the stage for further work.

The philosophy of virtues in Christian rites that follows is theistic and involves making claims about God's activity as Creator, Sustainer, and Redeemer of the cosmos. In other words, I do not seek to reconcile Christian ritual with naturalism, atheism, or agnosticism.[2] I also intend this account to cover a wide array of Christian rites found in the Western Churches (Catholic and Protestant) and Eastern Orthodoxy, but I have no doubt that there are some liturgical rites which will not be covered. For the sake of simplicity, I make the Eucharist my chief reference point. I offer a short description of the Eucharist below along with a brief sketch of the rite that provides access to the Eucharist, Baptism.

II. The practice and virtues of liturgy

The Eucharist, along with Baptism, are the two principal rites in the Christian tradition. Baptism is the rite of initiation that, in most churches, enables the believer to full participation in the Eucharist. Baptism involves sprinkling or bathing a person in water in God's Triune Name – Father, Son, Holy Spirit – either on the profession of that person's faith or (as in the case of infants) through the sponsorship of individuals or a Christian community. Baptism, in the majority of Christian traditions, is considered a singular event, though for many Christians the Baptismal covenant is renewed at different times during the year and, upon this renewal, believers may be sprinkled again with blessed or holy water. The Eucharist (also called the Last Supper, Holy Communion, and Mass) is the ritual re-enactment of, and thanksgiving for, Christ's redemptive life and sacrifice. Believers partake in bread and wine that is consecrated to God, in memory of Christ's giving his disciples bread and wine in his last supper before his passion, death, and resurrection. Unlike Baptism, the Eucharist is a rite that, in many regions of the world, is cele-brated daily throughout the year. The Eucharist as it is found in Roman, Eastern Orthodox, Anglican, and Protestant churches involves an invocation to prayer, praise or worship of God, a penitential prayer of confession, a profession of faith, petitionary prayer (typically for the world and the church), a sanctification of the elements (blessing bread and wine in the name of Christ), reverent receiving of the elements, and a prayer of thanksgiving. While the focus of this paper is on the Eucharist, the Eucharist is a complex rite involving so many aspects of Christian spirituality that much of what follows bears on Christian liturgy in general.

Before looking at the virtues to be found through the Eucharistic liturgy, let us consider the conditions for participants in this ritual. While infants regularly play roles in the Eucharistic rite (if only passively receiving the bread and wine), a paradigmatic, adult case of being a celebrant or commu-nicant (one who takes communion) is one who consciously is aware of the act as linked to Christ's passion, life, and sacrifice. Can one even observe the Eucharist if one has no idea whatever of Christ, God, thanksgiving, good and evil, the atonement? One who was said to observe the Eucharist under those conditions would be like one who was said to be in love with another under conditions in which he or she had no concepts whatever of love, inti-macy, and tender, subtle emotions. As Ninian Smart points out in *The Concept of Worship,* ritual practices are thoroughly intentional; they are no less intentional than meaningful speech:

> The usage of physical movements in ritual supplies a range of gestures, and these in a sense constitute a language. One can misuse gestures, as you can misuse words. ... If therefore I imagine that bowing down in the direction of an image of Ganesh I am really saluting an image of Christ behind my back, I fail to understand the gesture-language of worship.[3]
>
> (Smart 1972: 7)

As a kind of language, understanding ritual must involve a conceptual grasp of its fundamental components and rules.

A good illustration of a person who achieves only a tenuous foothold in Christian ritual is David Hume's tongue-in-cheek depiction of "a young Turk" in *The Natural History of Religion*:

> A famous general, at that time in the Muscovite service, having come to Paris for the recovery of his wounds, brought along with him a young Turk, whom he had taken prisoner. Some of the doctors of the Sorbonne (who are altogether as positive as the dervishes of Constantinople) thinking it a pity, that the poor Turk should be damned for want of instruction solicited Mustapha very hard to turn Christian, and promised him, for his encouragement, plenty of good wine in this world, and paradise in the next. These allurements were too powerful to be resisted; and therefore, having been well instructed and catechized, he at last agreed to receive the sacraments of baptism and the Lord's supper. The priest, however, to make everything sure and solid, still continued his instructions, and began the next day with the usual question, *How many Gods are there? None at all*, replies Benedict; for that was his new name. *How! None at all!* Cries the priest. *To be sure*, said the honest proselyte. *You have told me all along that there is but one God: And yesterday I eat him.*
>
> (Hume 2000: 155)

Alas, entering into the world of Christian practice requires a bit more work theologically.[4]

Apart from the bare awareness of the meaning of the Eucharistic rite, is it essential for a participant to believe each of the statements that he or she recites? The Eucharist traditionally involves a recitation of the Nicene Creed which begins: "We believe in one God ...." In reciting this, is a participant committed to a belief in monotheism?

Some theologians have advanced a form of Christian atheism along with a radical re-interpretation of Christian liturgical language; they say, for example, that to proclaim that there is a God of love is to profess the supreme importance of a life of compassion. While I indicated at the outset that my account of ritual in this paper is thoroughly theistic, I do not think that honest participation in the Eucharist requires theistic belief or adherence to all the claims of the Creed. Full belief in the Creed *et al.* marks an ideal or full integration of language and intent, but it has been argued plausibly by Louis Pojman and others that hope or faith may differ from belief and yet suffice to secure a person's fitting participation in the Eucharistic rite.[5] Another possible route to participating or even celebrating the Eucharist is doing so on behalf of others or as a representative of a community. Imagine a priest who does not believe in God, nor even hopes that God exists, but he is committed to the welfare of the church and wishes to promote its life.

While some of these positions may have some legitimacy, they do not seem paradigmatic or ideal, central cases of liturgical participation. The focal point of the liturgy with the renewal of a person through penance and then celebrating Christ's sacrifice and resurrection seems to require a participant actually participating in penance and celebration. The church – Eastern and Roman, Anglican and Protestant – has taught the importance of not just believing the creeds but participants actually seeking to live the life they profess: a life of obedience to the God of justice and mercy. In other words, for someone to take the Eucharist while bent upon malicious injustice would be a profound offense to God and to the rite itself (I Corinthians 5:8).

Having indicated some of the conditions for participation, what goods or virtues are in play in the Eucharistic rite? I believe that there are five key virtues. I shall be using the term "virtue" more broadly than one finds in, say, Aristotle's ethics. A virtue is an *excellent feature* or *good power* where the excellence or goodness involves more than moral goods. The first three virtues include the virtue of fidelity and solidarity with God's will; the virtue of worship; and the virtue of what I will describe as external goods sought in the Eucharist. I outline these three virtues only briefly below, and concentrate on the fourth, which involves the virtue or goodness of the believer's integrated, religious identity, and the fifth virtue, which involves a divine embodiment whereby the community of believers comes to constitute the Body of Christ.[6]

III. Four virtues in Christian rites

First, there is the virtue or good of acting in solidarity with, and fidelity to, the revealed will of God. Insofar as God has revealed sacramental rites that we ought to engage in, such practices are binding and it is a virtue to engage in them.[7] In the Anglican *Book of Common Prayer*, there is this invocation – which in the main is common to Roman Catholicism, Orthodoxy, and many Reformed churches:

> On the night he was handed over to suffering and death, our Lord Jesus Christ took bread; and when he had given thanks to you, he broke it, and gave it to his disciples, and said, "Take, eat: This is my Body, which is given for you. Do this for the remembrance of me."
>
> After supper he took the cup of wine; and when he had given thanks, he gave it to them, and said, "Drink this, all of you: This is my Blood of the new Covenant, which is shed for you and for many for the forgiveness of sins. Whenever you drink it, do this for the remembrance of me."[8]

Participating in the Eucharist may thereby be seen as a filial response to Christ's command or invitation to discipleship.

Acting in concord with God's will, whereby one re-enacts or re-capitulates the act of Christ, can be seen not just as a matter of obedience to an external command but as a participation in God's self-offering in Christ. Fidelity to God through the Eucharistic rite may be seen as uniting one's action to God's, thus securing a solidarity between the believer and her Creator-Redeemer. The virtue or excellence here is a combination of fidelity and solidarity with God through the faithful carrying out of a rite that Christ invites.

A second virtue pertains to worship. Insofar as we have a duty (or it is good) to praise a benefactor, God's overriding supreme benefaction as Creator and Redeemer warrants praise. The most central act of praise in the Eucharist is this exclamation: "Holy, holy, holy Lord, God of power and might, heaven and earth are full of your glory. Hosanna in the highest. Blessed is he who comes in the name of the Lord. Hosanna in the highest."[9] There is also adoration and worship over God's redemption in Christ and for the good of creation.[10]

The good or virtue of worship may be understood as a complex good in the tradition of Franz Brentano, G. E. Moore, Roderick Chisholm, and others. These philosophers hold that, *ceterus paribus*, if something is good, to take pleasure in that good is itself a good. Insofar as worship involves the pleasure, adoration, veneration of a reality of great goodness, such worship is itself good (Chisholm 1986). As an example, consider The Song of Mary, "My soul doth magnify the Lord." The notion of magnification fits the Brentano-Moore-Chisholm thesis that one's affective response to a value magnifies or intensifies the total value at hand. Using Christian ritual out of inordinate self-love is systematically and rigorously condemned in classic Christian spirituality. Witness, for example, the insistence that sorrow over sin should be out of *contrition* (genuine love of God), not *attrition* (e.g. injured self-love, self-hate, or other inferior motives such as the fear of hell).

A third virtue involves all the external goods that are prayed for or sought in the Eucharist. If, for example, the Eucharist is offered as part of a prayer for peace in the Middle East, then part of the value of the Eucharist lies in the resulting (looked for) peace. The virtue of achieving goods as a result of a rite is perhaps the most dangerous religiously, for Christian ethicists have long pointed out the inferiority of a love of God that is prompted by self-love. Inferior love of God has sometimes been called concupiscential and servile love.[11] But insofar as petitionary prayer for good ends is defensible, as I believe it is, seeking such good in ritual can be good. The Lord's Prayer commends this petition: "Give us this day, our daily bread."[12]

The fourth virtue involves the goodness of the believer's religious identity. This good builds on the other virtues, but I single it out as it involves the integration of one's affective and bodily life.

The Eucharistic memorial of Christ's life, death, and resurrection is laced around a moral and spiritual death and re-birth of the participant. In the confession of sins, the participant confesses past failings, renounces the prior intentions and omissions behind wrongdoing, intends (or expresses the intention) to lead a new life in orientation to God. Christian tradition speaks of the believer becoming a new person (Romans 6). This renewal extends well beyond a sacramental rite in terms of one's life, but it is crystallized and articulated liturgically.

In the Eucharist, ideally, there is the good of affectively internalizing and then embodying the good of living in relation to God. Given that the God of Christianity exists, it is good to act in solidarity with God's will (the virtue of fidelity and solidarity); it is good to contemplate, take pleasure in, be in awe of this divine presence (the virtue of worship); and it is good to seek good ends through liturgy as is the case in worthy petitionary prayer (the virtue of external goods). And it is a further good to affectively embody and then physically express one's relation to God.

Concerning the value of embodiment, consider an analogy. Imagine you see someone whom you care about, after a long absence. Compare these cases: (A) you see the person, take note of your affection but merely walk by; (B) you see the person, feel an affectionate care, and say something like "Good to see you!"; or (C) you see the person you care about and embrace them. The first state of affairs is good, but it is a better good (other things being equal) to express the good of affection, and (again, assuming there are no competing factors about propriety) an even better good to embody the affection. Similarly, if it is good to contemplate, worship, and petition the divine, it is an even better good to do this in an expressive, embodied fashion, and this may involve liturgy as a specific good.

The recognition of the value and possible dangers of an integrated affective internalization of emotion and expression has been long noted in the history of aesthetics. The key debate over the value of poetry and rhapsody in Plato's work takes up precisely this issue. In the *Republic*, Plato questions the good of Homeric poetry for it involves the display of evil – jealousy, murderous rage, and so on. If these states of character were bad, the poet's assimilation and imitation of them were (at least prima facie) bad. Part of the history of the philosophy of art is the history of justifying such displays by pointing to greater goods that may be achieved through the display (manifestation, imitation) of evil. Aristotle, famously, replied to Plato by appealing to the greater good of moral education and catharsis. None of this debate makes sense unless one believes that the physical expression of affective states (from love to hate) can itself be a value or disvalue.

To further support the recognition of such values, consider a thought experiment that reverses the earlier case expressing affection. Imagine these cases: (D) you hate me for no good reason and yet you pass by without any expression of this; (E) you express your anger by shaking your fist and reporting, "I hate you;" or (F) you assault me with hatred. The cases have a diminishing value, each case is worse than the other, and a parallel diminishment would also occur if we imagine some sinister religion of hatred. Imagine you are not only misanthropic, but sacramentally venerate *the spirit of misanthropy*. I suggest that such sacramental veneration would be a worse evil. I submit that "F" is worse than "D," just as "C" is better than "A."

Of course, the modest appeal to these thought experiments and the historical debate on the ethical critique of art hardly amount to a case for highly formal liturgy, let alone a case for a spirituality that is limited only to liturgy. (Imagine that the friend or misanthrope in each thought experiment only commends or insults the other person in rigorous ritual. We might well think that some more unfettered, free form affection or malice would add something good or bad.) But what I am highlighting is the good of some fitting bodily display of religious life, and the wisdom of there being a structured liturgy can be seen when one appreciates the corporate, public nature of Christian spirituality. In his magisterial work, *The Shape of Liturgy*, Dom Gregory Dix writes about the function of liturgy as a practice that is open to all those who are interested:

> We regard Christian worship in general, not excluding the Eucharist, as essentially a public activity, in the sense that it ought to be open to all comers, and that the stranger (even the non-Christian, though he may not be a communicant) ought to be welcomed and even attracted to be present and to take part.
>
> (Dix 1982 [1945])

A public liturgy with a repeatable pattern, rhythmic phrases that may be easily memorized and trusted, allows for different individuals to incorporate individual petitions and desires into a united practice. By fostering an ongoing liturgy that has continuity between primitive Christian communities and today's religious practices, participants have the virtue of a solidarity with other Christians over time.[13]

The integrated liturgical identity of the believer is reflected in this passage from Augustine's *De Cura Pro Mortus*:

> Those who pray by using the members of the body, as when they bend the knees, when they extend the hands, or even prostrate themselves upon the ground, or whatever else they do in a visible manner, they do that which indicates that they are suppliants although their invisible will and the intention of their heart is known to God, for He has no need of such outward signs to indicate that the human mind is in a state of supplication to Him. By doing this a man excites himself more to a proper state for praying and lamenting more humbly and fervently, and, somehow or other, since these movements of the body cannot be made except by a previous movement of the mind, by these same actions of the visible man, the invisible soul which prompted them is strengthened. Then, by reason of this the devotion of one's heart is strengthened, because he has resolved that these prayers be made and has made them.
>
> (1955: 360)

Augustine's portrait of the mind-body relationship in prayer may seem somewhat disjointed and instrumental. Is bodily posture of importance largely to help focus the mind? While bodily assistance may be at work, there is also, in Augustine, the notion that in intentional action and speech something immaterial (the soul) may become visible (Augustine 1998: Book X, ch. 13). The great virtue (powerful excellence) in coordinated soul-body prayer is that the participant comes to make visible the affective internalization of the relationship between God and the creature. As the relationship with God may be complex, involving awe, penance, petition, love, and so on, there is a fitting diversity in Christianity's many liturgical traditions.

To summarize the account thus far, the four virtues involved in Christian ritual, especially the Eucharist, include the virtue of fidelity and solidarity; the virtue of worship; the virtue of external goods; and the virtue of affective formation and expression of the believer's identity in relation to God. The fifth virtue or good involves a complex divine action, which I seek to describe in the next section.

IV. The body of Christ

There are considerable differences in how Christians (philosophers, theologians) have understood the efficacy and nature of the sacraments, especially the Eucharist. Despite great variation, I suggest that there is a widespread belief that in gathering for the rites of prayer, God is present in a special, distinctive way. Christ promises in Scripture that when two or three are gathered in His Name, He is in their midst (Matthew 18:20). Traditionally, this has been understood as a distinctive presence. God is omnipresent throughout the cosmos, but God's relation to each part of the cosmos is not the same. For example many Christian theists hold to the Biblical picture of God hating injustice. From this perspective, God may be present in (or to) some world event but as one who condemns the malice involved. In the rites of Christianity, God is present (or believed to be present) as the lover and beloved, the nurturing, self-giving creator, atoning savior, sustaining spirit. It is through the world of a merely earthly transaction (eating bread and wine, sharing "the Kiss of Peace") that the lives of believers become uplifted into a greater world, God's world. I suggest that while many Christians have divergent views on how the sacraments "work," there is a common conception that in Christian practices like Baptism and the Eucharist, earth and heaven intermingle so that God becomes actively present and is revealed to participants (see Danielou 1956: 50).

In the New Testament and in much Christian tradition, this conviction is expressed by saying that Christian believers make up *the body of Christ* in the world. The action of believers in, say, corporeal acts of mercy and charity may be seen as God acting in the world. Augustine writes of God's love taking embodiment in the world,

> What sort of face does [divine] love have? What sort of form does it have? What sort of stature does it have? What sort of feet does it have? What sort of hands does it have? ... [Yet love] does have feet, for they lead to the Church. It does have hands, for they are stretched out to the poor man. It does have eyes; for he who is in need is understood thereby.
>
> (Augustine 1995: 225)

The believers who make up the body of Christ exhibit this love in non-ritual events. The explicit sacramental rites are, however, central acts in which the church itself consciously and deliberately seeks to embody this love.[14] As

J. D. Crichton writes of the Eucharist: "It is the communal celebration by the Church, which is Christ's body and in which he with the Holy Spirit is active, in the paschal mystery" (1978: 28).

In the era of logical positivism after World War II, philosophers like Paul Edwards, Kai Nielsen, and others critiqued theism on the grounds that it promoted a disembodied view of God. Paul Edwards' complaint that follows is representative:

> I have no doubt that when most people think about God and his alleged activities, here or in the hereafter, they vaguely think of him as possessing some kind of rather large body. Now if we are told that there is a God who is, say, just and good and kind and loving and powerful and wise and if, (a) it is made clear that these words are used in one of their ordinary senses, and (b) God is not asserted to be a disembodied mind; then it seems plain to me that *to that extent* a series of meaningful assertions has been made. And this is so whether we are told that God's justice, mercy, etc., are "limitless" or merely that God is superior to all human beings in these respects. However, it seems to me that all these words lose their meaning if we are told that God does not possess a body. Anyone who thinks otherwise without realizing this I think is supplying a body in the background of his images. For what would it be like to be, say, just without a body? To be just, a person has to *act* justly – he has to behave in certain ways. This is not reductive materialism. It is a simple empirical truth about what we mean by "just." But how is it possible to perform these acts, to behave in the required ways without a body? Similar remarks apply to the other divine attributes.
>
> (1961: 242, 243)

I have argued elsewhere against Edwards, Neilsen, and others. I believe that materialism is implausible and that it is perfectly intelligible to think of a non-physical reality acting justly, showing mercy, and so on. A physical event need not have a physical cause (see Taliaferro 1994; for a more recent defense, see Hoffman and Rosenkrantz 2002: ch. 3). But there is an element in Edwards' position that may resonate with Augustine and a traditional Christian perspective. In Christian tradition, it is held that God's justice, wisdom, kindness, mercy, and love must be given embodiment in the life of the Church. The "must" here is not akin to Paul Edwards' philosophical materialism (which may not be "reductive materialism," but it still rules out in principle nonphysical agency). The "must" is a kind of moral or spiritual imperative. The term "supernatural" might be fitting here if one imagines that, in coming to participate in the life of God through sacramental rites, the natural world gets taken up, animated, and enlarged by a greater, divine reality.[15]

The function of the church is to display in its moral agency and sacramental life a coordination of human and divine virtue. In so doing, it functions as the body of Christ. I believe that the plausibility of this understanding of the church as a coordination or concert of human and divine action is testified to (in part) by the outrage by believers and non-believers when the church so evidently fails to display love, mercy, justice, or its rites become merely routine acts with no animating deep conviction or feeling. The crimes of the institutional church are often judged so harshly by Christian believers because such crimes are understood to be a sacrilege, the damaged defilement of something of God.

Some readers will notice that I have offered a philosophical overview of five virtues that come to the fore in religious rites but skirted the central, historical philosophical dispute about the Eucharist in particular. Does the consecrated bread and wine change in the rite such that they (in some way) *become* the body and blood of Christ? Thomas Aquinas developed his account of *transubstantiation* at this point to account for the bread and wine to retain their appearances ("accidents") while altering in substance. There are other theories, including *consubstantiation* (Luther), *virtualism* (Calvin), and treating the Eucharist as a simple memorial. The Eastern orthodox and Anglican churches have elected not to define as a matter of doctrine the "real presence" of Christ in the Eucharist; they affirm Christ's presence without commitment as to how this presence is achieved.

I have not taken on this topic because the account offered here is compatible with each of the historically significant theories about the elements themselves. As an Anglican, I side with the more general thesis that the elements are, in the old scholastic saying, efficacious signs (*significando causant*) while not committing to the metaphysically richer accounts like transubstantiation. Still, in defense of taking the more general account sketched above which focuses on the shared virtues of God and human being, I have followed the direction of the liturgical renewal in the Anglican and Roman Churches, which emphasizes the complete Eucharistic rite rather than focus on the host.[16]

V. Ritual and philosophy of religion

I began this essay with lamenting the neglect of work on ritual by mainstream philosophers of religion, especially in the analytic tradition. If there were an expansion of the field to take ritual and other components of Christian practice seriously, would this amplification have an impact on other components of business-as-usual philosophy of religion? I believe it would.

The treatment of theistic attributes such as omnipotence, omniscience, and goodness would be less abstract. From the standpoint of a sacramental philosophy, a central question would be one of fundamental values: Is a being with such attributes worthy of worship? What are the consequences of worshipping a God of essential goodness versus a God of pure, unbridled power? How would belief in omniscience affect prayer? Is a God that is atemporally eternal a God whom one may meet in the celebration of the Eucharist? Beliefs about God's relation to time directly impact different treatments of the sacraments. Some Christian philosophers have held that in the sacraments one may transcend one's temporal place in the present and somehow partake in the events of Christ's life. Participating in liturgy is often explicitly outlined as an act of observing Christ's passion and other sacred events.

More attention to the virtues involved in the sacraments would also, I think, provide an interesting concrete context by which to debate God's action in the world. To what extent does the notion that the church functions as the body of Christ involve the miraculous? I have described the church becoming the body of Christ while retaining the classic theistic distinction between creator and creation. But to what extent does this risk an *identity* between the church and God? Would some form of panentheism or process theology be more credible here?[17]

Finally, I suggest that a philosophy of the sacraments may well lead to taking more seriously aspects of the philosophy of art. Philosophers have long debated the nature of representation in art, how it is that one thing (a painting) may represent something else. Some aestheticians speak of how one may see something (a person or mind) in a painting or *through* a painting.[18] Such language may be useful for spelling out different ritual ways of seeing God.[19] This, I hope, will be the topic of another paper.[20]

Notes

1 It must be conceded that, to their credit, philosophers of religion inspired by Wittgenstein and some continental philosophers of religion have given more attention to religious practices than those in the (broadly speaking) analytic tradition. This is curious as there is nothing about analytic philosophical tools that should inhibit taking religious ritual more seriously. I suggest analytic philosophers tend to give more prominence to the coherence and credibility of religious belief rather than practice because they see the latter as grounded in the former. This is plausible, but it can still promote a lopsided view of religion that is more theoretical than affective, historical, and practical. See Taliaferro (1998: ch. 2).

2 I do not seek, for example, a naturalistic account of ritual like Wettstein 1997. My essay is specifically and unapologetically theistic. For all that, however, I believe that the interest that non-theistic naturalists have in accommodating theistic rites is testimony to the latter's beauty and value. Wettstein writes: "Having great value in the power of religious practice and the virtues of the religious life, I will freely employ terminology central to that practice and life. . . . Concerning my own outlook . . . I am with those who reject belief in the supernatural" (1997: 258).

3 A full treatment of religious ritual as a kind of language should, I think, highlight the values involved in rational, cooperative activity that H. P. Grice underscored (Grice 1989). Some Christian theologians speak of the essential need for proficiency when it comes to the religious life, and this is very similar to the concept of proficiency in language use (see Thornton 1988).

4 On the indispensability of belief in religious practice, see Godlove (2002).

5 See Pojman (1986). While I believe Pojman offers a robust account of how hoping for the truth of theism may legitimate theistic religious practices such as prayer, participation in the Eucharist *et al.*, I think some theistic passions (such as awe, joy, celebration, and profound gratitude) may be difficult unless a person actually believed in the truth of the relevant religious beliefs.

6 For a defense of the terminology of virtues which include moral *and* non-moral goods, see Taliaferro (2001).

7 I am assuming that a divine command theory is defensible. For a modest defense, see Taliaferro (1992). Divine command theories have been advanced by R. M.

Adams, T. Carson, W. Alston, P. Quinn, J. Hare, and J. Idziak. An alternative grounding of this virtue of solidarity and fidelity may be found in Murphy (2002).

8 These passages are derived from the New Testament (Matthew 26:26–28; Mark 14:22–24; Luke 22:19–20; I Corinthians 11:23–29).

9 As before, I take this from *The Book of Common Prayer* but this is representative of most Eucharistic rites.

10 Arguments for worship on the grounds of gratitude for God's goodness are plentiful. For a modern source, see Swinburne (1977).

11 Christian philosophers and theologians, classically, stand at odds with the ancient (and, alas, sometimes contemporary) treatment of prayer as "a mutual art of commerce" (from Plato's *Euthyphro* 14:e).

12 For an overview of the case for petitionary prayer, see Stump (1997).

13 Indeed, a Christian may well see liturgy as itself formed by the guidance of God as the Holy Spirit throughout time (Luke 12:12).

14 In support of this picture of the church, consider these passages from the Catechism in *The Book of Common Prayer*: "Q: How is the Church described in the Bible? A: The Church is described in the bible as the Body of which Jesus Christ is the Head and of which all baptized persons are members . . . Q: What is the mission of the Church? A: The mission of the Church is to restore all people to unity with God and each other in Christ. Q: How does the Church pursue its mission as it prays and worships, proclaims the Gospel, and promotes justice, peace, and love" (*Book of Common Prayer* 1979: 854, 855).

15 There are some interesting parallel issues in philosophy of mind and what may be called a philosophy of the church. If the church – the general body of "believers," not necessarily a specific denomination – is to have "the mind of Christ," what is the relation of that mind to the body? The debate over mind-body interaction, the indivisibility of the self, the unity of apperception, and so on, all have theistic analogues. The many bizarre thought experiments in philosophy of mind can be formatted to address a philosophy of the Church as the body of Christ, e.g. Searle's use of the Chinese Room, Chalmer's speculation over the zombie problem, Nagel on split brains, etc. For philosophical work on the soul-body, God-church relation, see Gilson (1955: 10–11) and elsewhere.

16 The liturgical renewal, which was marked, among other events, by Vatican II, places greater emphasis on communal liturgical rites in community rather than on the sacred status of the elements as objects of wonder and veneration.

17 While I resist the physicalist tendency in David Paulsen's theology, he and Carl Griffen offer a fascinating portrait of corporeal views of God in Paulsen and Griffen (2002). At the end of the day, however, I side more with the traditional understanding of God's nonmaterial nature as one finds in, for example, Gilson's *History of Christian Philosophy in the Middle Ages*.

18 For a succinct introduction to some of these issues which would be useful to draw on in a philosophy of ritual, see Rollins (2001).

19 Older philosophical work by Malebranche and Berkeley may also be relevant here. Perhaps their account of perceiving objects in God is mistaken when it comes to garden variety secular matters, but a version of their account is viable in the context of sacramental rites in which (or through which) one may see God.

20 I thank Kevin Schilbrack and Sarah Campbell, Jen Dotson and Paula Schanilec for comments on an earlier version of this paper.

Bibliography

Augustine (1955) "The Care to be taken for the Dead," *Treatises on Marriage and Other Subjects*, New York: Fathers of the Church.

—— (1995) *Tractates on the Gospel of John 112–24; Tractates on the First Epistle of John*, trans. J. Rettig, Washington: Catholic University of America.

—— (1998) *The City of God against the Pagans*, ed. and trans. R. W. Dyson, Cambridge: Cambridge University Press.

The Book of Common Prayer (1979), New York: Seabury Press.

Chisholm, R. (1986) *Brentano and Intrinsic Value*, Cambridge: Cambridge University Press.

The Cloud of Unknowing (1957) trans. I. Progoff, New York: A Delta Book.

Crichton, J. D. (1978) "A Theology of Worship," in C. Jones, G. Wainwright, and E. Yarnold (eds), *The Study of Liturgy*, New York: Oxford University Press.

Danielou, J. (1956) *The Bible and the Liturgy*, Notre Dame: University of Notre Dame Press.

Dix, G. (1982) *The Shape of the Liturgy*, New York: Seabury Press.

Edwards, P. (1961) "Some Notes on Anthropomorphic Theology," in S. Hook (ed.), *Religious Experience and Truth*, 242–3, New York: New York University Press.

Gilson, E. (1955) *History of Christian Philosophy in the Middle Ages*, London: Sheed and Ward.

Godlove, T. (2002) "Saving Belief," in N. Frankenberry (ed.), *Radical Interpretations of Religion*, Cambridge: Cambridge University Press.

Grice, H. P. (1989) *Studies in the Way of Words*, Cambridge: Harvard University Press.

Hoffman, J. and Rosenkrantz, G. S. (2002) *The Divine Attributes*, Oxford: Blackwell.

Hume, D. (2000) *The Natural History of Religion*, Chicago: LaSalle.

Murphy, M. C. (2002) *An Essay on Divine Authority*, Ithaca: Cornell University Press.

Paulsen, D. and Griffen, C. (2002) "Augustine and the Corporeality of God," *Harvard Theological Review* 95: 97–118.

Pojman, L. (1986) "Faith Without Belief?" *Faith and Philosophy* 3: 157–76.

Rollins, M. (2001) "Pictorial Representation," in B. Gaut and D. M. Lopes (eds), *The Routledge Companion to Aesthetics*, London: Routledge.

Smart, N. (1972) *The Concept of Worship*, London: St Martin's Press.

Stump, E. (1997) "Petitionary Prayer" in P. Quinn and C. Taliaferro (eds), *A Companion to Philosophy of Religion*, Oxford: Blackwell.

Swinburne, R. (1977) *The Coherence of Theism*, Oxford: Oxford University Press.

Taliaferro, C. (1992) "God's Estate," *Journal of Religious Ethics* 20: 69–92.

—— (1994) *Consciousness and the Mind of God*, Cambridge: Cambridge University Press.

—— (1998) *Contemporary Philosophy of Religion*, Oxford: Blackwell.

—— (2001) "The Virtues of Embodiment," *Philosophy* 76: 111–25.

Thornton, M. (1988) *Christian Proficiency*, Cambridge: Cowley Press.

Wettstein, H. (1997) "Awe and the Religious Life: A Naturalistic Perspective," in P. A. French, T. E. Ueling, Jr., and H. Wettstein (eds), *Midwest Studies in Philosophy, Vol. XXI: Philosophy of Religion*, Notre Dame: University of Notre Dame Press.

13 Religious rituals, spiritually disciplined practices, and health

Peter H. Van Ness

I. Methodological introduction: the promise of epidemiology

In the last century, social scientists sought to understand rituals and ritualistic behaviors in terms of the social functions they served and the cultural practices they embodied. Early in the century, Émile Durkheim and Alfred Reginald Radcliffe-Brown described how rituals promote social unity and address other enduring aspects of social structure (Durkheim 1995 [1912]; Radcliffe-Brown 1952). More recently, Clifford Geertz and Pierre Bourdieu have emphasized the role of rituals in resolving problems of meaning and negotiating questions of power in specific historical circumstances (Geertz 1973; Bourdieu 1977 [1972]). In neither perspective do rituals of healing and health-related practices figure prominently. They are only somewhat more prominent in the thinking of ritual theorists who stress notions of performance. Victor Turner includes "curative cults" within the broader rubric of "rituals of affliction," and these he contrasts with "life-crisis rituals" (Turner 1967: 7–15). Ronald Grimes lists healings rites as one of sixteen types of rituals (Grimes 1985: v–vi).

Medical anthropologists have given the most sustained scientific attention to healing rituals and practices. With ethnographic methodology they have provided many culturally detailed accounts of how diverse peoples marshal social and symbolic resources for coping with illnesses whose etiologies their specialists do not understand. Robert Hahn, both an anthropologist and epidemiologist, provides a perspective on healing rites in which qualitative ethnographic methods are primary but in which quantitative epidemiological techniques supply related empirical data (Hahn 1995). Hahn first notes the differences between anthropologists and epidemiologists: "Anthropologists focus on the uniqueness of particular settings and on meanings determined by the interconnections of local details ... Epidemiologists strive to eliminate local detail in order to achieve universal principles" (Hahn 1995: 102–3). Hahn proceeds to make a case for the complementary character of the two disciplines. Especially relevant here is his claim that epidemiologists aspire to identify causal relationships between risk factors and disease, not merely in order to attain generalizable knowledge, but because such knowledge allows for interventions that can cut the causal chain from risk factor to disease and thereby promote human health and well-being. A similar turn to abstraction in search of pragmatic benefits motivates this reflection on ritual and health.

The research of social epidemiologists into the impact of various aspects of religiousness on health outcomes offers a perspective on ritualistic behaviors complementary to the one provided by medical anthropologists. In the case of epidemiology, statistical methodology predominates. Attendance at religious services and frequency of private prayer are two of the most common dimensions of religiousness that have been measured in epidemiological studies. These measures are brief compared to the "thick descriptions" recommended by anthropologists like Geertz (Geertz 1973: 3–30): they are not intended to capture subtle differences in religious motivations, hopes, or feelings. They can, though, reflect either public behaviors like religious service attendance or subjective dispositions, for instance, self-reported degrees of religiousness. Because such epidemiological measures of religiousness are quantitatively represented as ordinal scales, they can, however, be related to specific biomedical outcomes that, in the best of circumstances, are observed during many years of follow-up. Such longitudinal results present distinct advantages compared with the mostly anecdotal observations of events consequent to ritualistic behaviors in classic ethnographic literature. They allow for an empirical assessment of how regular participation in religious rituals is related to specific health outcomes and to general measures of human well-being.

Social epidemiologists are not specifically interested in understanding the nature of religion or ritual. As I have argued elsewhere, however, epidemiological studies of religious predictors yield methodological insights that can contribute to more incisive ways of studying religion (Van Ness 2003). This reflection on religious ritual and health will attempt to substantiate this conviction. Like the works of medical anthropologists, it will seek to be an empirically informed account. Its empirical frame of reference, however, will be statistical rather than ethnographic. Also, its empirical evidence comes mostly from studies of contemporary US populations characterized by Western monotheistic faiths and advanced market economies. Its theoretical perspective on ritual and health will be more abstract and speculative than a culturally specific "thick description" of a healing ritual. These traits make it suitable for inclusion in a volume collecting diverse philosophical perspectives on ritual.

Most epidemiological researchers acknowledge that high levels of attendance at religious services are often associated with reduced rates of mortality (Hummer *et al.* 1999; Strawbridge *et al.* 1997) and high levels of devotional practices like prayer are frequently associated with lower subjective morbidity (Ellison *et al.* 1989; Musick 1996). In attempting to explain how people's religiousness promotes good health, epidemiologists have drawn upon themes present in the social scientific literature. Specifically, some have proposed that attendance at religious services provides social cohesiveness that, in turn, promotes healthy lifestyle choices and effective coping strategies. Also, it has been noted that practices like prayer in times of illness promote cognitive coherence by placing troubling events in a larger framework of meaning that then helps people cope with the stress that illness causes.

Beginning with the work of Walter Cannon and Hans Selye, biomedical researchers have proposed specific physiological models for the phenomenon of stress (Cannon 1932; Selye 1976 [1956]). Deeper understanding of the physiological expressions of stress has provided opportunities for understanding how psychosocial factors like social support promote successful coping with stress and reduce morbidity (Seeman and McEwen 1996; Seeman *et al.* 1997; McEwen and Stellar 1993). Accompanying these developments in stress research has been a growing insight into the role of periodic biological rhythms in the physiology of living organisms. Franz Halberg's research into the daily "circadian" rhythm of mammals in the 1950s has led to the development of the discipline of "chronobiology" which has begun to receive popular and practical exposition in the 1990s (Smolensky and Lamberg 2000: 4). This theoretical ferment has exciting possibilities for understanding the religion and health relationship when it is realized that most religious worship and practice occur as nested series of periodic religious behaviors having daily, weekly, yearly, and lifetime schedules. Of course, some religious, and especially healing rituals, are occasional in a nature, occurring in response to life crises like sudden illness. The ideas developed here are less directly applicable to this sort of ritual viewed by itself (see Appendix A).

This chapter will sketch how the temporal structure of religious rituals and spiritually disciplined practices – along with their other salient characteristics – might contribute to human health. It will not marshal empirical evidence in support of the physiological impact of participation in religious rituals. For one reason, work in this area is only just beginning. Also, the character of this contribution is intended to be philosophical. It will involve empirically informed philosophical reconnoitering of a new research field. Hopefully it will contribute to research that will illuminate the relationship between religion and health and thereby provide guidance for how religiousness and spirituality might be used as effective resources for overcoming illness and for achieving well-being generally. The type of research that should be done to test this hypothesis and advance this agenda will be indicated. The philosophical implications of the verification of this hypothesis will be discussed. Specifically, implications for the study of religion and for the role of religion in contemporary culture will be delineated.

II. Rituals as nested periodic behaviors

Catherine Bell's influential book, *Ritual: Perspectives and Dimensions*, includes a summary of the characteristics of "ritual-like activities" (Bell 1997: 138–69). She wisely declines to offer a concise definition of ritual and thereby become enmeshed in futile efforts to capture the essence of ritual. Showing less caution, Victor Turner has defined "ritual" to mean "prescribed formal behavior for occasions not given over to technological routine, having reference to belief in mystical beings or powers" (Turner 1967: 19). Although much about this definition is debatable, Bell and most other ritual theorists agree with Turner to the extent of making formalism a chief characteristic of ritual-like behaviors. She says that rituals are formal in the sense that they "involve the use of a more limited and rigidly organized set of expressions and gestures" (Bell 1997: 139). They have an expressive simplicity because choices of words or gestures are circumscribed by traditional practice.

Traditionalism in turn is cited by Bell as a second characteristic of ritual-like activities. Great value is customarily given to engaging in what are supposedly the same ritual activities as were performed by previous generations. Mircea Eliade interprets such traditionalism as involving an attempt – at least in archaic cultures – to repeat the words and gestures of supernatural precursors who existed in a pre-historical epoch: "Myth tells how through the deeds of Supernatural Beings, a reality came into existence, be it the whole of reality, the Cosmos, or only a fragment of reality – an island, a species of plant, a particular kind of human behavior, and institution" (Eliade 1963: 5–6). By emulating mythical or traditional models, rituals become authoritative as explanations for how things come to be as they are. For Eliade, creation myths and rituals are paradigmatic: the Akitu or new year festival of ancient Babylonia is an influential example he frequently cites (e.g. Eliade 1959: 77–8). The social functions of ritual are achieved because the communities who engage in them respect their ontological authority.

Regardless of whether the models emulated are historical or pre-historical, there is an attempt in ritual behavior to repeat what has been done before. Bell describes invariance as the third of her characteristics of ritual-like activities. It consists of "precise repetition" and "physical control" (Bell 1997: 150). People engaged in ritual subordinate spontaneity and individuality to formal adherence to traditional models of speech and action; this adherence is signaled by precise repetition of words and gestures. Song and dance, for instance, require physical control. Fasting and other ascetic practices are frequently made requirements for effective ritual experience, and they represent a broader dimension of physical control. The traditional Christian practice of performing baptisms on Easter morning after the forty days of Lent illustrates this point.

Under the rubric of "rule-governance" Bell summarizes a yet broader sphere of disciplined activity (Bell 1997: 153). Ritual bears comparison to moral mandates in the sense that not only does it stipulate that physical actions must be controlled but also social roles must be observed and prescriptive objectives met. Ritual activities associated with observance of the Jewish Sabbath suggest this broader dimension of disciplined behavior by the ways in which men's and women's roles are carefully prescribed. For instance, traditionally women light the ceremonial candles on Friday night, the eve of the Sabbath, and they do this in association with preparation of Sabbath bread that suggests both divine sustenance of the Jewish community and also the domestic sphere of traditional female social roles. At the end of the Sabbath, the male head of the household also lights candles and performs related ritual activities, invoking the prophet Elijah and blessing God for "separating the holy from the profane, Israel from the heathen, and Sabbath from weekdays" (Gaster 1952: 275). The traditionally more public and theological role of Jewish men in regulating the behavior of Jews is evident in this formula.

Rules of ritual behavior take on different meanings when a naive acceptance of the ontological explanations stressed by Eliade is no longer possible because of consciousness of alternative explanations, e.g. scientific cosmologies, or because of critiques of mythological modes of thought. Sigmund Freud's characterization of religion, with specific reference to religious rituals, as "a universal obsessional neurosis" is a prominent example of such a critique (Freud 1959: 126–7). The modern Olympics represent a ritual-like activity that continues a Greek tradition of athletic contestation that probably had religious origins in the sort of ritual combat evident in the Akitu festival. After its devolution into vulgar nationalistic competition as evidenced in the 1936 Berlin Olympics, efforts were made to invest the Olympics with secular spiritual meanings intended to inspire peaceful relations among diverse human communities (De Coubertin 1967). Ritual rules in this case no longer serve metaphysical ideals situated *in illo tempore*; rather, they serve moral ideals hopefully manifest in the near future.

Rituals in a modern or contemporary context may involve a relinquishment of naive conceptions of Turner's "mystical powers" or Eliade's "Supernatural Beings." Nevertheless, some notion of sacred or spiritual symbolism – however understood – is requisite and is proposed by Bell as her final characteristic of ritual-like activities. She writes:

> What makes activities around certain symbols seem ritual-like is really two-fold: they way they differentiate some places from others by means of distinctive acts and responses and the way they evoke experiences of a greater, higher or more universalized reality – the group, the nation, humankind, the power of God, or the balance of the cosmos.
>
> (Bell 1997: 159)

Ritual symbolism is thus characterized by its powers of differentiation and transcendence, and in contemporary contexts this differentiation may be more social than geographic and the transcendence may be more semiotic than metaphysical. Quite differently, new spiritual beliefs and behaviors might emerge that proclaim themselves independent of traditional religious communities and their practices, but that still lay a claim to something distinctively spiritual. There are many possible illustrations of this phenomenon (Van Ness 1996); the modern Olympic movement is one among this multitude.

Traditional ritual symbolism might be reinvigorated with meaning upon attaining what Paul Ricoeur aptly calls a "second naïveté" (Ricoeur 1969: 351). To attain this renewed openness, Ricoeur advocates an intellectually critical but also imaginatively sympathetic engagement with traditional myths and rituals. Weberian disenchantment need not be the consequence of the social scientific study of religious phenomena such as religious rituals and spiritually disciplined practices. Certainly it is not the consequence intended by this philosophical appreciation of what social epidemiologists might contribute to the study of these topics.

Like Bell, I decline to offer essential traits of ritual; I accede to the contemporary ethos that forsakes quests for metaphysical essences and remains content with Wittgensteinian "family resemblances" (Wittgenstein 1968: 32 [67]). Rituals, then, constitute a family of related behaviors having resemblances to one another sufficient to allow for their proximate identification by overlapping traits. Bell's characteristics of formalism, traditionalism, invariance, rule-governance, and sacred symbolism are insightful summary descriptions; however, they are incomplete in one important respect. (Bell includes a final characteristic called "performance," but its inclusion seems to be more a concession to contemporary theorists who stress the similarities between ritual activities and artistic performances than an independent identifying characteristic.) Bell's characteristics are incomplete because they mostly identify rituals in isolation from one another and ignore their usual configurations into larger wholes. When viewed in this more encompassing perspective – for example, within the context of a seasonal calendar of ritual activities – then rituals occur characteristically as nested periodic behaviors. One aspect of their invariance is that they occur periodically – at regular times during the day, week, or year, or during a person's lifetime. Furthermore, an aspect of their rule-governed character is the stipulation that the ritual context of one level of periodicity determines the ritual behaviors occurring at another level of periodicity nested within it. Within the lifetime schedule of periodic behaviors, a person usually undertakes an adolescent rite of passage to full membership in a religious community. For instance, Roman Catholic Christian youth prepare for the sacrament of confirmation, or a Baptist Protestant adolescent prepares for a believer's baptism. In turn, preparations for the Christian rituals that accompany these transitions include mandatory weekly regimens of religious studies and prayer.

Lack of completeness in Bell's list of ritual characteristics is paralleled by a lack of integration in her summary of the history of academic thinking about ritual. In her presentation of various perspectives on ritual, Bell treats the views of scholars in three loosely organized and historically progressive chapters. These chapters record a history in which key insights are too rigidly applied, and then because of ensuing reaction and controversy, become too thoroughly segregated from one another. I recommend the integration of three crucial points that are present but unrelated in Bell's intellectual history of ritual scholarship.

First, she summarizes the so-called "myth and ritual school" inaugurated by Edward Tylor and James Frazer and represented above by the scholarship of Mircea Eliade. Members of this school, and especially Frazer in *The Golden Bough*, emphasized the theme of the death and resurrection of a god or divine king that, when properly facilitated by ritual activities, secured the natural fertility of crops and livestock and the general well-being of the people

(Frazer 1955 [1911]). In *Thespis*, a study of ancient ritual and drama, Theodor Gaster articulated this theme in terms of a seasonal calendar of ritual activities that prescribed a periodic process of emptying and filling, of kenosis and plerosis (Gaster 1961). Originally, this process reflected astronomical and agricultural regularities – fallow seasons preceding growing seasons in accordance with periodic climate changes – but even in archaic times it encompassed social, political, and economic cycles of activities. The limitation of this point of view was that it tended to impose explanatory structures on diverse cultures in ways not well supported by ethnographic evidence.

In her account of the history of interpretation of ritual activities, Bell proceeds next to the social functionalism initiated by William Robertson Smith and most influentially exemplified by Émile Durkheim's contention that religion is "an eminently social thing" (Durkheim 1995 [1912]: 9). Durkheim's key idea is that ritual activities and other expressions of religion can serve constructive social ends even when their religious practitioners do not expressly intend to do so. The Talmudic requirement that Jews wash their hands before meals, though motivated by concerns for religious purity, had a positive impact on adherents' health (Dorff 1998). Thus religion can serve rational ends with non-rational means. Also, rituals that have the greatest health benefits might not be those that are most directly intended to be healing rites. Periodic rituals may establish the context of behavior and belief that enable occasional healing rites to enhance health and well-being.

Durkheim most instructively documented the social implications of religion in his quantitative studies showing that high degrees of social integration achieved by traditional religious communities, e.g. Southern European Roman Catholic Christianity and European Judaism are correlated with low levels of certain pathological behaviors such as suicide (Durkheim 1966 [1897]). Unfortunately, Durkheim's flawed appreciation of statistical laws led him to interpret regularities in suicide rates and other social phenomena in ways that slighted the individuality of human agents and overemphasized analogies with physical science. His claim that rates of suicide are caused by "suicidogenetic currents" running through societies much like electromagnetic currents run through conductors has been especially criticized by subsequent theorists (Hacking 1990: 177). Durkheim is in some respects guilty of the methodological excess of scientism to which a current generation of ritual scholars has strongly reacted.

Finally, Bell looks at an even yet more diverse collection of ritual scholars who insist upon the culturally conditioned and individualistically complex character of ritual and related practices. These scholars look to the study of language as a model of studying cultural practices like religious rituals and they de-emphasize the importance of cosmology and physical science. To comprehend ritual activities, one must learn its language and this requires the intuitive insights that ethnographers are privy to because of their immersion in the cultures they study. Claude Lévi-Strauss writes, "Myth is language, functioning on an especially high level," and recommends the study of "mythemes" in analogy to the study of phonemes in structural linguistics

(Lévi-Strauss 1963 [1958]: 210–11). Other anthropologists concur with the structuralist emphasis on myth and ritual as semiotic systems akin to natural languages, but they draw upon different techniques of studying language. The reflective writings of Clifford Geertz, for instance, challenge systematic theorizing about ethnographic data and favor more literary approaches. In *Works and Lives: The Anthropologist as Author*, he treats anthropology as a genre of literature (Geertz 1988). In his most recent reflective writings, he continues to recommend empathetic engagement with different forms of life and hermeneutic engagement with their distinctive symbol systems in preference to currently fashionable postmodern alternatives to ethnographic fieldwork. Geertz, however, sides with postmodernists by expressing suspicions about the statistical methodology used by Durkheim and elaborated in contemporary social epidemiology (Geertz 2000).

The distinctive emphases of these three perspectives are often viewed as incompatible and even antagonistic; Bell portrays these tensions. The vantage point on rituals suggested by the social epidemiological study of religious factors influencing health offers the possibility of integrating their respective key insights while avoiding their characteristic excesses. It is proposed here that rituals be examined as nested periodic behaviors that sometimes have salutary associations with clinically determined health outcomes by means of the mediation of psychosocial and physiological factors. By looking at ritual behaviors as nested periodic behaviors, this approach incorporates the insight of the myth and ritual school that ritual provides a structuring of people's temporal experience. Although not understandable in the archaic terms applicable to agrarian societies, periodic experiences associated with religious rituals retain importance in the contemporary world because they are about the only calendar of events that can compete with the temporal imperatives of the market economy in shaping people's lives. As sociologists like Talcott Parsons have contended, religion in recent centuries no longer provides the inclusive ideological and social structure in which political, economic, and medical institutions are situated. Rather, religion has become a differentiated part of social structures largely determined by the market economy. Thus the temporal ordering of people's dispositions and behaviors achieved by the observance of a series of religious rituals serves less the cosmogonic functions that Eliade describes and more the social therapeutic functions that Turner highlights. In *The Ritual Process*, Turner says that ritual observance carves out "liminal" periods from the schedule of secular activities that allows experiences of "*communitas*" – of less structured and more spontaneous relationships – to briefly prevail (Turner 1969: 94–130). The alternative structures of ritual allow for temporary and periodic experiences of "anti-structure." These periodic experiences, in turn, promote the relaxation of social tensions. I would add also that they can contribute to stress reduction and, thereby, to individual mental and physical health.

Social epidemiological studies dealing with religion should be interpreted in the context of Durkheim's insight that religion and its rituals can serve social functions that are not expressly intended by their practitioners. The most securely established findings in this field are ones that posit an association between high levels of religious attendance and low levels of all-cause mortality. The people who attend religious services regularly are not specifically attending healing rites, although such rites may be integrated into worship life in a way that also allows congregants to participate in them when they are ill. (See Appendix B.) The most controversial studies in this field are ones that have claimed to find evidence for the health benefits of intercessory prayer on behalf of ill persons who were unaware that devout people were praying for them. Given these experimental circumstances, known psychosocial mechanisms could not account for positive results; supernatural explanations seem at least implicitly invoked. Studies by Byrd, Harris, and others have reported evidence of cardiovascular benefits for people who were unknowingly the subject of intercessory prayers offered by religiously devout petitioners (Byrd 1988; Harris *et al.* 1999). Numerous critics have challenged these results (Sloan *et al.* 1999). If Durkheim's excess is a reductionistic scientism, then it is mirrored by an approach that seeks to use scientific methods to establish supernatural truths.

In interpreting studies of religious predictors such as attendance at religious services, epidemiologists have attributed importance to the social and regular character of this type of behavior and to the psychological dispositions they may engender. Supernatural factors are almost never invoked and "superempirical" forces are rarely considered (Levin 1996: 66). Mere social conformity such as is central to Allport's conception of "extrinsic religiosity" does not seem to play an explanatory role (Allport and Ross 1967: 442). Some studies show that only intrinsic religiosity – the type that values religious beliefs and behaviors for their own value rather than for what values they might mediate – is associated with good health outcomes like reduced depression and anxiety (Tapanya *et al.* 1997; Koenig *et al.* 1998). Of greater explanatory relevance is Bourdieu's notion of *habitus* as "a socially constituted system of cognitive and motivating structures" that is not reducible to a conscious attempt to achieved desired ends (1977 [1972]: 72–8). For Bourdieu, "[u]nderstanding a ritual practice is not a question of decoding the internal logic of a symbolism" and it "has nothing to do with an act of empathic projection" (Bourdieu 1977 [1972]: 114). While it is clear that he rejects Lévi-Straussian structuralism and Geertzian ethnography, it is not clear what he recommends when he directs attention to "the language of the body" revealed in ritual practice and to "the real conditions of its genesis" (Bourdieu 1977 [1972]: 120). Social epidemiology generally avoids such methodological vagueness while offering a more specific interpretation of the role of cultural factors in the religion and health relationship.

The ideal of disease ascertainment in epidemiological studies is a clinical diagnosis based upon physician examinations of patient symptoms and laboratory tests for relevant biomarkers. For instance, diagnosis of coronary heart disease is often based upon interpretation of patient complaints of chest pain and shortness of breath along with an interpretation of the results from electrocardiograms and CAT scans. Unfortunately, most epidemiological

studies are not sufficiently well-funded to employ such a comprehensive determination of disease status. (A different misfortune is that some physicians
don't really listen to patients' subjective reports and rely too exclusively on
presumably objective test results.) Yet the interpretation of symptoms is part
of the social epidemiological model and it highlights the hermeneutic dimension of the process of investigating the relationship between aspects of religiousness and selected health outcomes. The fact that many epidemiological
studies ascertain a participant's health status through a self-reported checklist
of symptoms doesn't deny the fact that interpretation is occurring; it just
means that what is interpreted is not as complete and subtle as one might like.

Viewing religious rituals as nested periodic behaviors that have salutary
associations with clinically determined health outcomes by means of the
mediation of psychosocial and physiological factors has several advantages.
It addresses a characteristic of many ritual-like activities that supplements
Bell's list of characteristics. Also, it integrates insights regarding ritual that
various schools of thought have tended to treat as points of differentiation
and controversy. Finally, and perhaps, most importantly, it contributes to
an explanation of how religious rituals might promote reduced morbidity
and mortality. Before proceeding to an exposition of this point, I will briefly
indicate how the remarks made thus far about religious rituals might be
extended to a broader category of spiritually disciplined practices.

III. Spiritually disciplined practices as "ritual interiorization"

The perspective offered above for studying religious rituals can be extended
to the study of persons engaged in spiritually disciplined practices. An intuitive way of thinking about this extension is to view regular regimens of
prayer, meditation, or yoga as rituals that have been personalized and so
rendered more individualistic. Among Christians, many regimens of personal
prayer follow communal patterns, such as the reciting of the Lord's Prayer
in Christian worship or the following of the Daily Office among medieval
monks. With some appropriateness, these respective devotional practices have
been called "personal worship" and "corporate worship" by one prominent
commentator (Underhill 1989 [1936]: 163). Mircea Eliade describes the
emergence of yogic practices within the history of Indian Vedic religion as
a process of "ritual interiorization" and he describes the practice of yogic
asceticism as an "inner sacrifice" in which physiological functions take the
place of libations and ritual objects (Eliade 1969: 111).

In addition to historical ties between religious ritual and spiritually disciplined practices, there is a conceptual continuity. Disciplined behavior has
some characteristics of formalism and rule-governance that Bell cited in her
identification of ritual-like activities; practices share aspects of invariance and
traditionalism, and spiritual and sacred meanings themselves have overlapping
semantic content. In other writings, I have presented a philosophical reconception of the notion of a spiritually disciplined practice that shares key
features with Bell's characteristic of ritual-like activities (Van Ness 1992). I

will not repeat this material here. I will only note briefly that practices like Hatha yoga have traditionally been conceived to be a regular, periodic practice. In this regard, it is similar to ritualistic behavior. Spiritually disciplined practices like yoga differ from ritual in that they are generally less fully social, yet more fully embodied.

There are several respects in which doing Hatha yoga is a good example of a periodic human practice. To do yoga authentically one should do it regularly. Regular repetition of a behavior is part of what is meant by the word "practice." Playing a musical instrument daily or engaging in a team sport are commonly called practices. In the *Yoga-sūtras*, Pantañjali recounts earlier tradition that says yoga is a practice (*abhysa*) in the sense of being "effort toward steadiness of mind" (*The Yoga Sutras of Patanjali* 1990: 1.13; cf. *Yoga Philosophy of Pantanjali* 1983). Such steadiness is not achieved by merely closing one's eyes and holding one's breath. Rather, the steadiness consists of a more comprehensive and enduring ability to prevent sensations and conceptions from distracting the mind from concentration and meditation. "Practice becomes firmly grounded when well attended to for a long time, without break and in all earnestness" (*Yoga-sūtras* 1.14).

As a type of practice, yoga is more disciplined than celebratory or devotional. Disciplined activities are usually the products of instruction; often they involve emulation of rule-governed behaviors. Indeed, the Latin root form *disciplina* primarily means instruction or teaching, and only secondarily does it connote the learning and customs so taught. Yoga is a disciplined practice because instruction by a teacher is virtually essential for doing it. Books and videotapes about yoga are now widely available, but the human exemplar remains crucial. The *Hatha Yoga Pradipika*, the first surviving written text on Hatha yoga, begins with a long list of yoga masters (*siddhas*) before it proceeds to a careful description of various body postures, breathing practices, and the other "limbs" of yoga (1.1–8). Accompanying these descriptions are claims that Hatha yoga can only be undertaken properly under the instruction of a *guru* (*Hatha Yoga Pradipika* 1992: 1.14, 2.50.13, 3.77 and 122, 4.8–9). In this sense, it is ineluctably social. Yet the goal of yoga is more individual liberation than liberation of a religious community. In fact, it is the liberation of the individual through his or her realization of unity with other people and all reality. In the *Yoga-sūtras*, the true self is *purua* and the ultimately desired self-transformation is *samādhi* – a state of consciousness where sensations and conceptions have been restrained completely and where true self realizes its identity with all reality.

A second trait of a disciplined practice is the careful equilibrium maintained between embodied self-supervision and unconscious effort. Athletes and artists know about this balance well: too much conscious effort at physical control can be counterproductive. The practice of yoga, though not explicitly athletic or aesthetic, does involve the cultivation of bodily perfections (*Yoga-sūtras* 3.46); and it also encourages practitioners to follow instruction and thus control their bodily movement and mental focus, while at the same time being sensitive to an esoteric dynamic of bodily energy. Specifically, the yogin should attend to the flow of *prāna* through body channels (*nādīs*) and amidst energy centers (*chakras*). The liberation of this esoteric energy, while cultivated by yogic practices, is not something completely at the disposal of conscious effort (*Hatha Yoga Pradipika* 2.50.4 and 3.2; also *Siva Samhita* 1990: 1.2).

Even though the word "discipline" in English has the connotation of corrective punishment in some usages, yoga is not punitive. Athletes, artists, and spiritual tyros all receive instruction about how to undertake their respective practices; they also are told what is proscribed and what is superfluous. An ethos of simplicity prevails. Yoga is basically privative in the sense that it is devoted to "the restraint of the modifications of the mind-stuff" (*Yoga-sūtras* 1.2). *Āsanas* and *prānāyāmas* are physical practices that are intended to make the practitioner less attached to physical sensations and perceptions. For the most part, they promote the higher limbs of yoga – concentration, meditation and liberated consciousness. Still, there is an undeniable depreciation of bodily existence in classical yoga texts. In the *Yoga-sūtras*, there occurs this statement: "By purification there arises disgust for one's own bodies and for contact with other bodies" (2.40). In a following verse of the *Yoga-sūtras* (2.43; also 2.1) it is urged that acceptance of *tapas* – sometimes translated as "austerity," sometimes as "pain" – is a means of purification. The next step, however, is not taken: the active infliction of bodily pain is not prescribed as a means of purification. Yoga shuns mortifying asceticism. For instance, the *Hatha Yoga Pradipika* explicitly rejects severe fasting (1.63–65); the *Siva Samhita* (3.33, 5.4) confirms this sentiment.

Yoga, in summary, is a disciplined practice. It is an inherently valuable variety of regular human behavior that is privative in character, instructive in adoption, and equilibrated in the sense of involving modulated degrees of both self-supervision and unconscious effort. It is also a spiritual practice in that it is oriented toward a human excellence achieved by transforming the self by means of encountering reality as an inclusive whole. In its original context, yoga was both a religious and spiritual practice. Today in the West, I contend, it is often spiritual without being specifically religious in the sense of having ties of doctrine and community with any institutional religion (Van Ness 1999). It is less social though more embodied than most religious rituals. This embodied character is something that theorists as diverse as Mary Douglas and Pierre Bourdieu have emphasized as important for doing what rituals do. More recent theorists have lamented the decline of embodied participation in contemporary American religious ritual life (Driver 1998). The nature of Hatha yoga as an intensely embodied spiritually disciplined practice has made it the subject of numerous epidemiological studies, many of which have reported positive results.

IV. Explaining the health benefits of religion

Religious rituals often occur as nested, periodic behaviors that foster habitual dispositions associated with healthy lifestyles, hopeful attitudes, supportive communities, and meaningful worldviews. A recommendation for thinking about rituals in this way is that it allows for an explanation of their association with low rates of mood disorder and heart disease and high levels of subjective well-being and longevity. The following explanatory hypothesis is offered: religious rituals contribute to periodic experiences of renewal, often communal in nature, which produce salutary benefits by reducing the harmful consequences of stress, and specifically, by partially diminishing and systematically varying the allostatic load borne by religious individuals. Spiritually disciplined practices that are not tied to religious traditions might yield benefits for similar reasons. The healthful impact of religiousness is probably mediated by other biological mechanisms than stress reduction. Immune system function is another possible biological mediator although the evidence here is thus far weaker. Stress reduction seems especially relevant to religious ritual and seems especially promising for social epidemiological research in the near future.

Religiousness and spirituality are here conceived naturalistically as an attribute of human organisms that strive to grow, develop, and flourish in natural and social environments through equilibrating strategies of adaptation and accommodation. Confessional theological affirmations are not addressed in these concluding reflections because the vantage point adopted is one of a philosophically-minded social epidemiologist. No view is advocated regarding, for instance, the salvific power of prayer and the salutary power of salvation. Contrary to positivistic naturalists, however, it is assumed to be meaningful to speak of organisms responding to a global environment in addition to proximal, particular aspects of their ambient reality. A spiritual dimension to human experience is deemed intelligible and spirituality or religiousness is deemed a part of a person's character in the Aristotelian sense of being the product of a history of habitual actions and a source of dispositions to act in regular ways.

Three salient features of Western Biblical religious traditions attune them to the elements of time, habit, and decision featured so prominently in this explanation of the health benefits of religious ritual. First, in the Bible God is revealed in both primordial time as creative agent establishing the natural world and in historical time as a redemptive presence communicating God's law and intentions through the activity of prophets. The Biblical God is not primarily revealed in the sphere of nature as in many Native American and Chinese religious traditions. This dual relation of the Biblical God to human temporality accords well with the hypothesis's emphasis on temporally periodic practices that promote health during human lifetimes. Second, the most important Biblical religious trait is faith in God rather than knowledge of divine things. Biblical religions differ in this respect from gnostic or occult spiritual traditions of the Hellenistic era or of recent times. Faith is consonant with the perspective on religion adopted here that accents adaptive and therapeutic habits of belief and behavior. Faith, like habit, can shape action without explicit appeal to rational calculation. Thus it can become a means by which religiousness promotes health without specifically intending to do so, as Durkheim insightfully noted. Finally, the most important religious experience in Western Biblical religion is arguably repentance or conversion – an intentional turning toward God. Authentic participation in religious rituals implies a conscious act of fidelity to God – a decision to pursue this allegiance over competing alternatives. This focus on repentance suggests compatibility with the decision-theoretic framework employed frequently in public health, social epidemiology and the social scientific study of religion. Citation of these features of Western Biblical religion is not meant to imply that such religious traditions promote health most effectively. Another explanatory hypothesis might best be illustrated by non-Western religious traditions.

Good health in the Western Biblical traditions is a synecdochal sign of salvation or right relationship with God: the favored Israelites are spared plagues that beset the Egyptians (Exodus 7–12). The Latin root "salus" of the English word "salvation" has the multiple connotations of health, wholeness, and deliverance. Although good health as measured by physiological and psychological indices is not the intended consequence of religious activities, it can plausibly be claimed that the alleviation of harmful stress is a desideratum of persons seeking a right relationship with God and is a consequence for those who attain this right relationship. The concluding line of the Christian Mass is a request for peace. It has been correctly noted that reducing religion to a quest for natural benefits trivializes it (Sloan *et al.* 2000); yet religion is trivialized in a different way if religious concerns are so thoroughly referred to a supernatural realm that their connections are severed to common human feelings of fear, despair, pain, and distress.

Stress is understood in this hypothesis as it is in the tradition of physiological research inaugurated by Walter Cannon and Hans Selye. Cannon coined the word "homeostasis" to refer to the relatively steady states of the internal chemical and physical environment maintained by the coordinated activity of numerous body systems. Such equilibrating processes have become the organizing principles of modern physiology. Cannon also first systematically identified the "fight-or-flight response" as the coordinated means by which the body's sympathetic nervous system prepares people to cope with situations of perceived danger (Cannon 1915). This concept also had wide influence, for instance, becoming renamed the "alarm reaction" as the first of three stages in Selye's model of the "stress" syndrome. Selye gave the word "stress" its scientific meaning as "the nonspecific response of the body to any demand" (Selye 1976 [1956]: 74). By this definition, not all stress is bad; ineffective stress responses and chronic stress, however, have been shown to be deleterious to health.

In the second half of the last century, the legacies of Cannon and Selye have been challenged and expanded. Two developments are worthy of note in this context. Shelly Taylor and colleagues have recently proposed the "tend-and-befriend" response as a complement to Cannon's fight-or-flight response (Taylor *et al.* 2000: 411). This response, most appropriate for threats to safety that are less acute than physical attack, emphasizes nurturant activities intended to protect oneself and others, especially children, and socializing activities designed to expand and strengthen social networks that might provide needed support in situations of crisis. Taylor contends that these sorts of behavior may be especially efficacious for women who are often disadvantaged in fighting by physical limitations and who are often prevented from fleeing because of maternal responsibilities.

The neuroendocrinologist Bruce McEwen has been especially concerned with the dynamic nature of biological processes of equilibration and with the harms of chronic stress. He has formulated notions of "allostasis" and "allostatic load" to convey more adequately what Cannon and Selye spoke about as homeostasis and chronic stress respectively. "Allostatic load" he defines as "the strain on the body produced by the repeated ups and downs of physiologic response, as well as by the elevated activity of physiologic systems under challenge ... changes in the metabolism and the impact of wear and tear on a number of organs and tissues ... [that] can predispose the organism to disease" (McEwen and Stellar 1993: 2094). In clinical research, McEwen and his colleagues have operationalized the notion of allostatic load by representing it as the sum of a number of biological parameters such as blood pressure, serum cholesterol levels, blood sugar levels, and urinary stress hormone levels (Seeman *et al.* 1997). They found that greater allostatic load defined in this way is associated with lower levels of cognitive and physical functioning and with increased risk of cardiovascular disease. In more recent work with laboratory animals, McEwen has shown that acute stress enhances certain aspects of immunologic functioning but that chronic stress compromises these same functions (Dhabhar and McEwen 1997).

Epidemiologists looking at the impact of religiousness on health have studied repeatedly only one of the dimensions of allostatic load postulated by McEwen and colleagues. Various aspects of religiousness have been shown to be associated with lower blood pressure, especially lower diastolic blood pressure (Koenig *et al.* 1998; Levin and Vanderpool 1989). Comparing periodic changes in blood pressures with periodic religious behaviors offers the greatest opportunity for epidemiological investigation that might soon yield specific and consistent results relevant to the proposal articulated above. Study of the impact of religious service attendance and other religious behaviors on the functioning of the human immune system has only just begun; some evidence of a salutary effect of religiousness has been reported (Koenig *et al.* 1997; also Koenig and Cohen 2002).

Ritual practices of archaic Middle Eastern religion – which Jews, Christians, and Muslims have adopted and transformed – and contemporary medical practices addressing people suffering from stress – informed by the insights of Cannon, Selye, Taylor, and McEwen – differ in significant respects: historical origins, descriptive levels, affective concomitants, intellectual procedures, and more. Yet they share a basic important feature also: they are human efforts to cope with natural and social changes that threaten aspects of human equilibrium and well-being. From a functionalist point of view, many archaic Middle Eastern religious practices are efforts to cope with externally imposed social and economic conditions of alternating seasons of fecundity and fallowness. Modern techniques for managing stress seek to bring moderation and variation to physical and psychological processes induced by chronic stress. Both, then, are striving to identify and effect cycles of change that are adaptive to the environment and compatible with human flourishing, and so both can be viewed under the rubric of biological equilibration broadly conceived.

V. Philosophical conclusion: ritual as resistance

How people work and what they consume are major determinants of their personal freedom, physical health, and spiritual well-being. Occupational epidemiologists document the health consequences of factors to which people are exposed at work and nutritional epidemiologists conduct studies about health consequences of what people choose to eat, drink, and smoke. In many instances, their message to the public is clear – for instance, eat more fruits and vegetables – but the public response is equivocal at best. People agree that they should make lifestyle changes, but then they fail to do so. Bad habits are hard to change.

Powerful institutions and the people who share their interests often profit from the unhealthy choices of American workers and consumers. Constitutional rights and egalitarian laws insure that their exercise of power is not direct and tyrannical, but they allow that it be indirect and persuasive. Hence as the world has become at least nominally more democratic, the agents of powerful institutions – certainly governments and corporations, but also churches and professional organizations – have been led to seek less coercive means of social control. Advertising pitches, political sloganeering, and related promotions are ubiquitous in popular mass media.

If profit follows from the ability to control how people work and consume, and if direct coercion is outlawed, then attention and effort become directed toward acquiring the ability to instill habitual patterns of behavior. Via advertising pitches and expert advice, powerful institutions today achieve this control by inculcating habitual patterns of consumption in malleable human populations. Revelations about the deliberate efforts of tobacco companies to increase the addictive nicotine component of cigarettes even while reducing the tar content show how calculating corporations can be in this regard (Kessler 2001). At the same time as the federal government funds research that shows pathological gambling to be a health problem for some persons who undertake this activity, state governments promote gambling as a source of tax revenue (Welte, G. *et al.* 2001; Walters 2001).

In this situation where individuals struggle to change unhealthy behaviors that powerful institutions encourage and promote, it is not surprising that people turn to religion as a social institution that might be their ally. This trend is especially evident in regard to substance abuse. The American Temperance Movement had strong roots in Christian churches; Bill Wilson consciously incorporated religion-like elements into the program of Alcoholics Anonymous; substance abuse among today's homeless is increasingly being addressed by the religious groups that provide food and housing to this population. Religious ritual and spiritually disciplined practices are frequently enlisted in these activities.

Engaging authentically and regularly in religious rituals and spiritually disciplined practices in contemporary America can have the salutary benefits of breaking bad habits and fostering good habits. Observing the Sabbath or holy day breaks the habitual pattern of work and consumption that characterizes life shaped by the market economy. In physiological terms, such observance can relieve the allostatic load of stress by providing a period of required relaxation and redirected attention; stress is not magically relieved, but its chronic grip is loosened by intermittent periods of ritual and prayer. Aspects of a healthy lifestyle are realized in at least a part of the workweek.

As cooperative social activities, ritual behaviors enlist other like-minded individuals in the various struggles in which religious congregants are engaged. Given the ethical tenor of most American religious communities, this collective response to temptations and stresses may have the more irenic traits of Taylor's "tend-and-befriend" response rather than the bellicose attributes of the "fight-or-flight" response. People help one another cope with problems through nurturant behaviors that address needs in ways not often done in the work world where people are assumed to be autonomous individuals rather than petitioners dependent upon God's grace.

Finally, as Charles Sanders Peirce noted in "The Fixation of Belief," arguably the founding document of American philosophical pragmatism, "All belief is the nature of a habit" (Peirce 1935–1958: 5:370). Religious behaviors are born from and also engender religious beliefs. Pascal frankly recommended the example of religious behavers become believers: "They behaved just as if they did believe, taking holy water, having masses said, and so on. That will make you believe quite naturally, and will make you more docile" (Pascal 1966: 152 [418]). Although Pascal's advice may not attain the intended result with the certainty he implies, it is generally true that rituals are accompanied by myths or theologies that give them meaning and that offer a broad conceptual framework for activities both sacred and secular. This sense of coherent meaning, along with healthy lifestyle choices and supportive communities, is prominent in the thinking of social scientists seeking to explain the health benefits of religion. The concentrated attention here on religious ritual and its capacity for relieving harmful stress concurs with this broader line of thought and gives it specification.

Religious ritual is many things. In some circumstances, it can be a salutary practice of resistance. It can help people resist chronically stressful regimens of work life and the unhealthy compensations of food, drink, and meretricious entertainments. In other circumstances, religious rituals might induce acute stress by modeling beliefs and behaviors that challenge secular worldviews. Both by the chronic stress they relieve and the acute stress they induce, religious rituals can plausibly foster healthier lifestyles. Social epidemiologists are now pursuing this empirical question as to whether participation in religious activities helps people resist the advent of disease and disability. By exploring the relationship between ritual activities and health outcomes in social scientific and philosophical investigations, one does not necessarily gainsay its distinctly salvific meanings and benefits. Research efforts such as those that have been exhibited and recommended here do, however, seek to ascertain whether embodied physical and mental health are among the worldly rewards of religious rituals and spiritually disciplined practices.

VI. Appendices

Appendix A Religious timelines

Daily Religious Timeline

Instructions: Place the appropriate letter on each timeline at every point when you regularly engage in that activity.

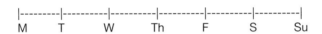

```
|---------|----------|----------|----------|----------|----------|
12am    4am       8am      12pm      4pm       8pm       12am
```

P = prayer   M = meditation   S = scripture reading   W = worship
T = television or radio program with religious content   O = Other

Weekly Religious Timeline

```
|---------|----------|----------|----------|----------|----------|
M       T        W         Th        F         S         Su
```

P = Group prayer meetings   S = Group scripture study
W = Group worship services   O = Other group religious activity
T = Other individual religious activity

Yearly Religious Timeline

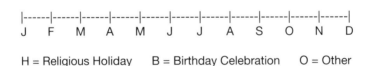

```
|------|------|------|------|------|------|------|------|------|------|------|
J      F      M      A      M      J      J      A      S      O      N      D
```

H = Religious Holiday   B = Birthday Celebration   O = Other

Lifetime Religious Timeline

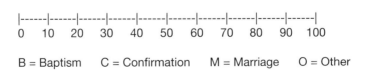

```
|------|------|------|------|------|------|------|------|------|------|------|
0     10     20     30     40     50     60     70     80     90     100
```

B = Baptism   C = Confirmation   M = Marriage   O = Other

Appendix B The Natural History of Disease with Correlated Religious Phenomena

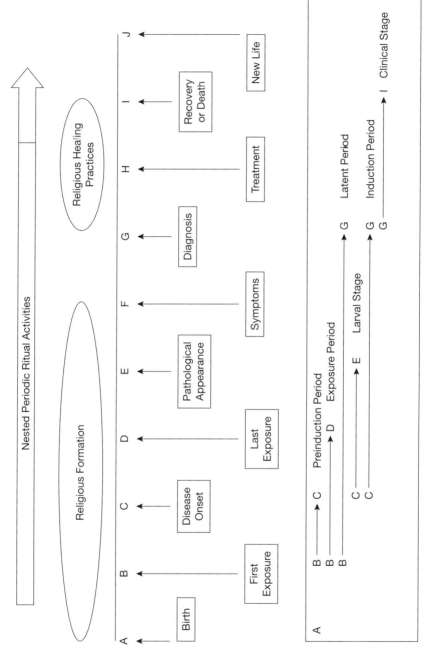

Bibliography

Allport, G. W. and Ross, C. E. (1967) "Personal religious orientation and prejudice," *Journal of Personality and Social Psychology* 5: 432–43.

Bell, C. (1997) *Ritual: Perspectives and Dimensions*, New York: Oxford University Press.

Bourdieu, P. (1977 [1972]) *Outline of a Theory of Practice*, trans. R. Nice, Cambridge: Cambridge University Press.

Byrd, R. C. (1988) "Positive therapeutic effects of intercessory prayer in a coronary care unit population," *Southern Medical Journal* 81: 826–9.

Cannon, W. B. (1915) *Bodily Changes in Pain, Hunger, Fear, and Rage*, New York: D. Appleton and Company.

—— (1932) *The Wisdom of the Body*, 2nd ed., New York: W. W. Norton.

De Coubertin, P. (1967) *The Olympic Idea: Discourses and Essays*, ed. Carl-Diem-Institut, Stuttgart: Hoffman.

Dhabhar, F. S. and McEwen, B. S. (1997) "Acute stress enhances while chronic stress suppresses cell-mediated immunity in vivo: a potential role for leukocyte trafficking," *Brain, Behavior, and Immunity* 11: 286–306.

Dorff, E. N. (1998) "The Jewish Tradition," in R. L. Numbers and D. W. Amundsen (ed.), *Caring and Curing: Health and Medicine in the Western Religious Traditions*, Baltimore: Johns Hopkins University Press.

Driver, T. F. (1998) *Liberating Rites: Understanding the Transformative Power of Ritual*, Boulder, CO: Westview Press.

Durkheim, E. (1966 [1897]) *Suicide: A Study in Sociology*, New York: Free Press.

—— (1995 [1912]) *The Elementary Forms of Religious Life*, trans. K. E. Fields, New York: Free Press.

Eliade, M. (1959) *The Sacred and the Profane: The Nature of Religion*, New York: Harcourt, Brace, and World.

—— (1963) *Myth and Reality*, New York: Harper and Row.

—— (1969) *Yoga: Immortality and Freedom*, trans. W. R. Trask, Princeton: Princeton University Press.

Ellison, C. G., Gay, D. A., and Glass, T. A. (1989) "Does religious commitment contribute to individual life satisfaction?," *Social Forces* 68: 100–23.

Frazer, J. G. (1955 [1911]) *The Golden Bough: A Study in Magic and Ritual*, 10 vols., London: Macmillan.

Freud, S. (1959) "Obsessive actions and religious practices," in J. Strachey (ed.), *The Standard Edition of the Complete Psychological Works of Sigmund Freud*, London: Hogarth Press.

Gaster, T. H. (1952) *Festivals of the Jewish Year*, New York: William Morrow.

—— (1961) *Thespis: Ritual, Myth, and Drama in the Ancient Near East*, 2nd ed., Garden City, N.Y.: Doubleday.

Geertz, C. (1973) *The Interpretation of Cultures*, New York: Basic Books.

—— (1988) *Works and Lives: The Anthropologist as Author*, Stanford: Stanford University Press.

—— (2000) *Available Light: Anthropological Musings on Philosophical Topics*, Princeton: Princeton University Press.

Grimes, R. L. (1985) *Research in Ritual Studies*, Metuchen, N.J.: Scarecrow Press.

Hacking, I. (1990) *The Taming of Chance*, Cambridge: Cambridge University Press.

Hahn, R. A. (1995) *Sickness and Healing: An Anthropological Perspective*, New Haven: Yale University Press.

Harris, W. S., Gowda, M., Kolb, J. W., Strychacz, C. P., Vacek, J. L., Jones, P. G., Forker, A., O'Keefe, J. H., and McCallister, B. D. (1999) "A randomized, controlled trial of the effects of remote, intercessory prayer on outcomes in patients admitted to the coronary care unit," *Archives of Internal Medicine* 159: 2273–8.

Hatha Yoga Pradipika (1992) trans. P. Singh, New Delhi: Munshiram Manoharlal Publishers.

Hummer, R. A., Rogers, R. G., Name, C. B., and Ellison, C. G. (1999) "Religious involvement and US adult mortality," *Demography* 36: 273–85.

Kessler, D. A. (2001) *A Question of Intent*, New York: Public Affairs.

Koenig, H. G., Cohen, H. J., George, L. K., Hays, J. C., Larson, D. B., and Blazer, D. G. (1997) "Attendance at religious services, interleukin-6, and other biological indicators of immune function in older adults," *International Journal of Psychiatry in Medicine* 27: 233–50.

—— , George, L. K., Hays, J. C., Larson, D. B., Cohen, H. J., and Blazer, D. G. (1998) "The relationship between religious activities and blood pressure in older adults," *International Journal of Psychiatry in Medicine* 28: 189–213.

—— , —— , and Peterson, B. L. (1998) "Religiosity and remission of depression in medically ill older patients," *American Journal of Psychiatry* 155: 536–42.

—— , McCullough, M. E., and Larson, D. B. (2001) *Handbook of Religion and Health*, New York: Oxford University Press.

Koenig, H. G., Cohen, H. J. (eds) (2002) *The Link Between Religion and Health: Psychoneuroimmunology and the Faith Factor*, New York: Oxford University Press.

Lévi-Strauss, C. (1963 [1958]) "The Structural Study of Myth," in *Structural Anthropology*, trans. C. Jacobson and B. G. Schoepf, New York: Basic Books.

Levin, J. S. (1996) "How prayer heals: a theoretical model," *Alternative Therapies in Health and Medicine* 2: 66–73.

—— , and Vanderpool, H. Y. (1989) "Is religion therapeutically significant for hypertension?" *Social Science and Medicine* 29: 69–78.

McEwen, B. S. and Stellar, E. (1993) "Stress and the individual: Mechanisms leading to disease," *Archives of Internal Medicine* 153: 2093–101.

Musick, M. A. (1996) "Religion and subjective health among black and white elders," *Journal of Health and Social Behavior* 37: 221–37.

Oman, D. and Reed, D. (1998) "Religion and mortality among the community-dwelling elderly," *American Journal of Public Health* 88: 1469–75.

Pascal, R. (1966) *Pensees*, Harmondsworth, Middlesex: Penguin Books.

Peirce, C. S. (1935–58) *Collected Papers of Charles Sanders Peirce*, ed. C. Hartshorne, P. Weiss, and A. Burks, Cambridge: Harvard University Press.

Radcliffe-Brown, A. R. (1952) "Religion and Society," in E. E. Evans-Pritchard (ed.), *Structure and Function in Primitive Society: Essays and Addresses*, Glencoe, IL: Free Press.

Ricoeur, P. (1969) *The Symbolism of Evil*, trans. E. Buchanan, Boston: Beacon Press.

Seeman, T. E. and McEwen, B. (1996) "Impact of social environment characteristics on neuroendocrine regulation," *Psychosomatic Medicine* 58: 459–71.

—— , Singer, B. H., Rowe, J. W., Horowitz, R. I., and McEwen, B. S. (1997) "Price of adaptation – Allostatic load and its health consequences," *Archives of Internal Medicine* 157: 2259–68.

Selye, H. (1956/1976) *The Stress of Life*, rev. ed., New York: McGraw-Hill.

Siva Samhita (1990), trans. R. B. S. C. Vasu, New Delhi: Munshiram Manoharlal Publishers.

Sloan, R. P., Bagiella, E., (1999) "Data without a prayer," *Archives of Internal Medicine* 160: 1870–6.

——, ——, VandeCreek, L., Hover, M., Casalone, C., Hirsch, T. J., Hasan, Y., Kreger, R., and Poulos, P. (2000) "Should physicians prescribe religious activities?" *New England Journal of Medicine* 342: 1913–16.

Smolensky, M., and Lamberg, L. (2000) *The Body Clock Guide to Better Health: How to Use Your Body's Natural Clock to Fight Illness and Achieve Maximum Health*, New York: Henry Holt.

Strawbridge, W. J., Cohen, R. D., Shema, S. J., and Kaplan, G. A. (1997) "Frequent attendance at religious services and mortality over 28 years," *American Journal of Public Health* 87: 957–61.

Tapanya, S., Nicki, R., and Jarusawad, O. (1997) "Worry and intrinsic/ extrinsic religious orientation among Buddhist (Thai) and Christian (Canadian) elderly persons," *International Journal of Aging and Human Development* 44: 73–83.

Taylor, S. E., Klein, L. C., Lewis, B. P., Gruenewald, T. L., Gurung, R. A. R., and Updegraff, J. A. (2000) "Biobehavioral Response to Stress in Females: Tend-and-Befriend, Not Fight-or-Flight," *Psychological Review* 107: 411–29.

Turner, V. (1967) *The Forest of Symbols: Aspects of Ndembu Ritual*, Ithaca, N.Y.: Cornell University Press.

—— (1969) *The Ritual Process: Structure and Anti-Structure*, Ithaca, N.Y.: Cornell University Press.

Underhill, E. (1989 [1936]) *Worship*, New York: Crossroad Publishing.

Van Ness, P. H. (1992) *Spirituality, Diversion, and Decadence: The Contemporary Predicament*, Albany, N.Y.: State University of New York Press.

—— (1999) "Yoga As Spiritual But Not Religious: Pragmatic Perspective," *American Journal of Theology and Philosophy* 20: 15–30.

—— (2003) "Epidemiology and the study of religion," *Religion* 33(2), April: 147–59.

—— (ed.) (1996) *Spirituality and the Secular Quest*, New York: Crossroad Publishing Company.

Walters, G. D. (2001) "Behavior genetic research on gambling and problem gambling: a preliminary meta-analysis of available data," *Journal of Gambling Studies* 17: 255–71.

Welte, J. G. B., Wieczorek, W., Tidwell, M. C., and Parker, J. (2001) "Alcohol and gambling pathology among U.S. adults: prevalence, demographic patterns and comorbidity," *Journal of Studies on Alcohol* 62: 706–12.

Wittgenstein, L. (1968) *Philosophical Investigations*, trans. G. E. M. Anscombe, 3rd ed., New York: Macmillan Company.

Yoga Philosophy of Pantanjali (1983) trans. S. H. Aranya and P. N. Mukerji, Albany: State University of New York Press.

The Yoga Sutras of Patanjali (1990) trans. S. S. Satchidananda, 2nd ed., Yogaville, VA: Integral Yoga Publications.

Index